Building Resilient IP Networks

Kok-Keong Lee, CCIE No. 8427

Cisco Press

800 East 96th Street
Indianapolis, IN 46240 USA

Building Resilient IP Networks

Kok-Keong Lee

Copyright© 2006 Cisco Systems, Inc.

Published by:
Cisco Press
800 East 96th Street
Indianapolis, IN 46240 USA

Printed in the United States of America   1 2 3 4 5 6 7 8 9 0

First Printing December 2005

Library of Congress Cataloging-in-Publication Number: 2004112420

ISBN: 1-58705-215-6

Warning and Disclaimer

This book is designed to provide information about building resilient IP networks. Every effort has been made to make this book as complete and as accurate as possible, but no warranty or fitness is implied.

The information is provided on an "as is" basis. The author, Cisco Press, and Cisco Systems, Inc., shall have neither liability nor responsibility to any person or entity with respect to any loss or damages arising from the information contained in this book or from the use of the disks or programs that might accompany it.

The opinions expressed in this book belong to the author and are not necessarily those of Cisco Systems, Inc.

Trademark Acknowledgments

All terms mentioned in this book that are known to be trademarks or service marks have been appropriately capitalized. Cisco Press or Cisco Systems, Inc. cannot attest to the accuracy of this information. Use of a term in this book should not be regarded as affecting the validity of any trademark or service mark.

Corporate and Government Sales

Cisco Press offers excellent discounts on this book when ordered in quantity for bulk purchases or special sales.

For more information please contact:
U.S. Corporate and Government Sales 1-800-382-3419 corpsales@pearsontechgroup.com

For sales outside the U.S. please contact: **International Sales** international@pearsoned.com

Feedback Information

At Cisco Press, our goal is to create in-depth technical books of the highest quality and value. Each book is crafted with care and precision, undergoing rigorous development that involves the unique expertise of members from the professional technical community.

Readers' feedback is a natural continuation of this process. If you have any comments regarding how we could improve the quality of this book, or otherwise alter it to better suit your needs, you can contact us through e-mail at feedback@ciscopress.com. Please make sure to include the book's title and ISBN in your message.

We greatly appreciate your assistance.

Publisher	John Wait
Editor-in-Chief	John Kane
Cisco Representative	Anthony Wolfenden
Cisco Press Program Manager	Jeff Brady
Production Manager	Patrick Kanouse
Development Editor	Dayna Isley
Editorial Assistant	Raina Han
Project Editor	Marc Fowler
Copy Editor	Keith Cline
Technical Editors	Roland Dobbins
	Ian Foo
	Mark Gallo
	Steve Moore
Book/Cover Designer	Louisa Adair
Composition	Mark Shirar
Indexer	WordWise Publishing

CISCO SYSTEMS

Corporate Headquarters
Cisco Systems, Inc.
170 West Tasman Drive
San Jose, CA 95134-1706
USA
www.cisco.com
Tel: 408 526-4000
    800 553-NETS (6387)
Fax: 408 526-4100

European Headquarters
Cisco Systems International BV
Haarlerbergpark
Haarlerbergweg 13-19
1101 CH Amsterdam
The Netherlands
www-europe.cisco.com
Tel: 31 0 20 357 1000
Fax: 31 0 20 357 1100

Americas Headquarters
Cisco Systems, Inc.
170 West Tasman Drive
San Jose, CA 95134-1706
USA
www.cisco.com
Tel: 408 526-7660
Fax: 408 527-0883

Asia Pacific Headquarters
Cisco Systems, Inc.
Capital Tower
168 Robinson Road
#22-01 to #29-01
Singapore 068912
www.cisco.com
Tel: +65 6317 7777
Fax: +65 6317 7799

Cisco Systems has more than 200 offices in the following countries and regions. Addresses, phone numbers, and fax numbers are listed on the
Cisco.com Web site at www.cisco.com/go/offices.

Argentina • Australia • Austria • Belgium • Brazil • Bulgaria • Canada • Chile • China PRC • Colombia • Costa Rica • Croatia • Czech Republic Denmark • Dubai, UAE • Finland • France • Germany • Greece • Hong Kong SAR • Hungary • India • Indonesia • Ireland • Israel • Italy Japan • Korea • Luxembourg • Malaysia • Mexico • The Netherlands • New Zealand • Norway • Peru • Philippines • Poland • Portugal Puerto Rico • Romania • Russia • Saudi Arabia • Scotland • Singapore • Slovakia • Slovenia • South Africa • Spain • Sweden Switzerland • Taiwan • Thailand • Turkey • Ukraine • United Kingdom • United States • Venezuela • Vietnam • Zimbabwe

About the Authors

Kok-Keong Lee, CCIE No. 8427, graduated from the University of Singapore, where he majored in computer and information systems sciences. From 1991 to 1993, Kok-Keong worked as a response center engineer for Hewlett-Packard, helping customers solve networking problems. From 1993 to 1999, Kok-Keong worked for IBM as a network systems engineer. Currently, he works as a consulting systems engineer for Cisco Systems, focusing on network architecture and IP core technologies. Kok-Keong lives with his wife in Singapore.

Fung Lim, CCIE No. 11970, joined Cisco Systems in October 1999 and has been working closely with Internet service providers (ISPs) in areas pertaining to network design and operations, as well as service provider security. He also assisted in the rollout of one of the first MPLS networks in Asia Pacific. He graduated from the National University of Singapore, majoring in electrical engineering with a minor in management of information systems. Fung Lim is also a Certified Information Systems Security Professional (CISSP No. 64090). Prior to joining Cisco Systems, Lim Fung was working as a systems engineer for Pacific Internet. Lim Fung lives with his wife in Singapore.

Beng-Hui Ong started his career as a system administrator for an ISP in Singapore. He then went to Digital Equipment Corporation (DEC) working with various ISPs to implement Internet application services. While at DEC, he implemented a large-scale video server with an ATM network for a local ADSL provider. Later, Beng-Hui worked for Cisco Systems as a consulting system engineer on network design and implemented various networks for ISPs and cable operators. Beng-Hui now holds a managerial position at Starhub Cable Vision, heading product management on broadband access products, value-added services, and new technologies development. Beng-Hui currently works for Cisco System as a product manager for the Broadband Edge And Midrange Routing Business Unit. Beng-Hui is married with a daughter and lives in Singapore.

About the Technical Reviewers

Mark Gallo is a systems engineering manager at Cisco Systems within the Channels organization. He has led several engineering groups responsible for positioning and delivering Cisco end-to-end systems, and for designing and implementing enterprise LANs and international IP networks. He has a bachelor of science degree in electrical engineering from the University of Pittsburgh and holds Cisco CCNP and CCDP certifications. Mark resides in northern Virginia with his wife, Betsy, and son, Paul.

Steve Moore, CCIE No. 4927, is an engineer with the Cisco IP Routing Deployment and Scalability Team, which is a part of the IOS Technologies Division of Cisco Engineering. He is responsible for discovering, testing, validating, and assisting in the customer deployment of new ideas relating to the scalability of routing protocols. He works closely with development, support, testing, and consulting groups within Cisco Systems as well as customers. A part of Steve's job is to educate, and he does so by working with customers directly and by writing white papers and speaking at various networker conferences. During the nine years Steve has worked at Cisco Systems, he has become known for his experience with routing protocols, as well as WAN technologies and optical networking.

Dedications

To my wife, Serene, for her endless support and unconditional sacrifice.
—KK

To my parents, and my wife, Andrea, for her constant support and encouragement.
—LF

To my wife, Nancy, for her constant support and to my daughter, Chloe, for her endless laughter and joy.
—BH

Acknowledgments

This has been an ambitious project, and we want to thank everyone who has helped us in this long process: our editor-in-chief, John Kane, for showing faith in unknown authors halfway around the globe, and for his patience and understanding; our development editor, Dayna Isley, for her patience and encouragement; the rest of the editorial team from Cisco Press for their assistance; and especially our reviewers, Roland Dobbins, Mark Gallo, and Steven Moore, for their precious time and comments. This book would not have been possible without your assistance.

KK would like to thank Paul Chen for his support to embark on this project. Finally, KK would like to thank Lim Fung and Beng-Hui for agreeing to collaborate on this project on such short notice.

Lim Fung would like to thank Sew Hoon for her guidance, encouragement, and support at Cisco Systems, and would like to thank KK and Beng-Hui for being such great working partners in the project.

Beng-Hui would like to thank KK and Lim Fung for the invitation and for being great working partners. Beng-Hui would like to thank Paul Chen for his encouragement to start this project. Beng-Hui would also like to thank Sew Hoon for her constant encouragement and support at Cisco Systems.

Finally, the author team would like to thank Seo-Boon Ng for his ideas and contribution to the structure of this book. More importantly, we would like to thank him for his friendship.

This Book Is Safari Enabled

The Safari® Enabled icon on the cover of your favorite technology book means the book is available through Safari Bookshelf. When you buy this book, you get free access to the online edition for 45 days.

Safari Bookshelf is an electronic reference library that lets you easily search thousands of technical books, find code samples, download chapters, and access technical information whenever and wherever you need it.

To gain 45-day Safari Enabled access to this book:

- Go to http://www.ciscopress.com/safarienabled

- Enter the ISBN of this book (shown on the back cover, above the bar code)

- Log in or Sign up (site membership is required to register your book)

- Enter the coupon code 9QAZ-DSSB-1DU9-IWC6-EV9M

If you have difficulty registering on Safari Bookshelf or accessing the online edition, please e-mail customer-service@safaribooksonline.com.

Contents at a Glance

Contents

Icons Used in This Book

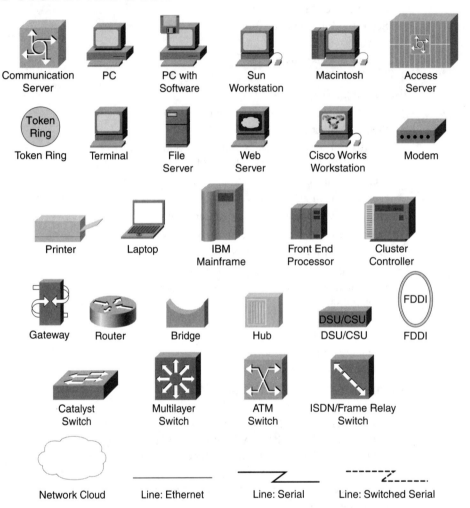

Command Syntax Conventions

The conventions used to present command syntax in this book are the same conventions used in the IOS Command Reference. The Command Reference describes these conventions as follows:

- **Boldface** indicates commands and keywords that are entered literally as shown.

- *Italics* indicate arguments for which you supply actual values.

- Vertical bars (|) separate alternative, mutually exclusive elements.

- Square brackets [ ] indicate optional elements.

- Braces { } indicate a required choice.

- Braces within brackets [{ }] indicate a required choice within an optional element.

Introduction

Over the years, many excellent books have been written on IP technology, and these books tend to focus on a specific topic, such as Open Shortest Path First (OSPF) or Border Gateway Protocol (BGP). However, building a resilient IP network requires a holistic approach to design and implementation. Various building blocks need to work together, most of which have seen enhancements and new features introduced. These features are scattered, mostly in the form of numerous Requests For Comments (RFCs), IOS features and documentations, and many Cisco Technical Assistance Center (TAC)-authored white papers.

The goal of this book is to provide a central resource for the features that focus on IP network resiliency. It covers a wide range of topics and serves as a foundation for anyone who needs a deeper understanding about IP network resiliency.

Who Should Read This Book?

This book is intended to increase your knowledge with respect to improving the resiliency of an IP network. It is not meant to be an introduction to IP network design. This book helps you understand what network availability means and introduces new features and tools that have been developed to improve resiliency in IP networks. Anyone who is involved in the design and implementation of a large-scale IP network and would like to understand ways to improve its resiliency will benefit from this book.

How This Book Is Organized

Although this book could be read cover to cover, it is designed to be flexible. You can easily move between chapters and sections of chapters to cover just the material that you need more information on.

- **Chapter 1, "Rise of the IP Transport System,"** provides a backdrop to the usage and new expectations of the IP network.

- **Chapter 2, "Establishing a High-Availability Network,"** takes a closer look at the real meaning of network resiliency and suggests a practical approach to tackling the "five-nines" availability challenge.

- **Chapter 3, "Fundamentals of IP Resilient Networks,"** serves as a refresher to the TCP/IP protocols and the various hardware and switching implementations that affect network resiliency. It also proposes a modular approach to solving the network resiliency problem.

- **Chapter 4, "Quality of Service,"** examines the relevancy of quality of service (QoS) with respect to network resiliency. Different QoS models and queuing techniques are examined, and a practical approach to a QoS architecture is presented.

- **Chapter 5, "Core Module"** examines the enhancements made to the various Interior Gateway Protocols to improve the resiliency of a network backbone.

- **Chapter 6, "Access Module,"** showcases the design guide for a resilient campus access network. Enhancements to the relevant protocol and first-hop gateways are highlighted.

- **Chapter 7, "Internet Module,"** focuses on resilient connectivity to the Internet. Improvements to the Exterior Gateway Protocol and addressing and routing solutions for redundancy are highlighted.

- **Chapter 8, "WAN Module,"** showcases improvements made to the various traditional WAN connectivity technologies.

- **Chapter 9, "Data Center Module,"** examines factors that influence data center network design. It highlights new technologies and a design guide to constructing the data center to support new application requirements.

- **Chapter 10, "Beyond Implementation: Network Management,"** looks at what more needs to be done beyond the basic configuration of hardware and routing protocols in a resilient IP network. The concept of proactive management is proposed, and the various supporting features are introduced.

- **Appendix A, "Calculating Network Availability,"** discusses mathematical calculations to evaluate network availability.

- **Appendix B, "RFCs Relevant to Building a Resilient IP Network,"** lists RFCs that are relevant to building resilient IP networks.

- **Appendix C, "The Cisco Powered Network Checklist,"** is an extract from the Cisco Powered Network data center best practices checklist.

This chapter covers the following topics:

- The Internet Explosion
- Next-Generation IP Applications
- MPLS: New Kid on the Block
- Next-Generation IP Transport System
- Continuous Improvements of Protocols

CHAPTER 1

Rise of the IP Transport System

The IP network has grown into an important asset for most organizations today. As a technology, IP has passed the phase of requiring justification for its existence. In fact, the problems faced by network managers today are not justification or construction of an IP network. The real challenge is to keep the IP network up and running continuously, around the clock.

Over the years, networking hardware and software enhancements have addressed throughput and capacity issues. With improvement in application-specific integrated circuit (ASIC) design and overall hardware features, network capacity has increased accordingly (and so has the complexity). For example, with more memory and faster processors, network devices can store more information and process that information faster (and, thus, facilitate bigger and more complex networks).

Not too long ago, OC-3 (155 Mbps) transmission speeds were prevalent as corporate network backbones. In contrast, the latest desktop computers come with a Gigabit Ethernet connection; the backbone of yesteryear seems small when compared with the current desktop standard. Today, most enterprises build their network backbone with Gigabit Ethernet technology. For service providers, the norms are OC-48 (2.4 Gbps) and OC-192 (10 Gbps) network backbones.

The CRS-1 router from Cisco Systems enables speeds of OC-768 (40 Gbps) on a single link. The CRS-1 router might make some people believe that the networking world is interested only in speed and feed. After all, we build an OC-768 IP network the same way we built OC-3 networks: We just connect some routers and turn on some routing protocols; for the most part, the network takes care of itself. Consider the following calculations, however:

- With a Gigabit Ethernet backbone, a link failure that lasts 10 seconds could result in a loss of more than 1 GB of data.
- With an OC-768 backbone, a link failure that lasts 10 seconds could result in a loss of 50 GB of data.

You can imagine the consequences of a prolonged network failure when information is being carried at these speeds. Important data is lost, as are business connections. After all, connectivity equates to business connections; lose one, and you lose the other. Therefore, you cannot run networks today like you did in the past. And although many network managers would agree that it is now easy to pump up the link speeds and capacity of a network, managing the network and keeping it running smoothly is a whole other issue.

Taking a step backward, you might even question the need for such zealous reliance on the IP network and whether that reliance is just a ploy by the equipment vendors to promote products. After all, the Internet is not always reliable. Some network managers might even wonder whether it is technically possible to operate an IP network with minimal failures. After all, most network managers have changed from one design to another only to find out that they are still dealing with that dreadful midnight phone call.

A few key networking developments address these concerns. This chapter discusses some of these developments, including the dependence on the Internet, use of next-generation applications such as Voice over IP (VoIP), adoption of Multiprotocol Label Switching (MPLS), and changes in IP transport systems. An understanding of these developments and of the continuous improvement of IP-related protocols is the first step toward building resilient IP networks.

The Internet Explosion

Nobody would have guessed that a project by the name of ARPANET, funded by the Defense Advanced Research Projects Agency (DARPA) in the 1960s, would eventually change the way we live today. From its humble beginning as a research project on packet switching technology, the Internet has evolved into an important communication medium today.

Consider the following effects of the Internet's global reach:

- In the United States, telecommuters prefer to check into a hotel room that comes with broadband access.
- In Europe, businessmen are reading e-mails and surfing the Internet, while flying at 35,000 feet.
- In Singapore, you rent an office that comes standard with space, electricity, and an Internet connection.

The Internet, which is a network of IP networks, has effectively changed the way applications are developed and how services are delivered. From the initial e-mail and web applications, more legacy applications are being migrated to IP platforms, and demand for IP network resiliency has risen. As users, we are accustomed to the convenience and services that the Internet brings, and we expect to be able to go online anywhere and anytime. We do not expect the Internet to stop functioning completely. In fact, businesses place significant confidence in the technology of the Internet. Consider, for example, the following:

- More than 93 percent of the Cisco System $20 billion business is done through the Internet.
- Stock brokerages allow customers to trade online around the clock.
- Surgeons in Canada perform telerobotic surgery via the network.

It is hard to imagine the consequence of a broken down Internet. A minute of downtime equates to a $35,000 loss in revenue for Cisco. In the case of the surgery, downtime is not an option. The Internet is a network of networks, consisting of organizations of all sizes connected together. The challenge for network managers is how to be part of this community all the time. Effectively, no one can afford to be left out of this community.

Next-Generation IP Applications

Just like e-mail and web applications facilitated the use of the Internet, some new applications are going to affect us in a significant manner. These applications are going to require a level of network resiliency that has never before been demanded. Some of these applications even demand resiliency that only traditional transport systems can deliver. VoIP and IP storage applications are two examples.

Voice over IP

VoIP is a packet-based voice technology that has evolved from an application for a cheap Internet phone call to a mainstream business-class application that corporations rely on. Cisco runs its entire voice system on VoIP technology. As a technology, VoIP imposes the strictest requirement on an IP network in terms of jitter and delay. It also expects the underlying IP network to be able to work around failures in the order of milliseconds so that users on both ends of a call will not notice the failure. This is certainly one requirement that is not easily achievable without understanding the latest networking technology.

As packet-based voice looks set to replace the traditional voice system in both service provider and enterprise networks, network managers must prepare their networks for the challenge of what VoIP demands.

IP Storage

Another application that will demand network resiliency is IP storage. Just like the voice world, the storage world is undergoing changes. IP storage is another area of technology that has enjoyed much progress. Technologies such as Fibre Channel over IP (FCIP) and Internet Small Computer System Interface (iSCSI) enable system managers to run their system over an IP network, thus reducing cost of ownership and maximizing operational efficiency.

The demand from applications such as VoIP and IP storage brings network resiliency to a level never seen before. For many network managers, providing and maintaining such resiliency is quite a daunting task.

MPLS: New Kid on the Block

The massive increase in Internet traffic has resulted in service providers questioning the merits of running IP networks over traditional Layer 2 technologies such as ATM and Frame Relay. To keep costs down while generating new services, service providers must find new ways to build IP networks.

MPLS is one of the most significant networking technologies thus far developed. The MPLS standard is published by the Internet Engineering Task Force (IETF) and enjoys wide support both from vendors and end users. Although originally based on tag switching, MPLS has evolved into a family of technologies that are capable of providing services like Virtual Private Network (VPN) and traffic engineering.

MPLS is a new forwarding mechanism that is based on label swapping. When an IP packet reaches the edge of an MPLS network, a label is imposed on the packet, and that label is removed only when the packet leaves that MPLS network. Packet forwarding within the MPLS network is performed with a label lookup for an incoming label, and then that packet's label is swapped for an outgoing label and the packet is sent on to the next hop. Labels are assigned to packets based on groupings, called Forwarding Equivalence Class (FEC), and packets within the same FEC receive the same treatment from the MPLS network.

Under the MPLS family of technologies is an area called MPLS Traffic Engineering (MPLS-TE). One function that MPLS-TE enables is Fast Reroute (FRR). FRR allows for an extremely fast recovery of the network in the event that a link or a node within the network encounters a failure. In contrast to the long failover time that network managers had to deal with in the past, FRR allows recovery in milliseconds. New tools and features such as FRR enable network managers to build resilient networks as never before possible.

Today, MPLS is considered to be a promising technology that can be used to address network-resiliency issues. Some network managers have deployed FRR as a way to improve their network resiliency and are seeing positive results.

Next-Generation IP Transport System

Search for the phrase "next-generation IP transport system" on the Internet and you will end up with tens of thousands of ideas, products, and advertisements "related" to this phrase.

In the past, IP networks generally were constructed as an overlay network above other transport networks such as ATM or Synchronous Optical Network/Synchronous Digital Hierarchy (SONET/SDH). Progress in optical technology and IP-related protocols has resulted in the introduction of a new category of product that is a fusion of many areas of technology. These so-called next-generation IP transport systems promise to deliver systems with the intelligence of IP and resiliency of the SONET/SDH or optical world.

A good example of a next-generation IP transport system is the Cisco ONS 15454 series, which combines optical transport technology with IP routing intelligence. This category of networking equipment enables network administrators to consider adopting a different IP network architecture to harness the new capability.

Another area of interest is the standardization of the IEEE 802.17 Resilient Packet Ring (RPR) technology. This technology derives from the Cisco Dynamic Packet Transport (DPT) technology, which provides SDH- or SONET-like resiliency to an IP backbone. The packet-ring architecture reduces complexity in IP backbone design and can be found in many service provider and large enterprise networks. With the standardization effort, it is expected that the RPR technology will generate wide interest among the network community. Chapter 8, "WAN Module," discusses RPR technology in more detail.

Continuous Improvements of Protocols

In addition to developing new technologies for improved network resiliency, the industry continues to improve upon IP and its related protocols, such as Open Shortest Path First (OSPF) and Border Gateway Protocol (BGP). Consider BGP, for example. It was proposed in 1995, and since then many new ideas and enhancements have been proposed. The following are just some of these enhancements:

- RFC 2547: *BGP/MPLS VPN*
- RFC 2858: *Multiprotocol Extensions for BGP-4*
- RFC 3065: *Autonomous System Confederations for BGP*
- RFC 3392: *Advertisement Capabilities with BGP-4*

As with BGP, interior routing protocols such as OSPF and Intermediate System-to-Intermediate System (IS-IS) have many enhancements and continue to evolve. Even Layer 2 protocols such as Spanning Tree Protocol (STP) have had enhancements, and these will also continue to change. Some of these changes are vendor proprietary implementations; others are *de facto* standards or come in the form of an IETF draft.

Security is another important area that is being enhanced. IP network security can also contribute to the network's resiliency. Protecting the network from denial-of-service (DoS) attacks, viruses, and worms ensures that network resources are not consumed unnecessarily.

Regardless of their "official" status, improvements to these protocols and other new ideas have resulted in many enhanced features that appear in vendor products. Some of these features tackle specific problems in building a resilient IP network. This book brings you up-to-date on these improvements and illustrates how these new features work.

This chapter covers the following topics:

- Understanding the Five-Nines Availability Debate
- A Practical Approach to Achieving High Availability

CHAPTER 2

Establishing a High-Availability Network

The aim of building a resilient IP network is to achieve high availability. This chapter takes a closer look at the issues surrounding IP network availability. Understanding these issues is crucial because it will help you focus on what is really important in achieving high availability for the network.

Understanding the Five-Nines Availability Debate

A term that is always associated with availability is *five nines*. Most network managers use it in their procurement specification, and most vendors print it on their product brochure. You will often encounter terms such as *five-nines network*, *five-nines availability*, *five-nines reliability*, and so on. Many network managers use these terms to describe the state of their network or to describe their expectations of a particular product from the equipment vendors. However, the topic usually ends up with the network managers and equipment vendors arguing over the real meaning of the term.

The confusion surrounding the term is understandable. After all, to some people *five nines* means literally 5 minutes and 15 seconds of downtime per year. Others people believe that scheduled maintenance periods do not count as downtime. Some people think that a *five-nines network* can be built only with equipment that comes with five-nines certification on the brochure. Some people believe that *five nines* is an old concept from the legacy voice world and should not be imposed on the data network at all.

This section differentiates two concepts often used interchangeably when discussing five nines: reliability and availability. It also discusses the origins of the five-nines concept and how it contributes to real availability and reliability of a network.

Differentiating Between Reliability and Availability

Two words are commonly mentioned alongside five nines: *reliability* and *availability*. Although they have different meanings, network managers use these terms interchangeably, which clouds the resiliency issue even more.

Before beginning the discussion about five nines, it is important to be able to distinguish between reliability and availability.

Reliability is the probability that a product can perform a required function for a given time interval. Reliability is generally used to describe the quality of a product through *mean time between failure* (*MTBF*) data provided by the equipment vendor. MTBF is the average time taken for a component to transit from an operation state to a failure state.

Availability, on the other hand, is the total amount of time a system is up and functioning properly to accomplish its mission. When talking about five nines, availability is what you are interested in. Bear in mind, however, that reliability is also an important contributing factor. Those who prefer the MTBF approach would suggest the following formula for availability:

$$\text{Availability} = \frac{\text{MTBF}}{(\text{MTBF} + \text{MTTR})}$$

where

- MTBF (mean time between failure) is the average time taken for a component to transit from an operation state to a failure state.

- MTTR (mean time to restore) is the average time taken to reinstate a failed component to a functioning state.

The MTBF approach focuses on calculating a theoretical availability of a system. In doing so, you look at how a system is constructed out of its components. These components are inevitably arranged in one of two fashions:

- Series
- Parallel

The overall availability of a system is the summation of the availability of these components. Figure 2-1 shows two systems, each built with different components. The system that was built in a series relies on both components A and B to be functional. The system breaks down when either one of these components fails. On the other hand, in a parallel arrangement, as long as one of its components, B1 or B2, is working, the system is functional. Therefore, the overall availability of a system using components arranged in a series has a different availability from those that are arranged in a parallel fashion.

Figure 2-1   *Series Versus Parallel Components*

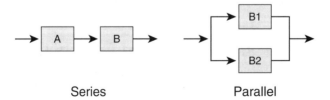

Series   Parallel

Appendix A, "Calculating Network Availability," shows the formula for calculating availability of systems built in both manners. Because a network is a collection of devices deployed in a series or parallel manner, by applying these formulas repetitively, you can arrive at a figure that indicates the overall availability number of the network.

NOTE   For a detailed description of the MTBF approach, refer to the book *High Availability Network Fundamentals* by Chris Oggerino (Cisco Press 2001, ISBN: 1587130173).

After going through some of the calculations via the MTBF approach, you might realize that you are dealing with the concept of estimation rather than a metric with absolute value. Consider, for example, MTBF values. It is not uncommon to come across products with an MTBF value in the range of a few hundred thousand hours. How would you verify the accuracy of this data when you have yet to encounter a product that really ran for that many hours before failure? The derivation of the MTBF is based merely on the summation of a set of series and parallel components from a manufacturing point of view. The final figure might also be determined by placing the device under the test within accelerated or exaggerated conditions to simulate aging and environmental effects. It is, therefore, an estimate.

In addition, you might run into a peculiar situation in which you have a product that has high availability but a bad reliability record—it just keeps going up and down, in rapid turnaround states.

Conversely, you might end up with a product that has high reliability—it went down only one time in its lifetime—but it took three days to restore to its original state. This is an example of a product with bad availability.

The discussion of availability and reliability is not an easy one to understand. Because of the complexity of the MTBF approach, some people might choose a more straightforward concept that is easily understood—the "five-nines" approach.

The Five-Nines Approach

After going through the MTBF way of defining availability, network managers soon realized that it is a theoretical calculation. The simple numeric value does not convey the expectation of a network's availability. That is probably why the five-nines approach is preferred, because it actually lists a quantifiable challenge. This approach comes in the form of a percentage table of downtime that is based on a simple case of mathematics, as outlined in Table 2-1.

Table 2-1   *Five Nines and Network Availability*

Number of Nines	Downtime per Year = (100 – Uptime)(365 * 24 * 3600) / 100
99.999	5 minutes, 15 seconds
99.99	52 minutes, 36 seconds
99.9	8 hours, 46 minutes
99	3 days, 15 hours, 40 minutes

Table 2-1 is probably every network manager's introduction to the concept of five-nines availability. This approach sets the expectation of network availability, and ultimately impacts how the network is designed and what type of equipment must be purchased. With this approach, however, network managers debate what counts toward downtime (the yardstick of a five-nines system). Therefore, it is common to see network managers referencing some standards documents or network characteristics when trying to clarify their expectations, in addition to referencing the actual five-nines availability requirement. For example, the Telcordia GR-512-Core document will be used as a reference for downtime, or a 50-millisecond (ms) reroute capability will be used to measure resiliency. Unfortunately, such references might not actually help to express the real expectation.

Idiosyncrasies of the Telcordia GR-512-Core Document

It is hard to discuss the expectation of a five-nines system without mentioning the Telcordia (originally Bellcore) GR-512-Core document. The focus of the document is a set of recommended hardware and field reliability performance requirements for Local Access and Transport Area (LATA) switching systems. This includes the LATA end office and tandem switching systems, both ISDN and non-ISDN. The document stipulates conditions when a service or system is considered down. Many network managers use this document in their Request For Proposals (RFPs) for building a data network to indicate their expectations of downtime for the proposed systems. However, the GR-512-Core document also states what the exceptions to downtime are—an area not many network managers are familiar with.

Think of these exceptions as the idiosyncrasies of the GR-512-Core document. The best way to illustrate them is via the private branch exchange (PBX) system. The PBX was chosen as the gold standard of a five-nines system. Everyone seems to agree that indeed it is, without realizing the odd way of calculating downtime in a PBX system under the GR-512-Core guidelines.

Figure 2-2 shows the basic components of the PBX system.

Figure 2-2   *PBX System Components*

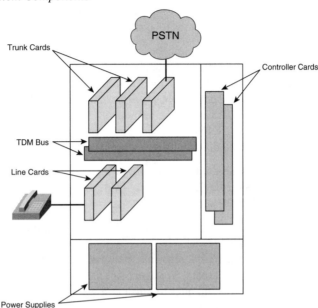

As Figure 2-2 illustrates, the important components that are crucial to the calculation of the availability of the PBX system are as follows:

- **Line cards**—To which devices such as phones and faxes are connected
- **Trunk cards**—Provide connectivity to the Public Switched Telephone Network (PSTN) world
- **Controller cards**—The processor components that comprise the brain of the system
- **Time-division multiplexing (TDM) bus**—The switching fabric that connects all cards
- **Power supply**—Provides power to the entire system

For redundancy, you usually see duplication of the controller cards, TDM bus, and power-supply components. The line and trunk cards are never duplicated.

When calculating the availability of the PBX system in Figure 2-2, you must consider which of the following constitute a downtime:

- Failure of a line card, rendering numerous devices such as phones and faxes out of service
- Failure of a trunk card, rendering numerous bearer channels out of action
- Loss of a few attendant consoles

If you were to follow the GR-512-Core standard, none of these count toward system downtime. If you were to scrutinize the standard, any problems that affect the service of 64 ports or fewer do not count toward system downtime.

Whenever a line card failure occurs, the PBX vendor usually offers a 4-hour response time to replace the faulty card. Remember that to achieve five-nines uptime, you can afford only 5 minutes and 15 seconds of service interruption. So does that mean that the system described in the preceding paragraphs is not five-nines certified? The answer is that PBX is still a five-nines system. It would take a shutdown of the entire system to constitute a downtime. That is why PBX vendors can always meet the so-called five-nine standard—they simply provide enough redundant power supply and controller cards.

In fact, the expected availability of the entire PBX system, according to the Telcordia document, is 99.94 percent. This is a far cry from what we thought a PBX system ought to be—maintaining a 99.999 percent uptime.

When superimposing the concept of the GR-512-Core documents onto a data network, you encounter arguments about what constitutes IP network availability. If you were to apply the GR-512-Core document model to an IP network, the network would still be considered up and running in the event that fewer than 64 users are affected. In addition, a file transfer that takes hours rather than minutes to finish is considered in normal working condition because service is still available.

The data network introduces new areas of challenges that the GR-512-Core document might not be able to address. Figure 2-3 shows a typical setup of an IP network, with all the major components in place.

Figure 2-3 *Typical IP Network*

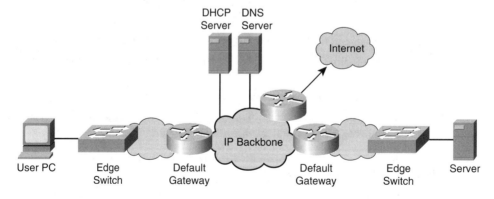

From Figure 2-3, you can see that the IP network is made up of components that are entirely different from the PBX world. It is difficult to superimpose the specifications spelled out in the GR-512-Core document onto the IP network in Figure 2-3. The truth is, you are dealing with a completely different technology now, and you are applying an old-world concept to a new one. In the legacy voice world, you never encounter poor response time after a call has been made. Speaking slowly to combat network congestion is not necessary. When the call connection is established, network congestion in the legacy voice world is not an issue. Data networks are different. Congestion after the connection is established is an issue. Anyone who has used FTP over the Internet, for example, knows about the erratic performance issue. The users of IP networks expect consistent network performance. Any degradation in response time is considered failure, even though the service might be available.

The Truth About 50-ms Resiliency

As mentioned earlier in the "The Five-Nines Approach" section, besides referencing the GR-512-Core document for expectations of downtime, the 50-ms reroute capability is often used to dictate expectations of network resiliency. This is another concept that plagues the networking community, and many managers demand it without realizing its relevancy and implications. A little history lesson will shed light on this subject.

In the 1980s, the International Telecommunication Union-Telecommunication Standardization Sector (ITU-T) introduced the G.841 document, which specifies the Synchronous Digital Hierarchy (SDH) network protection standard. The 50-ms protection time was introduced so that a network fault could be corrected within that short duration. The reason for introducing the 50-ms protection time has to do with the standard of the voice channel banks technology. In the early days, the voice channel banks terminated all calls being carried over a trunk if a failure lasted more than 200 ms. Taking other activities such as fault detection into consideration, the 50 ms was adopted and has since been the standard. With newer technology being introduced—for example, the new-generation digital phone—the tolerance for failure has been increased to 2 seconds. There is no longer the need for the 50-ms reroute capability. However, the original requirement of 50 ms still stays in the document.

In the data world, things work in a different way. If you look at the way a TCP application behaves, it is elastic in nature in a sense that it can tolerate high failure duration and can recover by itself. In other words, a network that recovers in 50 ms and another one that recovers in a few seconds would probably be the same to a TCP application. Although new applications such as Voice over IP (VoIP) might require a more stringent resiliency, because of the nature of human conversation, the effect of a 50-ms failure recovery and one that takes 1 second might still be the same—users at both ends of a VoIP call might not notice the delay at all.

Note that to build a network with 50-ms recovery capability, you might need to invest a lot (both money and human engineering resources). This capability can be expensive, with the difference in cost easily 50 or even 100 percent. The design philosophy behind such a network differs from the rest of the network, too. Therefore, network managers should understand the implication of requesting that a network have 50-ms recovery. Network managers should make this request only if they absolutely understand the traffic nature and fully understand the costs involved. Failure to understand can result in costly expenditures or, in the worst-case scenario, network inefficiency. Depending on the network design, some might end up with 50 percent bandwidth waste just to achieve a protection capability that applications might not need.

In some cases, however, a 50-ms recovery is a goal worth pursuing—for example, if you are running a service provider network with a strict service level agreement (SLA) to honor. Considering the number of end users who are going to be affected by your network and the potential penalty, you have no other choice. Another example is when the link speed of your network gets faster and faster, such as in the case of an OC-192 or OC-768 network, and so you might truly require such resiliency. In addition, sometimes applications require the 50-ms recovery capability. Time-sensitive applications such as securities exchange and order systems used by brokerage firms are just some examples. Any delays, even with the prevention of loss of data by retransmission and application recovery, could mean pricing fluctuations and significantly impact the business.

A network manager must remember this: The user experience matters most. When users are unhappy with the services delivered by the network, it does not matter whether the network is rubber stamped with four-nines, five-nines, or even a 50-ms recovery capability. A satisfactory user experience depends on more than the technology portion.

A Practical Approach to Achieving High Availability

As you should understand by now, the ability to achieve high availability in a data network should not be a stamped approval about a product or design. Do not confuse it with the specifications listed in the GR-512-Core document either.

In fact, five-nines availability is the result of how well a network operation is being run (which includes the hardware that makes up the network, software, design, error-handling capability, and processes that keep the network running). To achieve fine-nines availability requires the following:

- Setting a standard to measure network availability
- Defining a metric for what is important with respect to business goals
- Understanding the issue of network availability
- Setting a strategy to achieve high availability

Measuring Availability

A suggested way to measure network availability is to put in place a process such as the following:

1 Measure against a list of parameters, such as equipment availability, link utilization, and application response times.

2 Tabulate and compile the results to reflect a trend.

3 Act to address those areas that are falling short.

Figure 2-4 illustrates this concept. Figure 2-4 shows a typical campus network setup where the edge of the network is fronted by all the access switches. The assumption here is that as long as the edge switches are up, users should be able to gain access to the network. The status of the edge switches can be determined by pinging them via a network station every 30 seconds. This way, the results of the pings are collected and over a period of time, you can plot a graph to reflect the status of the access network.

Figure 2-4   *Measuring Network Availability*

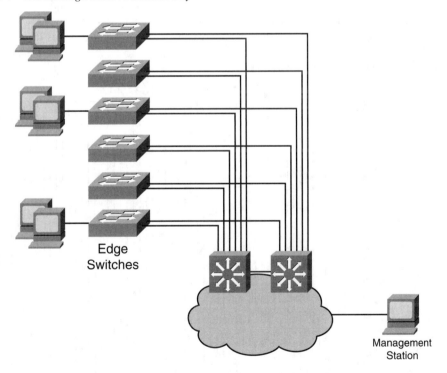

Edge
Switches

Management
Station

Keep in mind, however, that gaining access to the network is only one aspect of measuring network availability. The user experience—getting a job done—is what counts. In this case, the job can be opening up a web page, transferring some data files, or performing a transaction on an online application. Therefore, measurement of the network availability needs to include the following activities:

- Server administrators keeping track of their application servers
- Webmasters monitoring the status of the web servers
- Database administrators monitoring the database transactions

The statistics collected will be compiled by the network operation team and put into a graph to reflect the uptime of these important resources. You can introduce the concept of raw availability and an adjusted availability to take system maintenance into consideration:

- Raw availability reflects the availability of a device, with all outages considered.
- Adjusted availability does not include outages due to maintenance activities.

When documenting these two measurements of availability, a high score on both reflects the quality of the network experience; huge differences in the scores reflect something more. When you have a low score on the raw availability, and a higher score on the adjusted availability, you should look into the operational aspects. You should explore the reasons for the high frequency of maintenance, some of which might be due to network design changes or patching of software due to bug or feature enhancement. Figure 2-5 illustrates this concept.

Figure 2-5   *Raw Versus Adjusted Availability*

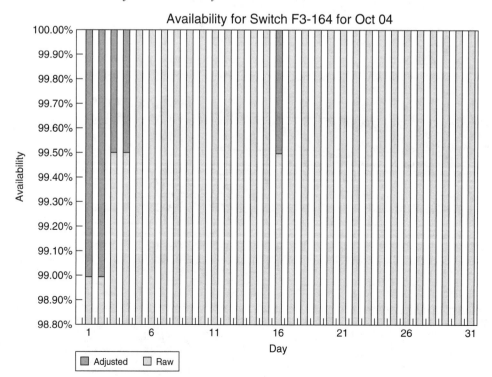

Of course, this measurement strategy cannot quantify special cases of downtime. For example, under a denial-of-service (DoS) attack, users might still be connected, but there is no response from a particular server. Someone might have introduced a rogue Dynamic Host Configuration Protocol (DHCP) server, and although the network is up from a connectivity perspective (the network management station can still ping the switch), some users on the same segment are not going to be able to do productive work at all. In this case, collection of statistics is just one facet of network availability measurement. Another important activity that you must do is to keep track of the problems filed by the users. You should deal with high-severity problems immediately and monitor these cases closely. Problem resolution and monitoring might require a trouble-ticketing application both for collection of statistics and tracking of the status.

By now, you have concluded that you should adopt a holistic approach when determining network availability via the collection of statistics on the uptime of devices, as well as when looking into user reported problems.

After a period of time, you might end up with an availability status that looks something like the results in Table 2-2.

Table 2-2   *Availability Status for Major Network Modules*

Category	Adjusted Availability	Raw Availability
Server Farm	99.996%	99.954%
WAN	99.992%	99.853%
Desktop Access	99.995%	99.99%
Development	99.85%	99.753%
Overall	99.95%	99.9%

Notice that different categories have different results. This is because a network is usually divided into major modules. These modules might be owned and managed by different groups within an IT department. With different budget allocations and perceived importance, their design and resiliency strategy might differ from each other.

Now that you have a clearer picture of the overall user experience, you can tackle the area that needs improvement. Perhaps you can do something to boost the availability of the server farm, or perhaps someone needs to speak to the service provider about the SLA.

After deciding what needs to be done, repeat the entire exercise all over again. This way, you can keep track of the results of the suggested improvement.

Defining a Metric

One of the IT department's important roles within an organization is to support activities that help meet the company's goals. There will be resources within the IT department that are crucial to the company's success. Likewise, there will be certain categories of resources within the network that are crucial to its operation. The failure of these resources has a wide impact on the overall functionality of the network. In establishing the network availability as a whole, these components will be more important than others, and you might need to assign weights to these categories. For example, a problem encountered on the WAN is more critical than a lab network going down. Because the WAN is the company's connection to the rest of the business world, you cannot afford the problem to exist in the first place. You should deal with errors immediately and explore areas of improvement to ensure that the problem does not occur again.

Having a metric helps network managers decide what is more important so that resources can be spent to help solve a problem or improve on a situation. You can achieve maximum impact this way. For example, you can have the ticketing system queuing cases based on weights. This way, the system highlights a WAN failure as highest priority and puts the case before others, even though the failure happened much later than the others.

Understanding the Issue of Network Availability

When dealing with network availability, you must understand the cause of network downtime. As long as network managers know where the prospective problems lie, they can act to prevent the problems from happening. After all, prevention is better than cure.

Over the years, many surveys have been done on the major causes of network failure. Although the results might differ somewhat, you can probably guess that the causes include the following:

- Software-related problems
- Hardware-related problems
- WAN link issues

Note that contrary to popular belief, link failure is not the major contributor of network downtime. In the past, connectivity such as the WAN circuit was blamed for most network outages. With improvement in access technologies and other factors, this is no longer so. Nowadays, software-related problems represent the major contributor to downtime.

Considering the industry trends and technology innovations, you should not find this fact surprising. As the IP network takes its place in enterprise networks and service provider networks, it continues to evolve so as to cater to the ever-increasing new feature requirements. In addition, IP is an open standard, which also means that there is more opportunity for multivendor equipment to be put together within a network. Interoperability is always an issue when dealing with multivendor equipment. Finally, the code that runs the networking equipment has grown in size and complexity. Code, like any other application software, has bugs that surface only after being put into production.

Besides code, if you were to focus on user experience, any of the following incidents can cause what can be considered a network outage:

- **Hardware failure**—Includes power supply failure, line card failure, as well as component failure

- **Software failure**—Includes software defects; might result from a hardware failure (for example, memory corruption)

- **Network failure (upstream)**—Usually happens in the service provider's network and is beyond control

- **Server failure**—Could be hardware failure, or it could be caused by an operating system failure

- **Application error**—Includes application defects, or it might be a design fault

- **Human error**—Usually misconfiguration, causing software failure

- **Disaster**—Acts of nature beyond your control

- **Capacity problem**—An overwhelming number of user requests might congest the network, server, or application

- **Attacks**—Caused by introduction of a virus into the system, or it might be a case of sabotage such as a denial-of-service (DoS) attack

Therefore, no matter how well designed a resilient network is, a number of external factors might still cause network failure. You can mitigate some of these factors, such as attacks, but the topic of mitigations is beyond the scope of this book. Others, such as disaster, play to chance and can be mitigated only via risk-analysis and risk-management techniques.

Setting a Strategy to Achieve High Availability

Achieving high availability in a network requires planning and execution. It is about knowing what problems to address and how to deal with them appropriately. In addition, unseen problems might occur, and having a plan to handle these problems is crucial to achieving the overall result.

A network manager should draw up a strategy that includes the following:

- Designing a network for high availability

- Establishing continuous fault detection and measurement of network availability

- Making full use of scheduled downtime

- Instituting a disciplined approach to network operation and processes

Designing a Network for High Availability

Designing a network for high availability takes more than just redundant power supplies for the equipment and lots of redundant links between devices. On the other hand, deploying too many high-availability features, be it hardware or software, might actually render the network unstable (and, therefore, potentially less reliable). Network equipment has come a long way since the days of the coaxial cable and the hub. Not only has the hardware become faster, the software has also become richer in terms of features. As a result, the number of knobs that a network manager can use has increased. These knobs are introduced as software version progressions, and their function might not be well understood. The best way for a network manager to understand and appreciate the functionality of these features is to divide the network into various domains, as shown in Figure 2-6.

Figure 2-6 *Main Areas of an IP Network*

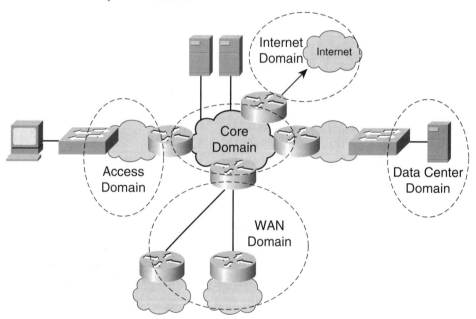

Each domain has features that are relevant and important to maintaining network high availability. The following chapters cover these features in detail.

Establishing Continuous Fault Detection and Measurement of Network Availability

The ability to detect faults and correct them immediately to minimize disruption is important in maintaining network availability. In addition, it is important for you to minimize the damaged area by isolating it so that the least number of users are affected.

Network availability measurement is an important aspect of network operation. A baseline is important so that you have a "snapshot" of the health of the network. Knowing which part of the network is not performing to expectation and needs improvement is crucial. After attempting to remedy the problem, you must take another snapshot to see whether the remedy is working. As mentioned earlier, achieving high availability is an ongoing process. Network managers must continuously improve on network processes, as illustrated in Figure 2-7.

Figure 2-7 *Network Measurement Process*

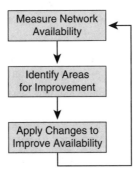

Fault detection and measurement is one area where network management plays a pivotal role. Many tools and features are required in this area, and they are discussed in Chapter 10, "Beyond Implementation."

Making Full Use of Scheduled Downtime

Because downtime has a direct correlation to the overall availability of a network, one obvious strategy is to minimize it as much as possible. Although you cannot prevent unforeseen downtimes such as power failures or hardware failures, you can certainly improve network availability by keeping track of what is happening around the network. For example, be sure that you continually track announcements from vendors about bugs, announcements from the Product Security Incident Response Team (PSIRT) about the latest exploits, and even incident reports from within the network. Events such as these are important because they tell you whether your network will encounter problems and cause subsequent downtime.

You must note announcements from vendors about software rebuilds for bugs or feature improvements so that they can be applied to the network to avoid trouble. Announcements from PSIRT are extremely crucial because they usually relate to exploits and attacks that will paralyze the network. Usually, a recommendation is given accompanying each announcement, and network managers must decide whether the recommendation is relevant to their network.

Internal trouble-ticket events can usually tell a network manager something about the health of the network. An incident that falls into a pattern or looks suspicious usually spells trouble and might require special network settings to deal with it.

Scheduled downtime, or maintenance windows, allows the network manager to take a breather and arm the network with the necessary armory to fight downtime. Applying patches to the currently running software prevents a known bug from hitting the network. Scheduled downtime also proves useful for solving problems that need re-creation. For example, network sniffing might be set up to investigate a difficult problem. Finally, you can use a maintenance window to verify redundancy in the network. Without a scheduled "crash test," you cannot determine that a redundant design will actually work in the event of a real failure.

You should take complete advantage of scheduled downtime to keep the network running smoothly. It is just like sending a vehicle for routine maintenance—the regular battery check, motor oil replacement, and brake pad inspection.

Instituting a Disciplined Approach to Network Operation and Processes

A disciplined approach to network operation and processes is vital and relates directly to network high availability. One example of a disciplined operation is the inclusion of change management. Change management not only provides documentary proof of what has been introduced or changed in the network, it also requires a step-by-step approach to the change itself to minimize user impact. A good change-management process should require that requests be filled out on a form that states the reason for the change and when, how, and where the change is going to be made. In addition, affected users must be notified via e-mail or phone regarding downtime duration and when the network will be back to normal. A documented change request will make troubleshooting easier in the event of an oversight or error.

Because good change management requires request forms to be completed and approval given, it allows for a sanity check to prevent the implementation of conflicting requests. In addition, it is also possible to implement a few nonrelated changes to be made within a single downtime, thus cutting down on total downtime. The process also allows for the help desk to digest what will happen and perhaps stand by with an answer in case users call to ask for information.

Remember that a disciplined network operation is also about managing the user's expectations. If users are kept well informed of the activities in the network and do not encounter surprises during their course of work, they will not be dissatisfied with the network service. Note, however, that managing user expectations is not an easy task and might prove to be a challenging topic by itself.

After you map out a strategy, you must create a design that embraces the points mentioned in the preceding section. Chapter 3, "Fundamentals of IP Resilient Networks," covers design principles that will help achieve the goal of a resilient network.

Summary

It is important to have a clear understanding of the various concepts involved in IP network availability. Many of these concepts derive from the voice world, and you should be careful with their application in the data world. If you apply these concepts incorrectly, you might end up spending money and effort but yet achieve little. On the other hand, if you understand and treat IP network resiliency as a process, you can draw up a series of tasks to create and maintain a highly resilient network. Such tasks include developing an overall strategy, designing and incorporating resiliency features, establishing network operation procedures, and most important, managing user expectations. Successful completion of these activities takes you halfway to your goal.

This chapter covers the following topics:

- Revisiting IP, TCP, and UDP
- Device-level resiliency
- Impact of different switching paths
- Key principles for designing resilient networks

CHAPTER **3**

Fundamentals of IP Resilient Networks

Building a resilient IP network requires more than just putting in duplicate devices and turning on every feature available. A network manager must understand how those relevant protocols work, the architecture of the hardware being deployed, how to predict traffic growth, and how to evolve the network architecture.

This chapter revisits the mechanics of three major protocols: IP, TCP, and UDP. Especially of interest to you will be some of the behaviors of these protocols with respect to network resiliency. This chapter also examines how improvements in hardware features help contribute to network resiliency. Most important, you must have a strategy in place, with a few important design principles that we have learned from those who have done it.

Revisiting IP, TCP, and UDP

This section examines the IP, TCP, and UDP protocols. The building of a resilient network is all about managing these protocols. So a good understanding of how they function is crucial to understanding and resolving the basic challenges that you face.

Internet Protocol

The IP protocol corresponds to the network layer (Layer 3) of the Open Systems Interconnection (OSI) reference model. Its function is to transmit a data block, called a *datagram*, from a source to a destination. Part of its functionality includes fragmentation and reassembly. As a protocol, IP does not provide for data integrity, reliability of transmission, or sequencing.

Figure 3-1 illustrates the IP datagram format.

Figure 3-1 *The IP Datagram Format*

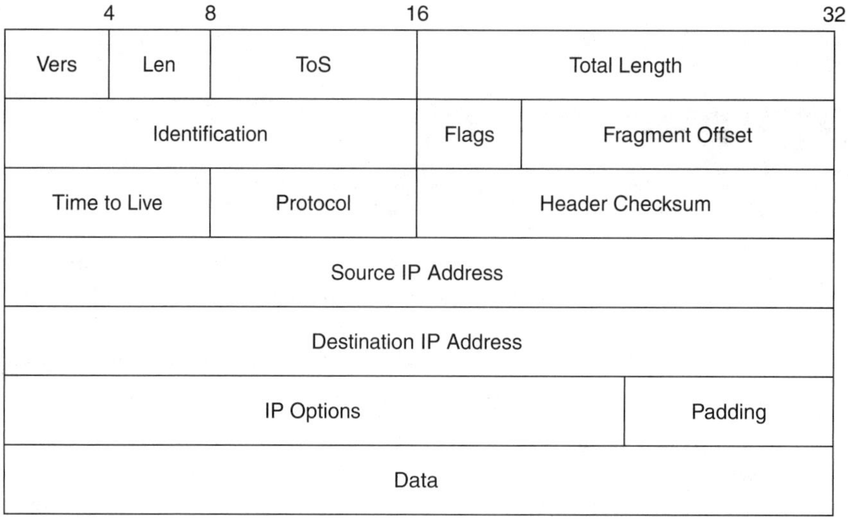

4	8	16	32

Vers	Len	ToS	Total Length		
Identification			Flags	Fragment Offset	
Time to Live		Protocol	Header Checksum		
Source IP Address					
Destination IP Address					
IP Options				Padding	
Data					

The nature of how IP behaves and the functions of some of the fields illustrated directly impact the resiliency of the network, as follows:

- IP cannot handle signal degradation during transmission. For example, when the quality of a pair of fiber has degraded and is causing a high burst error rate, IP continues to transmit packets, even though it is sending garbage. Therefore, selection of Layer 2 technology is important because the right one can complement this deficiency. For example, a Packet over SONET (PoS) interface is always preferred as compared to Gigabit Ethernet. A PoS interface monitors the quality of its transmission and can declare itself unusable so that a reroute can take place.

- IP does not retransmit data in the event of a missing packet. It treats every packet as an independent entity and has no knowledge of whether other related packets are transmitted successfully. It is the job of the upper-layer protocol to deal with this. Therefore, selecting the right upper-layer protocol is crucial for applications that want resilient capability.

- Because IP treats every packet independently, packets for an application might not arrive at the destination in sequence. This happens when multiple paths are made available to a router along the transmission. Although it is the duty of the destination host to handle this situation, this might not be ideal for applications such as voice. Therefore, the forwarding decisions the router makes, whether per-destination load balancing or per-packet load balancing, directly impact applications.

- IP can fragment and reassemble packets. And it can work with different transmission technologies, such as Ethernet, PoS, and so on. These technologies have different maximum transmission unit (MTU) sizes, and traversing from one to another might require the IP protocol to break bigger packets into numerous smaller ones. However, if in the case of a misconfiguration, fragmentation taxes the processing power of the router, this might impact the performance of the network. When critical resources such as CPU of the router is taxed, resiliency is compromised. Therefore, fragmentation is one area that you want to avoid.

- The Type of Service (ToS) field has mostly been ignored until recently when the concept of quality of service (QoS) has become critical. QoS is the basis of identifying different classes of traffic within a network. In the event of network congestion, certain classes of traffic might be deemed less important and be dropped by the network. In this case, network service is affected for some users. Chapter 4, "Quality of Service," discusses QoS in more detail.

- The Options field is also one that is mostly ignored but has an impact on the performance of the network, which ultimately affects network services. Because of the specification of the IP protocol, any IP packet that has an Options field filled must be examined for further action. The packet has to be sent to the router's CPU for processing before being forwarded. In this case, the CPU is being hit by extra work and might potentially slow down the router.

- The length of the IP header is fixed, but the data portion is variable. This means that its efficiency might not be great when the actual payload is small. What this means is that the size of the payload traversing the network does impact the efficiency of the network. Although a larger payload is always preferred in applications such as a file transfer, some applications (Voice over IP [VoIP], for example) send traffic in small packet sizes. Therefore, it is important to have a traffic matrix utilizing the network so that a more accurate capacity can be planned for.

As you might have realized by now, one just needs to review the protocol more thoroughly to realize its impact on network resiliency. This is especially so when some of the fields are used to implement features such as QoS. If you are thinking that the IP protocol is dated and no more work is being done on it, you just might be proven wrong. One just needs to trace the development work from the various RFCs to know that experts have worked on it continuously. To stay informed of the latest development, visit the Internet Engineering Task Force (IETF) website at http://www.ietf.org.

Transmission Control Protocol

The TCP protocol provides reliable transmission of data over an IP network. It works around transmission errors by resending packets. TCP corresponds to the transport layer (Layer 4) of the OSI reference model. As a complement to the IP protocol, it provides functionality that is missing in IP.

Figure 3-2 shows the TCP packet format.

Figure 3-2 *TCP Packet Format*

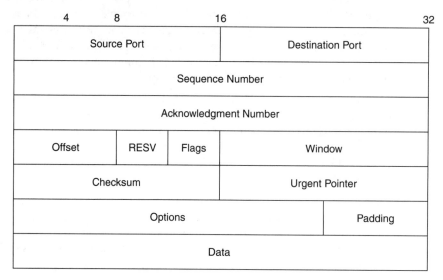

Figure 3-2 illustrates the TCP packet format. Similar to IP, the nature of how TCP behaves and the functions of the fields within the TCP packet have the following implications with respect to resiliency:

- TCP delivers an unstructured stream of bytes identified by sequence numbers, which is called *stream data transfer*. This service benefits applications because they do not have to chop data into blocks before handing it off to TCP. TCP accomplishes this by grouping bytes into segments and passing them to IP for delivery.

- TCP provides connection-oriented, end-to-end reliable packet delivery through an IP network. It does so by sequencing bytes with a forwarding acknowledgment number indicating to the destination the next byte the source expects to receive. Bytes not acknowledged within a specified time period are retransmitted. The reliability mechanism of TCP allows hosts to deal with lost, delayed, duplicate, or out-of-order packets that might happen as they move through an IP network. This ability to recover from errors is sometimes exploited by network managers when dealing with network congestion via features such as weighted random early detection (WRED), as discussed in Chapter 4.

- When sending acknowledgments back to the source, the receiving TCP process indicates the highest sequence number it can receive without overflowing its internal buffers. This flow-control capability of TCP dictates bandwidth consumption, and in fact, affects how fast an application appears to a user.

- TCP processes can both send and receive at the same time. This means fewer flows to keep track of within the network, which is good in the event that you need to deal with per-flow types of operations (for example, accounting). With fewer flows to keep track of, the network saves on critical resources, such as memory, that are important in maintaining the resiliency.

- The TCP process also allows for multiplexing, which enables numerous upper-layer conversations to take place over a single connection. Again, this decreases the number of flows within the network.

Beside these points, two other important characteristics of TCP need special attention: the three-way handshake and the sliding window.

TCP Three-Way Handshake

One of the important characteristics of TCP is the way it establishes a connection between two hosts. The so-called *three-way handshake* is a signature of TCP and is a basis of how some technology works. One good example is a server load-balancing technique, which Chapter 9, "Data Center Module," discusses.

Because of the way resources have to be allocated for a three-way handshake to work, many network attacks exploit this characteristic to compromise the resiliency of the network.

When a pair of devices wants to initiate a TCP connection, they undergo a process known as a three-way handshake. The initiating side sends a SYN packet to the peer, which replies with an ACK and a SYN of its own. Sequence number negotiation occurs here. Finally, the initiator sends an ACK for the peer's SYN. Figure 3-3 illustrates the TCP three-way handshake.

Figure 3-3 *TCP Three-Way Handshake*

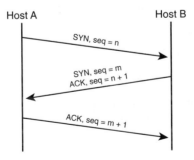

After the connection has been established, data begin to flow between the two hosts. The two hosts then maintain states of the connection, which consume memory resources. Therefore, in a form of a denial-of-service (DoS) attack, the attacker issues numerous SYN requests to a target host, which cause a SYN_ACK response from the target. The target host will soon run out of resources trying to maintain the various SYN requests and eventually not be able to process legitimate SYN requests from other hosts. Even worse, the target host might not even function properly at all because of a lack of memory resources. Therefore, it is critical that important resources within the network, such as the servers and routers, be protected from attacks that exploit the three-way handshake.

TCP Sliding Window

The TCP sliding window is another important characteristic of the TCP protocol. It is a flow-control mechanism used by TCP to regulate the amount of traffic received from a sender at any one time. Data received from the sender is stored in a buffer that feeds the data to an application. If the application is slow in removing the data from the buffer, TCP slows down the sender in transmission. On the other hand, if the application can retrieve data faster than the buffer can be filled up, TCP informs the sender to speed up. The speed to send is determined through a negotiated entity called a *window size*. Window size refers to the number of messages that can be transmitted while awaiting an acknowledgment. After a host transmits the window-size number of messages, it must receive an acknowledgment before any more messages can be sent.

With a window size of 1, each segment must be acknowledged before another segment is transmitted. This methodology results in inefficient use of bandwidth by the hosts.

Figure 3-4 shows a window size of 3.

Figure 3-4 *TCP Sliding Window*

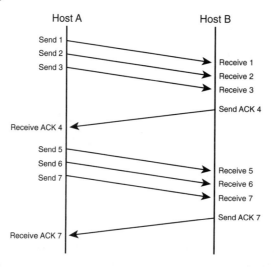

A larger window size allows more data to be transmitted pending acknowledgment, which improves the performance of data transmission, as shown in Figure 3-4.

TCP uses expectation acknowledgments, meaning that the acknowledgment number refers to the packet that is expected next. The "sliding" part of "sliding window" refers to the fact that the window size is negotiated dynamically during the TCP session. Because it is dynamic, it can be increased or reduced during the life of the conversation. Because of this characteristic, the sliding window may be exploited to slow down an application when network congestion occurs. This allows for other more important applications to get service from the network and, hence, improves resiliency for those classes of traffic.

User Datagram Protocol

As opposed to the TCP, User Datagram Protocol (UDP) is a connectionless protocol. It is simpler than TCP in implementation and does not have overheads such as the three-way handshake. UDP corresponds to the transport layer (Layer 4) of the OSI reference model. As a complement to the IP protocol, it serves as a transport mechanism to applications that need efficiency in transmission rather than reliability, and is used when error correction or even resend does not make sense. Examples of such applications are video streaming and voice applications.

Figure 3-5 shows the UDP datagram format.

Figure 3-5   *UDP Datagram Format*

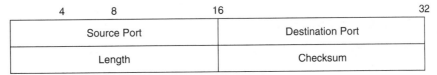

4   8   16   32
Source Port	Destination Port
Length	Checksum

The nature of how the UDP protocol behaves and its format have the following implications with respect to resiliency:

- As you can see, the UDP datagram format is much simpler than that of TCP. It does not have most of the characteristics of TCP recovery. Because UDP does not provide a recovery function, it depends on higher-layer applications to do so.

- You might wonder why you should implement UDP if it does not provide for a reliable transmission. UDP does one thing better than TCP: performance. It is useful in situations where performance is preferred over reliability of the protocol. Some applications work on the basis of short message passing with a small chance of error. The application might provide its own error-recovery mechanism. The following applications use UDP:

  — Network File System (NFS)

  — Simple Network Management Protocol (SNMP)

  — Domain Name System (DNS)

  — Trivial File Transfer Protocol (TFTP)

- UDP does not have a flow control mechanism like that of TCP. In other words, features such as WRED will not work on the UDP protocol. Therefore, in the event of network congestion, an application that uses UDP cannot be slowed down by the network. The throttling mechanism must come from the application itself. From a network-resiliency perspective, these applications become more difficult to control. Although you may choose to police the transmission rate of these applications, dropping too many packets might affect its quality.

- If you are not familiar with UDP, familiarize yourself now. Most video and VoIP applications run on UDP. Learning to deal with UDP will prove important as you try to keep your voice network running continuously.

So far, this chapter has highlighted the characteristics of the major protocols such as IP, TCP, and UDP and how their behaviors impact the resiliency of the network. Another area that contributes to the resiliency of the network is the high-availability feature of the hardware that supports the running of these protocols.

This chapter now looks at how fast the hardware can recover from a failure so as not to affect the running of these protocols, which ultimately affect the applications that are running on them. The following section discusses the development of these hardware features and how the improvements seek to complement the behaviors of the major protocols in supporting a resilient IP network.

Device-Level Resiliency

Device reliability directly impacts the overall resiliency of the network. Many protocol enhancements have been based on improvements made to device-level resiliency. The sections that follow trace the development work done on device-level resiliency, including the following:

- Online insertion and removal (OIR)
- Single line card reload
- High system availability (HSA)
- Route processor redundancy (RPR)
- Route processor redundancy plus (RPR+)
- Stateful switchover (SSO)
- Nonstop forwarding (NSF)

Online Insertion and Removal (OIR)

The online insertion and removal (OIR) feature was developed to enable network managers to replace faulty parts on a hardware device without affecting system operation. For example, when a replacement card is inserted, power is available on the card, and it initializes itself to start working. This feature is also referred to as *hot swap capability.*

Hot swap capability on a card, for example, allows the system to determine when a change occurs in the unit's physical configuration, and reallocates the unit's resources to allow all interfaces to function adequately. This feature allows interfaces on the card to be reconfigured while other interfaces on the router remain unchanged.

The software performs the necessary tasks involved in handling the removal and insertion of the card. A hardware interrupt is sent to the software subsystem when a hardware change is detected, and the software reconfigures the system accordingly. When a card is inserted, it is analyzed and initialized in such a way that the end user can configure it properly. The initialization routines used during OIR are the same as those called when the router is powered on. System resources are allocated to the new interface so that it can begin functioning. Likewise, when a card is removed, the resources associated with the empty slot must either be freed or altered to indicate the change in its status.

Although the concept of OIR might sound simple enough, it is important to know what exactly is happening within the hardware. When an OIR is performed on a Cisco router, the following will happen:

1 The router rapidly scans the backplane for configuration changes.

2 The router initializes all newly inserted interfaces and places them in the administratively shutdown state. This is the default.

3 The router brings all previously configured interfaces on the card back to the state they were in when they were removed. Any newly inserted interfaces are put in the administratively shutdown state.

The effect on the routing table of the router is that routes learned through the removed interface are deleted. Likewise, the Address Resolution Protocol (ARP) cache is selectively flushed. If the card is reinserted into the same slot from which it was removed, or if an identical card is inserted in its place, many of the control blocks from the previous installation are reused.

Almost all Cisco routers today support OIR, but some hardware requires special attention. One good example is the FlexWAN module on the Cisco 7600 series router. The FlexWAN module acts as a carrier module for you to insert port adaptors such as those used on the 7200 and 7500 series into the 7600 series router. Before a port adaptor is removed or inserted into the FlexWAN module, the module has to be removed. In this case, the FlexWAN module is OIR capable, but not the port adaptors. On the other hand, this caveat does not apply to the Port Adaptor Carrier module on the Cisco 7300 series.

If a router does not support OIR and an interface is inserted or removed from it, it might impact traffic being processed by the router, and, in a worse situation, the router might simply reboot. Therefore, it is crucial that you read the installation guide of all modules and port adaptors carefully. A mistake can be costly; it might mean permanent damage done to the card, or worse, the router.

Single Line Card Reload

Before the introduction of the Cisco 7500 single line card reload feature, the only way to correct a line card hardware failure or a severe software error for one line card on a Cisco 7500 series router was to execute a Cbus Complex—a process that reloaded every line card on the network backplane. The time taken to complete the Cbus Complex was often inconvenient, and no network traffic could be routed or switched during the Cbus Complex process.

The Cisco 7500 single line card reload feature enables users to correct a line card failure on a Cisco 7500 series router by automatically reloading the microcode on a failed line card. During the single line card reload process, all physical lines and routing protocols on the other line cards of the network backplane remain active. A single line card reload is also significantly faster than the Cbus Complex process.

Figure 3-6 illustrates the concept of the single line card reload.

Figure 3-6 *Single Line Card Reload*

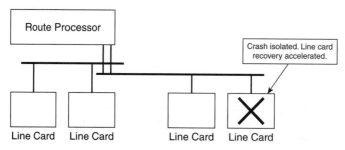

Because the Cisco 7500 single line card reload feature reloads only the line card with the hardware failure rather than all the line cards on the network backplane, the active line cards can continue to forward network traffic.

Use the **show running-config** command to verify that single line card reloading has been successfully enabled on the Cisco 7500 series router. If the "service single-slot-reload-enable" line appears in the command output, the Cisco 7500 single line card reload feature is enabled. If this line does not appear in the command output, the Cisco 7500 single line card reload feature is disabled.

Example 3-1 demonstrates how to configure single line card reload.

Example 3-1 *Configuring Single Line Card Reload*

```
7507#config t
Enter configuration commands, one per line.  End with CNTL/Z.
7507(config)#service single-slot-reload-enable
```

The output in Example 3-2 shows the status of the configuration.

Example 3-2 *Verifying Single Line Card Reload Configuration Status*

```
7507#show running-config
8w1d: %SYS-5-CONFIG_I: Configured from console by consoleun
Building configuration...
Current configuration : 3587 bytes
!
version 12.0
no service pad
service timestamps debug uptime
service timestamps log uptime
no service password-encryption
service multiple-config-sessions
service single-slot-reload-enable
```

For the rest of the chassis-based routers that were developed after the Cisco 7500 series (for example, the Cisco 12000 and the 7600 series routers), this capability is a default rather than a feature that needs configuration. You may reload a line card on the Cisco 12000, 10000, and the 7600 series router without affecting the functioning of the router. It is also available on the Catalyst range of switches.

High System Availability

The HSA feature first appeared on the Cisco 7507 and Cisco 7513 routers. This feature enables you to install two route processor (RP) cards in a single router to improve system availability. HSA is not available on routers such as the Cisco 7200 series because it supports only one processor.

The two RP cards in a router provide the most basic level of increased system availability through the so-called *cold restart feature*. A cold restart means that when one RP card fails, the other RP card reboots the router. In this way, your router is never in a failed state for very long, and, hence, system availability is increased.

When one RP card takes over operation from another in HSA, system operation is interrupted. This change is similar to issuing the **reload** command. The following events occur when one RP card fails and the other takes over:

1 The router stops passing traffic.

2 Route information is lost.

3 All connections are lost.

The backup or "slave" RP card becomes the active or "master" RP card that reboots and runs the router. Thus, the slave has its own image and configuration file so that it can act as an independent processor.

Figure 3-7 illustrates the concept of HSA.

Figure 3-7 *High System Availability*

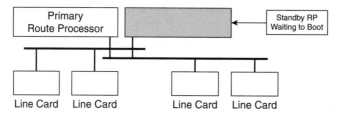

In the HSA process, the time from initial failure to first packet transmission is the aggregate of the times required for each of the following:

1 Identify failure.

2 Load and boot software on standby RP.

3 Load new configuration on standby RP.

4 Reset and reload line cards.

5 Load new configuration on line cards.

6 Learn routes, pass keepalive message, and forward traffic.

7 Route convergence at routing protocol level.

The HSA way of resiliency is also called *cold standby*, which implies that the entire system will lose function for the duration of the restoration via cold restart. All traffic flowing through the router is lost during this time. The benefit of using cold standby is that the device will restart without manual intervention by rebooting with the standby RP taking control of the router.

Taking into consideration how HSA operates, there are two common ways to use HSA, as follows:

- **Simple hardware backup**—Use this method to protect against an RP card failure. With this method, you configure both RP cards with the same software image and configuration information. Also, you configure the router to automatically synchronize configuration information on both cards when changes occur.

- **Software error protection**—Use this method to protect against software errors in a particular release. With this method, you configure the RP cards with different software images but with the same configuration information. If you are using new or experimental software, you might want to consider using the software error-protection method.

You can also use HSA for advanced implementations. For example, you can configure the RP cards with the following:

- Similar software versions, but different configuration files
- Different software images and different configuration files
- Widely varied configuration files (For example, various features or interfaces can be turned off and on per card.)

Example 3-3 shows the configuration steps for HSA setup.

Example 3-3 *HSA Setup Configuration*

```
7507#config t
Enter configuration commands, one per line.  End with CNTL/Z.
7507(config)#redundancy
7507(config-red)#mode hsa
```

When the system has been successfully configured, you can verify the HSA status using the **show redundancy** command, as demonstrated in Example 3-4.

Example 3-4 *Verifying HSA Status*

```
7507#show redundancy
Redundant System Information :
------------------------------
        Available system uptime = 8 weeks, 1 day, 10 hours, 11 minutes
Switchovers system experienced = 0
              Standby failures = 1
          Last switchover reason = none
                 Hardware Mode = Duplex
      Configured Redundancy Mode = hsa
      Operating Redundancy Mode = hsa
              Maintenance Mode = Disabled
                Communications = Down       Reason: Simplex mode
Current Processor Information :
------------------------------
               Active Location = slot 2
          Current Software state = ACTIVE
        Uptime in current state = 8 weeks, 1 day, 10 hours, 10 minutes
                 Image Version = Cisco Internetwork Operating System Software
IOS (tm) RSP Software (RSP-PV-M), Version 12.0(27)S1, EARLY DEPLOYMENT RELEASE )
Technical Support: http://www.cisco.com/techsupport
Copyright© 1986-2004 by cisco Systems, Inc.
Compiled Mon 23-Feb-04 01:14 by nmasa
                          BOOT = ,1;disk0:rsp-pv-mz.120-21.S8,1;
                    CONFIG_FILE =
                      BOOTLDR =
          Configuration register = 0x2102
Peer (slot: 3) information is not available because it is in 'DISABLED' state
7507#
```

Route Processor Redundancy

The route processor redundancy (RPR) feature provides an improvement to the HSA feature. HSA enables a system to reset and use a standby RP in the event of a failure of the active RP.

With RPR, you can achieve a quicker switchover between an active and standby RP in the event of a fatal error on the active RP. When you configure RPR, the standby RP loads a Cisco IOS image upon boot up and initializes itself in standby mode. In the event of a fatal error on the active RP, the system switches to the standby RP, which reinitializes itself as the active RP, reloads all the line cards, and restarts the system.

Figure 3-8 illustrates the concept of RPR.

Figure 3-8 *Route Processor Redundancy (RPR)*

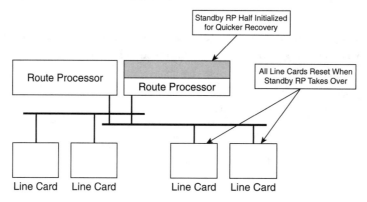

The RPR feature eliminates the following in the HSA switchover process, and, thus, reduces the failure recovery time:

- Step 1: Load and boot software on standby RP.
- Step 2: Load new configuration on standby RP.

The recovery time is now reduced because the standby RP has already started the boot-up process before taking control of the router. This is also called *warm standby mode*.

Example 3-5 demonstrates how to configure RPR.

Example 3-5 *Configuring RPR*

```
7507#config t
8w1d: %SYS-5-CONFIG_I: Configured from console by console t
Enter configuration commands, one per line.  End with CNTL/Z.
7507(config)#redundancy
7507(config-red)#mode rpr
```

Example 3-6 shows sample output of the RPR status.

Example 3-6 *Verifying RPR Configuration Status*

```
7507#show redundancy
Redundant System Information :
------------------------------
        Available system uptime = 8 weeks, 1 day, 10 hours, 25 minutes
 Switchovers system experienced = 0
               Standby failures = 2
           Last switchover reason = none
                  Hardware Mode = Duplex
       Configured Redundancy Mode = rpr
       Operating Redundancy Mode = rpr
               Maintenance Mode = Disabled
                 Communications = Down        Reason: Simplex mode
Current Processor Information :
------------------------------
                Active Location = slot 2
          Current Software state = ACTIVE
       Uptime in current state = 8 weeks, 1 day, 10 hours, 24 minutes
                  Image Version = Cisco Internetwork Operating System Software
IOS (tm) RSP Software (RSP-PV-M), Version 12.0(27)S1, EARLY DEPLOYMENT RELEASE )
Technical Support: http://www.cisco.com/techsupport
Copyright©  1986-2004 by cisco Systems, Inc.
Compiled Mon 23-Feb-04 01:14 by nmasa
                           BOOT = ,1;disk0:rsp-pv-mz.120-27.S1.bin,1;
                  CONFIG_FILE =
                      BOOTLDR =
          Configuration register = 0x2102
Peer (slot: 3) information is not available because it is in 'DISABLED' state
7507#
```

Route Processor Redundancy Plus

Building on the RPR feature, the RPR+ feature further eliminates steps in the HSA switchover process:

- Step 3: Reset and reload line cards.
- Step 4: Load new configuration on line cards.

RPR+ on the router keeps the line cards up and running during the switchover. The line cards will not be reloaded or reinitialized, and they continue to forward traffic. This feature reduces the route processor switchover time by 90 percent (down to 30 to 40 seconds) compared to RPR.

Figure 3-9 illustrates the concept of RPR+.

Figure 3-9   *Route Processor Redundancy Plus (RPR+)*

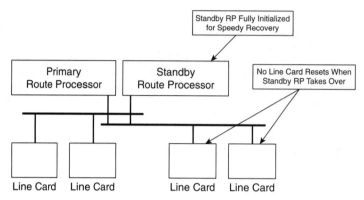

Example 3-7 demonstrates how to configure RPR+.

Example 3-7   *Configuring RPR+*

```
7507#config t
Enter configuration commands, one per line.  End with CNTL/Z.
7507(config)#hw-module slot 2 image disk0:rsp-pv-mz.120-27.S1.bin
7507(config)#hw-module slot 3 image disk0:rsp-pv-mz.120-27.S1.bin
7507(config)#redundancy
7507(config-red)#mode rpr-plus
```

The output in Example 3-8 shows the status of the router after RPR+ has been configured. Notice the peer status shows STANDBY COLD-CONFIG.

Example 3-8   *Verifying RPR+ Configuration Status*

```
7507#show redundancy
Redundant System Information :
------------------------------
         Available system uptime = 8 weeks, 1 day, 10 hours, 38 minutes
Switchovers system experienced = 0
               Standby failures = 4
          Last switchover reason = none
                  Hardware Mode = Duplex
        Configured Redundancy Mode = rpr-plus
         Operating Redundancy Mode = rpr-plus
               Maintenance Mode = Disabled
                 Communications = Up
Current Processor Information :
------------------------------
                Active Location = slot 2
          Current Software state = ACTIVE
         Uptime in current state = 8 weeks, 1 day, 10 hours, 37 minutes
                  Image Version = Cisco Internetwork Operating System Software
IOS (tm) RSP Software (RSP-PV-M), Version 12.0(27)S1, EARLY DEPLOYMENT RELEASE
```

Example 3-8 *Verifying RPR+ Configuration Status (Continued)*

```
SOFTWARE (fc2)
Technical Support: http://www.cisco.com/techsupport
Copyright© 1986-2004 by cisco Systems, Inc.
Compiled Mon 23-Feb-04 01:14 by nmasa
                        BOOT = ,1;disk0:rsp-pv-mz.120-27.S1.bin,1;
                 CONFIG_FILE =
                     BOOTLDR =
         Configuration register = 0x2102
Peer Processor Information :
--------------------------
            Standby Location = slot 3
         Current Software state = STANDBY COLD-CONFIG
      Uptime in current state = 1 minute
               Image Version = Cisco Internetwork Operating System Software
IOS (tm) RSP Software (RSP-PV-M), Version 12.0(27)S1, EARLY DEPLOYMENT RELEASE
SOFTWARE (fc2)
Technical Support: http://www.cisco.com/techsupport
Copyright© 1986-2004 by cisco Systems, Inc.
Compiled Mon 23-Feb-04 01:14 by nmasa
                        BOOT = ,1;disk0:rsp-pv-mz.120-27.S1.bin,1;
                 CONFIG_FILE =
                     BOOTLDR =
         Configuration register = 0x2102

7507#
```

Stateful Switchover

The stateful switchover (SSO) feature, which is based on RPR+, reduces the time in Step 5 in the HSA switching process:

- Step 5: Learn routes, pass keepalive message, and forward traffic.

The SSO allows the active RP to pass the necessary state information of key routing and interface protocols to the standby RP upon switchover, thereby reducing the time for the standby RP to learn and converge routes.

Figure 3-10 illustrates the concept of SSO.

Figure 3-10 *Stateful Switchover (SSO)*

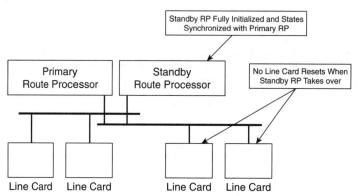

For any hardware device that is running SSO, both RPs must be running the same software and configuration so that the standby RP is always ready to assume control following a fault on the active RP. The configuration information is synchronized from the active RP to the standby RP at startup and whenever changes to the active RP configuration occur. Following an initial synchronization between the two processors, SSO maintains RP state information between them, including forwarding information.

During switchover, system control and routing protocol execution are transferred from the active processor to the standby processor. The time required by the device to switch over from the active to the standby processor ranges from platform to platform. The Cisco 12000 series switches immediately and can achieve zero packets dropped, whereas the Cisco 7500 series may take between 5 and 10 seconds.

Example 3-9 demonstrates the configuration required for SSO.

Example 3-9 *Configuring SSO*

```
7507#config t
Enter configuration commands, one per line.  End with CNTL/Z.
7507(config)#hw-module slot 2 image disk0:rsp-pv-mz.120-27.S1.bin
7507(config)#hw-module slot 3 image disk0:rsp-pv-mz.120-27.S1.bin
7507(config)#redundancy
7507(config-red)#mode sso
```

The output in Example 3-10 shows the status of the router after it has been configured for SSO. Notice the peer status shows STANDBY HOT.

Example 3-10 *Verifying SSO Configuration Status*

```
7507#show redundancy
Redundant System Information :
------------------------------
       Available system uptime = 8 weeks, 1 day, 10 hours, 43 minutes
Switchovers system experienced = 0
```

Example 3-10 *Verifying SSO Configuration Status (Continued)*

```
                Standby failures = 5
          Last switchover reason = none
                   Hardware Mode = Duplex
      Configured Redundancy Mode = sso
        Operating Redundancy Mode = sso
                Maintenance Mode = Disabled
                  Communications = Up
Current Processor Information :
------------------------------
                 Active Location = slot 2
           Current Software state = ACTIVE
         Uptime in current state = 8 weeks, 1 day, 10 hours, 42 minutes
                   Image Version = Cisco Internetwork Operating System Software
IOS (tm) RSP Software (RSP-PV-M), Version 12.0(27)S1, EARLY DEPLOYMENT RELEASE
SOFTWARE (fc2)
Technical Support: http://www.cisco.com/techsupport
Copyright© 1986-2004 by cisco Systems, Inc.
Compiled Mon 23-Feb-04 01:14 by nmasa
                            BOOT = ,1;disk0:rsp-pv-mz.120-27.S1.bin,1;
                     CONFIG_FILE =
                         BOOTLDR =
           Configuration register = 0x2102
Peer Processor Information :
--------------------------
                Standby Location = slot 3
           Current Software state = STANDBY HOT
         Uptime in current state = 0 minutes
                   Image Version = Cisco Internetwork Operating System Software
IOS (tm) RSP Software (RSP-PV-M), Version 12.0(27)S1, EARLY DEPLOYMENT RELEASE
SOFTWARE (fc2)
Technical Support: http://www.cisco.com/techsupport
Copyright© 1986-2004 by cisco Systems, Inc.
Compiled Mon 23-Feb-04 01:14 by nmasa
                            BOOT = ,1;disk0:rsp-pv-mz.120-27.S1.bin,1;
                     CONFIG_FILE =
                         BOOTLDR =
           Configuration register = 0x2102

7507#
```

Nonstop Forwarding

The NSF feature works with the SSO feature in the Cisco IOS Software. Whereas SSO solves an internal problem (RP failure), NSF prevents some external event that might prove harmful to the network from occurring.

Usually when a networking device restarts, all routing peers of that device detect that the device went down and then came back up. This transition results in a *routing flap*, which could spread across multiple routing domains. Although the device might be forwarding traffic, routing flaps caused by the switchover create routing instabilities, which are detrimental to overall network performance. NSF helps to suppress routing flaps in SSO-enabled devices, thus reducing network instability.

Figure 3-11 illustrates the concept of NSF.

Figure 3-11 *Nonstop Forwarding (NSF)*

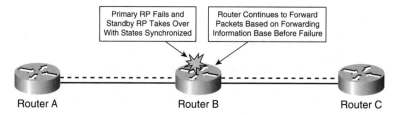

NSF allows for the forwarding of data packets to continue along known routes while the routing protocol information is being restored following a switchover. With NSF, routing peers do not experience routing flaps. Data traffic is forwarded through the line cards while the standby RP assumes control from the failed active RP during a switchover. The capability of line cards to remain up through a switchover and to be kept current with the Forwarding Information Base (FIB) on the active RP is key to NSF operation.

For NSF to function, protocols and applications must be high-availability (HA) aware. A feature or protocol is HA aware if it maintains, either partially or completely, undisturbed operation through an RP switchover. For some HA-aware protocols and applications, state information is synchronized from the active to the standby processor.

For NSF to work, enhancements to the routing protocols such as Open Shortest Path First (OSPF), Intermediate System to Intermediate System (IS-IS), and Border Gateway Protocol (BGP) have been made. These enhancements are also known as *graceful restart extensions* to the protocols. With the enhancements, these protocols have been made NSF capable and aware, which means that routers running these protocols can detect a switchover and take the necessary actions to continue forwarding network traffic and to recover route information from the peer devices. For example, the IS-IS protocol can be configured to use state information that has been synchronized between the active and the standby RP to recover route information following a switchover instead of information received from peer devices.

A device is said to be NSF capable if it has a redundant RP and has been configured to support NSF; therefore, it would rebuild routing information from NSF-aware or NSF-capable neighbors. A networking device is said to be NSF aware if it is running NSF-compatible software but it does not have redundant RP (for example, the Cisco 7200 series router).

For NSF to work, Cisco Express Forwarding (CEF) has also been enhanced, because each protocol depends on CEF to continue forwarding packets during switchover while the routing protocols rebuild the Routing Information Base (RIB) tables. When the routing protocols have converged, CEF updates the FIB table and removes stale route entries. CEF, in turn, updates the line cards with the new FIB information. CEF is discussed in detail in the section "Cisco Express Forwarding Switching" later in this chapter.

Example 3-11 demonstrates the configuration required for NSF. In this case, OSPF is configured to operate in NSF mode.

Example 3-11 *Configuring OSPF to Operate in NSF Mode*

```
7507#config t
Enter configuration commands, one per line.  End with CNTL/Z.
7507(config)#hw-module slot 2 image disk0:rsp-pv-mz.120-27.S1.bin
7507(config)#hw-module slot 3 image disk0:rsp-pv-mz.120-27.S1.bin
7507(config)#redundancy
7507(config-red)#mode sso
7507(config-red)#exit
7507(config)#router ospf 100
7507(config-router)#nsf
```

Although the status of the router shows that it is in SSO mode, the status of the OSPF process now reflects NSF in Example 3-12.

Example 3-12 *Verifying OSPF in NSF Mode*

```
7507#show ip ospf
 Routing Process "ospf 100" with ID 10.10.10.4
 Supports only single TOS(TOS0) routes
 Supports opaque LSA
 Supports Link-local Signaling (LLS)
 Supports area transit capability
 Initial SPF schedule delay 5000 msecs
 Minimum hold time between two consecutive SPFs 10000 msecs
 Maximum wait time between two consecutive SPFs 10000 msecs
 Incremental-SPF disabled
 Minimum LSA interval 5 secs
 Minimum LSA arrival 1000 msecs
 LSA group pacing timer 240 secs
 Interface flood pacing timer 33 msecs
 Retransmission pacing timer 66 msecs
 Number of external LSA 0. Checksum Sum 0x0
 Number of opaque AS LSA 0. Checksum Sum 0x0
 Number of DCbitless external and opaque AS LSA 0
 Number of DoNotAge external and opaque AS LSA 0
 Number of areas in this router is 1. 1 normal 0 stub 0 nssa
 Number of areas transit capable is 0
 External flood list length 0
 Non-Stop Forwarding enabled
    Area BACKBONE(0) (Inactive)
        Number of interfaces in this area is 5 (1 loopback)
        Area has no authentication
        SPF algorithm last executed 2w4d ago
        SPF algorithm executed 42 times
```

continues

Example 3-12 *Verifying OSPF in NSF Mode (Continued)*

```
        Area ranges are
        Number of LSA 1. Checksum Sum 0x3746
        Number of opaque link LSA 0. Checksum Sum 0x0
        Number of DCbitless LSA 0
        Number of indication LSA 0
        Number of DoNotAge LSA 0
        Flood list length 0
7507#
```

Besides getting a good grasp on the way the key protocols work and knowing the resiliency capability of the devices, it is also important to have a good understanding of the switching paths that an IP packet can possibly take within the router. This concept is important in the discussion of network resiliency, because it directly impacts how the hardware behaves as well as the resultant performance.

Impact of Different Switching Paths

A Cisco router can move a packet from one interface to another in various ways. These switching paths use different methods to achieve the same result, but the differences in the way they work affect how fast the router can perform its job. For obvious reasons, you want the router to work as fast as possible. However, depending on the network condition, the router might revert to the slowest method.

NOTE   Portions of this section are adapted from "How to Choose the Best Router Switching Path for Your Network," a white paper available at Cisco.com.

To understand how these switching paths work, it helps to first understand the basic functions of the router. The role of the router is to move packets. It does it through the following steps:

1 Receive the packet.

2 Perform additional services to the packet. For example, tagging the ToS field, or changing the source or destination IP address and so on.

3 Determine how to get to the destination of the packet.

4 Determine the next hop toward the destination and which interface to use.

5 Rewrite the Media Access Control (MAC) header so that it can reach its next hop.

Figure 3-12 illustrates how a router moves packets.

Figure 3-12 *Basic Function of a Router*

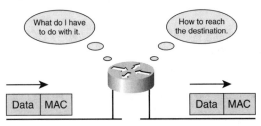

Process Switching

Process switching, or sometimes referred to as punting, is the slowest among all switching paths. This is the ancestor of all routing functions, and almost all features that you see within Cisco IOS Software originate from process switching.

During process switching, the forwarding decision is based on the Routing Information Base, or RIB, and the information necessary for the MAC rewrite is taken from the ARP cache. Depending on the configuration, additional services might also be performed. However, the most significant point about process switching is that it runs as a normal process in the CPU and competes for system resources with the rest of the processes. While the CPU is handling the switching process, all other activities have to be interrupted for the job.

In process switching, the processor is heavily involved in the work of forwarding IP packets. This has the effect of slowing down the performance of the router, because every packet needs to be handled in the same manner. Most of the value-added IP services such as Network Address Translation (NAT) were introduced via the process switching method. Over time, these features have been incorporated into other methods that are more efficient and even into the ASIC.

Process switching should be avoided at all costs because it hits the control-plane function, affects performance of the router, and, in a worst-case scenario, affects the stability of the network. With process switching, a router rated as capable of forwarding millions of packets per second can be running at just thousands of packets per second. Therefore, it is important that you know which features in the Cisco IOS code will be process switched and ascertain whether there are any alternatives to the solution. Note, however, that process switching provides the most flexibility for features support. Therefore, it does have its advantages when it comes to introduction of new features in the fastest manner.

Over the years, various switching methods were devised to overcome the performance limitation of process switching, including the following:

- Interrupt context switching
- Fast Switching

- Optimum switching
- CEF switching

Each of these switching methods stores the forwarding information in a different manner in a bid to speed up forwarding performance. In addition, each is an improvement as compared to previous ones, with CEF switching being the latest method.

Cisco Express Forwarding Switching

Cisco Express Forwarding (CEF) uses a 256-way data structure to store forwarding and MAC header rewrite information, but it does not use a tree, as do the previous methods. CEF uses a *trie*, which means the actual information being searched for is not in the data structure. Instead, the data is stored in a separate data structure, and the trie just points to it. In other words, instead of storing the outbound interface and MAC header rewrite within the tree itself, CEF stores this information in a separate data structure called the *adjacency table*, as illustrated in Figure 3-13.

Figure 3-13 *Cisco Express Forwarding (CEF)*

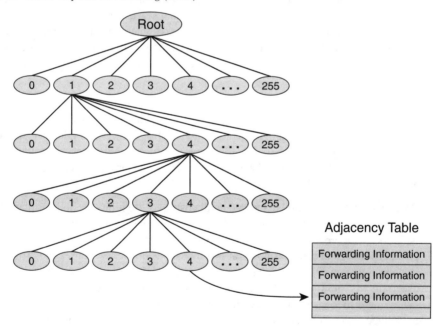

CEF uses a FIB to make IP destination prefix-based switching decisions. The FIB is conceptually similar to a routing table or information base. It maintains a mirror image of the forwarding information contained in the IP routing table. When routing or topology changes occur in the network, the IP routing table is updated, and those changes are reflected in the FIB. The FIB maintains next-hop address information based on the information in the IP routing table. Because there is a one-to-one correlation between FIB entries and routing table entries, the FIB contains all known routes and eliminates the need for route cache maintenance that is associated with switching paths such as fast switching and optimum switching.

Hosts in a network are said to be adjacent if they are directly connected. In addition to the FIB, CEF maintains an adjacency table to keep track of all MAC information of the adjacent hosts.

The separation of the forward information in the CEF table and the Layer 2 information in the adjacency table provides a number of benefits:

- The adjacency table can be built separately from the CEF table, allowing both to build without process switching being involved.

- The MAC header rewrite information that is used to forward a packet is not stored in the cache entries, so changes in this information do not require invalidation of cache entries.

- Recursive routes can be resolved by pointing to the recursive next hop, rather than directly to the forwarding information.

- The adjacency table can contain entries other than MAC header rewrite strings and outbound interface information. Some of the various types of entries that can be placed in the adjacency table include the following:

    - **Cache**—A MAC header rewrite string and outbound interface used to reach a particular adjacent host or router.

    - **Receive**—Packets destined to this IP address should be received by the router. This includes broadcast addresses and addresses configured on the router itself.

    - **Drop**—Packets destined to this IP address should be dropped. This could be used for traffic denied by an access list, or routed to a NULL interface.

    - **Punt**—CEF cannot switch this packet; pass it to the next-best switching method (generally fast switching) for processing.

    - **Glean**—The next hop is directly attached, but no MAC header rewrite strings are currently available.

- CEF is less CPU intensive than fast switching route caching. Therefore, more CPU resources can be dedicated to other critical activities.

- CEF offers an unprecedented level of switching consistency and stability in large dynamic networks. In a large network, fast switching cache entries are frequently invalidated because of routing changes. These changes can cause traffic to be process switched using the routing table, rather than fast switched using the route cache.

Because the FIB lookup table contains all known routes that exist in the routing table, CEF eliminates route cache maintenance and the fast switch/process switch forwarding scenario.

CEF also takes advantage of the separation between the CEF table and the adjacency table to provide a better form of load sharing than any other switching method. An extra hash table is inserted between the CEF table and the adjacency table, as illustrated in Figure 3-14.

Figure 3-14 *CEF Load Balancing*

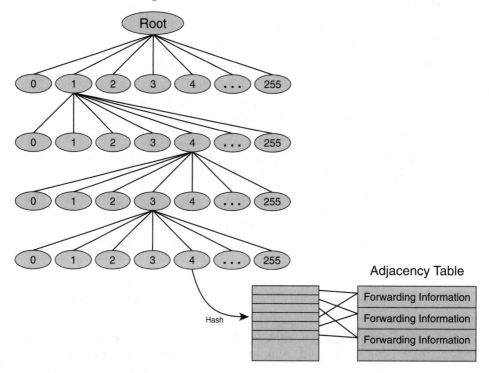

The CEF table points to the hash table, which contains pointers to the various adjacency table entries for available parallel paths. The source and destination addresses are passed through a hash algorithm to determine which table entry to use for each packet. Per-packet load sharing can be configured, in which case each packet uses a different hash table entry.

Each hash table has 16 entries among which the paths available are divided based on the traffic share counters in the routing table. If the traffic share counters in the routing table are all 1 (as in the case of multiple equal-cost paths), each possible next hop receives an equal number of pointers from the hash table.

With CEF, all cache aging is eliminated, and the cache is prebuilt based on the information contained in the routing table and ARP cache. Unlike process switching, there is much less processor involvement during the course of the operation. Because much less process switching is involved, the router boosts its performance, keeps its control-plane activity in check, and makes the network more robust.

Example 3-13 demonstrates the configuration for CEF.

Example 3-13 *Configuring CEF*

```
7507#config t
Enter configuration commands, one per line.  End with CNTL/Z.
7507(config)#ip cef
```

The output in Example 3-14 shows the switching status of the router.

Example 3-14 *Verifying Router Switching Status*

```
7507#show ip cef summary
IP CEF with switching (Table Version 218), flags=0x0
  18 routes, 0 reresolve, 0 unresolved (0 old, 0 new), peak 1
  0 load sharing elements, 0 references
  48 in-place/0 aborted modifications
  21268 bytes allocated to the FIB table data structures
  universal per-destination load sharing algorithm, id F968AD29
  2(0) CEF resets
  Resolution Timer: Exponential (currently 1s, peak 1s)
  Tree summary:
   8-8-8-8 stride pattern
   short mask protection disabled
   18 leaves, 16 nodes using 18688 bytes
  Transient memory used: 0, max: 112
  Table epoch: 0 (18 entries at this epoch)
7507#
```

Depending on the hardware architecture, you can run CEF in two ways:

- Central CEF
- Distributed CEF

Central CEF

In central CEF mode, both the FIB and adjacency tables reside within the route processor, and the route processor performs the switching function, as illustrated in Figure 3-15.

Figure 3-15 *Central CEF Mode Operation*

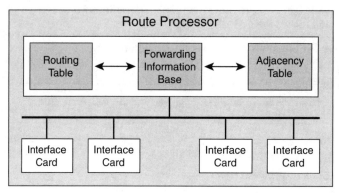

Central CEF switching mode is usually used in the lower end of the router family, because they do not support separate line cards.

Distributed CEF

In Distributed CEF (dCEF), line cards, such as the 7500 series Versatile Interface Processor (VIP) cards or Gigabit Switch Router (GSR) line cards, maintain an identical copy of the FIB and adjacency tables. The line cards perform the express forwarding between port adapters, relieving the route processor of any involvement in the switching operation. Figure 3-16 illustrates dCEF mode operation.

Figure 3-16 *Distributed CEF Mode Operation*

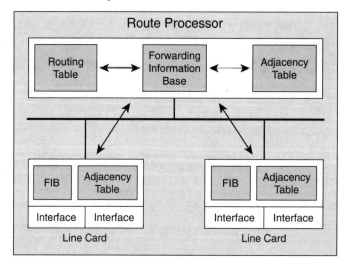

dCEF uses an interprocess communication (IPC) mechanism to ensure the synchronization of FIB tables and adjacency tables on the RP and line cards.

The development in the switching method not only enables a router to have better and more stable performance, it is also the basis for resiliency features such as SSO and NSF. Note that beginning from Cisco IOS Release 12.0, CEF is the preferred and default switching path, and dCEF is the only supported switching method for the Cisco 12000 series router.

Protecting the Control Plane and Data Plane

Although concepts such as control and data planes have been around for many years, not many network managers pay much attention to them—not until recently, when hackers started turning their attention to attacking the network itself.

A router, or rather, all networking devices, can be divided into three distinct components:

- **Control plane**—The brain of the hardware
- **Data plane**—The portion of the router where most of the user traffic traverses
- **Management plane**—Provides a way to configure and manage router resources

The control plane handles the well-being of the router and is responsible for activities such as routing updates, keepalives, and housekeeping of the many processes running. Recall that in CEF switching the processor has to maintain the FIB and adjacency tables. This is an example of a control-plane function. Of course, the rest of the caches, such as ARP, are also part of the function. These tables and processes that are running in the CPU of the router keep the router running properly and maintain states with the rest of the devices. If these are not properly maintained, the router will fail.

Because the control plane is such an important function, any disruption to it will have a detrimental effect. An example of an event that causes disruption of the control plane is a DoS attack. Such activity almost always causes one of the following to occur:

- Near or 100 percent CPU utilization, which inhibits the router from functioning properly
- Loss of routing protocol keepalives, which causes route flaps and network stability
- Loss of packets due to buffer exhaustion, causing dropping of legitimate IP traffic

Therefore, with more sophisticated attacks, more and more network managers are paying attention to control-plane protection. Chapter 7, "Internet Module," discusses this topic in more detail.

The data plane handles most of the traffic-forwarding function. Recall that in dCEF switching, the line cards are forwarding traffic among the interfaces, with minimal processor intervention. This is an example of a data-plane activity. Most of the activities that happen within the data plane are value-added services such as inspection, filtering, marking, and translation. For increased performance, most of these activities are done with the help of the ASIC within the line cards, which is sometimes called a *hardware assist*. In the event that a packet is not handled by the ASIC, it will be passed to the processor for processing, which you learned about earlier in the "Process Switching" section. Any activities that cause punting negatively affect performance and so should be avoided.

The management plane provides a way to configure and manage the network. Because it can change the way the network behaves, protecting it from unlawful use is of paramount importance. The management plane plays an important role in maintaining the resiliency of the network, because it is also responsible for performance information gathering.

Routers such as the Cisco 12000 and 10000 series adopt a separate control-, data-, and management-plane design in their hardware architecture. The advantage of separating these functions, beyond dramatic performance improvements, is that the separation provides stronger fault containment. If a control plane (route processor) fails or is restarted, for instance, traffic will continue to flow through the line cards. This is the basis of how SSO and NSF work.

Establishing a Resiliency Strategy

Building a resilient IP network is not just about having redundant links and turning on the SSO features in all routers. In fact, the most difficult aspects of achieving IP resiliency is establishing an overall resiliency strategy.

With an overall resiliency strategy, you can predict what needs to be done to the network in the next few phases. You should be able to map out the logical design, knowing how it will eventually grow. From the logical design, the corresponding physical design is mapped out. Finally, both the logical and physical design translate to what sort of hardware is required, and which capacity features have to be placed in the hardware.

The strategy has to remain consistent. Many times, the resiliency of a network is compromised because of inconsistency in strategy. Shortcuts are made or different hardware is selected to do a certain task, perhaps because of shortages of funds or maybe because of changes in decision-making personnel. Problems such as these ultimately create outages later on.

Redundancy Strategy

Part of the overall resiliency strategy is how to achieve redundancy in both the logical and physical networks. Many network managers find this task challenging. For example, you might achieve physical redundancy, but because of a lack of logical redundancy, the network still experiences failure.

Logical Resiliency

When we talk about logical redundancy, we are mainly protecting important parts of the network, such as the following, from failing:

- Network paths
- Functional entity

As mentioned previously, a network path is the route that traffic traverses between a source and a destination. It is a logical entity because network paths usually arise from some route calculations (for example, a shortest-path algorithm). The determination of the path is always done by the routing protocol and the results stored in the various routers within the network. As events occur within a network (for example, when a physical link fails), the network path for a source and destination pair may potentially change. This change might result in an alternative path, or it might result in a broken connection between the same source and destination. The task then is to make sure there is always a redundant network path to an important resource within the network (to a server, for example).

Functional entity refers to the logical functions that are performed by the routers (for example, a default gateway function or a multicast routing function). A host such as a personal computer usually needs a default gateway to help it send traffic to the rest of the world. If there is only one default gateway and it fails, the personal computer will never be able to contact any other hosts except those on the same subnet. Another example is the Area Border Router (ABR) function in the OSPF network. The multiple ABRs prevent the OSPF subarea from being disconnected from area 0.

Ensuring redundancy for these logical functions is critical, because it ensures a backup in the event of a failure. Information on logical resiliency in routing is usually found in the design guides for routing protocols such as OSPF and BGP:

- *OSPF Network Design Solution*, 2nd Edition, by Tom M. Thomas. (Cisco Press, 2003. ISBN: 1587050323)
- *BGP Design and Implementation*, by Randy Zhang and Micah Bartell. (Cisco Press, 2003. ISBN: 1587051095)

Physical Resiliency

You might find the task of ensuring physical redundancy easier because it is a more visual exercise. You should look at several areas with regard to physical redundancy:

- **Device**—For device-level resiliency, look into areas such as power supply and route processors. For example, if redundant power supplies are used, they should be connected to different power sources. You also need to know how a particular device behaves under certain physical conditions such as heat and humidity. This is when certification such as Network Equipment Building System (NEBS) proves helpful.

- **Link**—For link-level redundancy, look into areas such as the number of links required and how they map to the logical design. For example, you might choose to have multiple Ethernet links between two routers. If you choose to implement EtherChannel technology, these links appear as one logical interface in the logical network. On the other hand, if these links are used individually, there will be multiple logical links in the logical design. For link redundancy, having multiple logical links might not be advantageous. For one, cost might be prohibitive, as in WAN links, or some protocols might impose a limit on the number of links that it can support.

- **Site**—With device-level and link-level resiliency addressed, the next thing to look into is whether there is a need for the entire site to be protected from disaster. This is usually applicable to data centers and for disaster recovery purposes; a remote site may be required.

Scaling Strategy

Some people might find it strange how a scaling strategy affects resiliency of a network. For one, you might not be able to tear down everything in the network just to do improvement work on a congested link. With such high expectations on the uptime on a network (remember the five-nines challenge described in Chapter 2, "Establishing a High-Availability Network"), it is almost impossible to do maintenance work without affecting network services. Therefore, many things have to be "preprovisioned" so as to avoid downtime.

As with a redundancy strategy, a scaling strategy also involves logical and physical aspects. To scale a network logically, consider aspects such as the IP addressing scheme, subnet size, and the number of subnets available within a network. You also need to look at how the routing design scales. For example, consider how many routers should be within an OSPF area, how many subnets should belong to a specific area, how many areas the network should be, and how many ABRs your network needs.

In the physical aspect, look into areas such as scaling a link speed. For example, you must decide whether to scale a 1-Gb backbone link by adding another 1-Gb link or by upgrading to an OC-48 link. The first option is called *scaling horizontally*; the latter is called *scaling vertically*. The correct choice depends on resource availability.

You might also look at things such as interface capacity, or so-called real estate, and router performance. In a chassis-based router, the number of slots, and thus the number of ports that it can support, dictates how large a network it can connect to in terms of number of links. In addition, the performance of the same router, in both switching capacity and forwarding capability, affects how much traffic it can carry at any one time.

By relying on features such as OIR, you can keep adding interfaces to a router and grow the network without affecting the rest. However, you can do so only if the router has enough slots in the first place. Therefore, having a capacity-planning exercise is important, and right sizing has to be done on the hardware. You do not want too large a router that costs a lot of money, nor do you want to run out of slots on a router.

Failure in this area usually results in network congestion and costly downtime.

Key Principles for Designing Resilient Networks

Designing a resilient IP network depends on a multitude of variables such as resources, constraints, and funds. You might not be able to get a definite list of rules for network design, but a few principles are worth noting, including the following:

- Simplicity
- Modularity
- Security

These principles are tried and tested and have been proven to be effective in every successful network.

Simplicity

In IP network design, you might be able to achieve more by having less.

One of the common mistakes many network managers make when it comes to network resiliency is an "overdesigned" network. By provisioning more redundant components than required, a network manager might actually complicate things and make matters worse. The network might become too complex to implement, monitor, and troubleshoot. The result: The network suffers from more outages.

Simplicity is perhaps the most important principle of all. It advocates implementing the minimal hardware and features to achieve the desired result, and, thus, it ultimately drives cost-savings. However, network managers must tread a fine line, because excessive cost-savings often leads to running too many logical functions within a single box. Remember, there has to be a limit to cost cutting.

Modularity

If you view the entire network as one entity, it is a huge and complex system. The network, however, is more manageable if you break it into various smaller components, as shown in Figure 3-17.

Figure 3-17 *A Modular Network*

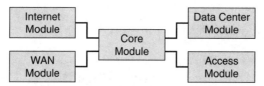

Figure 3-17 shows how a network can be broken into smaller modules, as follows:

- **Core**—The module that links the rest of the modules (commonly known as the backbone)

- **Access**—The module from which users interface with the network

- **Internet**—The module that connects the entire network to the Internet

- **WAN**—The module that connects remote branches

- **Data center**—The module that connects all the servers

Each of these smaller modules has its distinct role within the network. Because each of these modules has a unique function to perform, each requires different features to be effective in its work. For example, the features that you look for in the core module (mainly IP routing) differ from those in the access module (mainly Ethernet switching). This enables one to identify the suitable hardware to be deployed within the different modules.

In addition, it is clear that certain features may be important in a module but may not be so in another. Often, network managers ask for every feature on a particular piece of hardware, only to pay too much for a piece of hardware that eventually does little. The excuse for doing this is always the "just in case" mentality. However, with proper logical design in place, and most important, a consistent strategy, you can avoid this.

Another advantage of having a modular network design is it enables you to isolate problems within a module. If you contain the problem, the rest of the network can then continue to function, which means fewer users are affected and more overall uptime of the network.

Security

With hacking tools readily available now, it no longer takes a professional to do damage to your network. A youth sitting in his study room with broadband access to the Internet is all it takes. Therefore, security is paramount and should not be compromised when designing the network.

The job of the network is to transport IP packets from source to destination. Therefore, the resources required to perform the job, the routing information and the devices, become important entities and natural targets of attacks. Protecting these resources becomes a paramount task when designing the network. These resources can be exploited in many ways; the best source of information is a white paper under the Cisco SAFE Blueprint series:

> SAFE: Best Practices for Securing Routing Protocols, http://www.cisco.com/en/US/ netsol/ns340/ns394/ns171/ns128/ networking_solutions_white_paper09186a008020b51d.shtml

Securing the routing infrastructure is just one aspect of security. You should also look into many other areas, such as IP telephony, wireless network, as well as mitigating worm and virus attacks. A good reference to start with is the Cisco SAFE Blueprint, which you can find at the following URL:

> http://www.cisco.com/en/US/netsol/ns340/ns394/ns171/ns128/ networking_solutions_package.html

Summary

Building a resilient IP network requires you to thoroughly understand the way the three protocols—IP, TCP, and UDP—behave. It is also important to understand the factors that affect the performance of the network. Besides the software, understanding the high-availability feature of the hardware, and its impact on these protocols, helps you to choose the right device to build the network. However, the first step to a resilient network is to have a clear strategy as to how it should be achieved, bearing in mind that simplicity, modularity, and security play important roles.

This chapter covers the following topics:

- Protecting the control plane with QoS
- Protecting applications with QoS
- Building blocks of QoS
- Application QoS and control-plane traffic
- QoS deployment strategy

CHAPTER 4

Quality of Service

This chapter examines how quality of service (QoS) can be deployed to assist in building a resilient IP network. QoS refers to the ability of a network to enforce preferential treatment to applications, through a series of classification, policing, congestion avoidance, and queuing. Although QoS is not directly responsible for ensuring that the network is up and running all the time, it has a direct impact on the resiliency of the network.

It is important to remember that resilient networks must fulfill two requirements:

- Maintain high availability
- Ensure consistent user experience

The first requirement aims to keep the network running as long as possible and to recover from failures in an efficient and transparent manner. Two types of problems can adversely effect the availability of network:

- Physical failure
- Control-plane failure

Whereas redundant components and routing protocols are used to prevent physical failure, QoS can be used to prevent control-plane failure.

As stated in Chapter 2, "Establishing a High-Availability Network," it is the user's experience that matters. Users consider the network at fault when their applications suffer from performance or quality of delivery. This is another area where QoS comes in to help fulfill the second requirement of a resilient IP network.

Protecting the Control Plane with QoS

As discussed in Chapter 3, "Fundamentals of IP Resilient Networks," the control plane ensures the overall health of the router and its ability to forward traffic. A heavily loaded control plane is bad for the router, because the router might lose its ability to track changes in the network, recover from faults quickly, or, in the worst case, it might completely break down. The control plane of a router may be kept busy for many reasons. Some are intentional, such as a denial-of-service (DoS) attack, whereas some are inherent in the implementation of protocols.

Protecting the control plane is an important component of building a resilient network. A good understanding of the types of traffic that affect the control plane is crucial. In addition, knowing how different features can be used to protect the control plane is useful.

Traffic Types That Affect the Control Plane

One of the basic roles of a router is to forward packets from one interface to another. Packets that are not meant for the router itself but that require forwarding are called *transit packets*. Through the improvements made to the various switching technologies, routers can handle transit packets without the intervention of the CPU. In many situations, however, the service of the CPU is required:

- Process switching
- Transit packets with IP option
- Transit packets with Time-To-Live = 1
- Packets destined for the router (for example, ping)
- Management packets for the router (for example, Simple Network Management Protocol (SNMP) or Telnet)
- Routing protocol packets (for example, Open Shortest Path First (OSPF) and Border Gateway Protocol (BGP))
- Broadcast traffic
- Address Resolution Protocol (ARP)
- Layer 2 keepalives
- Traffic that needs fragmentation

Whenever a router receives packets that fall into the preceding list, its CPU has to be interrupted to process these packets. The rate at which these packets arrive at the router has a profound impact on the overall well-being of the router. In an extreme case, the rate of arrival can be so high that the router is so overwhelmed with the traffic that it cannot maintain the rest of the processes properly. When this happens, performance of the router suffers and the following can occur:

- The router cannot keep up with Layer 2 keepalive messages, which causes its peer to think that it has gone down.
- The router loses its Layer 3 keepalive messages, which causes its routing protocol peer to think that it has gone down.
- The router has a problem learning new routes (for example, processing new BGP updates).
- The router's routing table is not kept current.

When any of these things happen, the availability of the network is affected. Therefore, a control-plane failure is a serious problem and should be avoided.

Many features have been implanted in the Cisco IOS Software to protect the CPU of the router from overloading. The aim is to protect the CPU so that the router can function properly under all traffic conditions. Because the router receives all sorts of traffic that requires the attention of the CPU, the aim is to be able to prioritize and choose which traffic to process first. This is when QoS plays an important role.

For QoS to work, the various traffic must be sorted first. After that, you can prioritize traffic for the CPU to process. It is also necessary to choose what sort of traffic to process in the first place. After prioritizing the traffic, you want to have the additional ability to dictate at what rate the traffic should be processed.

Tagging Routing Protocol and Layer 2 Control Packets

Of all the packets that need the CPU's attention, the most important ones come from the routing protocols and the Layer 2 keepalives. These two categories of traffic are the most important, because losing routing protocol updates means having an invalid routing table, and losing Layer 2 keepalives may be misinterpreted as a link down.

To differentiate these packets from the rest, they have to be tagged so that they can be recognized and given priority for processing. There are two ways to tag these packets, depending on whether the router is sending packets out to a peer or whether the packet is to be used internally:

- IP Precedence
- The pak_priority flag

IP Precedence

The IP Precedence is used for tagging when routing protocol messages are sent to external peers by the router. As illustrated in Figure 4-1, the IP Precedence is made up of the first 3 bits within the Type of Service (ToS) byte of the IP packet.

Figure 4-1 *IP Precedence*

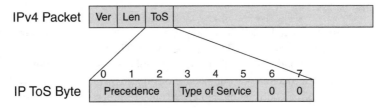

Depending on the setting of its 3 bits, the IP Precedence provides eight classifications, as illustrated in Table 4-1.

Table 4-1 *Original Meaning of the Precedence Bits*

Precedence Bits	Class	Name
000	0	Routine
001	1	Priority
010	2	Immediate
011	3	Flash
100	4	Flash override
101	5	Critic/ECP
110	6	Internetwork control
111	7	Network control

When sending out routing protocol updates, a router tags all the packets with an IP Precedence set to 6. This is enabled by default and does not need configuration. The following routing protocols use this feature:

- Routing Information Protocol (RIP)
- OSPF
- BGP

The pak_priority Flag

Whereas the IP Precedence is used when the router sends out routing protocol packets, the pak_priority is for use by Cisco routers internally. When a packet arrives at the interface of a router, the interface driver queues the packet with a packet header. The packet header indicates the type of information that has arrived. The pak_priority is a flag within the packet header that Cisco IOS Software uses to prioritize the treatment of this packet within the router.

Whereas the IP Precedence affects how external parties treat the packet, the pak_priority affects how packets are queued within the router. The tagging of these two fields is independent, and both might not be used by applications running within the router. For example, when a router sends out packets originating from OSPF, the IP Precedence is set to 6 with pak_priority turned on. However, only IP Precedence is set to 6 for BGP packets.

Besides IP routing protocols, the pak_priority is also used by other non-IP protocols and Layer 2 keepalives. The following are some of these protocols:

- RIP
- OSPF

- Intermediate System to Intermediate System (IS-IS)
- Point-to-Point Protocol (PPP)
- High-Level Data Link Control (HDLC)
- Asynchronous Transfer Mode (ATM)
- Frame Relay
- Spanning Tree Protocol (STP)

Through the use of IP Precedence and pak_priority, the router can differentiate high-priority control packets from normal traffic that is bound for the CPU. This capability is important for it to implement the next phase of control-plane protection, which is selective packet discard (SPD).

Selective Packet Discard

SPD is the ability of the router to give priority to the processing of the routing protocol packets. The routing protocol packets are given higher priority over other packets to reach the input queue of the CPU. This is to ensure that the router can maintain the integrity of its forwarding tables and its states first before processing other packets.

With SPD, traffic sent to the CPU is sorted, and checks are performed to decide whether to drop or to continue processing the traffic. Two queues are allocated for the sorting of the traffic: a general queue and a priority queue. Packets put into the priority queue are processed first regardless of other traffic conditions. Packets put in the priority queue include routing protocol packets or those with IP Precedence set to 6. The general queue is for holding packets from some other applications that also need the CPU's attention. In this case, the traffic might still be subjected to checks, and so a chance still exists that the traffic might be dropped. When the queue size of the general queue is in between a minimum and maximum threshold, packets are dropped randomly. These drops are called *SPD flushes*.

With SPD, the router does what is critical to its well-being: The router processes the most important messages from the routing protocol and Layer 2 keepalives first. By ensuring that its most precious resource is protected, the router can then maintain proper states and continue to forward traffic.

Receive ACL

Although SPD gives priority to the routing protocol traffic and Layer 2 keepalives, it is more important to ensure that the traffic destined for the CPU is indeed legitimate in the first place.

The receive access control list (RACL) complements the protection of the CPU by enforcing an external net of defense around it. RACL is implemented at the ingress interface of the router and is activated after the input ACL. Traffic destined for the router is subjected to the RACL, and depending on its configuration might be dropped even before the SPD is activated. RACL is useful in DoS attack prevention, because the router can be configured to respond only to queries from certain hosts and reject all other traffic.

The RACL works just like a normal ACL. Example 4-1 shows a sample that allows only ping and OSPF packets to be sent to the router.

Example 4-1 *Configuring RACL*

```
ip receive access-list 100
access-list 100 permit icmp any any echo
access-list 100 permit ospf any any precedence internet
access-list 100 deny ip any any
```

With SPD and RACL in place, the CPU of the router might still become overwhelmed (for example, when a DoS attack is launched at the router with the flooding of ping packets at the router). In Example 4-1, the RACL permits ping packets to the router. Because ping packets are allowed to pass through the RACL and fit the requirement to be processed by the CPU, precious CPU resources are spent on processing these packets. Under a DoS attack, the CPU can be crippled with this traffic. The control-plane policing (CPP) tightens the protection of the CPU, as you learn in the next section.

Control-Plane Policing

The CPP further tightens the protection of the CPU by applying the usual QoS mechanism of matching and policing on packets bound for the CPU. The Modular QoS command-line interface (CLI) (MQC) is used in this case to define the policy.

In CPP, the CPU is treated just as another host within the router where MQC can be applied to its ingress and egress interfaces. Ingress is for traffic bound for the CPU, whereas egress is for traffic originating from the CPU. Although CPP adopts the nomenclature of MQC, certain restrictions apply to the use of certain MQC features:

- The only actions allowed are police and drop.
- Matching is based on standard and extended ACLs, IP Differentiated Services Code Point (DSCP), and IP Precedence.

Because CPP can be configured via the MQC, you have flexibility in terms of defining different traffic types bound for the CPU with different treatment characteristics. Example 4-2 shows how to configure CPP to give priority to BGP and OSPF traffic, while policing on the management traffic and other IP traffic.

Example 4-2 *Configuring CPP*

```
access-list 100 permit tcp any any eq bgp
access-list 100 permit ospf any any precedence internet
access-list 101 permit icmp any any echo
```

Example 4-2   *Configuring CPP (Continued)*

```
access-list 101 permit tcp any any eq telnet
access-list 101 permit udp any any eq snmp
access-list 102 permit ip any any

class-map routing_traffic
match access-group 100
class-map management_traffic
match access-group 101
class-map normal
match access-group 102

policy-map cpp
class management_traffic
police 128000 1500 1500 conform-action transmit  exceed-action drop
class normal
police 64000 1500 1500 conform-action transmit  exceed-action drop

control-plane
service-policy input cpp
```

Protecting Applications with QoS

Protecting applications with QoS is the second requirement that a resilient network needs to fulfill. The previous sections in this chapter have described how you can deploy QoS to protect the control plane. Now, the following sections describe ways to ensure consistent user experience, especially in a converged IP network.

Understanding the Need for Application QoS

The concept of QoS has been around for quite some time. One topic of discussion among network managers has always been whether QoS is necessary in the first place. The most common misconception has been "throwing bandwidth at the problem." The reason for this misconception has been the mix-up between solving a capacity problem as opposed to solving a QoS problem.

In the past, many applications had their own dedicated network. Think of a bank, in the past, for example. The bank had at least a dedicated phone network to provide for voice service, an SNA network to run its banking applications, a separate network that provided for videoconferencing service, and maybe even a separate network for video surveillance. Each of these networks was running different protocols and different networking technologies. Voice was running on a time division multiplexing (TDM)-based network, while the SNA network had an automatic teller machine that connected to the network via 64-kbps leased lines. The videoconferencing solution was most likely running on ISDN, and the surveillance was on a proprietary technology. Collectively, these myriad of networks made up the communication infrastructure of the bank. Because each of these networks carried a single application, the only way to improve performance was via upgrades of hardware and bandwidth. To enable more calls to be made from a branch, the TDM connection had to be upgraded. To support new-generation automatic teller machines, the 64-kbps line had to be upgraded to 128 kbps. This kind of network conditioned network managers to think that upgrading bandwidth is the only way to solve a problem.

Today, the same bank has a totally new communication infrastructure consisting of a converged IP network: a single network that carries with it voice service that is based on VoIP, banking applications that are web based, videoconferencing that is done via IP-based software, and a video surveillance system that has IP-enabled cameras. "Throwing bandwidth" seems to continue to solve some of the problems, but it has come to a point where it is either too expensive to continue doing so, or it does not work anymore.

The reasons why this is so can be attributed to a few factors:

- Latency
- Jitter
- Loss

These factors might not be relevant in the communication infrastructure of the past, but they become apparent in a converged network infrastructure. The following sections describe these factors and the effects they have on the applications.

Latency

In an IP network, latency is defined as the time taken for a packet to enter and leave the network. As shown in Figure 4-2, packet A enters the network at time = t_0 and leaves the network at time = t_1. The latency of the network, t_2, for packet A, in this case, is $t_1 - t_0$.

Figure 4-2   *Network Latency*

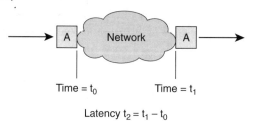

Time = t_0 Time = t_1

Latency $t_2 = t_1 - t_0$

Note that latency is an end-to-end measurement of network delay. The time, t_2, is the total delay introduced from various components of the network. These include transmission technology used, the speed at which packets can be forwarded at each intermediate node, and the various transmission speeds along the way.

Many network managers think that latency problems can be solved by adding bandwidth. This is not true, as can be illustrated in a simple example. Suppose that two towns, A and B, are connected by a single-lane highway that permits only a speed of 10 miles per hour. These towns are 100 miles apart. And suppose there is a car with two people who need to travel from town A to town B. It will take them 10 hours to reach town B. Now suppose the highway has been expanded to a two-lane highway. Each of the two people can now take two cars to go from town A to town B. They can even invite one more person each. But they will still take 10 hours, because the speed limit is still 10 miles per hour. Although the capacity of the highway has increased, the time taken to reach town B is still the same. The effect of adding bandwidth is like adding an extra lane to the highway. Because bandwidth solves only the capacity issue, it does not solve the latency problem.

Latency becomes a big issue in a converged network, because applications such as voice and video have stringent requirements regarding latency. For example, VoIP applications, such as the one used by the bank, generally require a one-way delay of 150 ms. A breach of this requirement might result in problems such as echo and incomprehensible conversation. Problems such as this, something that is audible, are apparent to users and totally unacceptable to them. The 150-ms requirement contrasts with having to wait 5 seconds for a file transfer to complete. With the introduction of each node or link within the network, latency adds up. The introduction of other applications on the same network that contend for the same resources might also increase the latency.

Jitter

Another factor that is closely related to latency is jitter. Jitter is defined as the rate of change in the time gap between consecutive packets. As shown in Figure 4-3, the time gap between packets A and B, t^0, might be different from that between packets B and C, t^1, after traversing through the network.

Figure 4-3 *Network Jitter*

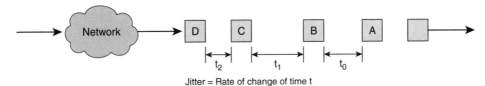

Jitter = Rate of change of time t

Just like latency, jitter is another key requirement for delivering good-quality voice or video applications. Consider video applications, for example. If the jitter is negligible, the image is delivered in a smooth manner to the end user. On the other hand, with high jitter, the video suffers from jerky images and, in the worst-case scenario, might not be visible at all.

Jitter is affected by the traffic condition in the network. As a video packet traverses the network, it has to contend with packets from other applications along the way (for example, FTP and web applications). The latter two applications have a very different characteristic from that of the video: They are bursty by nature and may transmit variable-sized packets.

The network needs to ensure that the jitter for the voice and video is not affected by these applications. This is when QoS is required.

Loss

Besides solving latency and jitter issues, preventing packet loss in applications such as voice and video is critical. Although losing one packet once every great while might not adversely effect these applications, losing too many might produce undesirable results. A long silence might interrupt a conversation, or a video screen might appear blank. In the case of the bank doing surveillance using an IP camera, losing images might have serious consequences.

Packet loss also results from the traffic condition in the network. A converged network carries different application types of data, video, and voice. These different applications must contend for the resources in the network. If the network is congested, packets are dropped because no resources are available. The network must be able to prevent the loss of packets that belong to voice and video applications. This is an area QoS can help in mitigating the risk of packet loss.

Determining When to Deploy QoS

With an understanding of the need for QoS to combat latency, jitter, and loss, it is also important to know when to deploy QoS. Many times, this is mixed up with the need to provision additional bandwidth. Sometimes you need only one of them to solve a problem, whereas at other times you might need both.

A few scenarios will help you decide when QoS is needed and when adding bandwidth will help within a network.

Scenario 1: Undercongested Link

The left side of Figure 4-4 shows that because the traffic load over a period of time is always less than the peak bandwidth, there is no congestion at all on the link.

Figure 4-4 *Scenario 1*

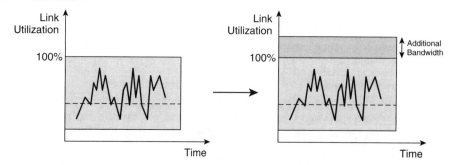

Because there is no congestion at all in this scenario, adding bandwidth does not contribute anything at all (as shown on the right side of Figure 4-4). No benefit derives from deploying QoS to prevent packet loss either. The only reason to deploy QoS is to tackle the latency and jitter issues, if they exist. One key consideration here is the link speed in this scenario. If it is a low-speed link, jitter becomes an issue if packets from a voice application have to be transported across the link behind other applications with large packets. For high-speed links, this problem might not be an issue at all. In this scenario, it is recommended that for link speed of 768 kbps or below that QoS be considered to meet the latency and jitter requirements.

Scenario 2: Occasionally Congested Link

The left side of Figure 4-5 shows the case when a link is occasionally congested. The right side shows when additional bandwidth was introduced just to cater to the spikes of traffic load that happened every once in a while.

Figure 4-5   *Scenario 2*

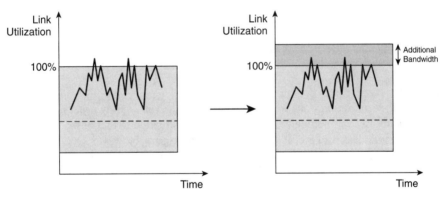

In this case, it might be too expensive to deploy the additional bandwidth in response to occasional spikes. This is when the benefits of QoS are most apparent. The occasional spikes are called *transient congestion*. They only happen occasionally, such as when month-end reports need to be churned out for reporting purposes. QoS is most effective in solving transient congestion because it eliminates the need for additional bandwidth, thus achieving cost-savings. This savings is most obvious when you are dealing with expensive WAN links. Multiply the cost of the WAN links a hundredfold for a bank, for example, and the savings can be quite substantial.

Another reason to deploy QoS in this case is to prevent loss of packets belonging to voice or video applications during period of transient congestion. You can achieve this via prioritization of the traffic and selectively dropping other traffic. The requirement for latency and jitter will be the same as that described in scenario 1.

Scenario 3: Badly Congested Link

Figure 4-6 shows a case when the traffic load is more than the original bandwidth most of time. This is a classic case of a capacity issue, and the addition of bandwidth is absolutely required. Without adding bandwidth, attempting to deploy QoS as in scenario 2 is not going to help much, because the traffic load just overwhelms the available bandwidth. This is also a classic case when QoS is being tasked to solve the wrong problem. It might be able to help some applications, but overall, too many applications are affected and the overall effect of the QoS implementation does not help.

Figure 4-6 *Scenario 3*

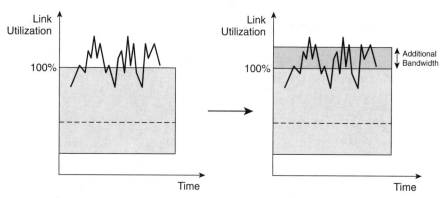

In this scenario, introduction of more bandwidth is absolutely necessary to solve the capacity issue. If adding bandwidth brings the situation to that of the first scenario, then preventing loss packets via QoS will not be necessary. However, QoS will still be required to solve the latency and jitter issues, just as in scenario 2.

Building Blocks of QoS

The Differentiated Services (DiffServ) model is the building block for QoS applications. DiffServ, defined in RFC 2475, is one of the two QoS architectures for IP networks defined by the IETF. It works on a provisioned QoS model and does not require the application to signal for reservation of network resources.

In the DiffServ model, the network attempts to segregate traffic into different classes based on the DSCP field in the IP packet. Based on the individual class, network nodes within the network then perform the following activities:

- Classification and marking
- Congestion avoidance
- Congestion management
- Traffic conditioning

Classification and Marking

Traffic classification is the most fundamental step that needs to be taken when deploying DiffServ model QoS. It is the action of separating different applications so that priority or special treatment can be accorded to them. Without traffic classification, all applications will look the same within the network, and all will be treated the same, which defeats the purpose of QoS. After the traffic classification has been done, there has to be a way to identify the traffic from different applications, which is where traffic marking, sometimes referred to as *coloring*, comes in. Traffic marking identifies these different applications by setting the ToS byte in every packet of the application; subsequent action can then be taken by the devices in the downstream direction.

Classification and marking should be done at ingress of the network so that time-sensitive applications can be recognized early and preferential treatment can be given.

Congestion Avoidance

Congestion avoidance is a QoS strategy that monitors network traffic in an effort to anticipate and avoid congestion before more severe problems occur. The concept of congestion avoidance is tightly linked to TCP's behavior under network overload situations. As discussed in Chapter 3, "Fundamentals of IP Resilient Networks," TCP can ensure a reliable transmission of data. The strength of the TCP protocol lies in its retransmission function and its capability to regulate traffic flow. However, this very strength also makes TCP susceptible to a phenomenon called the *global synchronization*. Global synchronization happens because different TCP flows tend to adjust their window sizes at the same time, in response to network congestion.

Global synchronization causes inefficient use of bandwidth and increases latency and jitter in the network. The solution to global synchronization lies in exploiting the retransmission characteristics of TCP via the deployment of feature called random early detect (RED). The purpose of RED is to address congestion in an active manner rather than in a reactive manner. It is a mechanism whereby an IP gateway can infer an impending congestion by calculating its average output queue size. The gateway then goes on to drop certain packets randomly or mark the packets to indicate probability of a drop. By relying on the sliding window mechanism of the TCP protocol, RED solves the problem of global synchronization by preventing different TCP sessions from adjusting their window size at the same time. An enhancement to RED is weighted RED (WRED), which enables you to separate traffic into different classes, each with different dropping rates.

As the network speed gets higher, the concept of RED is especially important to keep the network throughput high while maintaining a low delay. This throughput is important for applications such as voice and video. However, to ensure consistent delivery of voice and video applications, it is critical that they not be subjected to congestion avoidance. Regardless of the underlying protocols used, random dropping of packets from these applications should be prohibited.

Congestion Management

Congestion management is also known as queuing. All the packets that arrived at a router have to contend for the scarce resource of the output buffer for transmission. The management of the use of the buffers is important. Over the years, different queuing methods have been introduced, including the following:

- First-in, first out (FIFO)
- Priority queuing
- Custom queuing
- Weighted fair queuing (WFQ)
- Class-based weighted fair queuing (CBWFQ)
- Low-latency queuing (LLQ)

Choosing a right queuing strategy is critical to delivering the service that is expected of each application. In a converged network, to overcome the latency and jitter demand of delay-sensitive applications, LLQ is recommended for this class of application. The rest of the bandwidth is then shared by the rest of the applications via the CBWFQ.

Traffic Conditioning

Traffic conditioning is perhaps the easiest concept of all QoS tools to understand. Basically, the network avoids potential trouble by limiting the amount of traffic that an application can send at any one time. This limit can be achieved in either of two ways: via traffic policing or via traffic shaping.

Traffic policing enables you to manage traffic by specifying an allowable transmission rate and what action to be taken for excess traffic. The action to take is either dropping the traffic or marking the traffic with lower precedence. On the other hand, traffic shaping buffers the excess traffic and tries to smooth the flow by delaying the sending of the excess traffic.

Applications such as voice and video should not be subjected to shaping because this has the effect of increasing latency and jitter. However, the use of the policing function on this class of traffic may be considered as a safety measure to ensure that they transmit within the bandwidth allocated.

For more details about QoS and its building blocks, refer to *End-to-End QoS Network Design: Quality of Service in LANs, WANs, and VPNs* by Tim Szigeti and Christina Hattingh (Cisco Press, 2005).

Application QoS and Control-Plane Traffic

In the section "IP Precedence," you learned that a router makes use of the IP Precedence to tag the packets when sending out routing protocol messages. The IP Precedence is also used by routers to tag traffic of other applications. Therefore, it is important to understand how the router behaves when it also has QoS enabled for the applications in the network.

When it comes to classification and marking, IP routing protocol messages are tagged with IP Precedence of 6 before they are sent out by the router. This tagging has a significant impact on how the QoS should be designed. For one, no other applications should be using IP Precedence 6 or 7. Otherwise, packets from these applications might be confused with routing protocol updates, jeopardizing the control-plane stability. In fact, any traffic, other than routing protocol updates, with a IP Precedence of 6 and above should be disallowed to enter the network, or its IP Precedence reset to a lower level (a common practice for service providers). Likewise, it is also critical to ensure that when sending normal traffic to other external networks, the packets not be tagged with IP Precedence 6.

When it comes to congestion management, it is also important to understand how the router handles the routing protocol updates as well as Layer 2 control packets in its queuing. In distributed platforms such as the Cisco 7500 series, the packets with pak_priority set are placed in the default class if no separate QoS configuration is done. In this case, it has to share the queue with other applications, although its pak_priority setting ensures that it will not be dropped. For such platforms, it might be advisable to explicitly configure a separate class for the routing protocols and specify its own bandwidth requirement. Doing so will guarantee bandwidth availability for the updates and ensure consistent performance. Other Cisco routers, such as the 7200 and the lower-end series, deploy a totally different approach to handling these high-priority packets. Special queues are dedicated to processing these packets, and other queues are reserved for user-specified QoS configuration.

For the rest of the QoS tools, congestion avoidance and traffic conditioning should not be applied to the routing protocol messages at all. In fact, packets with a pak_priority flag set are never dropped by QoS implementations such as RED.

Understanding the way high-priority control packets are handled is crucial to maintaining a resilient network. Consider this fact when planning a QoS deployment strategy.

QoS Deployment Strategy

Much can be said about the development of the QoS architecture and technology within the IP world. However, the percentage of networks deploying an end-to-end QoS architecture is still low. As mentioned in the beginning of this chapter, part of the reason could be because throwing bandwidth is still practiced by many network managers. Another possibility is that network managers try deploying QoS, but no visible benefits derive from the deployment. Many times, QoS deployment in a network fails mainly because of a lack of strategy. Without a proper strategy, just turning on some fancy QoS features will not work (and in a worst-case scenario, might break the network).

As part of the effort in building a resilient IP network, a proper QoS architecture is mandatory. And that means a proper documentation that deals solely on the QoS matters.

One way to ascertain whether a network is well run is to ask for a QoS architecture documentation. Chances are, you will not find many.

The QoS deployment strategy should be worked out during the network design phase. It encompasses five major steps, as follows:

Step 1   Classify applications.

Step 2   Define policies.

Step 3   Test policies.

Step 4   Implement QoS features.

Step 5   Monitor.

Classifying Applications

The first step in the QoS deployment strategy is to identify all applications running within your network. You need to find out each application's ranking within the business organization, and determine whether it is mission critical. You also need to understand the nature of each of the applications in terms of behavior, protocol, bandwidth requirements, and network characteristics. This is perhaps the most difficult part of all because ranking an application might involve politics within the organization, and many parties might be involved in this exercise. For example, a networking person might not know the application as well as the application person or the developer. In this case, trying to find out network requirements might require the involvement of other departments.

A good way to start is to understand the different traffic classes. Put simply, you can group all IP applications under one of these classes.

Table 4-2 shows an example of how applications can fall into one of these classes.

Table 4-2   *Application Classes and Their Properties*

Application Class	Example Applications	Application/Traffic Properties	Packet/Message Sizes*
Real-time	VoIP application, IP phones	Voice bearer. Small packets. Well-defined maximum rate/flow. Sensitive to delay and latency.	Packet sizes G.729 20 ms = 60 bytes G.711 20 ms = 200 bytes
Signaling	VoIP and video applications	Voice and video signaling. Bursty flows. Traffic bursts occur when calls are established/torn down. Very little traffic while call is active.	Average message size = 100 bytes Maximum message size = 1000 bytes

Table 4-2 *Application Classes and Their Properties (Continued)*

Application Class	Example Applications	Application/Traffic Properties	Packet/Message Sizes*
Interactive	Telnet Citrix Instant Messenger Whiteboarding	Highly interactive applications with tight user feedback requirements. Examples: character echoing in Telnet, TN3270, and so on. Hosts generate small messages.	Average message size < 100 bytes Max message size < 1KB
Transactional	SAP B2B Applications Oracle Database Siebel Microsoft SQL Microsoft Outlook Lotus Notes BEA Systems E-mail Data-link Switching	Interactive query applications. Client/server protocol model. User-initiated client-based queries followed by server response. Query response may consist of many messages between client and server. Query response may consist of many TCP and FTP sessions running simultaneously (HTTP-based applications).	Number of bytes in total query response depends on application. Can be anywhere from 1 KB to 50 KB.
Financial market data	Tibco	Stream of packets containing financial information. Each financial feed has a well-defined maximum rate.	1500 bytes
Interactive video	NetMeeting	Video and audio bearer for videoconferencing applications. Variable packet sizes depending on image complexity, encoding algorithm, and frame type (I, P, or B frames in MPEG).	Maximum packet size ~= 1500 bytes

continues

Table 4-2   *Application Classes and Their Properties (Continued)*

Application Class	Example Applications	Application/Traffic Properties	Packet/Message Sizes*
Streaming video	Real video IP/TV	Video and audio bearer for streaming (not interactive) video. Variable packet sizes depending on image complexity, encoding algorithm, and frame type (I, P, or B frames in MPEG). Forward error correction for video sources is assumed to allow a 1% network drop rate.	Maximum packet size ~= 1500 bytes
Bulk	Database Synchronizations Network-based backup Video content distribution Large FTP transfer	Long file transfers. Rate between hosts always > available network bandwidth. Always need to be tamed.	Average message size = 512 KB or greater
Best-effort	All noncritical traffic, for example: HTTP web browsing Miscellaneous traffic	Bursty traffic. Always need to be tamed.	Average message size = 100 to 500 KB
Layer 3/2 control	Routing protocol traffic (OSPF, BGP, IS-IS, and so on) Bridge protocol data unit	Bursty traffic. Periodic Hello messages to maintain link state. Link failures cause burst of link-state update messages.	IGP Hello packets ~= 100 bytes Link-state packets 10010-500 bytes
Management	SNMP TFTP Configuration downloads	Transactional, like polling for MIBs.	Average message size 256 bytes

* Message sizes are the typical/maximum message sizes exchanged between applications. When messages are less than IP MTU size (and TCP MSS size for TCP applications), packet size = message size. When messages are greater than IP MTU size, each message becomes a burst of MTU-size packets.

Based on the characteristics of the traffic, you now have a good understanding of how each of these applications behaves. Most important, there is a way to help decide which traffic type gets assigned to a certain IP Precedence or DSCP class. With information such as packet size and protocol setup, you can select the correct queuing mechanism to support the workings of the applications.

Defining Policies

After categorizing the applications, you can define the class of service for the QoS architecture. You will now have a good indication of the number of classes in the network, as well as the nature of the traffic flow. You can define policies with respect to the identified classes of traffic.

During policy definition, make sure you have logical and physical network diagrams. The logical diagram indicates the traffic flow within each class of traffic. The physical diagram reveals the bandwidth capacity, as well as potential bandwidth choke points within the network. With these important characteristics clearly identified, you can define the type of policies on each node. For example, the first-hop nodes are called the edge of the network. This is the place to perform classification and marking. Queuing and LFI are most often found in the WAN links with low-speed connections. As the traffic flows toward the core of the network, it is mainly WRED and queuing that play a more critical role.

Testing Policies

Testing is the system verification exercise for the QoS architecture. It is recommended that this be done in a test lab first rather than in a live environment. The test-lab phase of the entire testing exercise verifies the individual configuration. It also gives you an indication of the behavior of the router with the necessary features turned on. For example, you would want to make sure that router performance is unhindered. For hardware assist features, you would want to make sure that the required features are not through the CPU of the router.

After this initial test-lab phase, you can move the testing phase to a small portion of the network (to verify the effects of the QoS architecture on a small controlled number of applications or users). Before the actual QoS features are turned on, you must take a snapshot of the condition of the network during peak and nonpeak hours. For example, the snapshot can include a typical response time of certain transactions, quality of voice calls, time taken for certain data transfers to be completed, and so on. Then, after the QoS features have been turned on, you need to record the same parameters again to ascertain the effect of the QoS features on the same applications or users.

Implementing QoS Features

After the testing phase comes the implementation phase, when the QoS features have to be turned on in most of the network. A good practice is to always implement the QoS policy in a controlled manner and incremental fashion. The classification and marking have to be done first. This means the implementation phase starts from the edge of the network and moves toward the core. During this phase, updating of documentation is of utmost importance, because the network is undergoing changes. Proper documentation also allows for rollback to be carried out in the event that the new configuration does not perform to expectations.

Monitoring

The monitoring phase starts right after the policies have been implemented. The focus of this phase is on data collection and answering questions such as whether the QoS architecture is working.

You have two sources for data collection regarding QoS features:

* Management Information Base (MIB)
* IP Service Level Agreement (IP SLA)

The Class-Based QoS MIB stores vital information that can tell you lots of details about the QoS implementation. For example, information such as the number of packets marked or dropped can be accessed. This information gives a good indication of the traffic load of the network, as well as how the network nodes are reacting to the situation.

The other great tool for monitoring the effects of the QoS architecture is the IP SLA, formally known as the Service Assurance Agent (SAA). IP SLA enables you to monitor key network parameters such as delay, jitter, and the health of important network resources. IP SLA is discussed in detail in Chapter 10, "Beyond Implementation."

The use of the Class-Based QoS MIB and the IP SLA give you a good indication of whether the QoS architecture is sound. In addition, as described in Chapter 2, during scheduled network maintenance you might want to verify that you have implemented the QoS strategy successfully. You can do so by using test equipment to generate a load on the network and verifying that the voice traffic is not affected or unimportant traffic is being dropped during congestion. However, the ultimate tool that will tell you whether the QoS features are working is the end users. Remember, there is no point configuring a complex queuing mechanism with the latest QoS features when the users still find that their application is not working. Therefore, besides collecting network statistics, user visits are mandatory to gather feedback.

Summary

Deployment of QoS is required in building a resilient IP network. It is needed in the areas of protection of the control plane, as well as ensuring consistent user experience. QoS is not an afterthought, and its implementation requires proper planning and should be done during the design phase of the network.

This chapter covers the following topics:

- Network Convergence in the Core
- OSPF Enhancements
- IS-IS Enhancements
- EIGRP Enhancements
- IP Event Dampening
- Multipath Routing
- MPLS Traffic Engineering
- Multicast Subsecond Convergence

CHAPTER 5

Core Module

In Chapter 3, "Fundamentals of IP Resilient Networks," you learned about the functionalities of the different modules that make up the building blocks of a network. The core module deals mainly with IP routing issues; it is designed to move packets from the ingress to egress of the core in the shortest amount of time, and its design is often kept as simple as possible to achieve this objective. Features that are configured at the core may include those associated with the guaranteed delivery of network services, such as quality of service (QoS) and fast network convergence. These features can be used to improve the overall resiliency of the network.

In this chapter, you focus on features that enable you to minimize downtime and achieve high resiliency in the network core. These features are classified broadly to those pertaining to the following:

- Fast link failure detection
- Fast failure propagation
- Fast routing convergence

You also learn about features that enhance the overall scalability and availability of the network.

Network Convergence in the Core

Network convergence in the core is defined as the time required for traffic to be rerouted to the alternative (backup) or more optimal path after a network topology change. For a link-state Interior Gateway Protocol (IGP) such as Open Shortest Path First (OSPF), it is the sum of the time required for the network to detect the event (link layer detection), signal the event throughout the network (link-state packet [LSP] flooding), process the event (Shortest Path First [SPF] calculation), and then update the routing table or forwarding table (update Forwarding Information Base [FIB]).

Network convergence can occur at different layers of the OSI stack (Layer 1 to 3) depending on whether the particular technology provides protection mechanisms. Examples of Layer 1 technologies that provide fast convergence include Synchronous Optical Network/Synchronous Digital Hierarchy (SONET/SDH) and Resilient Packet Ring (RPR). These technologies allow for recovery from link failures in the range of 50 to

100 milliseconds (ms), and potentially without the need for upper layers, such as the network layer being aware of the network event.

In some cases whereby there is no correlation between the link status and network connectivity (such as when two routers are connected to each other via an Ethernet switch), the network devices must rely on Layer 3 convergence. With OSPF, for example, Hello packets are sent once every 10 seconds, and by default it requires four Hello intervals to be missed before declaring a neighbor to be down. Thus, OSPF provides a convergence time of approximately just less than a minute.

Although this might be considered a "short" period of time for data traffic (and is sufficient for TCP to retransmit to recover lost segments), the IP networks of today no longer carry only bulk data but might also be used for voice and video. A 50-second delay in routing protocol convergence could mean several thousands of voice calls being dropped in the backbone of a service provider. A 50-second delay for a Gigabit Ethernet link implies about 6.25 GB of information lost.

This chapter introduces the different features and enhancements available to help you achieve the objective of building a highly resilient IP network.

OSPF Enhancements

The Open Shortest Path First (OSPF) routing protocol was formalized in 1991, with the original intention of creating a common interoperable IGP for the TCP/IP protocol family. OSPF is also one of the first protocols to depart from the Bellman-Ford vector-based algorithms used in routing protocols such as Routing Information Protocol (RIP) and instead uses the Link-State Protocol. A good read on OSPF technology is the whitepaper titled "OSPF Design Guide," written by Sam Halabi (Cisco Systems 1996, http://www.cisco.com/warp/public/104/1.html), or *OSPF Network Design Solutions*, 2nd Edition, by Tom M. Thomas (Cisco Press, 2003).

Because OSPF is a link-state routing protocol, it normally offers faster convergence as compared to routing protocols such as RIP. However, bear in mind that it has been proven for Enhanced Interior Gateway Routing Protocol (EIGRP), which is an advanced distance vector routing protocol, with a feasible successor to converge faster than OSPF. To understand the significance of the various enhancements made in OSPF, it is important to first understand the OSPF convergence process. Figure 5-1 illustrates this process using a simple network setup.

Figure 5-1   *Simple Network Setup*

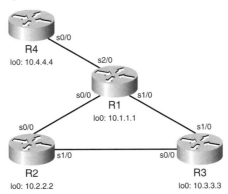

In the setup, the links of routers R1, R2, and R3 are running OSPF in Area 0, whereas R4 is a directly connected router that is not running OSPF. All the routers are connected using serial point-to-point interfaces. A loopback interface is defined on each router that is used for the unnumbered link addresses connecting to the rest of the routers.

NOTE

Figure 5-1 shows serial point-to-point links being used. In reality, Fast Ethernet or Gigabit Ethernet may be used instead. Because Ethernet is considered a multiaccess medium, OSPF will elect a designated router (DR) and backup designated router (BDR) for the segment. To avoid DR election and to prevent unnecessary OSPF Type 2 LSAs (network LSAs) from being generated, back-to-back Ethernet interfaces should be configured with **ip ospf network point-to-point**.

OSPF relies on the use of link-state advertisements to propagate the topology changes to its neighbors. Suppose there is a link failure between R1 and R2, as shown in Figure 5-2. R1 detects the failure before R2 (because we perform an administrative shutdown at R1), and waits for a **link-state advertisement delay** interval of 500 ms (or **initial link-state advertisement throttle delay** if it has been configured) before generating the link-state advertisement and flooding it to R3. Similarly, when R2 sees that the neighbor adjacency is down, it does the same. If packet pacing is active, the flooding of the link-state advertisements is also subject to the packet-pacing timer. This update is sent using OSPF packet Type 4 (link-state update). Note that both the link-state advertisement delay interval and the initial link-state advertisement throttle delay are applicable to locally originated link-state advertisements only. Link-state advertisements are uniquely identified by the link-state type (LS-Type), link-state ID (LSID), and the advertising router (Adv Rtr) fields in the LSA header.

Figure 5-2 *Link Failure Between R1 and R2*

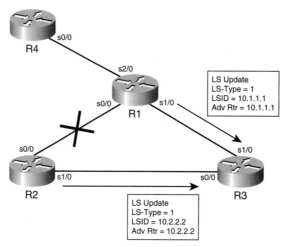

When R3 sees the link-state updates from R1 and R2, they will be flooded immediately to R2 and R1, respectively, as shown in Figure 5-3. This flooding is throttled by the packet-pacing timer if active. In this way, network topology changes are passed along to its neighbors in the shortest amount of time.

Figure 5-3 *Propagating the LSA Update to Neighbors*

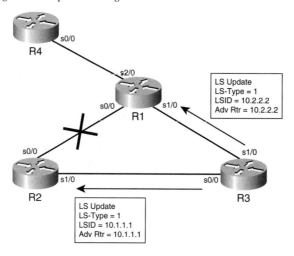

After the neighbors have received the link-state advertisement, they reply with a link-state acknowledgment, as shown in Figure 5-4, to indicate that the link-state update has been successfully received. Link-state acknowledgment are OSPF packet Type 5 packets, with the body containing a list of link-state advertisement headers for those link-state advertisements to be acknowledged. Note that in some cases, link-state acknowledgments may be implied by the use of link-state update packets. The acknowledgement is also usually delayed so that multiple acknowledgements can be placed into a single link-state packet.

Figure 5-4   *Link-State Acknowledgment Being Sent to Neighbors*

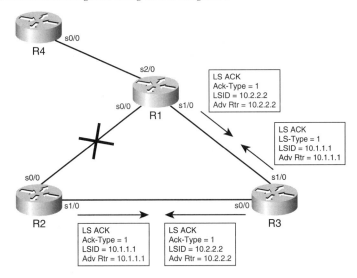

Following this step, all the routers in the OSPF area will proceed with running the SPF algorithm, as shown in Figure 5-5 (after waiting for an initial SPF schedule delay of 5000 ms, referenced from the time the topology change was first detected by the respective routers), to determine the shortest path cost to each destination. At this point, all the routers have received all the link-state advertisements pertaining to the failure. The SPF algorithm looks into the link-state database and goes through each link-state advertisement and into each individual link advertised by the link-state advertisements. In the case of R1, it proceeds with looking at the first router link-state advertisement (for example, link-state advertisement ID of 1.1.1.1), and then examining the three links advertised by that link-state advertisement before proceeding with other router link-state advertisements (link-state advertisement ID of 3.3.3.3, followed by link-state advertisement ID of 2.2.2.2).

Figure 5-5 *Running SPF on Each Router in the Area*

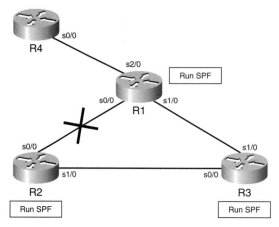

When the SPF algorithm concludes, each of the OSPF routers will have the lowest-cost path to each of the destinations installed on their respective routing tables. Djikstra's algorithm or its variation is typically used for SPF calculations. Depending on the implementation, the runtime for Djikstra's algorithm on a single node for m routers with a total of n paths is approximately proportional to $(m + n \cdot \log n)$. For more information on Djikstra's algorithm, refer to Chapter 5, "The Network Layer," of *Computer Networks*, 4th Edition, by Andrew S. Tanenbaum (Prentice Hall PTR, 2002).

The **debug** output in Example 5-1 illustrates the convergence of the simple network, and significant events in the convergence process on router R1 are highlighted.

Example 5-1 *Convergence for a Simple Network on Router R1*

```
R1#debug ip ospf spf
OSPF spf events debugging is on
OSPF spf intra events debugging is on
OSPF spf inter events debugging is on
OSPF spf external events debugging is on
R1#configure terminal
Enter configuration commands, one per line.  End with CNTL/Z.
R1(config)#interface s0/0
R1(config-if)#shutdown
R1(config-if)#^Z
Jun 25 10:57:39.684: %OSPF-5-ADJCHG: Process 100, Nbr 2.2.2.2 on Serial0/0 from
  FULL to DOWN, Neighbor Down: Interface down or detached
Jun 25 10:57:39.952: %SYS-5-CONFIG_I: Configured from console by console
Jun 25 10:57:40.188: OSPF: Inc retrans unit nbr count index 1 (0/1) to 1/1
Jun 25 10:57:40.188: OSPF: Set Nbr 3.3.3.3 1 first flood info from 0 (0) to
  32C953C (28)
Jun 25 10:57:40.188: OSPF: Init Nbr 3.3.3.3 1 next flood info to 32C953C
Jun 25 10:57:40.188: OSPF: Add Type 1 LSA ID 1.1.1.1 Adv rtr 1.1.1.1 Seq
  80000010 to Serial1/0 3.3.3.3 retransmission list
Jun 25 10:57:40.188: OSPF: Start Serial1/0 3.3.3.3 retrans timer
```

Example 5-1 *Convergence for a Simple Network on Router R1 (Continued)*

```
Jun 25 10:57:40.188: OSPF: Set idb next flood info from 0 (0) to 32C953C (28)
Jun 25 10:57:40.188: OSPF: Add Type 1 LSA ID 1.1.1.1 Adv rtr 1.1.1.1 Seq
  80000010 to Serial1/0 flood list
Jun 25 10:57:40.188: OSPF: Sending update over Serial1/0 without pacing
Jun 25 10:57:40.188: OSPF: Flooding update on Serial1/0 to 224.0.0.5 Area 0
Jun 25 10:57:40.188: OSPF: Send Type 1, LSID 1.1.1.1, Adv rtr 1.1.1.1, age 1,
  seq 0x80000010 (0)
Jun 25 10:57:40.188: OSPF: Create retrans unit 0x32C82CC/0x32C74DC 1 (0/1) 1
Jun 25 10:57:40.188: OSPF: Set nbr 1 (0/1) retrans to 4813 count to 0
Jun 25 10:57:40.188: OSPF: Set idb next flood info from 32C953C (28) to 0 (0)
Jun 25 10:57:40.188: OSPF: Remove Type 1 LSA ID 1.1.1.1 Adv rtr 1.1.1.1 Seq
  80000010 from Serial1/0 flood list
Jun 25 10:57:40.188: OSPF: Stop Serial1/0 flood timer
Jun 25 10:57:40.188: OSPF: Schedule SPF in area 0
      Change in LS ID 1.1.1.1, LSA type R, , spf-type Full
Jun 25 10:57:40.188: OSPF: Build router LSA for area 0, router ID 1.1.1.1,
  seq 0x80000010
Jun 25 10:57:41.224: OSPF: received update from 3.3.3.3, Serial1/0
Jun 25 10:57:41.224: OSPF: Rcv Update Type 1, LSID 2.2.2.2, Adv rtr 2.2.2.2,
  age 2, seq 0x8000000B
Jun 25 10:57:41.224: OSPF: Detect change in LSA type 1, LSID 2.2.2.2, from
  2.2.2.2 area 0
Jun 25 10:57:41.224: OSPF: Schedule SPF in area 0
      Change in LS ID 2.2.2.2, LSA type R, , spf-type Full
Jun 25 10:57:41.684: %LINK-5-CHANGED: Interface Serial0/0, changed state to
  administratively down
Jun 25 10:57:42.700: %LINEPROTO-5-UPDOWN: Line protocol on Interface Serial0/0,
  changed state to down
Jun 25 10:57:42.736: OSPF: Received ACK from 3.3.3.3 on Serial1/0
Jun 25 10:57:42.736: OSPF: Rcv Ack Type 1, LSID 1.1.1.1, Adv rtr 1.1.1.1, age 1,
  seq 0x80000010
Jun 25 10:57:42.736: OSPF: Dec retrans unit nbr count index 1 (0/1) to 0/0
Jun 25 10:57:42.736: OSPF: Free nbr retrans unit 0x32C82CC/0x32C74DC 0 total 0.
  Also Free nbr retrans block
Jun 25 10:57:42.736: OSPF: Set Nbr 3.3.3.3 1 first flood info from 32C953C (28)
  to 0 (0)
Jun 25 10:57:42.736: OSPF: Adjust Nbr 3.3.3.3 1 next flood info to 0
Jun 25 10:57:42.736: OSPF: Remove Type 1 LSA ID 1.1.1.1 Adv rtr 1.1.1.1 Seq
  80000010 from 3.3.3.3 retransmission list
Jun 25 10:57:42.736: OSPF: Stop nbr 3.3.3.3 retransmission timer
Jun 25 10:57:43.724: OSPF: Sending delayed ACK on Serial1/0
Jun 25 10:57:43.724: OSPF: Ack Type 1, LSID 2.2.2.2, Adv rtr 2.2.2.2, age 2, seq
  0x8000000B
Jun 25 10:57:45.208: OSPF: Begin SPF at 1766.164ms, process time 364ms
Jun 25 10:57:45.208:       spf_time 00:29:21.156, wait_interval 5000ms
Jun 25 10:57:45.208: OSPF: running SPF for area 0, SPF-type Full
Jun 25 10:57:45.208: OSPF: Initializing to run spf
Jun 25 10:57:45.208:  OSPF - spf_intra() - rebuilding the tree
Jun 25 10:57:45.208:  It is a router LSA 1.1.1.1. Link Count 2
Jun 25 10:57:45.208:   Processing link 0, id 1.1.1.1, link data 255.255.255.255,
  type 3
Jun 25 10:57:45.208:     Add better path to LSA ID 1.1.1.1, gateway 1.1.1.1,
```

continues

Example 5-1 *Convergence for a Simple Network on Router R1 (Continued)*

```
    dist 1
Jun 25 10:57:45.208:     Add path: next-hop 1.1.1.1, interface Loopback0
Jun 25 10:57:45.208:     Processing link 1, id 3.3.3.3, link data 0.0.0.3, type 1
Jun 25 10:57:45.208:     Add better path to LSA ID 3.3.3.3, gateway 0.0.0.3,
    dist 64
Jun 25 10:57:45.208: OSPF: putting LSA on the clist LSID 3.3.3.3, Type 1,
    Adv Rtr. 3.3.3.3
Jun 25 10:57:45.208:     Add path: next-hop 3.3.3.3, interface Serial1/0
Jun 25 10:57:45.208: OSPF: downheap LSA on the clist LSID 3.3.3.3, Type 1,
    Adv Rtr. 3.3.3.3, from index 1 to index 1
Jun 25 10:57:45.208:   It is a router LSA 3.3.3.3. Link Count 3
Jun 25 10:57:45.208:     Processing link 0, id 3.3.3.3, link data 255.255.255.255,
    type 3
Jun 25 10:57:45.208:     Add better path to LSA ID 3.3.3.3, gateway 3.3.3.3,
    dist 65
Jun 25 10:57:45.208:     Add path: next-hop 3.3.3.3, interface Serial1/0
Jun 25 10:57:45.208:     Processing link 1, id 1.1.1.1, link data 0.0.0.3, type 1
Jun 25 10:57:45.208:     Ignore newdist 128 olddist 0
Jun 25 10:57:45.208:     Processing link 2, id 2.2.2.2, link data 0.0.0.2, type 1
Jun 25 10:57:45.208:     Add better path to LSA ID 2.2.2.2, gateway 0.0.0.3,
    dist 128
Jun 25 10:57:45.208: OSPF: putting LSA on the clist LSID 2.2.2.2, Type 1,
    Adv Rtr. 2.2.2.2
Jun 25 10:57:45.208:     Add path: next-hop 3.3.3.3, interface Serial1/0
Jun 25 10:57:45.208: OSPF: downheap LSA on the clist LSID 2.2.2.2, Type 1,
    Adv Rtr. 2.2.2.2, from index 1 to index 1
Jun 25 10:57:45.208:   It is a router LSA 2.2.2.2. Link Count 2
Jun 25 10:57:45.208:     Processing link 0, id 2.2.2.2, link data 255.255.255.255,
    type 3
Jun 25 10:57:45.208:     Add better path to LSA ID 2.2.2.2, gateway 2.2.2.2,
    dist 129
Jun 25 10:57:45.208:     Add path: next-hop 3.3.3.3, interface Serial1/0
Jun 25 10:57:45.208:     Processing link 1, id 3.3.3.3, link data 0.0.0.3, type 1
Jun 25 10:57:45.208:     Ignore newdist 192 olddist 64
Jun 25 10:57:45.208: OSPF: Adding Stub nets
Jun 25 10:57:45.208: OSPF: delete lsa id 1.1.1.1, type 0, adv rtr 1.1.1.1 from
    delete list
Jun 25 10:57:45.208: OSPF: insert route list LS ID 1.1.1.1, type 0,
    adv rtr 1.1.1.1
Jun 25 10:57:45.208: OSPF: Add Network Route to 2.2.2.2 Mask /32. Metric: 129,
    Next Hop: 3.3.3.3
Jun 25 10:57:45.208: OSPF: Path left undeleted to 2.2.2.2
Jun 25 10:57:45.208: OSPF: delete lsa id 3.3.3.3, type 0, adv rtr 3.3.3.3 from
    delete list
Jun 25 10:57:45.208: OSPF: Add Network Route to 3.3.3.3 Mask /32. Metric: 65,
    Next Hop: 3.3.3.3
Jun 25 10:57:45.208: OSPF: insert route list LS ID 3.3.3.3, type 0, adv rtr 3.3.3.3
Jun 25 10:57:45.208: OSPF: Entered old delete routine
Jun 25 10:57:45.208: OSPF: Old STUB NET route 2.2.2.2, mask /32, next hop 2.2.2.2
    not exist
Jun 25 10:57:45.208: OSPF: delete lsa id 2.2.2.2, type 0, adv rtr 2.2.2.2 from
    delete list
```

Example 5-1   *Convergence for a Simple Network on Router R1 (Continued)*

```
Jun 25 10:57:45.208: OSPF: insert route list LS ID 2.2.2.2, type 0,
  adv rtr 2.2.2.2
Jun 25 10:57:45.208: OSPF: ospf_gen_asbr_sum_all_areas
Jun 25 10:57:45.208: OSPF: running spf for summaries area 0
Jun 25 10:57:45.208: OSPF: sum_delete_old_routes area 0
Jun 25 10:57:45.208: OSPF: Started Building Type 5 External Routes
Jun 25 10:57:45.208: OSPF: ex_delete_old_routes
Jun 25 10:57:45.208: OSPF: Started Building Type 7 External Routes
Jun 25 10:57:45.208: OSPF: ex_delete_old_routes
Jun 25 10:57:45.208: OSPF: End SPF at 1766.164ms, Total elapsed time 0ms
Jun 25 10:57:45.208:          Schedule time 00:29:26.164, Next wait_interval 10000ms
Jun 25 10:57:45.208:          Intra: 0ms, Inter: 0ms, External: 0ms
Jun 25 10:57:45.208:          R: 3, N: 0, Stubs: 3
Jun 25 10:57:45.208:          SN: 0, SA: 0, X5: 0, X7: 0
Jun 25 10:57:45.208:          SPF suspends: 0 intra, 0 total
```

Example 5-2 illustrates the convergence of the simple network, and significant events in the convergence process on router R2 are highlighted.

Example 5-2   *Convergence for a Simple Network on Router R2*

```
R2#debug ip ospf spf
OSPF spf events debugging is on
OSPF spf intra events debugging is on
OSPF spf inter events debugging is on
OSPF spf external events debugging is on
Jun 25 10:57:40.222: OSPF: received update from 3.3.3.3, Serial1/0
Jun 25 10:57:40.222: OSPF: Rcv Update Type 1, LSID 1.1.1.1, Adv rtr 1.1.1.1,
  age 2, seq 0x80000010
Jun 25 10:57:40.222: OSPF: Detect change in LSA type 1, LSID 1.1.1.1, from 1.1.1.1
  area 0
Jun 25 10:57:40.222: OSPF: Inc retrans unit nbr count index 2 (0/2) to 1/1
Jun 25 10:57:40.222: OSPF: Set Nbr 1.1.1.1 2 first flood info from 0 (0) to 32AB1AC
  (27)
Jun 25 10:57:40.222: OSPF: Init Nbr 1.1.1.1 2 next flood info to 32AB1AC
Jun 25 10:57:40.222: OSPF: Add Type 1 LSA ID 1.1.1.1 Adv rtr 1.1.1.1 Seq 80000010
  to Serial0/0 1.1.1.1 retransmission list
Jun 25 10:57:40.222: OSPF: Start Serial0/0 1.1.1.1 retrans timer
Jun 25 10:57:40.222: OSPF: Set idb next flood info from 0 (0) to 32AB1AC (27)
Jun 25 10:57:40.222: OSPF: Add Type 1 LSA ID 1.1.1.1 Adv rtr 1.1.1.1 Seq 80000010
  to Serial0/0 flood list
Jun 25 10:57:40.222: OSPF: Sending update over Serial0/0 without pacing
Jun 25 10:57:40.222: OSPF: Flooding update on Serial0/0 to 224.0.0.5 Area 0
Jun 25 10:57:40.222: OSPF: Send Type 1, LSID 1.1.1.1, Adv rtr 1.1.1.1, age 3, seq
  0x80000010 (0)
Jun 25 10:57:40.222: OSPF: Create retrans unit 0x32AA03C/0x32A939C 2 (0/2) 1
Jun 25 10:57:40.222: OSPF: Set nbr 2 (0/2) retrans to 4924 count to 0
Jun 25 10:57:40.222: OSPF: Set idb next flood info from 32AB1AC (27) to 0 (0)
Jun 25 10:57:40.222: OSPF: Remove Type 1 LSA ID 1.1.1.1 Adv rtr 1.1.1.1 Seq 80000010
  from Serial0/0 flood list
Jun 25 10:57:40.222: OSPF: Stop Serial0/0 flood timer
Jun 25 10:57:40.222: OSPF: Schedule SPF in area 0
```

continues

Example 5-2 *Convergence for a Simple Network on Router R2 (Continued)*

```
         Change in LS ID 1.1.1.1, LSA type R, , spf-type Full
Jun 25 10:57:40.450: %OSPF-5-ADJCHG: Process 100, Nbr 1.1.1.1 on Serial0/0 from FULL
  to DOWN, Neighbor Down: Dead timer expired
!Output omitted for brevity
Jun 25 10:57:45.246: OSPF: running SPF for area 0, SPF-type Full
Jun 25 10:57:45.246: OSPF: Initializing to run spf
!Output omitted for brevity
Jun 25 10:57:45.246: OSPF: End SPF at 1765.680ms, Total elapsed time 0ms
Jun 25 10:57:45.246:       Schedule time 00:29:25.680, Next wait_interval 10000ms
Jun 25 10:57:45.246:       Intra: 0ms, Inter: 0ms, External: 0ms
Jun 25 10:57:45.246:       R: 3, N: 0, Stubs: 3
Jun 25 10:57:45.246:       SN: 0, SA: 0, X5: 0, X7: 0
Jun 25 10:57:45.246:       SPF suspends: 0 intra, 0 total
```

Example 5-3 illustrates the convergence of the simple network, and significant events in the convergence process on router R3 are highlighted.

Example 5-3 *Convergence for a Simple Network on Router R3*

```
R3#debug ip ospf spf
OSPF spf events debugging is on
OSPF spf intra events debugging is on
OSPF spf inter events debugging is on
OSPF spf external events debugging is on
Jun 25 10:57:40.215: OSPF: received update from 1.1.1.1, Serial1/0
Jun 25 10:57:40.215: OSPF: Rcv Update Type 1, LSID 1.1.1.1, Adv rtr 1.1.1.1, age 1,
  seq 0x80000010
Jun 25 10:57:40.215: OSPF: Detect change in LSA type 1, LSID 1.1.1.1, from 1.1.1.1
  area 0
Jun 25 10:57:40.215: OSPF: Inc retrans unit nbr count index 1 (0/1) to 1/1
Jun 25 10:57:40.215: OSPF: Set Nbr 2.2.2.2 1 first flood info from 0 (0) to 32AB28C
  (29)
Jun 25 10:57:40.215: OSPF: Init Nbr 2.2.2.2 1 next flood info to 32AB28C
Jun 25 10:57:40.215: OSPF: Add Type 1 LSA ID 1.1.1.1 Adv rtr 1.1.1.1 Seq 80000010
  to Serial0/0 2.2.2.2 retransmission list
Jun 25 10:57:40.215: OSPF: Start Serial0/0 2.2.2.2 retrans timer
Jun 25 10:57:40.215: OSPF: Set idb next flood info from 0 (0) to 32AB28C (29)
Jun 25 10:57:40.215: OSPF: Add Type 1 LSA ID 1.1.1.1 Adv rtr 1.1.1.1 Seq 80000010
  to Serial0/0 flood list
Jun 25 10:57:40.215: OSPF: Sending update over Serial0/0 without pacing
Jun 25 10:57:40.215: OSPF: Flooding update on Serial0/0 to 224.0.0.5 Area 0
Jun 25 10:57:40.215: OSPF: Send Type 1, LSID 1.1.1.1, Adv rtr 1.1.1.1, age 2, seq
  0x80000010 (0)
Jun 25 10:57:40.215: OSPF: Create retrans unit 0x32AA03C/0x32A939C 1 (0/1) 1
Jun 25 10:57:40.215: OSPF: Set nbr 1 (0/1) retrans to 4633 count to 0
Jun 25 10:57:40.215: OSPF: Set idb next flood info from 32AB28C (29) to 0 (0)
Jun 25 10:57:40.215: OSPF: Remove Type 1 LSA ID 1.1.1.1 Adv rtr 1.1.1.1 Seq 80000010
  from Serial0/0 flood list
Jun 25 10:57:40.215: OSPF: Stop Serial0/0 flood timer
Jun 25 10:57:40.215: OSPF: Schedule SPF in area 0
         Change in LS ID 1.1.1.1, LSA type R, , spf-type Full
Jun 25 10:57:41.195: OSPF: received update from 2.2.2.2, Serial0/0
```

Example 5-3 *Convergence for a Simple Network on Router R3 (Continued)*

```
Jun 25 10:57:41.195: OSPF: Rcv Update Type 1, LSID 2.2.2.2, Adv rtr 2.2.2.2, age 1,
  seq 0x8000000B
!Output omitted for brevity
Jun 25 10:57:45.235: OSPF: running SPF for area 0, SPF-type Full
Jun 25 10:57:45.235: OSPF: Initializing to run spf
!Output omitted for brevity
Jun 25 10:57:45.235: OSPF: End SPF at 1763.760ms, Total elapsed time 0ms
Jun 25 10:57:45.235:         Schedule time 00:29:23.760, Next wait_interval 10000ms
Jun 25 10:57:45.235:         Intra: 0ms, Inter: 0ms, External: 0ms
Jun 25 10:57:45.235:         R: 3, N: 0, Stubs: 3
Jun 25 10:57:45.235:         SN: 0, SA: 0, X5: 0, X7: 0
Jun 25 10:57:45.235:         SPF suspends: 0 intra, 0 total
```

This example provides you with an understanding of the basic concepts behind OSPF convergence. With this understanding, you can now consider some of the features that will help improve the scalability and convergence of a network running OSPF.

Shortest Path First (SPF) Throttling

By default, a Cisco router running OSPF waits for 5000 ms (initial SPF schedule delay) upon detection of a topology change event before starting SPF calculations. You can observe this delay from the output of **debug ip ospf spf**, as shown in Example 5-4. You see that the SPF run occurs about 5 seconds after the SPF schedule time.

Example 5-4 *Output from* **debug ip ospf spf**

```
R1#debug ip ospf spf
OSPF spf events debugging is on
OSPF spf intra events debugging is on
OSPF spf inter events debugging is on
OSPF spf external events debugging is on
*Jun 14 17:23:13.937: OSPF: Schedule SPF in area 0
     Change in LS ID 200.200.7.225, LSA type R, , spf-type Full
*Jun 14 09:23:16.437: %LINEPROTO-5-UPDOWN: Line protocol on Interface Ethernet0/0,
  changed state to down
*Jun 14 17:23:18.969: OSPF: running SPF for area 0, SPF-type Full
*Jun 14 17:23:18.969: OSPF: Initializing to run spf
*Jun 14 17:23:18.969:  OSPF - spf_intra() - rebuilding the tree
```

This delay was originally introduced so that the router waits for other (possibly related) link-state advertisements to arrive before starting SPF calculations, to avoid the need to have multiple or too frequent SPF calculations. More important, after every SPF calculation, the RIB/FIB must be updated, which is a time-consuming process. When you reduce the number of SPF calculations required, you cut down on the corresponding amount of time spent on updating the RIB/FIB.

Using the previous example, if the link between two routers goes down, both routers generate link-state advertisements for the event to another connected router. Depending on the network topology and the situation, it might make sense to start to run the initial SPF calculation as soon as possible to achieve fast convergence. This is because the link-state advertisement from one router would be sufficient to indicate that the link was down and that SPF would fail the two-way connectivity check, and remove that link from the topology. However, you must be mindful of other considerations.

In the networks of today, waiting for initial SPF schedule delay might take too long, which inhibits you from achieving fast convergence. *SPF throttling* is a feature that makes it possible for you to configure SPF recalculations on network changes in the order of milliseconds rather than seconds. This feature also enables you to add delay to SPF calculations. SPF throttling is configured by the configuration commands shown in Example 5-5. In this case, we change the initial SPF schedule delay to 500 ms so that the first SPF calculation occurs in 500 ms rather than 5000 ms.

Example 5-5 *Configuring SPF Throttling*

```
R1#configure terminal
Enter configuration commands, one per line.  End with CNTL/Z.
R1(config)#router ospf 100
R1(config-router)#timers throttle spf 500 10000 10000
R1(config-router)#^Z
R1#
```

The first value is for the initial SPF schedule delay; the next two values are for the minimum hold time and maximum wait time between consecutive SPFs, respectively. You can see the currently configured values from the output of **show ip ospf** in Example 5-6.

Example 5-6 *Output from* **show ip ospf**

```
R1#show ip ospf
 Routing Process "ospf 100" with ID 200.200.7.225
 Supports only single TOS(TOS0) routes
 Supports opaque LSA
 Supports Link-local Signaling (LLS)
 Supports area transit capability
 Initial SPF schedule delay 500 msecs
 Minimum hold time between two consecutive SPFs 10000 msecs
 Maximum wait time between two consecutive SPFs 10000 msecs
!Output omitted for brevity
```

SPF uses an exponential back-off to prevent SPF from being run too frequently in times of network instability. When the router receives at least one topology change during the previous wait interval, the wait interval is doubled. When the maximum wait time has been reached, the wait interval remains the same until no further events are received in that interval, and further events are subjected to the initial SPF schedule delay.

As another example, the initial SPF schedule delay is configured to 5 seconds (s), and the minimum hold time and maximum wait time are configured to 10 seconds and 40 seconds, respectively. The partial output from **debug ip ospf spf** is as shown in Example 5-7, which illustrates the exponential back-off behavior for consecutive SPF runs.

Example 5-7 *Exponential Back-Off for SPF*

```
R1#debug ip ospf spf
.Jun 25 15:01:25.722: OSPF: Schedule SPF in area 0
.Jun 25 15:01:26.438: OSPF: Schedule SPF in area 0
.Jun 25 15:01:30.738: OSPF: Initializing to run spf
.Jun 25 15:01:31.394: OSPF: Schedule SPF in area 0
!Output omitted for brevity
.Jun 25 15:01:40.750: OSPF: Initializing to run spf
.Jun 25 15:01:41.394: OSPF: Schedule SPF in area 0
!Output omitted for brevity
.Jun 25 15:02:00.754: OSPF: Initializing to run spf
.Jun 25 15:02:01.882: OSPF: Schedule SPF in area 0
!Output omitted for brevity
.Jun 25 15:02:40.758: OSPF: Initializing to run spf
!Output omitted for brevity
```

In this case, the wait intervals for the SPF runs are 5.016, 9.356, 19.36, and 38.876 seconds, respectively, and you can see that each subsequent time interval is double that of the previous, because topology changes occurred within the previous wait interval.

Although it is possible to lower the initial SPF delay to achieve faster convergence, you might not want to configure the initial SPF schedule delay to be lower than the link-state advertisement delay interval (see the section "OSPF LSA Throttling") or the link-state advertisement throttle start interval (if it has been configured). In addition, it should also not be lower than the packet-pacing timer, because when SPF runs, flooding stops. Therefore, it might be desirable for the configured router to flood the link-state changes along to its neighbors before starting on SPF calculations. Otherwise, the router must wait for the SPF calculations to be completed before flooding out the changes.

A general guideline is to have the initial SPF schedule delay to be no less than three times the packet-pacing interval. The minimum hold time can be configured anywhere from about 20 milliseconds to an average SPF time. In addition, prior to the introduction of the SPF throttling feature, the default **timers spf spf-holdtime** was 10 seconds, so setting the maximum wait time to 10,000 ms provides the equivalent response. You should also ensure that the timers are configured consistently across the network.

In some sense, the SPF delay enables you to dampen the effect of an event, and prevents the configured router from overreacting to the link-state advertisement that has been received. It enables you to wait long enough for all the related link-state advertisements to arrive before starting on the SPF calculations.

OSPF LSA Throttling

Prior to the OSPF link-state advertisement throttling feature, link-state advertisement generation for the same link-state advertisement was rate limited for 5 seconds (MinLSInterval) as per RFC 2178, *OSPF Version 2*; and the originating router will wait for 1 second before generating a link-state advertisement to reflect a new network event. The purpose for this delay is to consolidate any other changes that might have occurred within this interval and have them included in the new link-state advertisement and to prevent the router from generating link-state advertisements too quickly. However, this delay prevents the routing protocol from being able to achieve subsecond convergence.

The OSPF link-state advertisement throttling feature allows for faster OSPF convergence by allowing millisecond timers to be used for link-state advertisement rate limiting. This feature allows the timings for both generating and receiving link-state advertisements to be configured and provides a dynamic mechanism to slow down the frequency of link-state advertisement generation during periods of network instability.

Example 5-8 shows the configuration commands for link-state advertisement throttling.

Example 5-8 *Configuring OSPF LSA Throttling*

```
R1#configure terminal
Enter configuration commands, one per line.  End with CNTL/Z.
R1(config)#router ospf 100
R1(config-router)#timers throttle lsa all 200 1000 2000
R1(config-router)#timers lsa arrival 500
R1(config-router)#^Z
R1#
```

The configured parameters are the start interval, hold interval, and maximum interval, respectively. For locally generated Type 1 (router link states, which are originated by all routers) and Type 2 (network link states, which are originated for broadcast and nonbroadcast multiaccess networks by the OSPF designated router) link-state advertisements, the link-state advertisement is subject to the fixed link-state advertisement delay interval of 500 ms, unless the link-state advertisement throttling has been explicitly configured. The next link-state advertisement is controlled by the minimum start interval (that is, the hold interval). Subsequent link-state advertisements with the same link-state advertisement ID, link-state advertisement type, and router ID (that is, same link-state advertisements) are rate limited until the maximum interval (max interval) is reached. The default values for the start interval, hold interval, and maximum interval are 0, 5000 ms, and 5000 ms, respectively, which provide the same behavior for MinLSInterval of 5 seconds.

You can use the **show ip ospf** command to find out whether LSA throttling is active. Example 5-9 shows that LSA throttling is not active, because the output makes references to the minimum link-state advertisement interval and minimum link-state advertisement arrival interval.

Example 5-9 *Output of* **show ip ospf** *When LSA Throttling Is Inactive*

```
R1#show ip ospf
 Routing Process "ospf 100" with ID 1.1.1.1
 Supports only single TOS(TOS0) routes
 Supports opaque LSA
 Supports Link-local Signaling (LLS)
 Supports area transit capability
 Initial SPF schedule delay 5000 msecs
 Minimum hold time between two consecutive SPFs 10000 msecs
 Maximum wait time between two consecutive SPFs 10000 msecs
 Incremental-SPF disabled
 Minimum LSA interval 5 secs
 Minimum LSA arrival 1000 msecs
 LSA group pacing timer 240 secs
 Interface flood pacing timer 33 msecs
 Retransmission pacing timer 66 msecs
 !Output omitted for brevity
```

Example 5-10 shows that link-state advertisement throttling is active, because the output makes references to the initial link-state advertisement throttle delay, minimum hold time, and maximum wait time for link-state advertisement throttle.

Example 5-10 *Output of* **show ip ospf** *when LSA Throttling Is Active*

```
R1#show ip ospf
 Routing Process "ospf 100" with ID 1.1.1.1
 Supports only single TOS(TOS0) routes
 Supports opaque LSA
 Supports Link-local Signaling (LLS)
 Supports area transit capability
 Initial SPF schedule delay 5000 msecs
 Minimum hold time between two consecutive SPFs 10000 msecs
 Maximum wait time between two consecutive SPFs 10000 msecs
 Incremental-SPF disabled
 Initial LSA throttle delay 0 msecs
 Minimum hold time for LSA throttle 5000 msecs
 Maximum wait time for LSA throttle 5000 msecs
 Minimum LSA arrival 1000 msecs
 LSA group pacing timer 240 secs
 Interface flood pacing timer 33 msecs
 !Output omitted for brevity
```

Example 5-11 shows the corresponding output for **debug ip ospf flood**, **debug ip ospf spf**, and **debug ip ospf database-timer rate-limit** for timer values of 200, 1000, and 2000 ms.

Example 5-11 *Output for* **debug ip ospf flood**, **debug ip ospf spf**, *and* **debug ip ospf database-timer rate-limit**

```
R1#debug ip ospf flood
OSPF flooding debugging is on
R1#debug ip ospf spf
```

continues

Example 5-11 *Output for* **debug ip ospf flood**, **debug ip ospf spf**, *and* **debug ip ospf database-timer**
          rate-limit *(Continued)*

```
OSPF spf events debugging is on
OSPF spf intra events debugging is on
OSPF spf inter events debugging is on
OSPF spf external events debugging is on
R1#debug ip ospf database-timer rate-limit
OSPF rate limit timer events debugging is on
R1#
.Jun 25 17:17:44.246: %OSPF-5-ADJCHG: Process 100, Nbr 2.2.2.2 on Serial0/0 from
  FULL to DOWN, Neighbor Down: Interface down or detached
.Jun 25 17:17:44.250: OSPF: Starting rate limit timer for 1.1.1.1 1.1.1.1 1 with
  200ms delay
.Jun 25 17:17:44.250: OSPF: Rate limit LSA generation for 1.1.1.1 1.1.1.1 1
.Jun 25 17:17:44.450: OSPF: Rate limit timer is expired for 1.1.1.1 1.1.1.1 1
.Jun 25 17:17:44.450: OSPF: For next LSA generation - wait : 1000ms
  next: 2000ms.
.Jun 25 17:17:44.450: OSPF: Inc retrans unit nbr count index 1 (0/1) to 1/1
.Jun 25 17:17:44.450: OSPF: Set Nbr 3.3.3.3 1 first flood info from 0 (0) to
  32C95AC (134)
.Jun 25 17:17:44.450: OSPF: Init Nbr 3.3.3.3 1 next flood info to 32C95AC
.Jun 25 17:17:44.450: OSPF: Add Type 1 LSA ID 1.1.1.1 Adv rtr 1.1.1.1 Seq
  8000005C to Serial1/0 3.3.3.3 retransmission list
.Jun 25 17:17:44.450: OSPF: Start Serial1/0 3.3.3.3 retrans timer
.Jun 25 17:17:44.450: OSPF: Set idb next flood info from 0 (0) to 32C95AC (134)
.Jun 25 17:17:44.450: OSPF: Add Type 1 LSA ID 1.1.1.1 Adv rtr 1.1.1.1 Seq
  8000005C to Serial1/0 flood list
.Jun 25 17:17:44.450: OSPF: Sending update over Serial1/0 without pacing
.Jun 25 17:17:44.450: OSPF: Flooding update on Serial1/0 to 224.0.0.5 Area 0
.Jun 25 17:17:44.450: OSPF: Send Type 1, LSID 1.1.1.1, Adv rtr 1.1.1.1, age 1,
  seq 0x8000005C (0)
```

Corresponding commands (**timers lsa arrival**) allow the receiving router to decide the
minimum allowed interval between instances of receiving the same link-state advertisement. RFC 2328, which obsoletes RFC 2178, sets the MinLSArrival to 1 second, and if
link-state advertisements are received that are less than this interval, they are just ignored.
For the same reason of maintaining compatibility with routers that do not support link-state
advertisement throttling, you might need to set the hold interval to be 1 second as per RFC
2328. If maintaining compatibility is not a concern, you may tune the hold time anywhere
from 20 ms to an average SPF time. This tuning is to ensure that even if all the link-state
advertisements have not been advertised by the first link-state advertisement, they will be
captured by the second.

OSPF LSA Flooding Reduction

The original OSPF specification requires link-state advertisements to be refreshed every 30
minutes, or they will expire in 60 minutes (even when the network topology is stable). This

periodic updating of link-state advertisements is intended to add robustness to the link-state algorithm. However with the growth of the IP-based networks, Internet service providers (ISPs) and large enterprises have noticed non-negligible routing protocol traffic even when their network topologies are stable.

RFC 1793, *Extending OSPF to Support Demand Circuits*, added enhancements to the OSPF routing protocol to support demand circuits. The enhancements allowed for the suppression of OSPF Hellos and periodic refresh messages over demand circuits such as ISDN and dial-up, which would otherwise result in unwanted usage charges by requiring the connection to be constantly open. One of the important changes this document has introduced is the ability for the high bit of the LS age field to be set, to indicate that the link-state advertisement should not be aged out (DoNotAge link-state advertisements) while they are being held in the link-state database.

The link-state advertisement flooding reduction mechanism works by leveraging on the use of DoNotAge link-state advertisements so that link-state advertisement refreshes are no longer required. This leveraging allows for OSPF to scale by reducing OSPF traffic overhead in stable network topologies. LSA flooding reduction is configured using the interface configuration command **ip ospf flood-reduction**, as shown in Example 5-12.

Example 5-12 *Configuring OSPF LSA Flooding Reduction*

```
R1#configure terminal
Enter configuration commands, one per line.  End with CNTL/Z.
R1(config)#interface ethernet 1/0
R1(config-if)#ip ospf flood-reduction
R1(config-if)#^Z
R1#
```

This command tells the configured routers to flood both self-originated and nonself-originated link-state advertisements with the DoNotAge bit set out the configured interfaces. As part of normal OSPF operation, any changes in the contents of the link-state advertisement will cause a reoriginated link-state advertisement to be flooded with the DoNotAge bit set. This allows for the protocol traffic overheads to be reduced, while still allowing changes to be flooded immediately.

OSPF DoNotAge link-state advertisements are indicated by a Do Not Age (DNA) in parenthesis next to the Age field in the **show ip ospf database** output, as shown in Example 5-13.

Example 5-13 *Output of* **show ip ospf database** *Showing LSA Flooding Reduction*

```
R2#show ip ospf database

            OSPF Router with ID (10.2.2.2) (Process ID 100)

            Router Link States (Area 0)

Link ID         ADV Router      Age          Seq#        Checksum Link count
10.1.1.1        10.1.1.1        1     (DNA) 0x80000004 0x000766 3
10.2.2.2        10.2.2.2        49          0x80000005 0x004321 3
10.3.3.3        10.3.3.3        70          0x80000003 0x00FA63 3
```

OSPF Fast Hello

The Hello protocol is responsible for establishing and maintaining neighbor relationships. Hello packets are sent out all router interfaces configured with OSPF periodically, and bidirectional communication is achieved when the router sees itself listed in the neighbor's Hello packet.

By default, the OSPF Hello interval is 10 seconds, and the OSPF dead interval is four times the OSPF Hello interval. This means that, in the worst case, if Hello packets are not seen from a neighbor in less than 50 seconds, it is declared to be down, as shown in Example 5-14. Note that OSPF requires these intervals to be exactly the same between two neighbors; otherwise they will not form an adjacency on a particular segment.

Example 5-14 *OSPF Neighbor Down Detection Using the Hello Process*

```
R2#debug ip ospf hello
OSPF hello events debugging is on
R2#
*Jun 15 04:12:07.551: OSPF: Send hello to 224.0.0.5 area 0 on Ethernet1/0 from
  10.1.1.2
*Jun 15 04:12:17.563: OSPF: Send hello to 224.0.0.5 area 0 on Ethernet1/0 from
  10.1.1.2
*Jun 15 04:12:27.571: OSPF: Send hello to 224.0.0.5 area 0 on Ethernet1/0 from
  10.1.1.2
*Jun 15 04:12:37.583: OSPF: Send hello to 224.0.0.5 area 0 on Ethernet1/0 from
  10.1.1.2
*Jun 15 04:12:41.291: %OSPF-5-ADJCHG: Process 100, Nbr 10.1.1.1 on Ethernet1/0 from
  FULL to DOWN, Neighbor Down: Dead timer expired
```

Cisco IOS Releases 12.0(23)S, 12.2(18)S, 12.2(15)T, and later added support for subsecond Hello intervals for OSPF, which allow for faster convergence. This feature proves especially useful in LAN segments, in which several routers might be connected to a switch and the data link is not affected by a neighbor loss. The OSPF Fast Hello feature is configured on a per-interface basis, as shown in Example 5-15.

Example 5-15 *Configuring OSPF Fast Hello on an Interface*

```
R1#configure terminal
Enter configuration commands, one per line.  End with CNTL/Z.
R1(config)#interface ethernet 1/0
R1(config-if)#ip ospf dead-interval minimal hello-multiplier 5
R1(config-if)#^Z
R1#
```

OSPF Fast Hello uses a dead interval of 1 second (which is the minimum allowed in the OSPF Hello packet) and allows the Hello interval multiplier (number of Hellos sent in

1 second) to be configured between 3 and 20 seconds. Example 5-16 shows the resulting output of the OSPF neighbor down detection using Fast Hello.

Example 5-16 *OSPF Neighbor Down Detection Using Fast Hello*

```
R2#debug ip ospf hello
OSPF hello events debugging is on
R2#
*Jun 15 04:29:40.571: OSPF: Send hello to 224.0.0.5 area 0 on Ethernet1/0 from
  10.1.1.2
*Jun 15 04:29:40.779: OSPF: Send hello to 224.0.0.5 area 0 on Ethernet1/0 from
  10.1.1.2
*Jun 15 04:29:40.987: OSPF: Send hello to 224.0.0.5 area 0 on Ethernet1/0 from
  10.1.1.2
*Jun 15 04:29:41.199: OSPF: Send hello to 224.0.0.5 area 0 on Ethernet1/0 from
  10.1.1.2
*Jun 15 04:29:41.407: OSPF: Send hello to 224.0.0.5 area 0 on Ethernet1/0 from
  10.1.1.2
*Jun 15 04:29:41.619: OSPF: Send hello to 224.0.0.5 area 0 on Ethernet1/0 from
  10.1.1.2
*Jun 15 04:29:41.687: %OSPF-5-ADJCHG: Process 100, Nbr 10.1.1.1 on Ethernet1/0 from
  FULL to DOWN, Neighbor Down: Dead timer expired
```

As you can see, the neighbor down is detected in approximately 1 second, which is more than a tenfold improvement as compared with the default setting.

Lowering the Hello interval can lead to substantial improvements in link failure detection, and subsequently, convergence times. However, as you reduce the Hello and dead interval, there might be an increased probability that congestions might cause Hellos to be lost and for a false link failure to be detected. If there is a surge of interrupt-level activities (such as process switching or packets being punted to the route processor [RP]) occurring, the CPU might not be able to process Hellos fast enough, leading to the same problem. Instead of using Fast Hellos in the routing protocol, *Bidirectional Forwarding Detection* (BFD), which is intended to provide a generalized framework for fast link failure detection, would eventually be the preferred way moving forward.

Another point to note is when Fast Hellos are configured on an interface, the HelloInterval field in the OSPF Hello packet (in the OSPF Hello packet that is being sent to the neighbor) is set to 0, and the Dead Interval field is set to 1 (because RFC 2328 specifies these fields in second, and we cannot specify subsecond timers to be used without making changes to the OSPF specifications). Within IOS, there is a separate internal HelloInterval field that, when set to all 1s (65536), would mean that the Hello Interval is of local significance. Also, when this internal HelloInterval is set to all 1s or if the interval is less than 3 and bit 32 of the internal RouterDeadInterval field is set, this timing in milliseconds for the dead interval is specified by the lower 31 bits of the internal RouterDeadInterval field.

Therefore, although the "normal" OSPF Hello configuration would not form an adjacency if the Hello and dead intervals do not match, if you are using Fast Hellos the neighbor adjacency would still form if the actual subsecond Hello interval does not match.

OSPF Update Packet-Pacing Timer

The OSPF update packet-pacing timer enables you to change the default timers to address CPU or buffer utilization issues that are associated with flooding very large numbers of link-state advertisements on the originating router. This feature enables you to configure the rate at which LSA floods, retransmissions, and group updates occur. Note that this pacing timer is applied on the link-state update (LSupdate) packets and not on the individual link-state advertisements. If a router has ten serial links, the LSupdate packet may contain approximately ten router link-state advertisements.

Initially, OSPF update packets were flooded upon receipt or generation without any delay, and the retransmission timer was tied to an individual OSPF neighbor. This was intended to achieve fast convergence whenever any network topology changes occurred. However, it was observed that there was no aggregation of updates, and it was easy to drop link-state update packets when the CPU load was high, causing retransmissions and slow convergence.

To address this, changes were made for each interface to send updates independently. In addition, a default of a 33 ms gap between update packets and a 66 ms gap between retransmission packets were added.

To configure the **flood packet pacing timer**, you must use the configuration in Example 5-17.

Example 5-17 *Configuring the OSPF Update Packet-Pacing Timer*

```
R1#configure terminal
Enter configuration commands, one per line.  End with CNTL/Z.
R1(config)#router ospf 100
R1(config-router)#timers pacing flood 50
R1(config-router)#^Z
```

Example 5-17 changes the interpacket spacing between consecutive link-state update packets in the OSPF transmission queue to 50 ms.

Similarly, for the retransmission packet-pacing timer, the configuration is as shown in Example 5-18.

Example 5-18 *Configuring the OSPF Update Retransmission Packet-Pacing Timer*

```
R1#configure terminal
Enter configuration commands, one per line.  End with CNTL/Z.
R1(config)#router ospf 100
R1(config-router)#timers pacing retransmission 100
R1(config-router)#^Z
R1#
```

Example 5-18 changes the interpacket spacing between consecutive link-state update packets in the OSPF retransmission queue to 100 ms.

Cisco IOS groups periodically refresh link-state advertisements to improve the link-state advertisement packing density for refreshes in large network topologies. The group packet-pacing timer controls the interval used for group link-state advertisement refreshment, and the commands to change the values are shown in Example 5-19.

Example 5-19 *Configuring the OSPF Update Group Packet-Pacing Timer*

```
R1#configure terminal
Enter configuration commands, one per line.  End with CNTL/Z.
R1(config)#router ospf 100
R1(config-router)#timers pacing lsa-group 200
R1(config-router)#^Z
```

You can verify the changes via the **show ip ospf** command, as shown in Example 5-20.

Example 5-20 *Output of the* **show ip ospf** *Command*

```
R1#show ip ospf
 Routing Process "ospf 100" with ID 200.200.7.225
 Supports only single TOS(TOS0) routes
 Supports opaque LSA
 Supports Link-local Signaling (LLS)
 Supports area transit capability
 Initial SPF schedule delay 5000 msecs
 Minimum hold time between two consecutive SPFs 10000 msecs
 Maximum wait time between two consecutive SPFs 10000 msecs
 Incremental-SPF disabled
 Minimum LSA interval 5 secs
 Minimum LSA arrival 1000 msecs
 LSA group pacing timer 200 secs
 Interface flood pacing timer 50 msecs
 Retransmission pacing timer 100 msecs
!Output omitted for brevity
```

Although this software feature provides the user with a knob for controlling the spacing between consecutive link-state update packets in the originating router, it should not be required most of the time. This feature should not precede other features to improve performance on OSPF networks such as summarization, stub area usage, queue tuning, and buffer tuning.

OSPF Incremental SPF

OSPF uses the Djikstra algorithm to compute the lowest-cost path to each router by building a shortest-path tree (SPT) that is rooted at the router running the algorithm. It does so by going through each of the link-state advertisements and all the links associated with that link-state advertisement. When changes to a Type 1 (router link state) or Type 2 (network link state) link-state advertisement occur in an OSPF area, the entire SPT is recomputed, even if there are no eventual changes to the final SPT topology.

Incremental SPF allows the system to recompute only the affected part of the SPT. Because the Djikstra algorithm has a runtime that is a function of the number of nodes and paths, this helps to reduce the amount of time required for calculation, which results in faster OSPF convergence and saves CPU resources. However, if the Type 1 or Type 2 link-state advertisement occurs in the calculating router, the full SPT calculation is performed. Incremental SPF provides more noticeable improvements in convergence time for networks with a high number of nodes and links, rather than for smaller ones. It also provides more significant advantage when the changes in the network topology are further away from the root of the SPT and when you have a wide network diameter.

Incremental SPF should not be confused with *partial SPF*, which means that the SPT is preserved (because there are no changes to the router or network link states), and only impacted prefixes need to be updated in the routing table. A partial SPF may be used for Type 3 (network summary), Type 4 (autonomous system boundary router [ASBR] summary), and Type 5 (AS external) link-state advertisements. An example might be when an external route has changed but there are no changes in the router link states.

Incremental SPF can interoperate with routers not running this feature on the same network. You can configure incremental SPF as shown in Example 5-21.

Example 5-21 *Configuring Incremental SPF in OSPF*

```
R1#configure terminal
Enter configuration commands, one per line.  End with CNTL/Z.
R1(config)#router ospf 100
R1(config-router)#ispf
R1(config-router)#^Z
```

As an illustration, a full SPF run for a 500-node, fully connected network may take approximately 50 ms to complete, whereas that for an incremental SPF might be in the range of 5 ms (a tenfold improvement).

OSPF Graceful Restart

Under normal circumstances when a router performs a RP failover, the routing protocol re-initializes the neighbor relationship, causing route flaps. Graceful restart enables you to resynchronize routing information between routing peers without causing traffic interruptions or route flaps. Graceful restart is implemented in Cisco IOS Software using the Nonstop Forwarding/Stateful Switchover (NSF/SSO) feature.

Graceful restart makes use of the fact that many of the routing platforms today implement separate control and forwarding functions, as can be seen most clearly on distributed platforms such as the Cisco 12000 series Gigabit Switch Router (GSR). Even on platforms such as the Cisco 10000, which is based on a centralized forwarding engine design, separate components make up the control and forwarding plane.

To minimize downtime, it is possible for a router to maintain its forwarding capability when a hardware or software problem causes a RP switchover in a redundant configuration. The

Cisco NSF/SSO implementation evolved from RP Redundancy (RPR) and RPR Plus (RPR+), which are a series of progressive enhancements to reduce the impact of a RP failure.

One may argue that continuing to forward packets while the control plane is nonfunctional may cause other problems, such as routing loops, or for the packets to be black holed. However, the only scenario whereby it is safe to keep the affected router on the forwarding path is when the network topology is stable (and it remains so), and if the affected router is able to be consistent in its forwarding table throughout the restart.

NSF uses the checkpoint and redundancy feature to replicate state information to the standby RP. However, when OSPF is configured on a router with dual RPs, only the primary or active RP is running OSPF. The standby RP does not contain any OSPF-related information, and when a switchover occurs, the neighbor relationship must be reestablished.

As you know by now, the OSPF Hello protocol is responsible for establishing adjacency. Bidirectional communications between neighbors are established when the router sees itself listed in its neighbor's Hello packets. When a switchover occurs, the restarting router attempts to reestablish its neighbor relationship by sending out Hello packets. Because the restarting router does not have any information in the neighbor list of the Hello packet, the routing adjacency is reset when a neighbor receives this Hello packet. The neighbor also floods link-state updates throughout the network to reflect the adjacency change, causing disruptions.

Routers that are capable of continuously forwarding traffic during a RP failover are known a *NSF-capable routers*; a router that has the capability to continue to forward traffic to a restarting router, and without introducing interruptions, is known as a *NSF-aware router*. NSF-aware routers "hide" the fact that the restarting router is restarting from the rest of the network. An NSF-capable router implies that it is also NSF aware but the reverse may not be true. An NSF-aware router could be a router that does not support redundant processors, such as the Cisco 2800 and 3800 series routers.

There are two implementations of a OSPF graceful restart: the Cisco implementation; and the IETF implementation, which is based on RFC 3623, *Graceful OSPF Restart*.

Although both the Cisco implementation and RFC 3623 try to achieve a graceful restart mechanism, there are differences in implementation, some of which are briefly described in the following sections.

RFC 3623

RFC 3623 uses the Link-Local Opaque link-state advertisement mechanism for capabilities exchange and signaling. It was originally designed to provide a mechanism for the router attempting a restart to announce its intention to its neighbors so that forwarding could continue unaffected, although an unscheduled restart would still work. This method makes use of a grace period, which is either specified by the user or calculated by the routing software. During this grace period, its neighbors announce this router as in their link-state advertisements as if it has full adjacency, if there are no other network topology changes. Link-state database synchronization is also provided by the mechanisms, as stated in RFC 2328, which is the same procedure as that during the neighbor adjacency establishment process. This section does not dwell too much on the specific details of the different implementations, because that is not in the scope of this book.

Cisco Implementation

The Cisco implementation is based on defining a link local signaling (LLS) mechanism in OSPF to perform an "out-of-band" capabilities exchange as well as the ability to perform "out-of-band" link-state database (LSDB) synchronization and restart notification. This is done by defining an L bit in the OSPF Options field (previously defined as the EA bit, which was deprecated). Any LLS information is then appended to the end of the OSPF Type 1 (Hello) or Type 2 (Database Description) packets.

Prior to the restart, the capability exchange is done using the LR bit (link-state database resynchronization bit) in the LLS Extended Options field. When the affected router is restarted, it is signaled by a restart bit (RS bit), which is carried in the LLS data block of an OSPF Hello packet. Figure 5-6 shows this process for the Cisco version of the OSPF graceful restart.

Figure 5-6   *Cisco OSPF Graceful Restart*

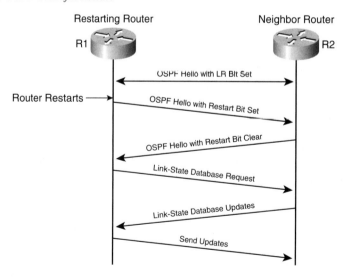

To use Cisco NSF, SSO is a prerequisite. NSF works with SSO to allow the forwarding plane to continue to forward IP packets after a RP failover. In addition, when a networking device restarts, all routing peers of that device may detect that the device went down and back up, which might cause route flaps. Cisco NSF helps to suppress route flaps in SSO-enabled devices, which increases network stability. Note that SSO may be turned on without NSF. However, doing so would result in a fast processor switchover, but the routing protocols will still have to be re-initialized, causing route flaps and interruption to traffic.

To configure NSF and SSO, you must use the configuration shown in Example 5-22 on the NSF-capable router.

Example 5-22 *Configuring OSPF NSF and SSO*

```
R1#configure terminal
Enter configuration commands, one per line.  End with CNTL/Z.
R1(config)#redundancy
R1(config-red)#mode sso
R1(config-red)#
R1(config-red)#router ospf 100
R1(config-router)#nsf
R1(config-router)#^Z
R1#
```

No configuration is required on the NSF-aware router.

When the router with redundant RP performs a RP failover, we observe the output shown in Example 5-23 from **debug ip ospf nsf** and **debug ip ospf adj**.

Example 5-23 *Output from* **debug ip ospf nsf** *and* **debug ip ospf adj** *on the Adjacent Router During a RP Failover*

```
R2#show ip ospf neighbor

Neighbor ID     Pri   State         Dead Time   Address       Interface
192.168.2.2      0    FULL/  -      00:00:03    192.168.2.2   GigabitEthernet2/0
R2#debug ip ospf nsf
OSPF non-stop forwarding events debugging is on
R2#
*Jun 28 14:28:49.663: OSPF: Rcv DBD (oob-resync) from 192.168.2.2 on
  GigabitEthernet2/0 seq 0x9DF opt 0x52 flag 0xF len 32  mtu 1500 state FULL
*Jun 28 14:28:49.663: OSPF: OOB-resync FROM Nbr 192.168.2.2 192.168.2.2
  GigabitEthernet2/0
*Jun 28 14:28:49.663: OSPF: Starting OOB-Resync with 192.168.2.2 address 192.168.2.2
  on GigabitEthernet2/0 (receiver)
*Jun 28 14:28:49.663: OSPF: Send DBD (oob-resync) to 192.168.2.2 on
  GigabitEthernet2/0 seq 0x9DF opt 0x52 flag 0xF len 32
*Jun 28 14:28:54.663: OSPF: Rcv DBD (oob-resync) from 192.168.2.2 on
  GigabitEthernet2/0 seq 0x9DF opt 0x52 flag 0xF len 32  mtu 1500 state EXSTART
*Jun 28 14:28:54.663: OSPF: NBR Negotiation Done. We are the SLAVE
*Jun 28 14:28:54.663: OSPF: Send DBD (oob-resync) to 192.168.2.2 on
  GigabitEthernet2/0 seq 0x9DF opt 0x52 flag 0xA len 72
*Jun 28 14:28:54.663: OSPF: Rcv DBD (oob-resync) from 192.168.2.2 on
  GigabitEthernet2/0 seq 0x9E0 opt 0x52 flag 0x9 len 32  mtu 1500 state EXCHANGE
*Jun 28 14:28:54.663: OSPF: Exchange Done with 192.168.2.2 on GigabitEthernet2/0*Jun
  28 14:28:54.663: OSPF: Synchronized with 192.168.2.2 on GigabitEthernet2/0, state
  FULL
```

continues

Example 5-23 *Output from* **debug ip ospf nsf** *and* **debug ip ospf adj** *on the Adjacent Router During a RP Failover (Continued)*

```
*Jun 28 14:28:54.663: %OSPF-5-ADJCHG: Process 100, Nbr 192.168.2.2 on
  GigabitEthernet2/0 from LOADING to FULL, Loading Done
*Jun 28 14:28:54.663: OSPF: OOB-Resync completed with 192.168.2.2 address
  192.168.2.2 on GigabitEthernet2/0
*Jun 28 14:28:54.663: OSPF: scheduling rtr lsa for area 0
*Jun 28 14:28:54.663: OSPF: Send DBD (oob-resync) to 192.168.2.2 on
  GigabitEthernet2/0 seq 0x9E0 opt 0x52 flag 0x8 len 32
*Jun 28 14:28:55.163: OSPF: no change in router LSA, area 0
R2#show ip ospf neighbor

Neighbor ID     Pri   State         Dead Time   Address       Interface
192.168.2.2       0   FULL/  -      00:00:03    192.168.2.2   GigabitEthernet2/0
```

There is no observed OSPF adjacency teardown during the RP failover, which is the expected behavior. To see whether an OSPF neighbor supports graceful restart, use the command **show ip ospf neighbor detail**, as shown in Example 5-24.

Example 5-24 *Determining Whether an OSPF Neighbor Supports Graceful Restart*

```
R1#show ip ospf neighbor detail
 Neighbor 192.168.2.2, interface address 192.168.2.2
    In the area 0 via interface GigabitEthernet2/0
    Neighbor priority is 0, State is FULL, 14 state changes
    DR is 0.0.0.0 BDR is 0.0.0.0
    Options is 0x52
    LLS Options is 0x1 (LR), last OOB-Resync 00:03:14 ago
    Dead timer due in 00:00:03
    Neighbor is up for 01:50:36
    Index 6/6, retransmission queue length 0, number of retransmission 1
    First 0x0(0)/0x0(0) Next 0x0(0)/0x0(0)
    Last retransmission scan length is 1, maximum is 1
    Last retransmission scan time is 0 msec, maximum is 0 msec
R1#
```

In this case, the neighbor has the link-state database resynchronization (LR) capability flag set in the LLS options, and that indicates that it is NSF aware.

To see whether the router has NSF configured, you can use the **show ip ospf** command, as shown in Example 5-25.

Example 5-25 *Checking Whether the Router Has NSF Configured from the Output of* **show ip ospf**

```
R2#show ip ospf
 Routing Process "ospf 100" with ID 192.168.2.2
 Supports only single TOS(TOS0) routes
 Supports opaque LSA
 Supports Link-local Signaling (LLS)
 Supports area transit capability
 Initial SPF schedule delay 5000 msecs
 Minimum hold time between two consecutive SPFs 10000 msecs
```

Example 5-25 *Checking Whether the Router Has NSF Configured from the Output of* **show ip ospf** *(Continued)*

```
Maximum wait time between two consecutive SPFs 10000 msecs
Incremental-SPF disabled
Minimum LSA interval 5 secs
Minimum LSA arrival 1000 msecs
LSA group pacing timer 240 secs
Interface flood pacing timer 33 msecs
Retransmission pacing timer 66 msecs
Number of external LSA 0. Checksum Sum 0x0
Number of opaque AS LSA 0. Checksum Sum 0x0
Number of DCbitless external and opaque AS LSA 0
Number of DoNotAge external and opaque AS LSA 0
Number of areas in this router is 1. 1 normal 0 stub 0 nssa
Number of areas transit capable is 0
External flood list length 0
Non-Stop Forwarding enabled
BFD is enabled
!Output omitted for brevity
```

Note that the NSF/SSO feature requires the restarting router to send the first Hello packet within the configured OSPF dead interval. Therefore, if the OSPF dead interval is too low, it would cause the dead time to expire and for the neighbor adjacency to change from full to down. A general guideline is to have a minimum of 4 to 5 seconds for the OSPF dead interval; the number will vary depending on the hardware platform. (For example, if you are using a Cisco 7500 with a Route Switch Processor 8 [RSP8] and below, it is recommended to have an OSPF dead interval of no less than 9 seconds.) For the same reason, this feature will also not interoperate well with the OSPF Fast Hello feature, which uses 1 second for the OSPF dead interval.

IS-IS Enhancements

Similar to OSPF, Integrated IS-IS is a link-state protocol that can be used to carry IP prefix information across the backbone. Comparisons between OSPF and IS-IS, and why some people prefer one to the other (including having a new routing protocol to list on a resumè), have been discussed in various other places, including North American Network Operator Group (NANOG) meetings; we do not attempt to cover the same discussion.

IS-IS uses a default of 3 and 10 seconds for the Hello multiplier and Hello interval, respectively, providing a default hold time of 30 seconds (hold time = Hello multiplier * Hello interval). If you want, you can tune the hold time to a lower value if the link layer does not offer fast enough failure detection, and BFD is not available. However, it is not recommended to have a dead interval less than 4 seconds, especially if you are using NSF/SSO.

The following subsections cover various enhancements that help improve the scalability and convergence of a network running IS-IS.

IS-IS SPF Throttling

Integrated IS-IS uses an exponential back-off mechanism for SPF calculations. You can configure the SPF timers as shown in Example 5-26.

Example 5-26 *Configuring IS-IS SPF Throttling*

```
R1#configure terminal
Enter configuration commands, one per line.  End with CNTL/Z.
R1(config)#router isis
R1(config-router)#spf-interval M I E
R1(config-router)#^Z
```

The parameters are the (M) maximum interval the router will wait between consecutive SPFs, the (I) initial delay before starting SPF, and the incremental interval (E), which is the time the router will wait before consecutive SPFs. The incremental interval will increase until it reaches the maximum interval value. The default values are 10 seconds, 5500 ms, and 5500 ms, respectively.

The initial SPF interval is the key to achieving fast convergence, and Example 5-27 shows the default SPF initial delay of 5500 ms from the **debug** output.

Example 5-27 *Router **debug** Output Illustrating the Initial SPF Interval*

```
R1#debug isis spf-events
*Jul  8 07:37:37.366: ISIS-Spf: L2 SPF needed, adjacency deleted, from 0xA9AEF4
*Jul  8 07:37:37.506: ISIS-Spf: L2, 0010.0100.1001.00-00 TLV contents changed, code 2
*Jul  8 07:37:42.878: ISIS-Spf:  Compute L2 SPT
*Jul  8 07:37:42.878: ISIS-Spf:  Compute L2 SPT
*Jul  8 07:37:42.878: ISIS-Spf: Starting level-2 SPF with 1 nodes into TENT
```

The optimal SPF interval values used to achieve fast convergence have high dependency on the network topology. As a general guideline, the initial SPF interval can be reduced, starting from a value of 150 ms. This is because you want to wait for all the relevant link-state advertisements to arrive before starting on SPF calculations, especially when node failures have occurred. When you can confirm that all the important LSPs have been fast flooded, you can further reduce this timer to a lower limit of approximately 50 ms.

The (M) maximum amount of time the router will wait between SPFs can be kept at the default, and the incremental interval may be tuned to a value between 20 ms and 100 ms.

Note that the command **spf-interval** changes the timer values for complete SPF calculations only. For partial route computations (PRC), the **prc-interval** command is used to change the timer values. The parameters that can be configured correspond to that for the complete SPF calculations, as shown in Example 5-28.

Example 5-28 *Configuring IS-IS Partial Route Computation Interval Timers*

```
R1#configure terminal
Enter configuration commands, one per line.  End with CNTL/Z.
R1(config)#router isis
R1(config-router)#prc-interval M I E
R1(config-router)#^Z
```

After the timers have been changed from their default values, you should ensure consistency throughout the network.

IS-IS LSP Generation

When a network topology change occurs, a LSP is generated to be flooded to other neighbors. Integrated IS-IS uses an exponential back-off timer for LSP generation that is trigged by network topology changes. You can adjust the timers with the command shown in Example 5-29.

Example 5-29 *Configuring IS-IS LSP Generation Interval Timers*

```
R1#configure terminal
Enter configuration commands, one per line.  End with CNTL/Z.
R1(config)#router isis
R1(config-router)#lsp-gen-interval M I E
R1(config-router)#^Z
R1#
```

The parameters are the same as that for SPF throttling, except that it is applied in the context of LSP generation rather than SPF runs. By default, the first LSP is generated 50 ms after receiving the event (initial interval), and it is recommended that this default value be used. It can be tuned downward to a minimal value of 1 millisecond, but with the consideration that if there are multiple network topology changes occurring (such as multiple interfaces on the same router going over the same physical infrastructure failing), there would be a high probability that a second LSP would need to be generated.

The maximum interval (M) has a default of 5 seconds and can be reduced to a value of around 1 second; the incremental interval could be a value from 20 ms to 100 ms. If the incremental interval is kept low, you can ensure that even if a second LSP would need to be generated for the failures, it would be promptly flooded onto the network.

IS-IS LSA Flooding Reduction

OSPF and Integrated IS-IS have different mechanisms to age and refresh LSAs. In OSPF, the ages of the LSAs are incremented starting from zero until it reaches the MaxAge value as they are held in the router's link-state database. The OSPF Demand Circuit feature (RFC 1793, *Extending OSPF to Support Demand Circuits*) is then used to enable you to tag certain link-state advertisements as DoNotAge to avoid these link-state advertisements from being aged, thus removing the need to refresh them (and to reduce flooding).

For IS-IS, every time a router originates an LSP, it tags the link-state advertisements with a lifetime or TTL value that is between 0 to 65,535 seconds, and the age of the link-state advertisements is decremented downward until it reaches 0. The benefit of such an approach is that individual LSPs can have different initial values to start aging from. By default, IS-IS refreshes LSPs every 900 seconds. For large integrated IS-IS deployments, it may be good to tune the following values to reduce the amount of LSA flooding done by IS-IS.

For IS-IS, reduction to the amount of link-state advertisement flooding may be achieved with the commands shown in Example 5-30.

Example 5-30 *Configuring IS-IS LSA Flooding Reduction*

```
R1#configure terminal
Enter configuration commands, one per line.  End with CNTL/Z.
R1(config)#router isis
R1(config-router)#max-lsp-lifetime 65535
R1(config-router)#lsp-refresh-interval 64000
R1(config-router)#^Z
R1#
```

In this case, the maximum LSP lifetime is set to the maximum allowed time of 65,535 seconds (about 18.2 hours) and the LSP refresh interval to a conservative value that is below the maximum LSP lifetime. This configuration prevents the unnecessary generation of refresh LSPs.

IS-IS Fast Hellos

Integrated IS-IS uses a default Hello timer value of 10 seconds for both Level 1 and Level 2 routes, with the exception of the designated IS (DIS), which uses 3.33 seconds for both levels of routing. This setup is intended for the DIS to be replaced quickly in case of a failure. The default dead interval is three times the Hello timer value, as shown clearly in Example 5-31.

Example 5-31 *Output of* **debug isis adj-packets**

```
R1#debug isis adj-packets
Jul  9 13:59:07.519: ISIS-Adj: Rec serial IIH from *HDLC* (Serial2/0), cir type L1L2,
  cir id 00, length 1499
Jul  9 13:59:07.519: ISIS-Adj: rcvd state UP, old state UP, new state UP
Jul  9 13:59:07.519: ISIS-Adj: Action = ACCEPT
Jul  9 13:59:07.983: ISIS-Adj: Sending serial IIH on Serial2/0, length 1499
Jul  9 13:59:16.371: ISIS-Adj: Sending serial IIH on Serial2/0, length 1499
Jul  9 13:59:25.195: ISIS-Adj: Sending serial IIH on Serial2/0, length 1499
Jul  9 13:59:32.783: ISIS-Adj: Sending serial IIH on Serial2/0, length 1499
Jul  9 13:59:37.527: %CLNS-5-ADJCHANGE: ISIS: Adjacency to Router3 (Serial2/0) Down,
  hold time expired
```

When the link layer is not affected by a neighbor loss, this feature may be used to allow for faster convergence. Compared to OSPF, IS-IS allows different Hello intervals to be configured for multiaccess media for Level 1 and Level 2 if desired, with the exception of point-to-point links (for which only a single Hello packet type is sent).

Fast Hello is configured on a per-interface basis, and two configuration statements are required, as shown in Example 5-32. The first statement states that a minimum of 1 second is to be used for the IS-IS dead interval, or hold time. After that has been configured, a second configuration statement can be used to configure the number of Hellos (n) that will be sent in 1 second. The default value is 3, effectively providing a Hello interval of approximately one-third second and an effective hold time of 1 second (because hold time = Hello interval * Hello multiplier).

Example 5-32 *Configuring IS-IS Fast Hello on an Ethernet Interface*

```
R1#configure terminal
Enter configuration commands, one per line.  End with CNTL/Z.
R1(config)#interface ethernet 0/0
R1(config-if)#isis hello-interval minimal
R1(config-if)#isis hello-multiplier N
R1(config-if)#^Z
R1#
```

IS-IS Update Packet-Pacing Timer

A default pacing value of 33 ms is applied for all LSPs that originate from the router. This pacing timer is intended to prevent too many LSPs from being sent back to back to its neighbor, causing drops on arriving LSPs because of input queue congestions and so on (which may then lead to retransmissions and subsequently higher convergence timings).

With faster processors being used in router control planes, this LSA packet-pacing timer may be reduced to between 5 to 10 ms, providing marginal improvements in sending consecutive LSPs. The packet-pacing timer is configured on a per-interface basis, as shown in Example 5-33.

Example 5-33 *Configuring the IS-IS Packet-Pacing Timer on a Serial Interface*

```
R1#configure terminal
Enter configuration commands, one per line.  End with CNTL/Z.
R1(config)#interface serial 1/0
R1(config-if)#isis lsp-interval I
R1(config-if)#^Z
```

In addition, IS-IS has a special knob known as fast flood. This feature tells the router to flood the first five (by default) LSPs that will trigger an SPF without any pacing. In addition, if these five LSPs are present in the input LSP queue and the **spf-interval** timer has expired, you will delay SPF execution in order to first flood these five LSPs.

The number of LSPs to fast flood (n) can be configured with the command shown in Example 5-34.

Example 5-34 *Configuring the IS-IS Fast Flood Feature*

```
R1#configure terminal
Enter configuration commands, one per line.  End with CNTL/Z.
R1(config)#router isis
R1(config-router)#fast-flood N
R1(config-router)#^Z
R1#
```

The number would correspond closely to the number of IS-IS neighbors per node. For example, for a network with ten neighbors connected to a node, fast flood ten might be required. This is because each of the ten neighbors connected to this node would generate and flood a new LSP for the event. If this is not done, only the first five LSPs would be fast flooded, and the pacing timers would delay the rest of the relevant or important LSPs, which might lead to multiple SPF runs. In an optimal situation, we wait just long enough to get the relevant information on the failure before flooding and running SPF.

NOTE   Note that if fast flood has been configured, you should not have to configure the packet-pacing timers.

IS-IS Incremental SPF

Incremental SPF can be configured in Integrated IS-IS to reduce the amount of time required to perform SPF calculations, especially when the affected nodes are farther away from the root of the SPT. In this manner, the Djikstra algorithm does not have to be run on the entire SPT but only on the part of the SPT that has changed. In IS-IS, incremental SPF can be turned on for Level 1, Level 2, or both, as shown in Example 5-35.

Example 5-35 *Configuring Incremental SPF in IS-IS*

```
R1#configure terminal
Enter configuration commands, one per line.  End with CNTL/Z.
R1(config)#router isis
R1(config-router)#ispf [level-1 | level-2 | level-1-2]
R1(config-router)#^Z
```

In IS-IS, if there are any changes to the topology, the SPT is computed and the RIB is updated. If there is only a leaf change (no change in link/node information), you perform a *partial route computation (PRC)*. In this case, the router keeps the existing SPT and just updates the RIB for the nodes whose leaf has changed. This is analogous to partial SPF for OSPF. However, integrated IS-IS offers the added benefit of running only the PRC even when the link layer address might have been changed, without any physical topology change. This is because IS-IS is not tightly coupled to IP, as OSPF is.

PRC is the process of calculating routes without performing an SPF calculation. This is possible when the topology of the routing system has not changed, but a change is detected in the information announced by a particular IS or when it is necessary to attempt to reinstall such routes in the RIB.

IS-IS Graceful Restart

Integrated IS-IS graceful restart works together with Stateful Switchover (SSO) to allow data traffic to continue to be forwarded between the restarting router and its peers to minimize disruption. The same feature also ensures that the peer does not declare the restarting router to be dead, and for link-state advertisements that originate from the restarting router to be flushed from routers in the same network.

Cisco implements two versions of IS-IS graceful restart: the IETF version based on RFC 3847, *Restart Signaling for Intermediate System to Intermediate System (IS-IS)*; and its own proprietary version. The key differences between these two implementations are that the IETF implementation requires additional Type-Length-Values (TLVs) to be defined in the IS-IS Hello (IIH) packets and that the peer router must be NSF aware.

Cisco Implementation

The Cisco version uses a check-pointing method in which IS-IS information is propagated from the active RP to the standby RP. Subsequently, a Complete Sequence Number Packet (CSNP) that references the entire LSP range, and a unique LSP that has never been sent by the issuing router, is used by the restarting router to trigger the synchronization of the restarting router's LSDB.

A Partial Sequence Number Packet (PSNP) is then originated by the neighbor to "acknowledge" the receipt of this special CSNP, followed by the neighbor sending all of its LSPs to the restarting neighbor. This is because a CSNP that references missing LSPs (which this neighbor has) will induce this neighbor to set its send routing message (SRM) bits and to flood the missing LSPs to the originator of the CSNP. Figure 5-7 shows this process.

From observation, you can deduce that the Cisco version of IS-IS graceful restart does not require a graceful-aware neighbor, because it makes use of existing IS-IS functionality for restart notification and database synchronization.

Figure 5-7   *The Cisco ISIS NSF Operation (P2P Link)*

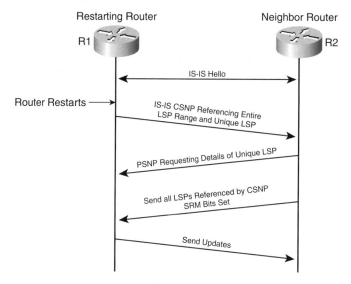

IETF Implementation

The IETF version uses the restart request (RR) bit, restart-acknowledgement (RA) bit, and Remaining Time field in the new *TLV* that is defined for the IIH packet. It also defines three additional timers—T1, T2, and T3—to be specified to support the functionality. Prior to RP switchover, the IS-IS neighbors perform a capability exchange by the mere fact that the restart TLVs (Type 211) always exist in the IIH *PDU*s in routers that support this capability. The RR bit is used to signal to the restarting router's neighbors that it is attempting a graceful restart, and the neighbor responds by sending an IIH with the RA bit set in the TLV. The neighbor also ensures that adjacency with this router is maintained in the up state. One node per interface per level then sends a set of CSNPs covering the entire LSP range, and the SRM flags are set on the interfaces for all LSPs in the local database for that level. The restarting router then uses these CSNPs to aid in rebuilding its link-state database.

Figure 5-8 shows the process for the IETF IS-IS graceful restart.

Figure 5-8   *IETF's ISIS Graceful Restart (P2P Link)*

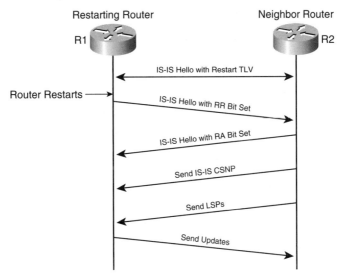

One key consideration for both the IETF and the Cisco version of the IS-IS graceful restart is to allow the restarting systems sufficient time for recovery and synchronization before the adjacency timers expire. Because IS-IS has more aggressive timers (a Hello interval of 3.33 seconds for a LAN segment, or 10 seconds for point-to-point links and a dead interval of 3 times the Hello interval) as compared to OSPF, it may be required for the Hello and dead interval to be configured above the default to allow a successful failover before the adjacency timer expires for platforms that cannot meet the aggressive timing constraints. In the worst-case scenario, for example, if a router fails immediately prior to sending an IIH packet, one complete Hello interval is lost and it must be able to send control packets following recovery in 6.66 seconds for the pseudonode, or 20 seconds for all other interfaces.

Increasing the timer values has the potential effect of slowing convergence, because they are directly involved in determining the time for signaling failed adjacencies. This work-around is often a tradeoff that you have between graceful restart functionality and your requirements for fast convergence during normal network operations.

To use IS-IS graceful restart, you need to turn on SSO. To configure NSF and SSO, use the configuration shown in Example 5-36 on the NSF-capable router.

Example 5-36 *Configuring IS-IS NSF and SSO*

```
R2#configure terminal
Enter configuration commands, one per line.  End with CNTL/Z.
R2(config)#redundancy
```

continues

Example 5-36 *Configuring IS-IS NSF and SSO (Continued)*

```
R2(config-red)#mode sso
R2(config-red)#
R2(config-red)#router isis
R2(config-router)#nsf [cisco | ietf]
R2(config-router)#nsf interval I
R2(config-router)#^Z
R2#
```

The **nsf interval** is an optional parameter and enables you to specify, roughly, the minimum time allowed between graceful restarts. In Cisco mode, this interval is the amount of time that the active RP must be up, and for the IETF mode, the value applies for the standby RP.

To check whether graceful restart has been configured and which version of graceful restart is running, you can use the command **show isis nsf**, as shown in Example 5-37. Note that you should see the line "NSF restart enabled," unless the interval timer is still running (and not expired).

Example 5-37 *Output from **show isis nsf** for the Cisco Mode of IS-IS NSF*

```
R2#show isis nsf

NSF is ENABLED, mode 'cisco'

RP is ACTIVE, standby ready, bulk sync complete
NSF interval timer expired (NSF restart enabled)
Checkpointing enabled, no errors
Local state: ACTIVE,  Peer state: STANDBY HOT,  Mode: SSO
```

If the router has been configured for the IETF mode for the IS-IS graceful restart, the output will be in the format shown in Example 5-38.

Example 5-38 *Output from **show isis nsf** for the IETF Mode of IS-IS NSF*

```
R2#show isis nsf
NSF is ENABLED, mode 'ietf'
NSF pdb state:
NSF L1 active interfaces: 0
NSF L1 active LSPs: 0
NSF interfaces awaiting L1 CSNP: 0
Awaiting L1 LSPs:
NSF L2 active interfaces: 0
NSF L2 active LSPs: 0
NSF interfaces awaiting L2 CSNP: 0
Awaiting L2 LSPs:
NSF T3 remaining: 0 seconds
Interface: POS2/0
    NSF L1 Restart state: Running
    NSF p2p Restart retransmissions: 0
```

Example 5-38 *Output from* **show isis nsf** *for the IETF Mode of IS-IS NSF (Continued)*

```
      Maximum L1 NSF Restart retransmissions: 3
      NSF L2 Restart state: Running
      NSF p2p Restart retransmissions: 0
      Maximum L2 NSF Restart retransmissions: 3
 R2#
```

Example 5-39 shows the output for **debug isis nsf**, **debug isis adj**, and **debug isis snp** for a successful graceful restart using the Cisco mode from the peer router. A successful graceful restart should never see the peer routing transiting into the down and init state, and this holds true for the IETF mode, too.

Example 5-39 *Output for the* **debug isis nsf**, **debug isis adj**, *and* **debug isis snp** *Commands*

```
R1#debug isis nsf
IS-IS NSF events debugging is on for router process null
R1#debug isis adj
IS-IS Adjacency related packets debugging is on for router process null
R1#debug isis snp
IS-IS CSNP/PSNP packets debugging is on for router process null
*Jul 17 23:06:38.851: ISIS-Adj: Sending serial IIH on POS3/0, length 4469
*Jul 17 23:06:42.475: ISIS-SNP: Rec L1 CSNP from 0040.0400.4004 (POS3/0)
*Jul 17 23:06:42.475: ISIS-SNP: CSNP range 0000.0000.0000.00-00 to
 FFFF.FFFF.FFFF.FF-FF
*Jul 17 23:06:42.475: ISIS-SNP: LSP not in CSNP (next entry 0040.0400.4004.FE-FE,
 seq 1), flooding 0010.0100.1001.00-00, seq 17
*Jul 17 23:06:42.475: ISIS-SNP: LSP not in CSNP (next entry 0040.0400.4004.FE-FE,
 seq 1), flooding 0040.0400.4004.00-00, seq 18
*Jul 17 23:06:42.475: ISIS-SNP: Entry 0040.0400.4004.FE-FE, seq 1 not in LSP
 database, adding dummy
*Jul 17 23:06:42.475: ISIS-NSF: Sched LSP - L1 R2.FE-FE (DROP dummy)
*Jul 17 23:06:42.475: ISIS-SNP: Rec L1 CSNP from 0040.0400.4004 (POS3/0)
*Jul 17 23:06:42.475: ISIS-SNP: CSNP range 0000.0000.0000.00-00 to
 FFFF.FFFF.FFFF.FF-FF
*Jul 17 23:06:42.475: ISIS-SNP: Same entry 0010.0100.1001.00-00, seq 17
*Jul 17 23:06:42.475: ISIS-SNP: Same entry 0040.0400.4004.00-00, seq 18
*Jul 17 23:06:42.475: ISIS-SNP: Rec L2 CSNP from 0040.0400.4004 (POS3/0)
*Jul 17 23:06:42.475: ISIS-SNP: CSNP range 0000.0000.0000.00-00 to
 FFFF.FFFF.FFFF.FF-FF
*Jul 17 23:06:42.475: ISIS-SNP: LSP not in CSNP (next entry 0040.0400.4004.FE-FE,
 seq 1), flooding 0010.0100.1001.00-00, seq 1A
*Jul 17 23:06:42.475: ISIS-SNP: LSP not in CSNP (next entry 0040.0400.4004.FE-FE,
 seq 1), flooding 0040.0400.4004.00-00, seq 20
*Jul 17 23:06:42.475: ISIS-SNP: Entry 0040.0400.4004.FE-FE, seq 1 not in LSP
 database, adding dummy
*Jul 17 23:06:42.475: ISIS-NSF: Sched LSP - L2 R2.FE-FE (DROP dummy)
*Jul 17 23:06:42.475: ISIS-SNP: Rec L2 CSNP from 0040.0400.4004 (POS3/0)
*Jul 17 23:06:42.475: ISIS-SNP: CSNP range 0000.0000.0000.00-00 to
 FFFF.FFFF.FFFF.FF-FF
*Jul 17 23:06:42.475: ISIS-SNP: Same entry 0010.0100.1001.00-00, seq 1A
*Jul 17 23:06:42.475: ISIS-SNP: Same entry 0040.0400.4004.00-00, seq 20
*Jul 17 23:06:42.479: ISIS-Adj: Rec serial IIH from *HDLC* (POS3/0), cir type L1L2,
 cir id 00, length 4469
*Jul 17 23:06:42.479: ISIS-Adj: rcvd state UP, old state UP, new state UP
```

continues

Example 5-39 *Output for the* **debug isis nsf**, **debug isis adj**, *and* **debug isis snp** *Commands (Continued)*

```
*Jul 17 23:06:42.479: ISIS-Adj: Action = ACCEPT
*Jul 17 23:06:42.479: ISIS-NSF: Adjacency timer refreshed: POS3/0
*Jul 17 23:06:42.479: ISIS-NSF: CP pending - ADJ R2.00 (PO3/0)
*Jul 17 23:06:43.475: ISIS-SNP: Rec L1 CSNP from 0040.0400.4004 (POS3/0)
*Jul 17 23:06:43.475: ISIS-SNP: CSNP range 0000.0000.0000.00-00 to
  FFFF.FFFF.FFFF.FF-FF
*Jul 17 23:06:43.475: ISIS-SNP: LSP not in CSNP (next entry 0040.0400.4004.FE-FE,
  seq 1), flooding 0010.0100.1001.00-00, seq 17
*Jul 17 23:06:43.475: ISIS-SNP: LSP not in CSNP (next entry 0040.0400.4004.FE-FE,
  seq 1), flooding 0040.0400.4004.00-00, seq 18
*Jul 17 23:06:43.475: ISIS-SNP: Entry 0040.0400.4004.FE-FE, seq 1 is newer than ours
  (seq 0), sending PSNP
*Jul 17 23:06:43.475: ISIS-SNP: Rec L1 CSNP from 0040.0400.4004 (POS3/0)
*Jul 17 23:06:43.475: ISIS-SNP: CSNP range 0000.0000.0000.00-00 to
  FFFF.FFFF.FFFF.FF-FF
*Jul 17 23:06:43.475: ISIS-SNP: Same entry 0010.0100.1001.00-00, seq 17
*Jul 17 23:06:43.475: ISIS-SNP: Same entry 0040.0400.4004.00-00, seq 18
*Jul 17 23:06:43.475: ISIS-SNP: Rec L2 CSNP from 0040.0400.4004 (POS3/0)
*Jul 17 23:06:43.475: ISIS-SNP: CSNP range 0000.0000.0000.00-00 to
  FFFF.FFFF.FFFF.FF-FF
*Jul 17 23:06:43.475: ISIS-SNP: LSP not in CSNP (next entry 0040.0400.4004.FE-FE,
  seq 1), flooding 0010.0100.1001.00-00, seq 1A
*Jul 17 23:06:43.475: ISIS-SNP: LSP not in CSNP (next entry 0040.0400.4004.FE-FE,
  seq 1), flooding 0040.0400.4004.00-00, seq 20
*Jul 17 23:06:43.475: ISIS-SNP: Entry 0040.0400.4004.FE-FE, seq 1 is newer than ours
  (seq 0), sending PSNP
*Jul 17 23:06:43.475: ISIS-SNP: Rec L2 CSNP from 0040.0400.4004 (POS3/0)
*Jul 17 23:06:43.475: ISIS-SNP: CSNP range 0000.0000.0000.00-00 to
  FFFF.FFFF.FFFF.FF-FF
*Jul 17 23:06:43.475: ISIS-SNP: Same entry 0010.0100.1001.00-00, seq 1A
*Jul 17 23:06:43.475: ISIS-SNP: Same entry 0040.0400.4004.00-00, seq 20
*Jul 17 23:06:45.495: ISIS-NSF: Pending LSP - L1 R2.00-00, seq 19, csum 7145, ht
  1199, len 88
*Jul 17 23:06:45.567: ISIS-NSF: Sched LSP - L2 R2.00-00, seq 22, csum 482E, ht 1199,
  len 97
*Jul 17 23:06:45.567: ISIS-NSF: UPD boolean
*Jul 17 23:06:46.751: ISIS-Adj: Sending serial IIH on POS3/0, length 4469
*Jul 17 23:06:50.187: ISIS-Adj: Rec serial IIH from *HDLC* (POS3/0), cir type L1L2,
  cir id 00, length 4469
*Jul 17 23:06:50.187: ISIS-Adj: rcvd state UP, old state UP, new state UP
*Jul 17 23:06:50.187: ISIS-Adj: Action = ACCEPT
*Jul 17 23:06:50.187: ISIS-NSF: Adjacency timer refreshed: POS3/0
*Jul 17 23:06:50.187: ISIS-NSF: CP pending - ADJ R2.00 (PO3/0)
*Jul 17 23:06:55.619: ISIS-Adj: Sending serial IIH on POS3/0, length 4469
*Jul 17 23:06:58.075: ISIS-Adj: Rec serial IIH from *HDLC* (POS3/0), cir type L1L2,
  cir id 00, length 4469
*Jul 17 23:06:58.075: ISIS-Adj: rcvd state UP, old state UP, new state UP
*Jul 17 23:06:58.075: ISIS-Adj: Action = ACCEPT
*Jul 17 23:06:58.075: ISIS-NSF: Adjacency timer refreshed: POS3/0
*Jul 17 23:06:58.075: ISIS-NSF: CP pending - ADJ R2.00 (PO3/0)
```

EIGRP Enhancements

The Enhanced Interior Gateway Routing Protocol (EIGRP) is an advanced distance vector protocol that provides the benefits of fast convergence and the simplicity of a distance vector protocol such as IGRP. It makes use of the diffusion update algorithm (DUAL) to calculate the shortest path to a destination.

EIGRP is distinct as a routing protocol, because it uses the idea of a feasible successor, which is a precomputed redundant next hop, to achieve fast convergence. In this manner, the failover path that packets should take after failover is precomputed prior to the link failure. EIGRP is also the first routing protocol to concurrently support IP, Internetwork Packet Exchange (IPX), and AppleTalk. As compared to distance vector protocols such as Routing Information Protocol (RIP), EIGRP plays an active role in the convergence process by querying neighbors instead of waiting for information to be propagated from neighbors, which is one major contributing factor that allows EIGRP to have fast convergence.

The following are some recent enhancements in EIGRP that relate to the areas of convergence and scalability. For more information on the features, refer to Cisco.com documentation.

EIGRP Graceful Shutdown

EIGRP supports the concept of a graceful shutdown. Graceful shutdown allows the router shutting down to inform its neighboring routers that it is doing so, so that those neighbors can remove the router from their adjacency table without needing the routing protocol hold timer to expire. Graceful shutdown minimizes the potential for traffic loss and for the neighbor to be in a stuck-in-active (SIA) state.

EIGRP Graceful Restart

NSF/SSO supports EIGRP, too. EIGRP graceful restart follows the same concept as that for OSPF and IS-IS. To achieve this, a new restart bit was introduced in the EIGRP update and Hello packets. At the same time, an End-of-Table (EOT) signal was introduced to allow the restarting router to begin topology and route calculation.

EIGRP Stub Router Functionality

When EIGRP routes to destinations are lost and no feasible successor routes exist, EIGRP sends a QUERY packet to each neighbor to discover whether alternative routes exist. These routers then propagate this QUERY until it reaches the edge of the network. In a typical redundant hub-and-spoke scenario, it is typical for the spoke site to be connected via redundant links to the hub site. In this case, the QUERY is propagated back to another router in the hub site, which may not be optimum. EIGRP has a functionality known as a stub router functionality that prevents this behavior. When a spoke router is explicitly configured to be so, a hub router does not send any QUERY packets to a stub router.

Bidirectional Forwarding Detection (BFD)

The capability to detect link failures quickly is becoming increasingly important for a network that is used for carrying voice, video, and data, regardless of the routing protocols being used. Although this does not present a challenge for situations where data-link hardware comes into play (such as SONET), it is a problem when the link layer does not provide the required signaling, or when it does not correlate with a failing link or node.

Bidirectional Forwarding Detection (BFD) provides a generalized framework to detect failures in the bidirectional path between two nodes, including that of interfaces, data links, and the forwarding engine itself. In some sense, BFD is a simple Hello protocol that is similar to mechanisms used by routing protocols to detect peer failures with the key difference that the peers can negotiate the speed at which BFD packets are originated, and echoed back to the originator. Its capabilities include providing fast failure detection times (potentially comparable to that of a Packet over SONET [POS] failure detection of ~50 milliseconds) for all media types, encapsulations, and topologies. In all fairness, although BFD provides fast failure detection, PoS's failure detection is absolute, and it requires far fewer overheads for failure detection and, therefore, it is still the media of choice for fast convergence.

The BFD protocol can operate in two modes:

- **Asynchronous mode**—Sends periodic BFD control packets to one another
- **Demand mode**—Sends short sequences of BFD control packets on an as-needed basis

The asynchronous mode emulates the existing IGP Hello protocols closely, and will declare the peer down if a number of these packets are not received. Both modes use an echo function such that a stream of BFD echo packets is transmitted for the other system to loop them back through the forwarding path.

In BFD, systems are defined as taking either an active or passive role in the initialization process. Passive systems never originate BFD packets until they have received BFD packets, and active systems always initiate BFD packets. Both ends of the system can take on an active role in the initialization process. A three-way handshake is used for the initialization process, whose completion is indicated by the "I Hear You" bit being set in both directions. When a session is declared down, it has to remain so until the remote end signals that it is down, thereby avoiding discrepancies.

BFD is configured in two steps, the baseline parameters for all BFD sessions on the interface and the routing protocol configuration, as shown in Example 5-40.

Example 5-40 *Configuring BFD on a Gigabit Ethernet Interface*

```
R1#configure terminal
Enter configuration commands, one per line.  End with CNTL/Z.
R1(config)#interface gigabit 2/0
R1(config-if)#bfd interval i min_rx rx multiplier m
R1(config-if)#^Z
R1#
```

The **interval** determines how often BFD sends packets to its peers, **min_rx** defines how frequently BFD packets are expected to be received from its peers, and **multiplier** defines the number of packets that must be missed before declaring the peer down.

The second part of the configuration deals with informing the routing protocol that BFD is to be used for failure detection. For our case, which is OSPF, the configuration commands look like Example 5-41. This configuration assumes that all OSPF neighbors have BFD implemented.

Example 5-41 *Configuring OSPF to Use All Interfaces for BFD Failure Detection*

```
R1#configure terminal
Enter configuration commands, one per line.  End with CNTL/Z.
R1(config)#router ospf 100
R1(config-router)#bfd all-interfaces
R1(config-router)#^Z
R1#
```

In platforms such as the Cisco 12000 series, BFD has an additional advantage in that it is implemented in a distributed manner on the linecards. As such, to look at the BFD neighbor status details, you need to use the **execute-on** *<slot>* command. On nondistributed platforms, the **show bfd neigh detail** command will suffice, as shown in Example 5-42.

Example 5-42 *Checking the BFD Neighbor Status on the Cisco 12000 Router*

```
R1#execute-on slot 2 show bfd neigh detail
========= Line Card (Slot 2) =========
Cleanup timer hits: 0
OurAddr        NeighAddr       LD/RD RH  Holdown(mult)  State     Int
192.168.2.1    192.168.2.2     32/33  1    94    (3 )     Up        Gi2/0
   Local Diag: 0, Demand mode: 0, Poll bit: 0
MinTxInt: 50000, MinRxInt: 50000, Multiplier: 3
Received MinRxInt: 50000, Received Multiplier: 3
Holdown (hits): 150(0), Hello (hits): 50(951953)
Rx Count: 954029, Rx Interval (ms) min/max/avg: 48/112/85 last: 4 ms ago
Tx Count: 951956, Tx Interval (ms) min/max/avg: 52/112/85 last: 24 ms ago
Last packet: Version: 0           - Diagnostic: 0
             I Hear You bit: 1    - Demand bit: 0
             Poll bit: 0          - Final bit: 0
             Multiplier: 3        - Length: 24
             My Discr.: 33        - Your Discr.: 32
             Min tx interval: 50000   - Min rx interval: 50000
             Min Echo interval: 0
```

continues

Example 5-42 *Checking the BFD Neighbor Status on the Cisco 12000 Router (Continued)*

```
Uptime: 22:25:39
SSO Cleanup Timer called: 0
SSO Cleanup Action Taken: 0
Pseudo pre-emptive process count: 9138323 min/max/avg: 8/16/8 last: 4 ms ago
 IPC Tx Failure Count: 0
 IPC Rx Failure Count: 0
 Total Adjs Found: 256
R1#
```

If a link failure due to BFD is detected, the **log-adjacency-changes** statement within OSPF causes the messages shown in Example 5-43 to be logged.

Example 5-43 *Router Logs Showing Neighbor Down Detection via BFD*

```
Jun 28 18:00:57.846: BFD Adj is Deleted Neighbor 192.168.2.2
Jun 28 18:00:57.846: %OSPF-5-ADJCHG: Process 100, Nbr 192.168.2.2 on
  GigabitEthernet2/0 from FULL to DOWN, Neighbor Down: BFD node down
```

Similar to OSPF Fast Hellos, BFD may not work very well with the NSF/SSO feature because of the nature of how the protocols operate. BFD supports the use of OSPF, IS-IS, and EIGRP.

IP Event Dampening

IP event dampening is a feature first introduced in the Cisco IOS Release 12.0(22)S to provide for a generic interface dampening mechanism. This mechanism provides a configurable exponential decay mechanism (such as BGP dampening) that can be used to suppress excessive interface flapping events on routing protocols and routing tables in the network. Dampening an interface effectively removes it from the network until the interface is stable and stops flapping (bouncing up and down). Configuring IP event dampening also improves stability and convergence time, because these disturbances are not propagated to other parts of the network, thus reducing the wastage of system resources required to process them.

NOTE   Note that this feature can be configured only on an interface, and all subinterfaces will inherit this feature. You cannot configure this feature on selective subinterfaces.

When configured, flapping interfaces are identified, assigned penalties, and suppressed if necessary. This means that as far as the supported routing protocols and HSRP are concerned, the interface is considered to be down, and connected routes for the suppressed interface are removed from the routing table.

Example 5-44 shows IP event dampening.

Example 5-44 *Configuring IP Event Dampening*

```
R1#configure terminal
Enter configuration commands, one per line.  End with CNTL/Z.
R1(config)#interface serial 2/0
R1(config-if)#dampening [half-life reuse-threshold suppress-threshold max-suppress
  restart-penalty]
R1(config-if)#^Z
R1#
```

If the default dampening parameters are to be used, you just have to configure dampening. Whenever the interface goes down, a default penalty of 1000 is added. This penalty value is halved every half-life seconds (exponential decay). When the penalty value exceeds the suppress threshold, the interface is dampened (prevented from going up), and after the penalty reaches below the reuse threshold, the dampening is disabled. The optional parameter **restart-penalty** allows a penalty to be applied to an interface the first time the router comes up.

Figure 5-9 shows the effect of configuring IP event dampening on a flapping interface. In the first instance when the interface goes down, a penalty of 1000 is added to the interface. When the interface goes up and down again, an additional penalty of 1000 is added. This addition causes the interface penalty to exceed the suppress threshold, which causes the interface to be dampened. Therefore, the interface status, as seen by the routing protocols, is down until the interface penalty reaches the reuse threshold. All the while, the interface penalty is subject to exponential decay.

Figure 5-9   *Effect of Configuring IP Event Dampening*

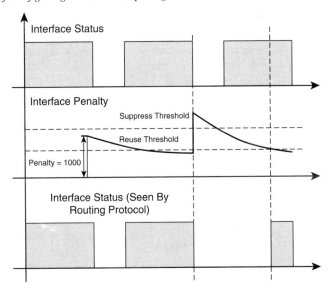

To illustrate the IP Interface dampening feature, Example 5-45 shows the **debug dampening interface** command.

Example 5-45 *Output of* **debug dampening interface**

```
R1#debug dampening interface
interface debugging is on
*Jun 30 08:07:13.207: IF-EvD(Ethernet0/0): IP Routing reports state transition from
  UP to DOWN
*Jun 30 08:07:13.207: IF-EvD(Ethernet0/0): setting merged state from UP to DOWN
*Jun 30 08:07:13.207: EvD(Ethernet0/0): charge penalty 1000, new accum. penalty
  1000, flap count 1
*Jun 30 08:07:13.207: EvD(Ethernet0/0): accum. penalty 1000, not suppressed
*Jun 30 08:07:13.207: IF-EvD(Ethernet0/0): update IP Routing state to DOWN,
  interface is not suppressed
!Output omitted for brevity
*Jun 30 08:07:16.899: EvD(Ethernet0/0): accum. penalty decayed to 1529 after 1
  second(s)
*Jun 30 08:07:16.899: EvD(Ethernet0/0): charge penalty 1000, new accum. penalty
  2529, flap count 3
*Jun 30 08:07:16.899: EvD(Ethernet0/0): accum. penalty 2529, now suppressed with a
  reuse intervals of 7
!Output omitted for brevity
*Jun 30 08:07:33.911: EvD(Ethernet0/0): accum. penalty decayed to 968 after 10
  second(s)
*Jun 30 08:07:33.911: EvD(Ethernet0/0): accum. penalty 968, now unsuppressed
*Jun 30 08:07:33.911: IF-EvD(Ethernet0/0): update IP Routing state to UP, interface
  is not suppressed
*Jun 30 08:07:41.667: IF-EvD(Ethernet0/0): IP Routing reports state transition from
  UP to UP
```

Multipath Routing

A basic strategy of building a resilient network is to build redundant links. The associated complication that comes with redundant links is the introduction of multiple paths that an IP packet can take as it traverses the network. Issues such as load balancing of packets have to be carefully considered.

Load Balancing

To understand load balancing, it is important to understand the process by which routes are selected from different routing protocols and installed into the routing table. A router always chooses the route with the longest prefix match, and if there are multiple routes to the destination with the same prefix length, it uses the one with the lowest administrative distance. If within the same routing protocol there are several candidate paths to the same destination, the path with the lowest path cost or metric is chosen.

Equal-Cost Multipath (ECMP)

If a router installs multiple paths with the same administrative distance and cost to a destination, load balancing can be achieved (with the exception of IGRP and EIGRP, which can load balance over unequal-cost paths using the concept of variance). This is known as equal-cost multipath (ECMP). By default, most routing protocols install a maximum of four paths, with the exception of BGP, which uses the single best path. Cisco IOS initially allows a maximum of six equal cost paths, but supports 32 equal cost paths in some of the newer software releases.

To check whether the router has installed multiple equal-cost paths for a destination, use the **show ip route** command as shown in Example 5-46.

Example 5-46 *Output of* **show ip route** *to Illustrate ECMP*

```
R1#show ip route 10.2.2.2
Routing entry for 10.2.2.2/32
  Known via "ospf 100", distance 110, metric 65, type intra area
  Last update from 192.168.0.2 on Serial0/0, 00:22:41 ago
  Routing Descriptor Blocks:
  * 192.168.3.2, from 10.2.2.2, 00:22:41 ago, via Serial3/0
      Route metric is 65, traffic share count is 1
    192.168.2.2, from 10.2.2.2, 00:22:41 ago, via Serial2/0
      Route metric is 65, traffic share count is 1
    192.168.1.2, from 10.2.2.2, 00:22:41 ago, via Serial1/0
      Route metric is 65, traffic share count is 1
    192.168.0.2, from 10.2.2.2, 00:22:41 ago, via Serial0/0
      Route metric is 65, traffic share count is 1
```

In Example 5-46, there are four equal cost paths to the destination address of 10.2.2.2 with a cost or metric of 65.

When there is more than one path to the destination, the router has to decide how it wants to distribute packets (load balance) across the multiple paths. There are two key methods for doing so: per-packet load balancing and per-destination load balancing as described next.

Per Packet

Per-packet load balancing occurs when multiple equal-cost paths exist, and the router is process switching or if it has been explicitly configured in Cisco Express Forwarding (CEF). Per-packet load balancing performs round-robin packet scheduling across the active paths.

The advantage of per-packet load balancing lies in its capability to achieve an almost perfect split of traffic across multiple links, because each subsequent packet is forwarded out the next active path. However, multiple packets from the same session may be forwarded via different paths in the network, thereby causing packet reordering and nondeterministic latency, which might cause problems with applications such as voice and video. In addition, TCP behaves by sending a duplicate acknowledgment (DUPACK) for every out-of-order segment it receives, and generally affects TCP throughput. Per-packet load balancing is generally not recommended.

To configure per-packet load balancing (in CEF), you must configure the **ip load-sharing per-packet** command on each interface where this behavior is desired, as shown in Example 5-47.

Example 5-47 *Configuring Per-Packet Load Balancing on Router Interfaces*

```
R1#configure terminal
Enter configuration commands, one per line.  End with CNTL/Z.
R1(config)#ip cef
R1(config)#interface serial 0/0
R1(config-if)#ip load-sharing per-packet
R1(config-if)#interface serial 1/0
R1(config-if)#ip load-sharing per-packet
R1(config-if)#^Z
R1#
```

Per Destination

The name *per-destination load balancing* is a bit of a misnomer. Cisco IOS uses both the source and destination IP address of the packet to create a hash that is used to decide which of the active paths are to be used for sending the packet. Therefore, the router is actually performing per-session load balancing. Per-destination load balancing is the default behavior if the router is running either fast switching or CEF switching.

NOTE   For a review of the different switching modes, see Chapter 3, "Fundamentals of IP Resilient Networks."

Per-destination load balancing has the advantage of allowing all packets with the same source and destination IP address pair to always traverse the same link. This advantage avoids problems such as packet reordering. When a router is performing per-destination load balancing for a small number of sessions, you might observe that the split of traffic between the links may be less than perfect. Statistically, however, if you have a large number of sessions, you might have an almost equal amount of traffic on the various load-shared links.

Per-destination load balancing also brings with it an issue known as *polarization*. Assuming that the same algorithm is being used on all routers, traffic traversing from a known source and destination will always use the first link in the load-share bundle, on every router. Additional modifications were made later whereby the hash functions are different in all routers in a given network, eliminating the polarization effect. The new hash function after the modification is known as the *universal load-sharing algorithm* and is the default mode for CEF. This algorithm uses an automatically calculated ID. The unique ID or "seed value" can also be fixed using the configuration command shown in Example 5-48.

Example 5-48 *Configuring the "Seed Value" for CEF Load Sharing*

```
R1#configure terminal
Enter configuration commands, one per line.  End with CNTL/Z.
R1(config)#ip cef load-sharing algorithm universal id
R1(config)#^Z
R1#
```

If the command is entered without the ID, a new ID value is generated and used by the algorithm. The net effect of this is the selected traffic path for a session is subject to the new "seed" value for the algorithm and it may take a different path.

Consider the scenario illustrated in Figure 5-10.

Figure 5-10 *Per-Destination Load Balancing*

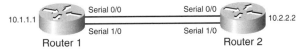

This scenario has a requirement for two hosts, 10.1.1.1 and 10.2.2.2, to load share traffic between the two links (serial 0/0 and serial 1/0). Our observation from the routing table on router R1 shows that there are two equal-cost paths, which are candidates for load sharing. Example 5-49 shows this setup.

Example 5-49 *Output of **show ip route** Showing Load Sharing Between Two Links*

```
R1#show ip route 10.2.2.2
Routing entry for 10.2.2.2/32
  Known via "ospf 100", distance 110, metric 65, type intra area
  Last update from 192.168.0.2 on Serial0/0, 00:02:01 ago
  Routing Descriptor Blocks:
  * 192.168.1.2, from 10.2.2.2, 00:02:01 ago, via Serial1/0
      Route metric is 65, traffic share count is 1
    192.168.0.2, from 10.2.2.2, 00:02:01 ago, via Serial0/0
      Route metric is 65, traffic share count is 1
```

The output from **show ip cef** is also consistent with the output of **show ip route**, and it shows that per-destination load sharing is active. See Example 5-50.

Example 5-50 *Output of **show ip cef** Showing Load Sharing Between Two Links*

```
R1#show ip cef 2.2.2.2
2.2.2.2/32, version 26, epoch 0, per-destination sharing
0 packets, 0 bytes
```

continues

Example 5-50 *Output of* **show ip cef** *Showing Load Sharing Between Two Links (Continued)*

```
  via 192.168.1.2, Serial1/0, 0 dependencies
    traffic share 1
    next hop 192.168.1.2, Serial1/0
    valid adjacency
  via 192.168.0.2, Serial0/0, 0 dependencies
    traffic share 1
    next hop 192.168.0.2, Serial0/0
    valid adjacency
  0 packets, 0 bytes switched through the prefix
  tmstats: external 0 packets, 0 bytes
           internal 0 packets, 0 bytes
```

However, when the hosts 1.1.1.1 and 1.1.1.2 start sending the same traffic to host 2.2.2.2, we notice that only serial 0/0 is utilized, as shown in Example 5-51.

Example 5-51 *Output of* **show ip cef exact-route**

```
R1#show ip cef exact-route 1.1.1.1 2.2.2.2
1.1.1.1          -> 2.2.2.2       : Serial0/0 (next hop 192.168.0.2)
R1#show ip cef exact-route 1.1.1.2 2.2.2.2
1.1.1.2          -> 2.2.2.2       : Serial0/0 (next hop 192.168.0.2)
```

For this specific scenario, the hash function for the load-sharing algorithm is biased toward serial 0/0. You need to "reseed" the algorithm and to get balanced traffic mix across the two links, as shown in Example 5-52.

Example 5-52 *Reseeding the CEF Load-Sharing Algorithm*

```
R1#configure terminal
Enter configuration commands, one per line.  End with CNTL/Z.
R1(config)#ip cef load-sharing algorithm universal
R1(config)#do show ip cef exact-route 1.1.1.1 2.2.2.2
1.1.1.1          -> 2.2.2.2       : Serial0/0 (next hop 192.168.0.2)
R1(config)#do show ip cef exact-route 1.1.1.2 2.2.2.2
1.1.1.2          -> 2.2.2.2       : Serial1/0 (next hop 192.168.1.2)
```

Now the two sources are hashed over the two equal-cost paths, serial 0/0 and serial 1/0. If for any reason the user needs to return to the old load-sharing algorithm, the global configuration command **ip cef load-sharing algorithm original** may be used. Note that load-sharing algorithms are available for platforms that use a software-forwarding path and for Engine 2 line cards on the GSR.

MPLS Traffic Engineering

One of the methods by which very fast convergence may be achieved is through the use of a precomputed backup path. MPLS Traffic Engineering Fast Reroute (MPLS-TE FRR) uses the same concept to achieve convergence in the range of 50 ms. In a network running MPLS, a traffic-engineering tunnel may be created to provide a backup path that traverses different nodes and links from those you want to protect against failure. When failure occurs, the traffic that would have traversed through the failed node or link is encapsulated into the backup LSP that bypasses the failure. In MPLS-TE FRR, the protection methods are broadly classified as *path protection* and *local protection*.

In path protection, you create a parallel traffic-engineering tunnel that uses a diversified path for the tunnel for which you are trying to provide protection. The unique characteristic of path protection is that the backup (or secondary) path is only protecting the original path (1:1), and the backup path is only used to carry traffic when there is a failure scenario. The primary and backup path should also have the same attributes, such as the same amount of bandwidth reserved. Note that having a second path option under the tunnel interface configuration will only result in an label switch path (LSP) reroute upon failure, and does not offer path protection. Path protection requires the LSP to be presignaled.

Local protection implies that the backup or protection path only covers a portion of the primary LSP; that is, you are only protecting a "local" link or node. However, it does not imply that the head end of the primary LSP and secondary LSP cannot be the same node. In local protection, a backup LSP is used to route traffic around a failed link (link protection) or failed node (node protection). In effect, the primary LSP, which would have traversed the failed link or node, is being encapsulated in the secondary or backup LSP. One of the key differences between path protection and local protection is that local protection allows a single backup LSP to provide backup to multiple primary LSPs (that is, 1:N), which makes it more resource efficient and, as a result, more scalable in its deployment.

NOTE   MPLS fast reroute tunnels, like regular MPLS traffic-engineering tunnels, are unidirectional. If you need to protect the link in both directions, you must create two separate fast reroute tunnels.

This section briefly explains how you can use MPLS-TE FRR to provide protection against failed links or failed nodes. For more details on the topic, an excellent reference is *Traffic Engineering with MPLS*, by Eric Osborne and Ajay Simha (Cisco Press, 2002).

Fast Reroute Link Protection

Fast reroute link protection, as its name implies, is intended to protect against failing links. In Figure 5-11, you set up a backup tunnel between R2 and R3 to protect against direct link failure between routers R2 and R3. Label allocation is signaled from downstream to upstream (from the tail end to the head end). The label binding is then done based on the signaled label allocation.

Figure 5-11 *Creation of Backup Path and Label Binding*

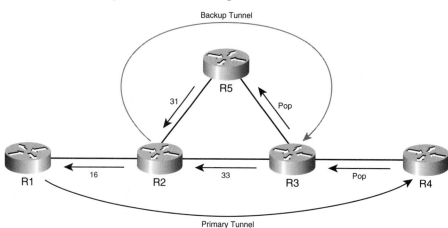

To understand MPLS-TE FRR, you first need to know some terminology. R2 is known as the *point of local repair* (*PLR*), which is the head end of the backup tunnel. R3 is known as the *merge point* (*MP*), which is where the backup tunnel terminates. R3 is the *next-hop router*, which is one hop away from the PLR.

You also need to understand two concepts that form the basis for MPLS-TE FRR: label stacking (when the PLR imposes another label, or pushes another label into the label stack), and global label space. Global label space is required so that when the MP sees a labeled packet entering the router, it can send it to the correct destination regardless of the interface from which the packet entered the router.

Under normal circumstances when packets are forwarded down the primary tunnel, the first-hop router R1 imposes a label of 16 on the packet. This packet is forwarded to router R2, which performs label swapping on the received label of 16, for 33, and forwards the labeled packet down to R3. Router R3, upon receiving this packet with a label of 33, performs *penultimate hop popping* (removing the top-level label prior to the last hop) and forwards the packet to the tunnel's tail end. Figure 5-12 shows this process.

If the protected link breaks, R2, which is the PLR, performs label stacking on the packet received from router R1. The original packet that was going to have a label of 33 is imposed with another label value of 31, because 31 is the label to be used for router R2 to switch packets toward R5 (allocated from global label space).

R5 is the penultimate-hop router for the backup tunnel and removes the top label, leaving the label of 33 for the packet forwarded to R3, the MP. R3 sees the label of 33 (which is the original expected label value if the path R1-R2-R3 was taken) and provides the packet with the same treatment as if it were received directly from Router 2. Figure 5-13 illustrates the process.

Figure 5-12 *Packet Forwarding for Primary Tunnel*

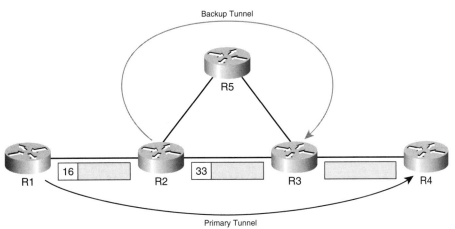

Figure 5-13 *Packet Forwarding for Backup Tunnel*

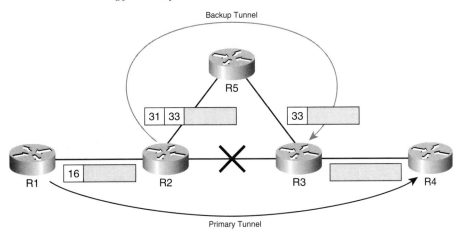

To configure MPLS-TE FRR link protection, you need to enable the primary or original MPLS TE for fast reroute. You do so with the configuration command **tunnel mpls traffic-eng fast-reroute** in the primary tunnel interface.

A secondary or backup tunnel is then created with explicit path routing to protect the primary tunnel. On the interface facing the link that needs to be protected, you specify the backup tunnel as the backup path using the command **mpls traffic-eng backup path tunnel**. Figure 5-14 shows a summary of the additional configuration commands required.

Figure 5-14 *Additional Commands for the Backup Path Tunnel*

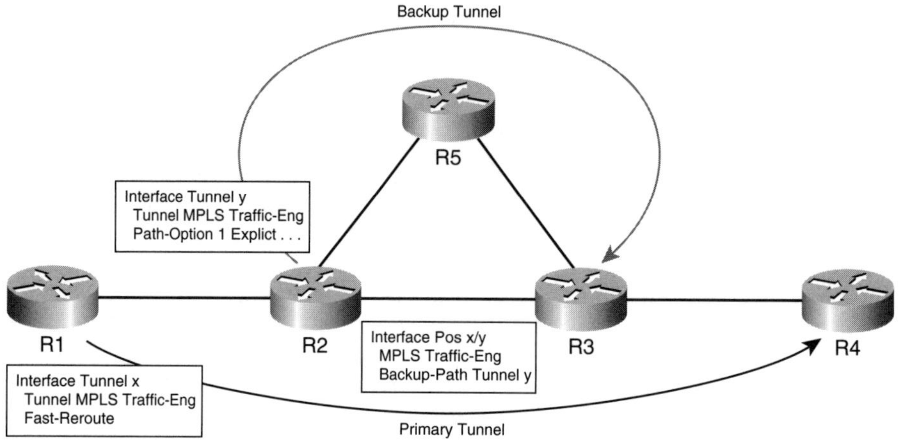

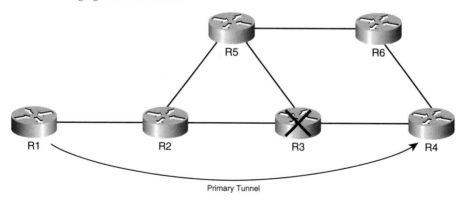

Fast Reroute Node Protection

The preceding section described how you can use MPLS-TE FRR to provide link protection. You can extend this concept to provide a protection mechanism for node failure.

Suppose that you change the network by adding a node, R6, and two links connecting to R5 and R4, as shown in Figure 5-15.

Figure 5-15 *Protecting Against Node Failure*

Now you want to protect against the failure of R3 (which, incidentally, most likely will bring down the links R2-R3 and R3-R4). If you provide for node protection against the failure of R3, you have provided for link protection for the links R2-R3 and R3-R4. You can achieve this protection by creating a backup tunnel that bypasses R3 but terminates at R4, as shown in Figure 5-16.

Figure 5-16 *Fast Reroute Node Protection*

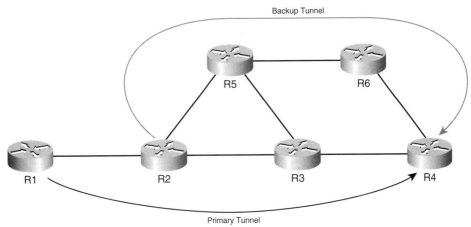

In terms of configuration, node protection is no different from link protection, with the exception that for node protection, the MP is now at the next-next hop (NNHop), which is two hops away from the PLR, and not the next hop. For MPLS-TE FRR link protection, RSVP is used to signal the label that the MP expects to receive to the PLR. In this case, label recording is required for the NNHop tunnel for the PLR to find out what label value it expects to receive.

Multicast Subsecond Convergence

IP Multicast is an extensive topic by itself, and the reader is assumed to have a good working knowledge of IP Multicast protocols such as Protocol Independent Multicast (PIM) and Internet Group Management Protocol (IGMP).

Multicast subsecond convergence was introduced in Cisco IOS Release 12.0(22)S and incorporated a couple of features to provide improved scalability and convergence in Multicast networks. Some of the features that were introduced include the ability to tune the PIM router query interval (PIM Hello timers) to millisecond intervals so that the PIM routers in the segment can sense the failure of their directly attached neighbors.

For the case of a DR failure, being able to tune the PIM router query interval will help in expediting the process of electing a new DR. Prior to these changes, it could take more than 90 seconds before a new DR was elected after a failure. DRs are responsible in PIM sparse mode networks for sending joins to the RP for members in the multiaccess network, and for sending registers for sources on the multiaccess network to the rendezvous point (RP). For dense mode operation, the DR has no significance.

The enhancements also included the triggering of Reverse Path Forwarding (RPF) checks for mroute states, using Unicast routing table updates. In this manner, users can set the periodic RPF check value to a relatively high value (or leave it as the default of 10 seconds) while still achieving subsecond failovers. As you know, IP Multicast uses RPF checks to verify that the IP Multicast traffic was received via the reverse path before it will forward the packet. For SPT forwarding, you use the IP address of the IP Multicast source for the check, whereas for shared tree, you use the IP address of the RP for the check.

For multicast subsecond convergence, the only parameter that should be configured by the user is the PIM router query interval, while leaving the other configurable items, such as RPF interval and back-off, to its defaults. This value may be changed in the interface configuration command, as shown in Example 5-53.

Example 5-53 *Changing the PIM Router Query Interval*

```
Router5#configure terminal
Enter configuration commands, one per line.  End with CNTL/Z.
Router5(config)#int e0/0
Router5(config-if)#ip pim query-interval I msec
Router5(config-if)#^Z
Router5#
```

Take care not to set the **pim query-interval** to too low a value, because routers that do not have enough CPU cycles to process the Hello interval might assume that the PIM neighbor is down, causing a PIM DR state change. To verify multicast subsecond convergence, you can use the **show ip pim interface** and **show ip pim neighbor** commands, as shown in Example 5-54.

Example 5-54 *Output of* **show ip pim interface** *Showing the Subsecond Query Interval*

```
Router#show ip pim interface

Address            Interface                    Ver/   Nbr    Query  DR      DR
                                                Mode   Count  Intvl  Prior
210.210.8.1        Ethernet0/0                  v2/SD  1      200 ms I       210.210.8.2

Router#show ip pim neighbor
PIM Neighbor Table
Neighbor           Interface                    Uptime/Expires    Ver   DR
Address                                                                 Priority/Mode
210.210.8.2        Ethernet0/0                  00:03:03/680 msec v2    1 / DR P
Router#
```

Note that all the routers on the same segment should be configured with the same PIM router query interval. To look at the information on the last 15 triggered multicast RPF check events, you can use the command **show ip rpf events**, as shown in Example 5-55.

Example 5-55 *Output of the* **show ip rpf events** *Command*

```
Router#show ip rpf events
Last 15 triggered multicast RPF check events

RPF backoff delay: 500 msec
RPF maximum delay: 5 sec

DATE/TIME              BACKOFF     PROTOCOL    EVENT       RPF CHANGES
Jul 22 10:47:50.339   500 msec    OSPF        Route UP    0
Jul 22 10:46:59.583   500 msec    OSPF        Route UP    0
Jul 22 10:45:03.651   500 msec    PIM         Nbr UP      0
Jul 22 10:39:17.639   500 msec    PIM         Nbr UP      0
Jul 22 10:30:23.279   500 msec    Connected   Route UP    0
```

Summary

This chapter covered the key enhancements made to the commonly used IGPs that may be used to improve the overall scalability and resiliency of the network. In addition, this chapter briefly covered other technologies, such as multipath routing, and introduced MPLS traffic-engineering fast reroute link and node protection, which you can use to improve the overall resiliency in the core of a network. This chapter explained that high system availability and fast convergence are sometimes mutually exclusive. For a network with multiple redundant links in the core, high system availability (such as that deployed using NSF/SSO) is typically deployed at the edge of a network, and fast convergence forms the key focus at the core.

This chapter covers the following topics:

- Multilayer Campus Design
- Access Module Building Blocks
- Layer 2 Domain
- Layer 3 Domain

CHAPTER 6

Access Module

The access module is a network's interface to the users or end stations, and challenges in the access module are often related to the physical or Layer 2 connectivity problems. Many Layer 2 technologies can be used to build the access module; however, the focus of this chapter is on the Ethernet technology because Ethernet has emerged as the *de facto* connectivity standard for end devices.

The ubiquity of the Ethernet technology lies in its simplicity and cost-effectiveness. The availability of Layer 3 switching technology brings IP and Ethernet together, and this has a profound impact on IP network design. For the first time, it is possible to build a complete network for an entire company using IP+Ethernet strategy, including workstation connections, servers in the data center, and connecting branches via a metro Ethernet offering from a service provider. The integration between IP and Ethernet here is so tightly coupled that problems found in the Layer 2 network directly impact the overall IP network availability.

This chapter focuses on Ethernet switching technology, specifically Layer 2 network resiliency and how it should be built to provide a solid foundation for the Layer 3 network.

Multilayer Campus Design

With the popularity of Layer 3 switching, the term *multilayer campus design* is almost synonymous with the Ethernet switching design. A multilayer campus design has two main characteristics:

- **Hierarchical**—Each layer has a specific role to play.
- **Modular**—The entire network is built by piecing building blocks together.

These two characteristics enable the network to scale in a deterministic manner, with efficient use of resources to provide a resilient network foundation.

Figure 6-1 shows the concept of a typical multilayer campus design. It has an access layer, which commonly consists of wiring closet switches. The access layer is connected to a distribution layer. The distribution layer is, in turn, connected to the core layer. From a high-level view, a group of access switches are connected to a pair of distribution switches to form a basic building block. Many of these building blocks exist within the network, and the core layer connects them. Designs such as this are also known as three-tier architecture.

Figure 6-1   *Three-Tier Multilayer Campus Design*

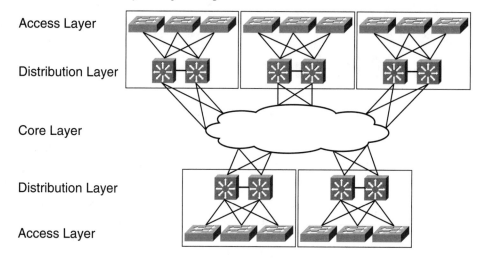

Access Layer

Distribution Layer

Core Layer

Distribution Layer

Access Layer

NOTE   For the discussion on resilient IP networks, the access module in this chapter refers to the access and distribution layers in the multilayer campus design. The core module, which has been discussed in Chapter 5, "Core Module," corresponds to the core layer.

Although Figure 6-1 shows a typical three-tier architecture, a smaller network may be built without the need of the core module at all, which makes it a two-tier design, as shown in Figure 6-2.

Figure 6-2   *Two-Tier Multilayer Campus Design*

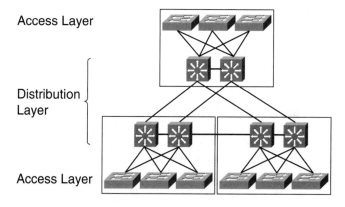

Access Layer

Distribution Layer

Access Layer

The benefit of adopting the multilayer campus design is clarity of roles performed by each layer. The role of each layer is translated to a set of features required, which in turn translates to which particular type of hardware is to be used.

Access Layer

The access layer within the multilayer campus design model is where users gain access to the network. Most of the features found within the access layer are geared toward collecting and conditioning the traffic that is coming in from the users' end stations. These features include the following:

- Aggregating all the user endpoints
- Providing traffic conditioning functions such as marking and policing
- Providing intelligent network services such as automatic IP phone discovery
- Providing network security services such as 802.1x and port security
- Providing redundant links toward the distribution layer

In the classic multilayer campus design, the access layer is mainly made up of Layer 2 switches. Therefore, most of the work done here is in optimizing the Layer 2 protocol that governs this layer. This helps to provide a robust Layer 2 environment for the functioning of the IP network.

Distribution Layer

The distribution layer within the multilayer campus design model aggregates the access layer. One of the most important characteristics of the distribution layer is that it is the point where the Layer 2 domain ends and where the Layer 3 domain begins. The features at the distribution layer include the following:

- Aggregating access layer switches
- Terminating virtual LANs (VLANs) that are defined within the Layer 2 domain
- Providing the first-hop gateway service for all the end stations
- Providing traffic conditioning services such as security, quality of service (QoS), and queuing
- Providing redundant links toward the core layer, if required

Because the distribution layer is the meeting place for both the Layer 2 and Layer 3 domains, it runs both Layer 2 and Layer 3 protocols. This is also the place where most of the network intelligence is found and is perhaps one of the most complex parts of the network.

Core Layer

The core layer within the multilayer campus design model has two important tasks:

- Interconnect all the distribution layer blocks
- Forward all the traffic as quickly as it can

As the backbone of the entire network, its function is quite different from that of the access layer and distribution layer. The features that are critical to the functioning of the core layer include the following:

- Aggregating distribution layers to form an interconnected network
- Providing high-speed transfer of traffic among the distribution layers
- Providing a resilient IP routing environment

Because speed is of the essence here, the core layer usually does not provide services that may affect its performance (for example, security, access control, or any activities that require it to process every packet).

In the discussion of multilayer campus design, the inclusion of a core layer is always an interesting question. For a small network, it is common to see a two-tier design, as shown earlier in Figure 6-2, for cost reasons. However, for bigger networks, inclusion of the core layer is always recommended to scale the network in a manageable fashion.

Access Module Building Blocks

This section focuses on the individual building blocks shown in Figure 6-3. Making these individual building blocks rock solid is critical, because it is how the end users are connected to the network. These building blocks are to be found in the data center module, too, which you learn about in Chapter 9, "Data Center Module." The well-being of an individual building block network relies on two factors:

- How well the Layer 2 domain behaves within the building block
- How its Layer 3 function interacts with the end devices and how well it is connected to the core layer

The rest of this chapter describes the Layer 2 and Layer 3 domains. Within the Layer 2 domain, the focus is on resilient switching design, whereas the focus for the Layer 3 domain is on resilient IP services and routing design.

Figure 6-3 *Building Blocks for the Access Module*

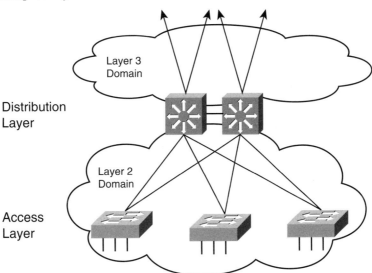

Layer 2 Domain

The access and distribution layers form the boundary for the Layer 2 domain of the building block network. This is an area where the Spanning Tree Protocol (STP) plays a critical role. Unfortunately, a common perception of STP is that it is a dated technology and has always been blamed for network disruptions. Whenever there is a network meltdown, chances are fingers will point toward the STP. The fact is, with proper design and configuration, STP is effective and useful.

It is absolutely critical that in the access and distribution layers, a steady state of a Layer 2 network is a prerequisite for a stable IP network. You can have a well-designed IP network, but without a proper underlying Layer 2 network design, you will not be able to achieve your goal. Therefore, besides paying attention to the IP network design, you need to have a Layer 2 network strategy thought out. In addition, having a well-documented Layer 2 network is as essential as that of the Layer 3 network.

Although STP was invented many years ago, it has been constantly improved to make it relevant in today's networks. The next few sections help you understand the original protocol and the subsequent improvements made. These include the following:

- The Spanning Tree Protocol (IEEE 802.1d)
- Trunking
- Per-VLAN Spanning Tree (PVST)

- Per-VLAN Spanning Tree Plus (PVST+)
- 802.1w
- 802.1s
- Channeling technology
- Best practices for the Layer 2 domain

The Spanning Tree Protocol: IEEE 802.1d

The purpose of the STP, or IEEE 802.1d specification, is to prevent loops forming within a Layer 2 network. In a bridge network, looping causes problems such as broadcast storms. During broadcast storms, frames circulate in the network endlessly, consuming bandwidth and control plane resources. In a bridge network, there can only be one active path between two end stations that are communicating with one another.

NOTE   For the discussion on STP and its related features, the word *bridge* is used, although the actual device you will be using is more likely a *switch*.

Essentially, the STP uses the spanning-tree algorithm to keep track of redundant paths, and then chooses the best one to forward traffic while blocking the rest to prevent loops. The result of the STP is a tree with a root bridge and a loop-free topology from the root to all other bridges within the network. A blocked path acts as a backup path and is activated in the event that the primary path fails. Each of the ports on a bridge may be assigned a role, depending on the resulted topology:

- **Root**—A forwarding port elected for the spanning-tree topology. There is always only one root port per bridge, and it is the port leading to the root bridge.

- **Designated**—A forwarding port elected for a LAN segment. The designated port is in charge of forwarding traffic on behalf of the LAN segment, and there is always only one designated port per segment.

- **Alternate**—A port that is neither root nor designated.

- **Disabled**—A port that has been shut down and has no role.

Depending on the port role, each port on a bridge will either be in forwarding state or blocked. The result is a tree topology that ensures a loop-free environment. Figure 6-4 shows a sample of a STP topology and the resulted role of the ports on the bridges.

Figure 6-4 *Port Roles of STP*

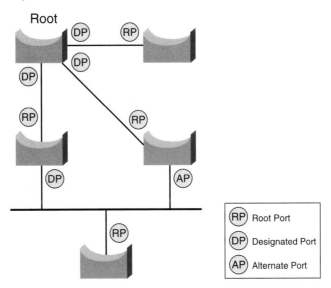

Every bridge participating in a STP domain is assigned a bridge ID (BID) that is 8 bytes long. The BID is made up of a 2-byte bridge priority and a 6-byte Media Access Control (MAC) address of the switch. In addition, each of the bridge ports on the bridge is assigned a port ID. The port ID is 2 bytes long, with a 6-bit priority setting and a 10-bit port number. Each port also has a path cost that is associated with it. The original default path cost was derived by dividing 1 gigabit by the link speed of the port. However, with the introduction of higher-speed links such as the 10 Gigabit Ethernet, the default cost has been updated, as shown in Table 6-1.

Table 6-1 *Default Path Cost for STP*

Link Speed	Path Cost
4 Mbps	250
10 Mbps	100
16 Mbps	62
45 Mbps	39
100 Mbps	19
155 Mbps	14
622 Mbps	6
1 Gbps	4
10 Gbps	2

NOTE   You can also overwrite the default path cost with your own. However, it is always
recommended that you keep the default values.

The formation of the spanning tree is determined by the following:

- The election of a root bridge
- Calculating the path cost toward the root bridge
- Determining the port role associated with each of the interfaces on the bridge

The election of the root bridge is an important event in the STP and has a direct bearing on
eventual traffic flow. Therefore, it is important for network designers to understand the
concept of the election of the root and its impact on the network.

The bridge with the lowest BID is always elected as a root bridge. Remember, BID is made
up of the bridge priority and the MAC address. The default value of the bridge priority is
32768. Therefore, by default, the bridge with the lowest MAC address is usually elected as
the root bridge. The root bridge acts like the center of a bridge network, and all traffic flows
toward it. The paths toward the root that are deemed redundant are put in a blocked state.

The STP is a timer-based protocol. As such, as a participant within the STP, a port goes
through a series of states, based on some configured timing, before it starts to forward
traffic. The cycle that a port goes through is reflected in Figure 6-5.

Figure 6-5   *The STP Cycle*

The states shown in Figure 6-5 are as follows:

- **Blocking**—No traffic is forwarded.
- **Listening**—First state whenever a port is first initialized. In this state, the bridge is
  trying to determine where the port fits in the STP topology.
- **Learning**—The port gets ready to forward traffic. In this state, the port is trying to
  figure out the MAC address information that is attached to the port.
- **Forwarding**—The port is forwarding traffic.
- **Disabled**—The port has been disabled.

In the discussion of optimizing a switched network, three parameters are of utmost importance:

- **Hello timer**—Determines how often a bridge sends out BPDUs

- **Forward delay timer**—Determines how long the listening and learning states must last before a bridge port starts forwarding traffic

- **Maximum age timer**—Determines the length of time a bridge stores its information received

As you can see in Figure 6-5, the time taken for transiting from power up to start of transmission for a bridge port is at least 35 seconds. That is, no IP traffic can be transmitted for at least that amount of time. Obviously, if the port goes up and down in a span of 35 seconds, no traffic actually flows through it.

Figure 6-6 shows a simple setup of three bridges connected together. After the STP has converged, the resulted topology is as show,n with bridge B being selected as the root bridge. The link between bridge A and C is blocked to prevent a loop.

Figure 6-6   *STP in Steady State*

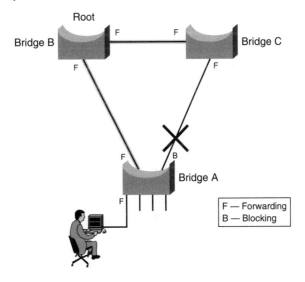

The following sections discuss various scenarios that can happen to this steady-state network. The behavior of STP is studied and suggestions are made on how to improve its capability to react to problems. The following features within the Catalyst series of switches are highlighted in the discussion of how to overcome problems:

- PortFast
- UplinkFast

- BackboneFast
- Unidirectional Link Detection (UDLD)
- RootGuard
- LoopGuard
- BPDUGuard

PortFast

As described in the preceding section, a port usually takes about 35 seconds before it starts to forward traffic. In some instances, this behavior is undesirable. One example is when an end station is connected to the port. Because the port takes 35 seconds to begin forwarding traffic, the following errors may potentially occur:

- If the end station is running a Windows client, it may encounter the error "No Domain Controllers Available."
- If the end station is trying to request an IP address via a Dynamic Host Configuration Protocol (DHCP) server, it may encounter the error "No DHCP Servers Available."
- If the end station is running the Internetwork Packet Exchange (IPX) protocol, it may encounter no login screen.

The errors may occur for a few reasons, such as a link-speed negotiation problem or duplex problems. However, the way the STP port behaves may have contributed to the problem. One of the reasons errors occur is that the port is still transiting to the forwarding state even after those protocol requests have been sent out by the end station. This is not uncommon, because advancement in end station technology has resulted in extremely fast boot time. The booting of the operating systems is so fast now that the system sends out requests even before the port goes into a forwarding state.

As shown in the STP topology illustrated earlier in Figure 6-6, user-facing ports are connected to end stations only. These ports do not connect to other bridges and are called *leaf nodes*. The use of the STP is to prevent loops between bridges. Therefore, there is no reason why a leaf node needs to toggle through the different states, because it will not be connecting to another bridge. It might be possible to bypass those transition states and put the port into forwarding mode immediately upon detection of a connection.

The **portfast** command in the Catalyst series switches is a feature that enables a leaf node in the STP topology to have such bypass capability. It can be configured at the global level, in which all ports are configured with the PortFast feature by default. It can also be configured at the individual port level.

It is critical that a port with the PortFast feature enabled should only be used for connection to end devices. It should never be connected to other Layer 2 devices such as a hub, switch, or bridge. For this reason, configuring the PortFast feature at port level is always preferred. Example 6-1 demonstrates how to configure the PortFast feature at the port level.

Example 6-1   *Configuring PortFast*

```
Cat3750#configure terminal
Cat3750(config)#interface GigabitEthernet 1/0/1
Cat3750(config-if)#spanning-tree portfast
```

UplinkFast

Figure 6-6 illustrated a simple Layer 2 network that is in steady state, with bridge A forwarding traffic toward bridge B. The link that is connected to bridge C is blocked and acts as a redundant link. By default behavior of STP, when the link between bridge A and B fails, the STP needs about 30 seconds before diverting traffic to the redundant link. Before the redundant link takes over, all user traffic from bridge A is not forwarded, as shown in Figure 6-7.

Figure 6-7   *Default STP Action on an Uplink Failure*

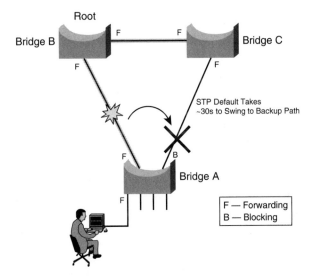

Because the backup link takes such a long time to forward traffic, one area of focus is how to accelerate the takeover process so that traffic is diverted to the redundant link immediately after the active link has failed.

The feature that makes this possible is delivered through the UplinkFast feature. Essentially, UplinkFast moves the original blocked port on bridge A to the forwarding state without going through the listening and learning states, as shown in Figure 6-8.

Figure 6-8 *STP Action with UplinkFast*

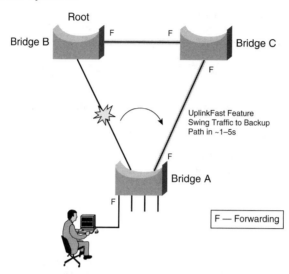

When the UplinkFast feature is enabled, the bridge priority of bridge A is set to 49152. If you change the path cost to a value less than 3000 and you enable UplinkFast or UplinkFast is already enabled, the path cost of all interfaces and VLAN trunks is increased by 3000. (If you change the path cost to 3000 or above, the path cost is not altered.) The changes to the bridge priority and the path cost reduce the chance that bridge A will become the root bridge.

It is important to note that the UplinkFast feature is most applicable to access switches only and may not be relevant in other parts of the network. In addition, it is a feature that is most useful in a triangular topology, such as the one previously shown. Its behavior may not be so predictable in other complex topologies, as discussed later in the section "Layer 2 Best Practices."

The **uplinkfast** command is issued at the global level. Example 6-2 shows an example configuration of the UplinkFast feature.

Example 6-2 *Configuring UplinkFast*

```
Cat3750#configure terminal
Cat3750(config)#spanning-tree uplinkfast
```

BackboneFast

In the steady-state network, sometimes links other than those connected directly to bridge A will fail, as shown in Figure 6-9.

Figure 6-9   *Default STP Action Without BackboneFast*

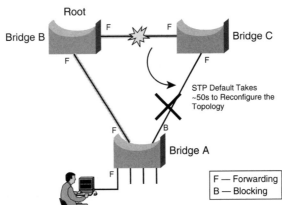

An indirectly connected failure causes bridge A to receive a type of BPDU called an *inferior BPDU*. An inferior BPDU indicates that a link that is not directly connected to this bridge has failed. Under STP default configuration, bridge A ignores the inferior BPDU for as long as the maximum aging timer; therefore, the STP topology is broken for as long as 50 seconds. That means no traffic flow from bridge A for 50 seconds.

The BackboneFast feature on bridge A circumvents this problem by initiating a state transition on the blocked port from blocked to listening state. This is done without waiting for the maximum aging time to expire and, thus, speeds up topology reconstruction to about 30 seconds, as shown in Figure 6-10.

Figure 6-10   *STP Action with BackboneFast*

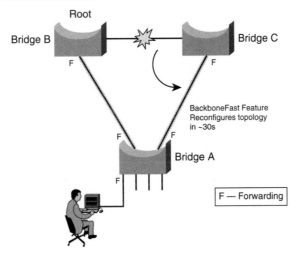

The **backbonefast** command is issued at the global level. Example 6-3 shows an example configuration of the BackboneFast feature.

Example 6-3 *Configuring BackboneFast*

```
Cat3750#configure terminal
Cat3750(config)#spanning-tree backbonefast
```

Unidirectional Link Detection (UDLD)

Up to this point, all the features discussed deal with a link or box failure scenario. However, there is still a possibility of a physical error that may wreak havoc in the access module and that is a unidirectional link error. A unidirectional link occurs whenever traffic sent by a device is received by its neighbor, but traffic from the neighbor is not received by the device. This happens, especially with fiber cabling, when only part of the fiber pair is working. A unidirectional link error can cause unpredictable behavior from the network, especially with the STP topology.

The situation depicted in Figure 6-11 does happen with fiber cabling systems that use a patch panel. In the figure, the switch ports are patched incorrectly at the patch panel, which may be located far away from the switches. The consequence of the erroneous cabling is unpredictable and may be difficult to troubleshoot just by issuing commands on the switch console. Even though the port status displays as up and working, errors will occur at the higher-layer protocol. In certain cases, the STP may still consider the link valid and move the effected port into a forwarding state. The result can be disastrous because it will cause loops to occur in the Layer 2 network.

Figure 6-11 *Possible Causes of Unidirectional Link Error*

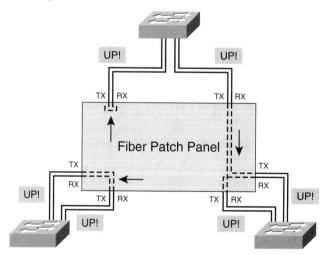

The UDLD feature provides a way to prevent errors such as the one depicted in Figure 6-11. It works with the Layer 1 mechanism to prevent one-way traffic at both physical and logical connections. The Layer 1 mechanism works by using the autonegotiation feature for signaling and basic fault detection. UDLD operates by having the devices exchange Layer 2 messages and detect errors that autonegotiation cannot. A device will send out a UDLD message to its neighbor with its own device/port ID and its neighbor's device/port ID. A neighboring port should see its own ID in the message; failure to do so in a configurable time means that the link is considered unidirectional and is shut down.

UDLD can be configured in two modes:

- **Normal**—If the physical link is perceived to be up but UDLD does not receive the message, the logical link is considered undetermined, and UDLD does not disable the port.

- **Aggressive**—If the physical link is perceived to be up but UDLD does not receive the message, UDLD will try to reestablish the state of the port. If the problem still persists, UDLD shuts down the port. Aggressive mode also supports detection of one-way traffic on twisted-pair cable.

You can configure UDLD at both the global level and at the port level. Example 6-4 shows how to configure UDLD at the global level.

Example 6-4 *Configuring UDLD Globally*

```
Cat3750#configure terminal
Cat3750(config)#udld enable
```

Example 6-5 shows how to configure UDLD at the port level.

Example 6-5 *Configuring UDLD at the Port Level*

```
Cat3750#configure terminal
Cat3750(config)#interface GigabitEthernet 1/0/1
Cat3750(config-if)#udld port
```

RootGuard

If you are running STP, the resulting topology always centers on the location of the root bridge. Whether a particular physical link is used or not depends on the port state of either forward or blocked. And this, in turn, depends on the location of the root bridge. It is possible that a certain topology was envisioned during the design phase so that traffic flows in a certain direction. However, the introduction of an additional bridge may turn things around and have an unexpected result, as shown in Figure 6-12.

Figure 6-12 *Result of Illegal Root Bridge Introduction*

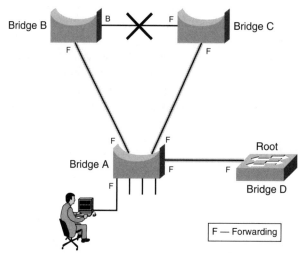

Before the introduction of the new bridge D, the topology of the network was intended as that shown earlier in Figure 6-6. However, the topology changes when bridge D is introduced. Because bridge D has a lower bridge priority, it begins to announce that it is the new root bridge for the Layer 2 topology. As a result, a new topology is formed to account for this new root bridge. As shown in Figure 6-12, the link between bridge B and bridge C has now been blocked. In other words, the communication path between the two bridges has to be via bridge A. If both links from bridge A are slow links, say 10 Mbps, this might have a performance impact between the two bridges B and C.

The RootGuard feature prevents the preceding scenario from happening. It is configured on a per-port basis and disallows the port from going into root port state. Example 6-6 shows how to configure the RootGuard feature.

Example 6-6 *Configuring RootGuard*

```
Cat3750#configure terminal
Cat3750(config)#interface fastethernet 1/0/24
Cat3750(config-if)#spanning-tree guard root
```

In Example 6-6, when a BPDU that is trying to claim root is received on the port, it goes into an error state called *root inconsistent*. The new state is essentially the same as the listening state and will not forward traffic. When the offending device has stopped sending BPDU, or the misconfiguration has been rectified, it will go into a forwarding state again. This way, a new bridge cannot "rob" the root away from the Layer 2 network. The following shows the error message that appears if RootGuard is put into action:

```
%SPANTREE-2-ROOTGUARDBLOCK: Port 1/0/24 tried to become non-designated in VLAN 10.
Moved to root-inconsistent state
```

To prevent the situation illustrated in Figure 6-12 from happening, you should introduce the RootGuard feature in bridge A on the port facing bridge D.

LoopGuard

Even if STP is deployed, loops might still occur. Loops happen when a blocked port in a redundant topology erroneously transits to a forwarding state, which usually happens because one of the ports of a physically redundant topology (not necessarily the STP blocking port) stopped receiving BPDUs. As a timer-based protocol, STP relies on continuous reception or transmission of BPDUs, depending on the port role (designated port transmits, nondesignated port receives BPDUs). So when one of the ports in a physically redundant topology stops receiving BPDUs, the STP conceives that nothing is connected to this port. Eventually, the alternate port becomes designated and moves to a forwarding state, thus creating a loop.

The LoopGuard feature was introduced to provide additional protection against failure, such as the one just described. With the LoopGuard feature, if BPDUs are not received any more on a nondesignated port, the port is moved into a new state, called the loop-inconsistent state. The aim is to provide a sanity check on the change in topology. Example 6-7 shows how to configure LoopGuard on all ports at the global level.

Example 6-7 *Configuring LoopGuard*

```
Cat3750#configure terminal
Cat3750(config)#spanning-tree loopguard default
```

The following shows the error message that appears on the console when an error is detected by LoopGuard:

```
SPANTREE-2-LOOPGUARDBLOCK: No BPDUs were received on port 3/4 in vlan 8. Moved to
    loop-inconsistent state.
```

NOTE   You cannot enable both the RootGuard and LoopGuard at the same time.

BPDUGuard

BPDUGuard is a feature that is recommended to be run together with the PortFast feature. Remember that the PortFast feature allows a port that has end systems connected to it to skip various STP states and go directly into a forward state. The port is not supposed to be connected to other bridges and, therefore, should not be receiving BPDUs. Any detection of a BPDU coming from the port is an indication that an invalid bridge has been introduced into the Layer 2 network. Upon detection of a BPDU, the BPDUGuard feature sends the port immediately into an error-disabled state, which enables you to investigate the problem, and rectify the situation before disaster strikes.

BPDUGuard can be enabled at the global command level as a global PortFast option. It can be also configured at the individual port level for granular control. Example 6-8 shows how to configure BPDUGuard.

Example 6-8 *Configuring BPDUGuard*

```
Cat3750#configure terminal
Cat3750(config)#spanning-tree portfast bpduguard default
```

VLANs and Trunking

Thus far, the discussion has focused on a common bridged network. The advent of Layer 2 switching technology introduces many new concepts that require further understanding and treatment for STP. For example, with Layer 2 switching comes the concept of VLANs and trunking.

A VLAN is basically a collection of network nodes that share the same broadcast domain. In a switched network design, an IP subnet is usually mapped to a VLAN, although there may be a rare exception. Because of their close association, the health of a VLAN directly impacts the functioning of the associated IP subnet.

The introduction of a VLAN brings about the concept of trunking, when many VLANs have to be transported across a common physical link. Figure 6-13 shows the trunking process.

Figure 6-13 *Nontrunking Versus Trunking Mode*

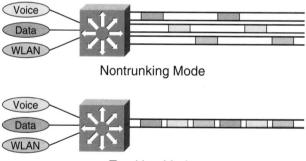

The reason for using the trunking mode feature varies, but the most obvious one is to save on ports that would have otherwise been spent on carrying each individual VLAN. This is especially true when connecting an access switch to the distribution layer. To carry multiple VLANs across the single physical link, a tagging mechanism or encapsulation has to be introduced to differentiate the traffic from the different VLANs. There are two ways of achieving this:

- Inter-Switch Link (ISL)
- IEEE 802.1q

ISL is a Cisco proprietary way of carrying different VLANs across a trunk. It is an encapsulation method whereby the payloads are wrapped with a header before transmission across the trunk. Figure 6-14 shows the format of an ISL frame.

Figure 6-14 *ISL Header*

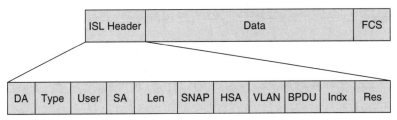

The fields in the ISL header are as follows:

- **DA**—Destination address
- **Type**—Frame type
- **User**—User-defined bits
- **SA**—Source address
- **Len**—Length
- **SNAP**—Subnetwork Access Protocol
- **HAS**—High bits of source address
- **VLAN**—Destination virtual LAN ID
- **BPDU**—Bridge protocol data unit
- **Indx**—Index
- **Res**—Reserved

ISL encapsulation adds 30 bytes to the original data frame. The implication of this is that you have to be careful of maximum transmission unit (MTU) size support on the various transmission interfaces. If the entire ISL-encapsulated frame size is bigger than the MTU size of the interface, fragmentation may occur. The largest Ethernet frame size with ISL tagging is 1548 bytes. Another point worth noting is that an ISL frame contains two Frame Check Sequence (FCS) fields: one for the original data frame, which is kept intact during encapsulation; and another one is for the ISL frame itself. Therefore, any corruption within the original data frame will not be detected until the ISL frame is de-encapsulated, and the original frame is sent to the receiver. ISL can carry up to 1000 VLANs per trunk.

Example 6-9 shows how to turn on trunking on a switch port using ISL.

Example 6-9   *Configuring ISL Trunking*

```
Cat3750#configure terminal
Cat3750(config)#interface fastethernet 1/0/24
Cat3750(config-in)#switchport mode trunk
Cat3750(config-in)#switchport trunk encapsulation isl
```

The other trunking mechanism is the IEEE 802.1q standard. It uses an internal tagging method that inserts a 4-byte Tag field into the original Ethernet frame. The Tag field is located between the Source Address and Type/Length fields, as shown in Figure 6-15.

Figure 6-15   *IEEE 802.1q Tag Field*

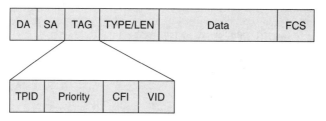

The Tag field is as follows:

- **TPID**—Tag protocol identifier
- **Priority**—User priority
- **CFI**—Canonical format indicator
- **VID**—VLAN identifier

For IEEE 802.1q tagging, there is only one FCS field. Because the frame is altered during the tagging, the FCS is recomputed on the modified frame. Because the tag is 4 bytes long, the resulting Ethernet frame size can be 1522 bytes. The IEEE 802.1q can carry 4096 VLANs.

Example 6-10 shows how to turn on trunking on a switch port using 802.1q.

Example 6-10   *Configuring 802.1q Trunking*

```
Cat3750#configure terminal
Cat3750(config)#interface fastethernet 1/0/24
Cat3750(config-in)#switchport mode trunk
Cat3750(config-in)#switchport trunk encapsulation dot1q
```

The 802.1q is the preferred method for implementing trunking because it is an open standard. In addition, 802.1q can carry more VLANs, a feature that is good to have in a metro Ethernet implementation.

The implication of VLANs and trunking is not so much having the concept of multiple broadcast domains within a single device, or the ability to carry multiple VLANs across a single physical link. It is the concept of multiple instances of STP that comes with it that is crucial in resilient network design. The following sections show how to deal with this challenge.

Common Spanning Tree (CST)

As discussed previously, the purpose of STP is to prevent loops from forming in a Layer 2 network. The introduction of the switch gives rise to many broadcast domains, called the VLANs. The IEEE 802.1d, as a protocol, does not have the concept of VLAN. The IEEE 802.q introduces the concept of VLANs, and it subjects the multiple VLANs to the control of a single STP instance by introducing a native VLAN that is not tagged during transmission. The STP state of the native VLAN governs the topology and the operation of the rest of the tagged VLANs. This mode of operation is commonly known as *Common Spanning Tree (CST)*.

Figure 6-16 illustrates the concept of a CST. Because there is only one instance of STP, all the VLANs share the same topology, with common forwarding ports and blocked ports, depending on the final STP state. In this case, no load balancing of traffic is possible and the redundant path does not carry any user traffic during normal operation.

Figure 6-16 *Common Spanning Tree Topology*

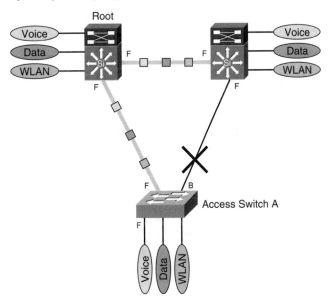

Per-VLAN Spanning Tree (PVST)

In contrast to CST, the Per-VLAN Spanning Tree (PVST) is a Cisco proprietary extension of IEEE 802.1d. It introduces an instance of STP process for each VLAN being configured in the Layer 2 networks. In this manner, each VLAN may have a different topology, depending on individual STP configuration. PVST works only with ISL trunking. Figure 6-17 illustrates the concept of a PVST implementation.

Figure 6-17 *PVST Topology*

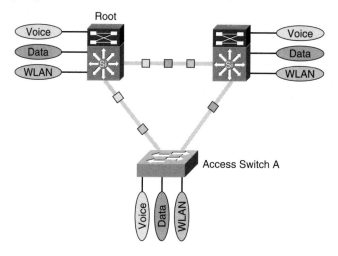

Because there is one instance of STP per VLAN, each VLAN can have its own topology, independent of the others. Figure 6-18 shows the topology of the voice VLAN.

Figure 6-18 *STP Instances for Voice VLAN*

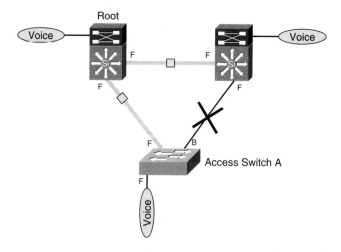

Figure 6-19 shows the topology of the wireless LAN virtual LAN (WLAN VLAN), which has the same uplink as that of the voice VLAN.

Figure 6-19 *STP Instances for WLAN VLAN*

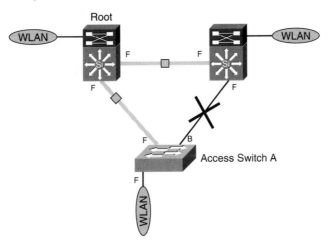

Unlike the voice and WLAN VLANs, the data VLAN has been configured to use the other uplink. This design allows for load balancing of traffic between the VLANs. Whereas the voice and WLAN VLANs use the uplink on the left, the data VLAN uses the uplink on the right. Figure 6-20 shows the data VLAN topology.

Figure 6-20 *STP Instance of Data VLAN*

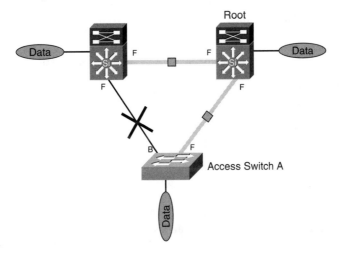

From an IP network perspective, regardless of the topology of the Layer 2 network, the logical IP networks of the three VLANs look exactly the same. The load balancing of traffic is achieved at a Layer 2 level and is transparent from an IP network perspective. The implication of this is that we have improved traffic-forwarding capability for all VLANs from switch A, utilizing both uplinks toward the distribution switches. In the event of a failure on any of the uplinks, all VLANs will be carried on the single remaining uplink.

Because PVST has each VLAN governed by its own STP instance, it still operates within the confines of STP and may exhibit problems that are typical of a STP implementation. Therefore, the following features are available with the implementation of PVST:

- PortFast
- UplinkFast
- BackboneFast
- BPDUGuard
- RootGuard
- LoopGuard

Per-VLAN Spanning Tree Plus (PVST+)

As mentioned in the preceding section, PVST gives you flexibility in creating a separate Layer 2 topology for each VLAN, thereby achieving Layer 2 load balancing toward the distribution layer. However, it runs only with the ISL trunking feature, not IEEE 802.1q.

Per-VLAN Spanning Tree Plus (PVST+) was introduced so that a network with PVST can interoperate with a network that runs IEEE 802.1q. When you connect a Cisco switch to other vendors' devices through an IEEE 802.1q trunk, PVST+ is deployed to provide compatibility.

The following features are available with the implementation of PVST+:

- PortFast
- UplinkFast
- BackboneFast
- BPDUGuard
- RootGuard
- LoopGuard

Although PVST and PVST+ give flexibility in terms of traffic distribution on the trunks, they tax the control planes of the switches implementing them. In both PVST and PVST+, each STP instance is a separate process and requires independent control a plane resources. Imagine if there are tens or hundreds of VLANs defined; there will be the same number of STP instances running in the switch. In the event of a topology change, these STP instances will have to go through the same steps to process the change. When this happens, the performance of the switch will be affected, and in some cases, no traffic can be forwarded at all because the control plane is overloaded. One solution to this is to implement 802.1s, which you learn about in the "IEEE 802.1s" section.

IEEE 802.1w

The IEEE 802.1d protocol was invented at a time when network downtime was not stringent at all. With the increase in networking speed and expectation of the network resiliency, the IEEE 802.1d protocol is finding it hard to keep up with the demand of the modern IP network. The enhancements discussed thus far have been Cisco proprietary enhancements, and interoperability with other vendors' implementation may not be possible.

IEEE 802.1w, or better known as Rapid Spanning Tree Protocol (RSTP), is the standard's answer to all the enhancements discussed so far. The motivations for the development of 802.1w include the following:

- Backward compatibility with the existing 802.1d standard
- Doing away with the problem with respect to long restoration time in the event of a failure
- Improvement in the way the protocol behaves, especially with respect to modern networking design

Because 802.1w is an enhancement of the 802.1d standard, most of the concepts and terminology of 802.1d still apply. In addition, because it is backward compatible with the IEEE 802.1d standard, it is possible to interoperate with older networks that are still running the original protocol.

As its name implies, the most important feature of 802.1w is its capability to execute transition rapidly. Whereas a typical convergence time for 802.1d is between 35 and 60 seconds, the 802.1w can achieve it in 1 to 3 seconds. In some cases, a subsecond convergence is even possible. The 802.1d protocol was slow in its operation because ports take a long time to move into a forwarding state. In 802.1d, the only way to achieve faster convergence is to change the value of the Forward Delay and Maximum Age timers. Even then, it is still a timer-based protocol. The 802.1w can achieve faster convergence because it can move a port to a forwarding state without waiting for any timer to expire. It does so via a few new features:

- New port roles and states
- New BPDU format and handshake mechanism
- New edge port concept
- New link type concept

In the original 802.1d standard, a bridge port may be in one of the five possible states: disabled, blocked, listening, learning, or forwarding. 802.1w reduces the port states to three: discarding, learning, and forwarding. Table 6-2 compares the port states of the two standards.

Table 6-2   *Comparison of 802.1d and 802.1w Port States*

802.1d Port States	802.1w Port State	Port Included in Active Topology?	Port Learning MAC Addresses?
Disabled	Discarding	No	No
Blocked	Discarding	No	No
Listening	Discarding	Yes	No
Learning	Learning	Yes	Yes
Forwarding	Forwarding	Yes	Yes

In the original 802.1d standard, a port can take on the role of a root, designated, or alternate. In the 802.1w, a port can take on a root, designated, alternate, or backup role. Table 6-3 compares the port role of the two standards.

Table 6-3   *Comparison of 802.1d and 802.1w Port Roles*

802.1d Port Role	802.1w Port Role
Disabled	Disabled
Root	Root
Designated	Designated
Alternate	Alternate
	Backup

In 802.1w, an alternate port is one that receives preferred BPDUs from other bridges, whereas a port is designated as backup if it has received preferred BPDUs from the same bridge that it is on. Figure 6-21 illustrates the concept of the new port roles.

The format of the 802.1w BPDU differs from that in 802.1d. In 802.1d, only the Topology Change (TC) and Topology Change Acknowledgement (TCA) were defined. In the new standard, the rest of the 6 bits are used to include the following flags:

- Proposal
- Port Role (2 bits)
- Learning
- Forwarding
- Agreement

Figure 6-21   *Port Roles of IEEE 802.1w*

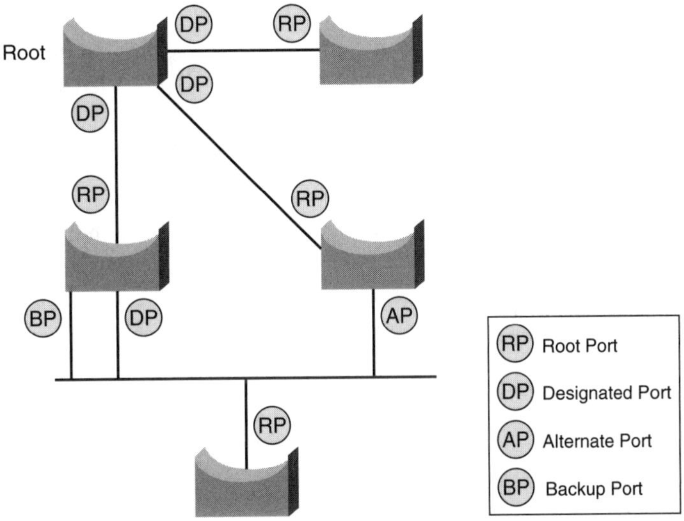

The inclusion of the new flags enables the bridges to communicate with each other in a new manner. In the 802.1d standard, BPDUs are propagated via a relay function. In other words, the root bridge sends out BPDUs and the rest will relay the message to the downstream.

Unlike 802.1d, 802.1w uses Hello packets between bridges to maintain link states and does not rely on the root bridge. In 802.1w, bridges send out BPDUs to their neighbors at fixed times, as specified by the Hello timer. When a bridge has not received a BPDU from its neighbor, it can assume that its neighbor is down. This reliance on Hello packets, rather than the Forward Delay and Maximum Age timers in the original 802.1d, enables the bridges to perform notification and react to topology change in a much more efficient manner.

In 802.1w, the edge port refers to a port that is directly connected to an end station. Because an end station is not a bridge and will not cause loops, the port can be put into a forwarding state immediately. This is exactly the same concept as that of the PortFast feature in the Cisco implementation. An edge port does not cause topology change, regardless of its link state. However, if it starts to receive BPDUs, it will lose its edge port status and become a normal STP port.

The advent of switching technology has resulted in changes to network design. Nowadays, switches are connected more in a point-to-point manner than through shared media. By taking advantage of the point-to-point link's characteristics, 802.1w can move a port into forwarding state much faster than before. The link type is derived from the duplex mode of the port. A link connected via a full-duplex port is considered to be point to point, whereas one that is connected via a half duplex is considered to be shared. The link type can also be configured manually in 802.1w. Therefore, a simple configuration of a port mode now significantly affects the behavior of the STP.

The 802.1w is made available on the Catalyst switches through the implementation of Rapid-PVST+. Rapid-PVST+ enables you to load balance VLAN traffic and at the same time provide rapid convergence in the event of a failure. 802.1w is also incorporated into the Cisco implementation of IEEE 802.1s. IEEE 802.1s is discussed in the following section.

Example 6-11 shows how to turn on Rapid-PVST+ in the global configuration mode.

Example 6-11 *Configuring Rapid-PVST+*

```
3750-A#configure terminal
3750-A(config)#spanning-tree mode rapid-pvst
```

Because 802.1w has introduced a few enhancements to the original 802.1d, not all features discussed in the section "The Spanning Tree Protocol: IEEE802.1d" are needed. The following features are available in conjunction with Rapid-PVST+:

- PortFast
- BPDUGuard
- RootGuard
- LoopGuard

As mentioned earlier, the 802.1w protocol can work with the 802.1d protocol to provide interoperability. However, all the 802.1w enhancements are lost, and the behavior will be that of the original standard.

IEEE 802.1s

The IEEE 802.1s protocol is another standard that deals with mapping VLAN topology with an independent instance of STP. To have a good understanding of IEEE 802.1s, you have to appreciate the differences between the CST model and PVST model.

In the deployment of CST, only one instance of STP is running in the switches, and as a result, all VLANs share the same Layer 2 topology. The characteristics of a CST implementation are as follows:

- Only one instance of STP is running for all VLANs; therefore, the CPU load on the switches is minimal.
- Because all VLAN topologies are governed by the same STP process, they all share the same forwarding path and blocked path.
- No load balancing of traffic is permitted.

By adopting a PVST strategy, you can achieve a different implementation, such as that shown earlier in Figure 6-17, with the following characteristics:

- Each VLAN is governed by a separate STP instance. Because of this, the CPU load on the switch has increased. With a network of 1000 VLANs, there are actually 1000 instances of STP running.

- Because each VLAN has its own STP instance, they can be configured differently to achieve different Layer 2 topology.

- Load balancing of traffic is achieved via configuration.

- There will be many VLANs sharing the same Layer 2 topology, and each VLAN will have its own STP instance.

Both of the preceding implementations have their pros and cons. CST achieves saving on CPU resources but sacrifices on topology flexibility and load-balancing capability. PVST sacrifices CPU resources to achieve better control of the topology and uplink capacity. The IEEE 802.1s standard aims to combine the benefits of the two implementations.

The idea behind the IEEE 802.1s standard is to map those VLANs that share the same topology to a common instance of STP. This way, you can reduce the number of instances of STP running, thus reducing the load on the CPU. At the same time, other VLANs may be mapped to another instance of STP for a different topology. This way, the flexibility of topology is made possible and load balancing can be achieved.

Figure 6-22 *STP Instances of IEEE 802.1s for Voice and Data VLANs*

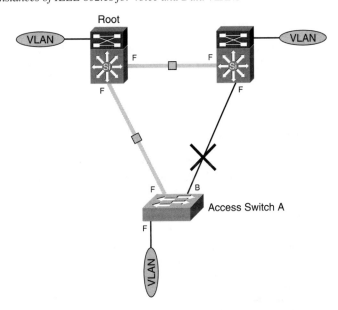

In Figure 6-22, both voice and data VLANs are mapped to STP instance 1, where the uplink on the right is blocked. On the other hand, as illustrated in Figure 6-23, the WLAN VLAN is mapped to STP instance 2, where the uplink on the left is blocked.

Figure 6-23 *STP Instances of IEEE 802.1s for WLAN VLANs*

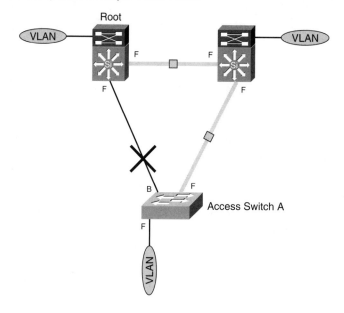

All in all, there are two instances of STP governing the topology of the three VLANs. With this implantation, it is possible to have, for example, 500 VLANs mapped to STP instance 1 and another 500 VLANs mapped to STP instance 2. Without 802.1s running, you need 1000 instances of STP running in the switch.

The benefit of the IEEE 802.1s is in saving CPU resources from managing too many STP instances. However, the drawback is that it adds complexity to the network design. Keeping track of which VLAN is mapped to which STP instance may be an administrative burden.

Example 6-12 shows an 802.1s configuration. The Catalyst series switches support a maximum of 16 instances of RSTP. Note that RSTP is enabled by default when you configure 802.1s.

Example 6-12 *Configuring 802.1s*

```
3750-A#configure terminal
3750-A(config)#spanning-tree mst configuration
3750-A(config-mst)#instance 1 vlan 5-10
3750-A(config-mst)#name HRServers
3750-A(config-mst)#revision 1
3750-A(config-mst)#exit
3750-A(config)#
```

The following error-prevention features are still made available to the instances of STP within 802.1s:

- PortFast
- BPDUGuard
- RootGuard
- LoopGuard

In the Catalyst series of switches, the 802.1s feature is implemented together with the 802.1w. Therefore, its implementation is not only capable of saving control-plane resources but also converging in subseconds in some cases.

Channeling Technology

The channeling technology enables you to use multiple Ethernet links combined into one logical link. This configuration allows for increments in transmission capability between devices and provides link redundancy. It can be used to interconnect LAN switches or routers and even improves the resiliency of a server connection to a switch.

The Cisco implementation of channeling technology is the EtherChannel. Depending on the connection speed, EtherChannel is referred to as Fast EtherChannel (FEC) for 100-Mbps links or Gigabit EtherChannel (GEC) for 1-Gbps links. The EtherChannel for 10-Gbps links is also available today. Figure 6-24 shows the basic concept of EtherChannel.

Figure 6-24 *EtherChannel*

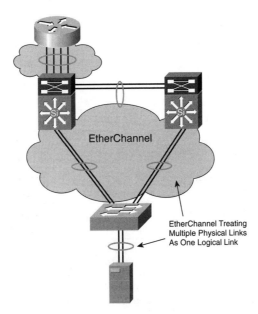

EtherChannel operation comprises two parts:

- The distribution of data packets on the multiple physical links
- A control portion that governs the working of the technology

The distribution of the packets is based on a hashing algorithm that derives a numeric value to decide which links to send the packet to. The algorithm may decide on the distribution based on the following:

- Source MAC address
- Destination MAC address
- Source/destination MAC address
- Source IP
- Destination IP
- Source/destination IP
- Source TCP port
- Destination TCP port
- Source IP/destination IP/TCP port

Based on the distribution criteria, the hashing is deterministic, and all packets that share the same characteristics are always transmitted via the same physical link to avoid sequencing errors. Depending on the hardware architecture, not all the Cisco devices support the algorithm.

The control portion of the EtherChannel governs the working of the EtherChannel. There are three ways to bring up EtherChannel:

- Manual configuration
- Port Aggregation Control Protocol (PAgP)
- IEEE 802.1ad, also known as Link Aggregation Control Protocol (LACP)

Before participating in the channeling operation, a port can be in one of the EtherChannel modes listed in Table 6-4.

Table 6-4 *Different Modes of EtherChannel*

Mode	Description
On	Forces the port to channel unconditionally. Ports configured in the on mode do not negotiate, and they only operate with a partnering port that has been configured to on mode.
Auto	PAgP mode that places a port into a passive negotiating state. It receives PAgP requests but does not initiate PAgP negotiation. This is the default.
Desirable	PAgP mode that places a port into an active negotiating state. The port sends out PAgP packets to initiate negotiations.
Passive	LACP mode that places a port into a passive negotiating state. It receives LACP requests but does not initiate LACP negotiation.
Active	LACP mode that places a port into an active negotiating state. The port sends out LACP packets to initiate negotiations.

The manual way to configure EtherChannel dictates that both ports must be set to on to form the EtherChannel.

The PAgP supports the autocreation of EtherChannel by the exchange of the PAgP packets between ports. This happens only when the ports are in auto and desirable modes. The basic rules for PAgP are as follows:

- A port in desirable mode can form an EtherChannel with another port in desirable mode.
- A port in desirable mode can form an EtherChannel with another in auto mode.
- A port in auto mode cannot form an EtherChannel with another also in auto mode, because neither one will initiate negotiation.

Likewise, the LACP supports the autocreation of EtherChannel by the exchange of the LACP packets between ports. This happens only when the ports are in active and passive modes. The basic rules for LACP are as follows:

- A port in active mode can form an EtherChannel with another port in active mode.
- A port in active mode can form an EtherChannel with another in passive mode.
- A port in passive mode cannot form an EtherChannel with another also in passive mode, because neither one will initiate negotiation.

Channeling technology is a good way to increase link capacity, provide link redundancy, and at the same time maintain the logical design of the IP network. However, care should be taken when deploying channeling technology, as discussed in the following section.

Layer 2 Best Practices

The health of the Layer 2 network plays an important role in maintaining the stability of the IP network within the access module. However, it is a common source of network error, with problems ranging from broadcast storms to complete network meltdowns. However, by following some simple principles, you can avoid these problems.

Simple Is Better

It cannot be stressed enough that in the Layer 2 network design, simple is more, and more may not be beautiful. What this means is that you have to keep the design as simple as possible, with easy-to-remember configuration settings. The following are some examples:

- If there is no uplink congestion problem, there is no need to load balance traffic.
- In the event that you load balance traffic, choose a simple formula. For example, the human resources (HR) department uses the left uplink as the primary path, and the finance department uses the right uplink as the primary path. Never try to formulate a

complex web of tables just to keep track of which VLAN has the left uplink as primary and which has the right as primary. A common approach is to have VLANs with even VLAN IDs going to the left and VLANs with odd VLAN IDs going to the right.

- If changing the bridge priority is enough, leave the path cost alone.

By keeping the Layer 2 design simple, you can actually improve the resiliency and convergence of the network. Another benefit is that it will make troubleshooting a lot easier in the event of a problem.

Limit the Span of VLANs

If possible, confine the span of the VLAN to a minimum. This means you should avoid building a VLAN that spans multiple access modules. Provided you are dealing with some legacy application that needs all hosts to be on the same subnet, there is no reason why you should build a campus-wide VLAN. Such a VLAN not only takes up too many resources to maintain topology, you will probably end up with a nonoptimized traffic path that uses bandwidth unnecessarily.

In addition, when there is an STP problem within the VLAN, too many switches will be involved in the convergence exercise. This increases the chance of a network-wide outage and should be avoided.

Build Triangles, Not Squares

Features such as UplinkFast and BackboneFast work best in a triangle topology—that is, a single access switch having dual uplinks to a pair of distribution switches. In some situations, access switches are daisy-chained via physical connections. With two access switches, you end up with a square topology. With more than two access switches, you end up with a ring architecture. Both the square and ring designs suffer from poorer convergence time in the event of a failure. Although RSTP may still achieve the desired convergence time, the resulting topology may be too difficult to manage and troubleshoot.

If you have to daisy chain the access switches, you should consider the StackWise technology available on the Catalyst 3750. With StackWise technology, you can stack up to nine access switches and yet they are seen as one device from a Layer 2 and 3 perspective. From an STP perspective, they are viewed as one bridge, and from an IP network perspective, they can be managed via a single IP address. Figure 6-26 shows three Catalyst 3750s connected to each other via the StackWise technology.

Figure 6-25 *Triangle and Square Topologies*

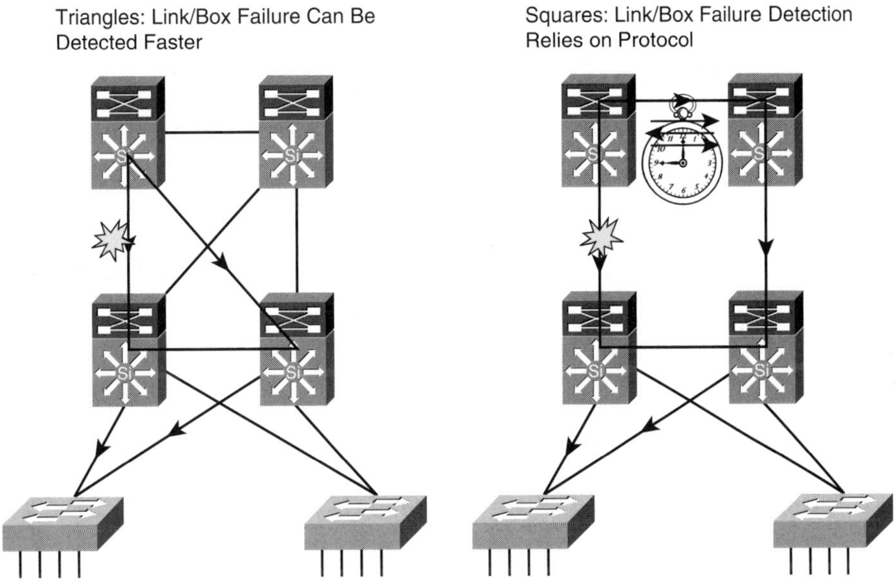

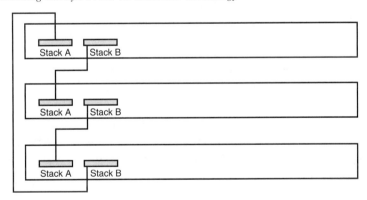

Triangles: Link/Box Failure Can Be Detected Faster
Squares: Link/Box Failure Detection Relies on Protocol

Figure 6-26 *Connecting Catalyst 3750s via StackWise Technology*

Stack A
Stack B
Stack A
Stack B
Stack A
Stack B

Protect the Network from Users

The access module is where users have a direct connection to the network. You can never trust that only end stations such as PCs and laptops are connected to the access switches.

The combination of users connecting a switch to the network and turning on the PortFast feature on that port could spell disaster for the STP topology. Therefore, the STP network has to be protected from all users via features such as BPDUGuard and RootGuard. You have to be cautious with the user-side connections to the network. Always imagine that users are going to put in technologies that are detrimental to the health of the network.

Selecting Root Bridges

The root bridge is the most important component in the Layer 2 network. Its location within the Layer 2 topology and the selection of hardware impact the health of the Layer 2 network.

Because all traffic in the Layer 2 network flows toward the root, the distribution layer switches are always good candidates. This corresponds to the way the IP traffic flows in the Layer 3 network. For redundancy purposes, there are usually two distribution switches per block, and they should be selected as the primary and secondary root bridge. Remember that in STP the bridge with the lowest BID is always elected as a root bridge. Therefore, you should not leave default values when configuring the BID of the switches. For this reason, part of the network design should include a BID assignment strategy.

One common mistake that network managers make is to leave the operation of STP to the default values and behavior. The problem with this is that the selection of the root is not deterministic, and the resulting Layer 2 topology might not be optimized. Worse still, in the event of a problem, you have to determine the location of the root bridge. The most difficult problem to troubleshoot is a floating network design, where it is difficult to determine how it should work in the first place. You should decide on a root bridge and a backup root bridge so that the Layer 2 topology is fixed and easily understood. With proper configuration and documentation, traffic has to flow in a certain manner. This way, any anomaly can be easily identified and the problem diagnosed. The root bridge has to be protected via features such as RootGuard, and if it is possible, no access switch should be elected as a root bridge.

Remember that the distribution layer is the most complex part of the access module, because it runs both Layer 2 and Layer 3 protocols. Therefore, the load on its control plane will be relatively higher than the rest of the switches in the network. For this reason, careful selection of hardware is important, and switches with higher-performance CPUs should be preferred.

Use Value-Added Features

You can also use the **diameter** keyword to specify the Layer 2 network diameter (that is, the maximum number of switch hops between any two end stations in the Layer 2 network). When you specify the network diameter, the switch automatically sets an optimal Hello time, forward-delay time, and maximum-age time for a network of that diameter, which can significantly reduce the convergence time. You can use the **hello** keyword to override the automatically calculated Hello time. Example 6-13 shows a configuration sample of limiting the diameter to four switches for VLAN 100.

Example 6-13 *Setting the Diameter of a Layer 2 Network*

```
3750#configure terminal
3750(config)#spanning-tree vlan 100 root primary diameter 4
```

EtherChannel Deployment

A common place to deploy EtherChannel is the connection between the distribution switches. Such a connection is usually configured as a switching trunk port, and, therefore, the bundling is called a Layer 2 EtherChannel. On the other hand, an EtherChannel may be deployed as a routed interface, such as that between a distribution layer switch and a core layer switch. Such an implementation is called a Layer 3 EtherChannel.

Extra care has to be taken with the implementation of a Layer 3 EtherChannel because many advanced IP features, such as Multiprotocol Label Switching-Traffic Engineering (MLPS-TE), Reservation Protocol (RSVP), and QoS, with complex configurations may not be supported in conjunction with a Layer 3 EtherChannel. Different linecards on different platforms may have an individual caveat with respect to this scenario, and it is important that you are familiar with these caveats. Because of the potential complexity that Layer 3 EtherChannel may introduce in such a scenario, link capacity scaling and resiliency in the core module require a different approach than that provided by EtherChannel.

EtherChannel Load Balancing

The default hashing algorithm for EtherChannel is based on the source/destination IP pair. This mode is adequate for most user access implementations. However, sometimes this might yield unexpected results. One good example is when a pair of servers is performing application synchronization. Because the source/destination IP pair remains constant throughout the transmission, you end up with only one of the links of an EtherChannel being utilized. This may have a performance impact if the transmission exceeds the transmission capacity of the single link.

One good way to overcome this problem is to adopt the source IP/destination IP/TCP port hashing algorithm for the EtherChannel. Including Layer 4 information allows for a more balanced use of the available links within the EtherChannel bundle.

Consistent EtherChannel Port Settings

When configuring EtherChannel, you have to ensure that all members of the bundle have the same port setting. This includes settings such as the link speed and duplex mode. If you have ports with different settings, you may face unexpected results and find troubleshooting more difficult. For example, ports belonging to the same EtherChannel configured with different trunking modes may produce undesirable STP behavior. All ports need to be in enabled mode, too. Having some ports in disabled mode will cause traffic to be diverted to the rest.

Layer 2 Setting for EtherChannel

When setting up the Layer 2 EtherChannel, take care with respect to the Layer 2 setting. For example, if the EtherChannel is to act as a logical access port for VLAN 10, all the switch ports that make up the EtherChannel have to be set to the same VLAN. If the EtherChannel is to act as a logical trunk port, however, all the switch ports that make up the EtherChannel have to be in trunk mode. In addition, the allowed range of VLANs has to be the same for all the ports. Failing to ensure port setting consistencies means that the EtherChannel will never be formed.

Turning Off Autonegotiation

Although the switches can autonegotiate for the formation of EtherChannel via protocols such as PAgP, it is better to configure them manually. For example, PAgP is on by default for switches running CatOS, whereas it is off by default for those running IOS. A mismatch PAgP setting can incur unnecessary negotiation time and may take a long time to restore connection.

Turning off autonegotiation on ports between servers and switches is also a good idea to improve resiliency of the network. Some server network interfaces might not negotiate the link properly and cause duplex mismatch. The server network interface card may think that the switch port is running as a half duplex, when in fact the switch port is a full duplex. Therefore, it is always recommended to explicitly set the duplex settings on both the server interface and the switch port.

So far, you have learned about all the Layer 2 building blocks that enable you to build a stable Layer 2 network. After the Layer 2 network is robust and has high resiliency, you can then build the corresponding IP subnets to be always reachable from other parts of the network.

Layer 3 Domain

The Layer 3 building block is found mainly in the distribution layer of the multilayer campus design. The function of the building block is mainly to provide for the following:

- A first-hop redundancy function to the hosts that are attached to the access layer
- To announce the routes of the IP subnet sitting behind the distribution layer to the rest of the network
- Other value-added functions that may help in the operation of the network (for example, access control, multicast forwarding, and QoS)

Because of the functions it provides, resiliency at the Layer 3 domain focuses on devices backing up each other in terms of providing all the previously described functions.

Hot Standby Routing Protocol (HSRP)

Most of the end devices such as PCs, laptops, and servers are usually configured with a single default IP gateway. What this means is that if the default IP gateway is unavailable, these devices cannot communicate beyond their subnet. Although a feature such as Router Discovery Protocol may help in looking for another default IP gateway, not many end devices support it. Therefore, ensuring the availability of the default IP gateway is a number one priority.

The Hot Standby Routing Protocol (HSRP) is the Cisco implementation of providing a redundant default gateway to the end devices. Essentially, HSRP allows a set of routers to work together so that they appear as one single virtual default gateway to the end devices. It does so by providing a virtual IP (vIP) address and a virtual MAC (vMAC) address to the end devices. The end devices are configured to point their default IP gateway to the vIP address. The end devices also store the virtual vMAC address via Address Resolution Protocol (ARP). This way, HSRP allows two or more routers to back up each other to provide first-hop resiliency. Only one of the routers, the primary gateway, does the actual work of forwarding traffic to the rest of the network. There will be one standby router, whereas the rest will be placed in the listen mode. These routers do not forward traffic from the end hosts. However, for return traffic, they may forward traffic to the devices, depending on the configuration of the IP routing protocol.

Figure 6-27 illustrates the concept of HSRP. When a router participates in a HSRP setup, it exchanges keepalive Hellos with the rest using User Datagram Protocol (UDP) packets via a multicast address.

Figure 6-27 *HSRP*

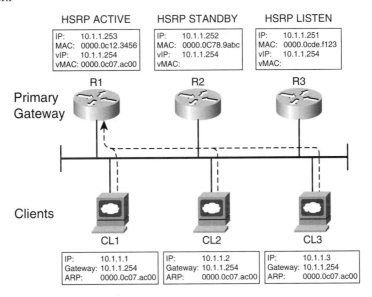

Table 6-5 lists the default configuration values of the HSRP parameters.

Table 6-5 *Default Values for HSRP Configuration*

Parameter	Default
HSRP group	Not configured
Standby group number	0
Standby MAC address	0000.0c07.acNN where NN is the group number
Standby priority	100
Standby delay	0
Standby track interface priority	10
Standby Hello timer	3 seconds
Standby Hello hold time	10 seconds

Here are some pointers about configuring HSRP:

- The role of primary and standby routers can be selected by assigning a priority value. The default value of the priority is 100, and its range is 0 to 255. The router with the highest priority is selected as the primary, whereas zero means the router will never be the primary gateway. In the event that all the routers have the same priority, the one with the highest IP address is selected as the primary router.

- The priority of the router changes if it has a standby track command configured and is brought into action. The tracking value determines how much priority is decremented when a particular interface that the router tracks goes down. A typical interface that is being tracked is the uplink toward the backbone. When the uplink toward the backbone fails, no traffic can leave the router. Therefore, the primary router should relinquish its role and have its priority lowered so that the standby router can take over its role.

- You can track multiple interfaces, and their failure has a cumulative effect on the priority value of the router, if it has a track interface priority configured. If no track priority value is configured, the default value is 10, and it is not cumulative.

- The default Hello timer is 3 seconds, whereas the hold time is 10 seconds. Hold time is the time taken before the standby declares the primary as unavailable when no more Hello packets are received.

From an IP resiliency standpoint, the focus is on how fast the standby gateway router takes over in the event that the primary gateway is down. Note that this is only for traffic going out from the end devices toward the rest of the network. The downtime experienced by the end devices will be the time it takes for the standby router to take over.

Although the standby router has taken over, its immediate neighbors may still keep the original primary router as the gateway to reach the access network. This happens because their routing tables have not been updated. In this case, for these routing tables to be updated, the routing protocol has to do its job.

The default Hello timer for HSRP is 3 seconds, and the hold time is 10 seconds. This means that when the primary router is down, end devices cannot communicate with the rest of the network for as long as 10 seconds or more. The Hello timer feature has since been enhanced so that the router sends out Hellos in milliseconds. With this enhancement, it is possible for the standby router to take over in less than a second, as demonstrated in Example 6-14.

Example 6-14 *Configuring HSRP Fast Hello*

```
Router#configuration terminal
Router(config)#interface fastEthernet 1/1
Router(config-if)#ip address 10.1.1.253 255.255.255.0
Router(config-if)#standby 1 ip 10.1.1.254
Router(config-if)#standby 1 timers msec 200 msec 750
Router(config-if)#standby 1 priority 150
Router(config-if)#standby 1 preempt
Router(config-if)#standby 1 preempt delay minimum 180
```

In Example 6-14, the router R1 has been configured with a virtual IP address of 10.1.1.254, and its priority is 150. For R1 to be the primary router, the rest will have a default priority value of 100. R1 sends out a Hello packet every 200 ms with a hold time of 750 ms. The function of the **preempt** command allows R1 to take over the forwarding function after it has recovered from its error, or after it has been reloaded. The preempt delay timer is to force R1 to wait for the indicated amount of time, in this case 180 seconds, before claiming back its role. This is to prevent it from taking over the HSRP primary role without a proper routing table.

Up to this point, HSRP may not seem like an efficient solution, because only one router, R1, is performing the forwarding function. The rest of the routers are simply not used at all. This might not even be a cost-effective solution, especially if all the HSRP routers are WAN routers with expensive WAN links as their uplinks. Because only the primary router is forwarding traffic, the rest of the WAN links on R2 and R3 will be left underutilized. The Multigroup HSRP (MHSRP) feature is used to solve this problem.

You can configure MHSRP on a pair of routers. Both the routers R1 and R2 are configured with multiple HSRP groups. For each of the HSRP groups, there is a unique virtual IP address with a virtual MAC address. Group 1 has R1 as the primary router and R2 as the standby. Group 2 has R2 as the primary and R1 as a standby. The end devices are separated into groups by configuring their default gateway to point to the different virtual IP addresses. Half the end devices will default the route to group 1's virtual IP address; the rest will default the route to group 2's virtual IP address. Figure 6-28 illustrates the concept.

Figure 6-28 *MHSRP*

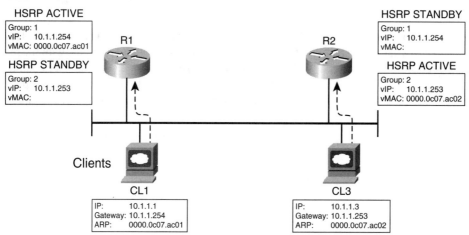

In this case, both the uplinks of R1 and R2 are utilized, because both are acting as the primary router for separate HSRP groups. Whenever the primary router of a group fails, the standby for that group takes over the duty of forwarding traffic.

Example 6-15 shows the configuration needed for R1.

Example 6-15 *Configuration of HSRP on R1*

```
R1#configuration terminal
R1(config)#interface ethernet1/0
R1(config-if)#ip address 10.1.1.250 255.255.255.0
R1(config-if)#standby 1 preempt
R1(config-if)#standby 1 ip 10.1.1.254
R1(config-if)#standby 1 track Serial0
R1(config-if)#standby 2 ip 10.1.1.253
R1(config-if)#standby 2 track serial 0
R1(config-if)#standby 2 priority 95
```

Example 6-16 shows the configuration needed for R2.

Example 6-16 *Configuration of HSRP on R2*

```
R2#configuration terminal
R2(config)#interface ethernet1/0
R2(config-if)#interface ethernet1/0
R2(config-if)#ip address 10.1.1.251 255.255.255.0
R2(config-if)#standby 1 ip 10.1.1.254
R2(config-if)#standby 1 track Serial0
R2(config-if)#standby 1 priority 95
R2(config-if)#standby 2 preempt
R2(config-if)#standby 2 ip 10.1.1.253
R2(config-if)#standby 2 track serial 0
```

MHSRP solves the problem of wasted uplink bandwidth of the standby router in HSRP. However, it adds complexity because the clients now have to have separate default gateway addresses. If the clients have their IP address assigned by a DHCP server, some mechanism has to be built in to distribute the clients to point to different default gateways. In this case, you might have added complexity for the sake of load balancing traffic on the various uplinks.

Virtual Router Redundancy Protocol (VRRP)

The Virtual Router Redundancy Protocol (VRRP), which is defined in RFC 2338, is the IETF standard version of a first-hop redundancy protocol. Its function is similar to that of HSRP. Routers participating in a VRRP setup are known as *VRRP routers*. These routers work together to provide what is known as a VRRP virtual router. There can be many virtual routers, each identified through a virtual router identifier (VRID). This is similar to the group ID assigned in MHSRP configuration.

In a similar concept as that of HSRP, VRRP routers elect a master router based on a priority value. The master router then sends out advertisements to the rest of the participating routers for keepalive. The minimum value of the advertisement interval is 1 second. In this case, the take over timing may not be as fast as that provided by HSRP. With VRID, VRRP can also provide a load-sharing mechanism to utilize all uplinks.

Global Load Balancing Protocol (GLBP)

In providing a first-hop redundancy solution, both HSRP and VRRP implement the concept of a single primary and multiple secondary gateways. Under normal working conditions, only the primary is actively forwarding traffic for the hosts; the secondary is not. This is costly, especially when both the uplinks from the gateways are expensive WAN circuits. Suppose the primary gateway has never encountered any problems; the secondary gateway may be forgotten after some time, or worse still, its failure may not be noticed.

MHSRP may be able to achieve a certain degree of load balancing for the uplinks; however, the complexity of configuring the end devices to have a different default IP gateway may outweigh the benefits. This is especially so if a DHCP is involved. Not many DHCP servers can assign a default IP gateway in a round-robin fashion.

The aim of the Global Load Balancing Protocol (GLBP) is to provide the basic function of first-hop redundancy, and at the same time achieve load balancing in terms of uplinks. GLBP combines the benefits of both HSRP and MHSRP. In a GLBP setup, routers work together to present a common virtual IP address to the clients. However, instead of using a single virtual MAC address tied to a virtual IP address, different virtual MAC addresses are tied to a single virtual IP address. These different virtual MAC addresses are sent to different end devices through the ARP process. This way, different end devices forward traffic to the different virtual MAC addresses for forwarding to the rest of the network.

In a GLBP setup, as shown in Figure 6-29, a router is elected to be the active virtual gateway (AVG). The AVG acts as the master of the group. In Figure 6-27, R1 has been elected as the AVG. The job of the AVG is to assign a virtual MAC address to each GLBP member. These members then become the active virtual forwarder (AVF) for that virtual MAC address. For example, R2 is an AVF for the virtual MAC 0007.b400.0102. The AVF is responsible for forwarding traffic that was sent to their virtual MAC address. Other members may be assigned as a secondary virtual forwarder (SVF) in case the AVF fails. In Figure 6-29, R3 is the SVF for R2. One important job of the AVG is to respond to all ARP requests sent out by the end devices. The end devices send out an ARP request for the common virtual IP address. The AVG assigns a different virtual MAC to different end devices based on a preset algorithm. It may be assigned the virtual MAC in a round-robin or weighted fashion. In this manner, all the clients share the same default gateway IP address, which resolves into different MAC addresses, depending on which AVF has been assigned.

Figure 6-29 *GLBP*

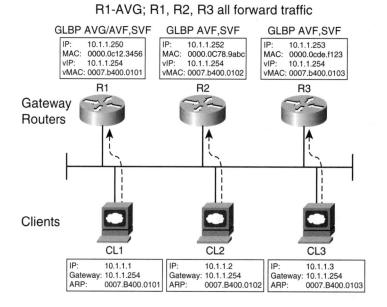

The election of the AVG is the same as that of HSRP. The candidate is elected based on the **glbp priority** command. The one with the highest priority is elected the AVG. In the event of a tie, the one with the highest IP address is elected. There is another one elected as the standby; the rest are placed in listen mode.

The members of the GLBP group communicate with each other via a multicast address 224.0.0.102 and UDP port number 3222. The virtual MAC address takes the form of 0007.b4nn.nnnn. The last 24 bits of the MAC address consists of six zeros, 10 bits for indicating the group number and 8 bits for the virtual forwarder number. This means GLBP can support 1024 groups, each with 255 forwarders. However, in practice, four virtual forwarders are configurable for each of the groups.

The virtual forwarders are each assigned a virtual MAC address and act as the primary forwarder for that MAC address instance. The rest of the routers in the group learn of this virtual forwarding instance via Hello messages and create their own backup instance. These are known as the secondary virtual forwarders. The working of the primary and secondary forwarders depends on the four timers that are important in the GLBP operation:

- **Hello time**—The Hello time is learned from the AVG, or it can be manually configured. The default is 3 seconds, and the range is 50 ms to 60 seconds.

- **Hold time**—The hold time is used to determine whether action is required to take over the virtual gateway or virtual forwarder function. This timer is reset whenever a Hello is received from the partners. The hold time must be greater than three times that of the Hello timer. The hold time can be learned from the AVG or manually configured. The default is 10 seconds, and the range is 1 to 180 seconds.

- **Redirect time**—This is the time in which the AVG continues to redirect clients to the AVF. The redirect time can be learned from the AVG or manually configured. The default is 5 minutes, and the range is 1 second to 60 minutes.

- **Secondary hold time**—This is the period of time for which an SVF remains valid after the AVF is unavailable. The SVF is deleted when the secondary hold time expires. When the SVF is deleted, the load-balancing algorithm is changed to allocate forwarding to the remaining VFs. This timer should be longer than the ARP cache age of the client. This timer can be learned from the AVG or manually. The default is 1 hour, and the range is 40 minutes to 18 hours.

There are three ways clients can be assigned to a particular virtual forwarder:

- **Weighted load balancing**—The number of clients directed to an AVF depends on the weight assigned to it. All the virtual forwarders within a router use this weight.

- **Host-dependent load balancing**—The decision of which AVF to direct to depends on the MAC address of the client. This way, a client is always directed to the same virtual MAC address.

- **Round-robin load balancing**—As the name implies, the virtual MAC addresses are assigned to the clients in a round-robin fashion. This method is recommended for a subnet with a small number of clients. This is the default method.

If no load-balancing algorithm is specified, the AVG responds to all ARP requests with its own VF MAC address. In this case, the whole operation is similar to that of HSRP.

Similar to HSRP, GLBP can track interfaces. In fact, with the introduction of the Enhanced Object Tracking feature in Cisco IOS, GLBP can track and react to errors arising from the following entities:

- Interfaces or subinterfaces

- IP routes

- All IP service level agreement (IP SLA) operations
- Object lists via Boolean operations (for example, AND and OR)

Example 6-17 shows how to configure GLBP on router R1.

Example 6-17 *Configuring GLBP on R1*

```
R1#configuration terminal
R1(config)#interface fastethernet 0/0
R1(config-if)#ip address 10.1.1.250 255.255.255.0
R1(config-if)#glbp 10 ip 10.1.1.254
R1(config-if)#glbp 10 forwarder preempt delay minimum 60
R1(config-if)#glbp 10 load-balancing host-dependent
R1(config-if)#glbp 10 preempt delay minimum 60
R1(config-if)#glbp 10 priority 254
R1(config-if)#glbp 10 timers 5 18
R1(config-if)#glbp 10 timers redirect 600 7200
```

GLBP combines the benefits of HSRP and MHSRP to achieve both first-hop resiliency and load balancing of traffic. It is especially important in a typical branch setup, which requires two WAN routers to provide a redundant setup. With GLBP, both the WAN links of the routers can be better utilized so that investment can be maximized. In addition, it is also good to use both links to verify their integrity. If a link is only used for redundancy purposes, it might not be possible to ascertain its quality until a failure has occurred. This may be too late.

Layer 3 Best Practices

This section looks at some Layer 3 best practices that focus on improving network resiliency. Besides providing a redundant first-hop gateway service to the access layer, another important task that the distribution layer has to perform is to provide robust IP connectivity for the access layer to the core layer. Besides providing a reroute capability in the event that a link for a device fails, the Layer 3 routing protocol can also provide load-balancing capability to achieve better throughput.

Adopt Topology-Based Switching

Recall in the previous section, "Layer 3 Domain," that the Layer 3 building blocks are found in the distribution layer. This is where Layer 3 switching products are deployed to fulfill the role. In the selection of a Layer 3 switch, it is important to note that the switching hardware architecture does have a bearing on the resiliency of the IP network.

Figure 6-30 shows a switching product that is based on flow-based architecture. In this architecture, the switch forwards traffic by sending the first packet of a traffic flow to the CPU. The CPU determines the outgoing port so that all subsequent packets are switched via hardware. The CPU also keeps a record of this flow in a hardware cache. In this architecture, the first packet of every flow involves the CPU of the switch. Flow-based architecture is a popular way to build a Layer 3 switch and can be found in many products on the market today.

Figure 6-30 *Flow-Based Switching Architecture*

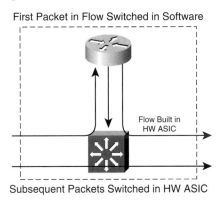

First Packet in Flow Switched in Software

Flow Built in HW ASIC

Subsequent Packets Switched in HW ASIC

The problem with flow-based architecture is that every traffic flow is maintained in the cache, and this takes up memory. For a Layer 3 switch performing the role at the distribution layer, it can potentially be supporting hundreds and even thousands of hosts. These hosts can create huge numbers of flows that need to be maintained in the cache. With hosts entering and leaving the network over time, huge amounts of CPU and memory resources are needed to maintain the cache. This strain on the control-plane resources is most pronounced when there is a DoS attack on the distribution layer. With a flow-based architecture, it will quickly run out of resources trying to maintain the millions of flows that were generated by the attack. The resiliency of the entire distribution building block will be jeopardized in this scenario, because the control plane has run out of resources.

In contrast to a flow-based architecture, a topology-based switching architecture is another way to build a Layer 3 switch. As discussed in the section "Cisco Express Forwarding" in Chapter 3, "Fundamentals of IP Resilient Networks," CEF is an example of a topology-based switching architecture.

Figure 6-31 shows the concept of a topology-based switching architecture. In this architecture, the CPU first builds the Forwarding Information Base (FIB) and adjacency table and pushes the information down to the ASIC in the line cards. Based on this information, the line card hardware can then forward traffic without the intervention of the CPU. With topology-based switching architecture, the CPU and its memory have been moved out of the way of all the traffic flows. Therefore, regardless of the number of hosts entering and leaving the network, the control plane of the distribution layer is not affected. Provided the DoS attack is targeted at the Layer 3 switch itself, the millions of flows that are created during the attack will have little impact on the control plane of the switch.

Figure 6-31 *Topology-Based Switching Architecture*

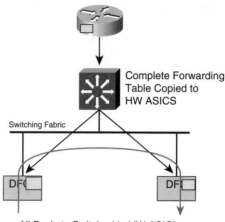

Therefore, a Layer 3 switch with a topology-based architecture is recommended to perform the role of the distribution layer. This is especially so if the Layer 3 switch is also to be used as in the core layer. Switches that incorporate topology-based architecture include the Catalyst 4500 and Catalyst 6500 series.

Using Equal-Cost Multipath

It is important to understand the routing protocol behavior with respect to topology so that you can exploit certain characteristics to achieve resiliency. Because protocols such as Open Shortest Path First (OSPF) and Intermediate System to Intermediate System (IS-IS) work on the basis of path cost, you should always try to strive for a equal-cost multipath (ECMP) topology. It just means trying to create a topology with at least two equal-cost paths between a source and a destination. An ECMP topology allows traffic to be load balanced on multiple paths, thus achieving better performance. In addition, in the event that one of the paths fails, ECMP can transfer traffic to the remaining working path in an instant. One simple rule to remember about constructing an ECMP environment is that triangular topology is always preferred, the same as in the Layer 2 network design. In addition, it is also important to know how the router behaves in an ECMP environment.

In an ECMP environment, the router takes advantage of the multiple links and tries to load balance traffic based on two algorithms: per destination or per packet.

With per-destination load balancing, the router sends packets destined on the same path. Unequal use of the multiple paths may occur if most traffic is bound for one particular host. For example, only two hosts are communicating, and they are sending out a huge amount of traffic. However, with more hosts receiving traffic, the multiple paths are better utilized. Prior to CEF, the route cache was used to maintain the distribution of traffic across the multiple paths for these hosts. And the router had to build an entry for every host. This may also be a strain on the control plane of the router.

With per-packet load balancing, the router sends packets across all the multiple paths in a round-robin fashion, which is a more balanced use of the multiple paths. Prior to CEF, this was done through process switching, and, therefore, this feature suffers from performance penalty.

Recall from the section "Cisco Express Forwarding" in Chapter 3 that CEF takes advantage of the separation between the forwarding table and the adjacency table to provide a better form of packet routing technology. With CEF, for per-destination load balancing, it does not need to build a cache entry for every host that needs load balancing. This frees up the control-plane resources and is especially important in building a resilient IP network. For per-packet load balancing, CEF does not need the help of the CPU to determine the next path for a packet to take. So there is minimal impact to the CPU load.

Therefore, to fully take advantage of the benefits of a multipath topology, you need a good understanding of the load balancing algorithms and their impact on the load on the control plane. CEF is again recommended for the implementation of an ECMP environment.

Conserve Peering Resources

The distribution layer terminates the VLANs coming from the access layer. Chances are, devices residing within these VLANs are end stations such as PCs or servers. These end stations rely on a default gateway to get connected to the rest of the network and do not normally run routing protocols. In this case, there is no need for the distribution layer to maintain any Layer 3 peering relationships with the devices in the VLANs. Cutting down on unnecessary peering will help conserve CPU and memory resources on the distribution layer switch, as shown in Figure 6-32.

Figure 6-32 *Limiting Peering at the Distribution Level*

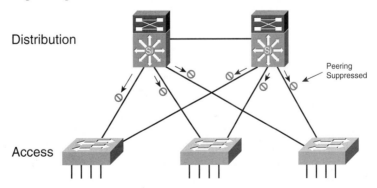

Adopt a Hierarchical Addressing Scheme

A basic rule that always holds true is this: The fewer the routes in the network, the faster it can converge. Therefore, it is worthwhile to adopt a hierarchical IP addressing scheme. A proper IP addressing scheme enables you to design the network in a hierarchical manner, where the routing table in the core should be less than that at the edge of the network.

In conjunction with concepts such as areas in the OSPF protocol, IP addresses at the edge of the network can be summarized and represented by a single entry in the core. There are at least two advantages in doing so. First, because of the area design, errors such as link failure are concealed from the rest of the network. The error messages are propagated only within the area. Second, when errors occur within the area, no changes are required in the routing table for routers in other areas, because the summarized entry is still valid. As long as there are minimal changes to the routing table, the network will always remain stable. Figure 6-33 illustrates the concept of using areas in OSPF.

Figure 6-33 *Summarization in OSPF*

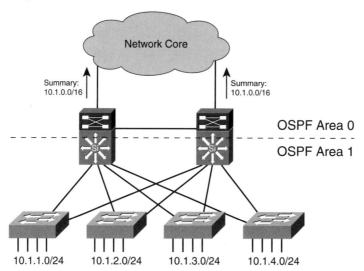

Summary

The access module deals mainly with Ethernet switch technology. As long as the intricacy of the STP protocol is well understood, it is possible to build a robust Layer 2 network in this module. Keeping the Layer 2 design simple and predictable is perhaps the best insurance for building a resilient IP network within the access module. The same principle applies to the Layer 3 domain. By adopting the best practices, you can improve the resiliency of the network and avoid unnecessary downtime.

This chapter covers the following topics:

- Understanding Addressing and Routing in the Internet Module
- Establishing Internet Module Redundancy
- Implementing Security Measures
- Resilient Border Gateway Protocol (BGP) Design
- Using Network Address Translation (NAT)

CHAPTER 7

Internet Module

The Internet module is the building block that connects a corporate network to the Internet. With increased reliance on the Internet for connectivity purposes, the Internet module design has also undergone changes with respect to redundancy and security to support business continuity. The security aspect has been under the spotlight because of the emergence of denial-of-service (DoS) attacks on critical business websites.

Regardless of your network requirement and design, connectivity to the Internet requires you to understand some basic rules. These rules govern how the Internet is operated, and they also influence how the service providers provision their services. Some of these rules can be found in the technical documentation within the Internet community, such as those listed in Table 7-1. This documentation is an essential read because it will help you develop a strategy for a resilient Internet module design. Another good source of reference is *Cisco ISP Essentials*, by Barry Raveendran Greene and Philip Smith (Cisco Press, 2002).

Given that the Internet module is responsible for the entire network's connection to the outside world, it is important that its design be well thought out. Although the best practices, such as a modular design concept, still hold, a few areas are most critical to the needs of the Internet module. These areas are important because they have implication on the overall resiliency of the Internet module. There is also a cost implication because connecting to the Internet involves paying a service provider for a service. The three major areas of concern in the Internet module design are as follows:

- Addressing and routing
- Redundancy
- Security

In addition to addressing these concerns, developing a resilient Internet module takes more than just redundant links. The routing of traffic for Internet access can be quite difficult and different from that of the internal network. For one, Internet routing requires different protocols and may involve cooperation from other parties, such as the service providers. In addition, special features are sometimes needed to overcome problems such as shortages of public IP address.

Internet module design involves careful planning and strategizing so that a certain level of resiliency can be achieved. The Border Routing Protocol (BGP) plays a vital role in the routing aspect. Depending on the addressing strategy and network design, another technology, Network Address Translation (NAT), also plays an important role. This chapter examines how the enhancements made to both BGP and NAT help in maintaining a highly resilient Internet module.

Understanding Addressing and Routing in the Internet Module

Addressing and routing are closely related when it comes to designing the Internet module. For connectivity to the Internet, you need to know the various addressing practices adopted by the service providers. In addition, you need to have a thorough understanding of various concepts such as public and private addresses and classless interdomain routing (CIDR).

You can build a good foundation on the topics of addressing and routing for the Internet module from the various RFCs that have been published, some of which are known as Best Current Practices (BCPs). The RFCs cover topics such as address allocation guidelines, rationale for adopting certain addressing schemes, and routing best practices. Table 7-1 lists some "must-read" RFCs if you are designing the Internet module.

Table 7-1   *"Must-Read" RFCs*

RFC	Title
1518	*An Architecture for IP Address Allocation with CIDR*
1519	*Classless Inter-Domain Routing (CIDR): an Address Assignment and Aggregation Strategy*
1918 (BCP 5)	*Address Allocation for Private Internets*
2008 (BCP 7)	*Implications of Various Address Allocation Policies for Internet Routing*
2050 (BCP 12)	*Internet Registry IP Allocation Guidelines*

It is important that you are familiar with these RFCs, especially if you are concerned with the availability of the Internet module as a whole. Having a good understanding of these concepts helps in avoiding unnecessary network migration later, as explained in the next section.

Address-Assignment Scheme

In the past, it was relatively easy to own a block of public IP addresses to gain access to the Internet. However, this has changed in recent times with the impending depletion of the Internet Protocol version 4 (IPv4) address in the Internet. Getting public IP addresses from the address registries now requires more justification and patience. What this means is that if you have a project on hand that requires a public address to be allocated, more effort and time have to be set aside as part of the planning process. In addition, this address-conservation exercise also means that you may have to find an alternative solution for the shortages of public IP address.

The Internet Assigned Numbers Authority (IANA) has reserved the following three blocks of the IP address space for private networks:

- 10.0.0.0–10.255.255.255 (10/8 prefix)
- 172.16.0.0–172.31.255.255 (172.16/12 prefix)
- 192.168.0.0–192.168.255.255 (192.168/16 prefix)

Adoption of the private address block is recommended for most enterprise networks because it provides the following advantages:

- You have the full flexibility of planning an optimized network with characteristics, such as route summarization, through the use of the address block such as 10.0.0.0. You would probably not enjoy such flexibility if you were using an allocated public IP address pool, provided your organization is one of the privileged few that has been allocated an entire Class A address. For private address deployment, it is recommended that the 10.0.0.0 block be used, because it gives you more headroom to plan for optimized routing through the use of consistent prefix size and route summarization.

- The private address has proven to be a useful tool in fighting DoS attacks launched from outside the network, because the hosts are not directly visible from the Internet. By placing checks and restrictions on the gateway devices, the public hosts are shielded from direct assaults when attacks are launched. However, it is important to note that although the hosts are protected, bandwidth saturation can still occur. Therefore, additional anti-DoS measures still need to be in place.

Although the adoption of private addresses is a common practice because of the benefits that it brings, there are some disadvantages in using private addresses, too:

- Access to the Internet for the private hosts need to go through an application layer gateway or address translation. This may prove to be a technical challenge for some applications, as discussed later in the section "Effects of NAT on Network and Applications."

- When it comes to the merger of two corporations that deploy the same private IP address block, connectivity of the two networks may not be as straightforward. For example, if two companies with networks that adopt the 10.0.0.0 address block were to merge, linking up these two networks would need some careful migration planning, because you must avoid the duplicate IP address issue.

In the event that the pool of public addresses has been allocated by a service provider, RFC 1518 and RFC 1519 specify ways for the service provider to summarize routes of its many customers to a single entry. This is done so as to contain the routing table size of the Internet. The implication of this practice is that it makes deploying multiple connections to the Internet complicated.

It is also important that you understand how the public address assignment schemes work in the Internet world, because it may mean avoiding painful migration of your network later. Network migration may potentially compromise the availability of the network, and so it is worthwhile to avoid it. RFC 2008 proposes the concept of the lending scheme with respect to public IP address assignment. Under the lending scheme, you acquire an Internet access circuit from a service provider. The service provider lends part of its public address block to you for connectivity. It can be a single IP address, or it may be a block of addresses carved from their address pool. The significance of building the Internet module under the lender scheme is that if you switch from one service provider to another, you have to change the IP addresses of your servers. This takes more than just a configuration change on the host portion. The name-resolution portion needs to be taken care of, and this may not be immediate. Meanwhile, connection to these hosts from the Internet will not be available, and the availability of the network is compromised.

Routing

The designs for both the Internet and data center modules are tightly coupled. Although the data center module, discussed in Chapter 9, "Data Center Module," holds the source of all information, it is the Internet module that provides reachability to the information residing within the data center. However, routing for the Internet module is not the same as that for an intranet. One of the major differences is that the Internet module has to take care of the data center's reachability for external users. Another difference is that the design is also dependent on the arrangement that you may have with the service provider. To understand the challenges involved in the Internet module design, you must know how to achieve the following:

- Provide reachability to a specific group of intranet servers for internal users only
- Provide reachability to a specific group of extranet servers, or demilitarized zone (DMZ) servers, for both internal and external users
- Provide reachability to the Internet for the internal users
- Prevent external users from reaching the intranet servers
- Provide a resilient connectivity to the Internet, capable of rerouting over failure of links or service providers

The routing task from the preceding requirements takes on a split-personality characteristic because you have to deal with both internal and external users. The best way to tackle the problem is to divide the problem into two smaller ones:

- Providing Internet reachability for the internal users
- Providing data center reachability for the external users

However, the addressing strategy of the data center has to be formulated before the routing comes into play. A common strategy is to assign a private address range for the intranet servers, whereas the DMZ servers will be assigned with a public address block. After the basic addressing scheme is taken care of, you can then decide how the routing should be done.

Routing for Internal Users

As illustrated in Figure 7-1, routing for internal users must provide reachability to the following:

- Intranet servers
- DMZ servers
- The Internet

Figure 7-1   *Routing for Internal Users*

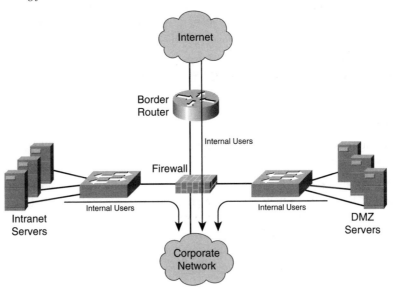

Routing for the internal users relies solely on the Interior Gateway Protocol (IGP) (for example, Open Shortest Path First [OSPF] or Enhanced Interior Gateway Routing Protocol [EIGRP]). In this case, both the address blocks of the intranet and DMZ server subnets are advertised by the IGP and made known to the rest of the network. For access to the Internet, a default route is injected into the network by the border router. In this manner, all traffic destined for the Internet is steered toward the border router.

One thing to take note of with Internet access is the method of routing required between the border router and the service provider. This method depends on the arrangement with the service provider in areas such as addressing, routing, and the redundancy strategy. One method is done via default routing, in which the border router just points a default route to the service provider's network. The other method is to have the border router run a dynamic protocol with the service provider.

The choice between default and dynamic routing depends on the redundancy strategy for the Internet module. When only a single link is providing the Internet access, pointing the default route to the service provider is always recommended, because it is simple to implement. However, the network design can get a little complicated, even with the internal routing, when a resilient design is involved. For example, you may choose to have multiple border routers to provide multiple exit points to the Internet. When there are multiple exit points to the Internet within the network, how do you then decide which border router to use? You may choose to route traffic by the proximity of the source to the border routers, but you may have to consider the cost of sending the traffic to a particular border router, the service level agreement that you may have with a particular service provider, or even performance implications when selecting a particular exit point. Also, you must take care to prevent suboptimal routing and traffic black holes in such a scenario.

The complication with multiple exit points for the Internet is discussed in further detail in the section "Establishing Internet Module Redundancy."

Routing for External Users

As illustrated in Figure 7-2, routing for external users involves providing reachability to the DMZ subnet.

A common strategy is to assign the DMZ servers a public address block. It may be possible for the DMZ servers to be assigned a private address block. However, this involves a more complex implementation with the involvement of NAT, which is covered in the section "Network Address Translation."

Figure 7-2   *Routing for External Users*

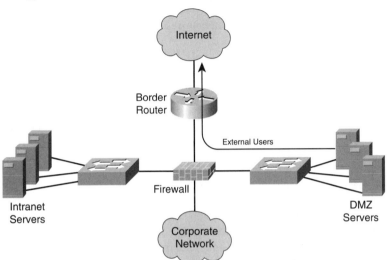

It is important to point out that providing reachability to the DMZ subnet for the external users is governed by the routing arrangement with the service provider. In the event of a corporate network receiving the public address block via the lending scheme and default routing being adopted, the service provider already knows how to reach the DMZ subnet. There is no need to advertise the DMZ address block to the service provider. However, the routing arrangement with the service provider can get really complicated, depending on the addressing scheme and the redundancy strategy being adopted. This is especially so for networks that require multiple connections to the Internet. Depending on the factors such as routing policy, cost of access, or load-balancing requirements, the network design typically involves running dynamic routing with the service providers, as discussed in detail in the next section.

Establishing Internet Module Redundancy

The availability of the Internet module is critical to an organization because business is conducted through the Internet. One important consideration when designing the Internet module is its redundancy strategy. You can achieve a redundant design for the Internet module in various ways, as follows:

- Link-level redundancy
- Device-level redundancy
- ISP-level redundancy
- Site-level redundancy

Each method provides protection against failure at a certain level of the network connectivity. When it comes to the differences between these methods, cost is often a major consideration because it is the single most expansive recurring cost when it comes to Internet connectivity.

Link-Level Redundancy

With Internet connections, the link between the corporate network and the service provider has traditionally been recognized as the weakest link. This is probably due to historical reasons when the WAN was considered unreliable as compared to the internal network links.

Figure 7-3 shows a border router with dual links connected to the service provider. You can achieve link-level redundancy in various ways, depending on the services made available from the service provider. One way is via link-bundling features, such as Multilink PPP (MLP). In MLP, multiple interfaces are bundled together and viewed as a single logical interface. This method achieves link redundancy and improves performance because multiple links are transmitting at the same time.

Figure 7-3 *Link-Level Redundancy*

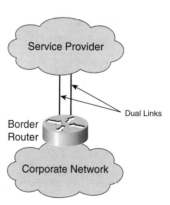

Another way to achieve link redundancy is via on-demand dial backup. In this scenario, an on-demand link is used for backup purposes. The on-demand link can be a simple dial-up line or ISDN. When the primary link fails, the border router brings up the on-demand interface for an alternate connection. With the availability of higher-speed Internet connectivity, the on-demand dial backup solution is becoming less popular because the technology lacks speed. It may not be as helpful to back up a high-speed link, such as a 100-Mbps Ethernet, with a 128-Kbps ISDN link.

For connection to the service provider via a Packet over SONET (POS) interface, link redundancy can be achieved through the implementation of the Automatic Protection

Switching (APS) feature. APS allows for a secondary POS connection to be a backup of the primary connection. In the event of a primary POS connection failure, the secondary takes over immediately.

Link-level redundancy protects the Internet module from a link-related failure. It is usually a straightforward solution, but the link-redundancy scenarios can get complicated as more devices are involved, as illustrated in the next section.

Device-Level Redundancy

Device-level redundancy takes the link-level redundancy strategy a step further. When links are protected, the next single point of failure is the border router itself. To remain connected when the border router fails, a secondary border router needs to be in place, as illustrated in Figure 7-4.

Figure 7-4   *Device-Level Redundancy*

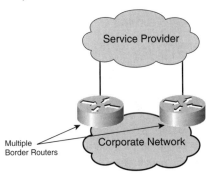

The complication with device-level redundancy lies in the routing design. Default routing is used when there is no routing protocol running between the corporate network and the service provider. The configuration at each of the border routers is straightforward in this case: They both point default routes to the service provider's router. However, it is the propagation of the routing information within the corporate network that is tricky. Because there will be two routers announcing a default route, you have to decide which takes precedence. This requires you to make a decision on how traffic is to leave the corporate network or how the traffic load is going to be split between the two links. In either implementation, you need to implement some form of a floating static route.

Another routing design is to run a dynamic routing protocol between the border routers and the service providers. This design can get really complex because of the various possible combinations of setup. The dynamic routing protocol used in this case will almost always be BGP. Implementation of BGP requires you to have knowledge of concepts such as autonomous system (AS) number and route control via policy propagation. More details on BGP can be found in the section "Border Gateway Protocol" later in this chapter.

ISP-Level Redundancy

ISP-level redundancy, or *multihoming*, is next when you take device-level redundancy one step further. By subscribing Internet connectivity through different service providers, your Internet module is protected when there is a problem in one of the service provider's networks. Another motivation is that it provides traffic load balancing across the multiple service providers. This is done at times when you are trying to improve application characteristics, such as performance and latency. Of course, multihoming design has cost implications and is mostly used by major corporate networks that cannot afford any failure in Internet connectivity.

The challenge with multihoming lies in its addressing and routing complexity, because the address blocks used will not solely belong to any service providers. Routing policy has to be carefully planned out, and you have to know the best practices to advertise routes in order to improve network resiliency. Another implication of multihoming is that service providers cannot aggregate this address block, which leads to an increased load on the overall routing of the Internet systems.

The two addressing options to consider with multihoming are as follows:

- The corporate network uses its own public address block. This is a straightforward implementation in which the address block is advertised to the upstream service providers.

- Use public address blocks assigned by the different service providers. This option is not as common because of the complexity of addressing and routing decisions. For example, you must determine how to allocate the various blocks of public addresses to the servers. In addition, because the addresses were obtained via the lending scheme, when there is a change in the service providers, the part of the server farm that had been using the old public address must be changed to the address provided by the new service provider. Solutions to such a scenario exist, one of which may involve the use of NAT.

Figure 7-5 shows a corporate network "multihomed" to two different service providers. A good place to start to appreciate what is involved in the addressing and routing of a multihomed scenario is RFC 2260, *Scalable Support for Multi-homed Multi-provider Connectivity.* The RFC discusses the implication of increasing multihomed corporate networks on the routing system within the Internet. RFC 2260 also describes various routing and addressing strategies to cater to multihomed networks. As such, it is critical that you have a good understanding of this RFC and its implication on your network.

Figure 7-5   *ISP-Level Redundancy*

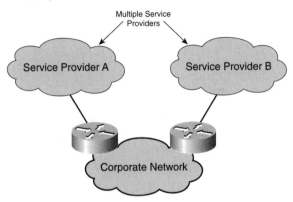

Site-Level Redundancy

Besides connecting to multiple service providers to increase the availability of the Internet module, another strategy is to have multiple border routers residing in multiple sites. This way, when disaster strikes at one location, the network is still reachable via another exit point provided by a remote site or, in some cases, multiple sites. As illustrated in Figure 7-6, a corporate network has two sites, site A and site B, connected via its internal WAN link. The different border routers in those sites connect to different service providers.

Figure 7-6   *Site-Level Redundancy*

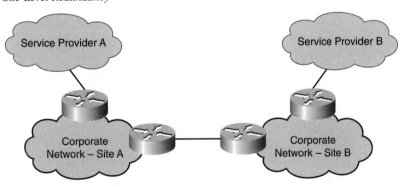

A multisite Internet module is the most costly of all resiliency strategies because real estate cost is involved. In some extremely large corporate networks, it is common to have more than one site residing in different countries. The Cisco Systems internal network is one good example.

Whichever resiliency strategy you adopt, it is always recommended that you are familiar with the BGP routing protocol and the NAT feature. Both of these are critical tools for the Internet module, and they are described in greater detail in the sections "Border Gateway Protocols" and "Network Address Translation."

Implementing Security Measures

With the proliferation of worms, viruses, and DoS attacks, it is not surprising that security is one critical consideration for the Internet module. Many network managers associate security at the Internet module with the placement of a firewall. However, you need more than just a box to protect the network from malicious attacks.

Because attacks such as worms and DoS can cripple a network, their effect is the same as that of a hardware failure or link failure to the Internet. Hence, you can no longer discuss resiliency to the Internet module without talking about security.

Security is a wide topic and warrants extensive research by itself. This section covers security policy and how it affects the design of the Internet module.

Security Policy

Many network managers recognize Figure 7-7 as the basic design of an Internet module: a firewall, border router, and a network carved out into an outside (Internet), inside (corporate network), and DMZ network.

Figure 7-7   *Basic Internet Module Design*

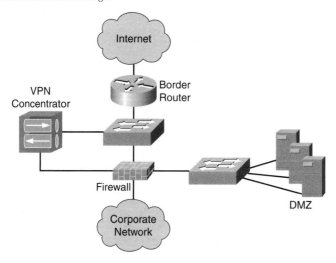

NOTE   This section, "Security Policy," is based on a Cisco Systems presentation titled *Internet-edge Routing Concerns* by James Christopher.

The design in Figure 7-7 may seem straightforward. However, the intricacy of the Internet module lies in the definition of the security policy rather than the actual physical connectivity.

Unlike the rest of the network modules, the starting point of the Internet module design is the security policy. As outlined by Cisco, the following are the five basic principles of a security policy:

- **Identity**—Identifies the hosts and applications that are affected by the policy. Address spoofing, or an attack based on a forged IP address, is a major identity concern in the Internet. As such, this portion of the security policy deals with the problem by taking action based on Layer 3 and Layer 4 information embedded within the IP packet.

- **Trust**—Determines under what condition hosts can communicate with each other. Whereas the traditional way of enforcing trust is via Layer 3 information, sophistication of technology enables you to enforce this even at Layer 2. One good example of the implementation of the private VLAN feature.

- **Enforcement**—Establishes how you implement the policy. The task of enforcement is further broken down to subtasks of secure, monitor, audit, and manage. Securing the infrastructure involves implementation of identity and authentication, encryption, and filtering and stateful inspection of traffic. Monitor deals with intrusion detection and traffic pattern monitoring. Audit is the process where security posture of the network is accessed and vulnerability of the network identified. Manage deals with the actual implementation of the devices, as well as event and data analysis on a day-to-day basis. Collectively, these subtasks help in enforcing the security policy for the network.

- **Risk assessment**—Determines the impact if the policy is breached. Hackers are constantly improving their ways of attack. Although the security policy is being enforced and the network is safe thus far, you will never be sure that it is going to be safe in the future. One important step is to study the impact of a breach. If the consequence proves too much for the corporation, perhaps connection to the Internet needs to be reassessed.

- **Incident response**—Establishes what actions to take when the policy is breached. Network managers should ask themselves whether they know exactly what to do when there is a security breach. In fact, there should be different actions drawn up with respect to different security breaches. Security breaches come in different levels of severity. There are basically five levels of breach:

    - **Known vulnerability**—A defect may be discovered because of a security audit or a vendor's announcements about code defects. This is the least severe because you have time to reconfigure or to apply patches.

— **Reconnaissance**—The network is being scanned and probed and this is when you realize that there may be an impending attack on your network, or at least there is some interest in gaining unlawful access to the network.

— **Misuse**—This is when unauthorized or inappropriate network activity is discovered.

— **Attack**—This is when the actual action of compromising the network resources is taking place.

— **Compromised**—This is when the attack was successful and the resulting network may or may not be functioning, depending on the severity of the attack.

Basic security policies for the network should encompass these five principles. An essential part of the configuration of the Internet module encompasses these principles and is done through a series of filtering, as shown in the next section.

Filtering at the Internet Module

Part of the security requirement for the Internet module is achieved through the implementation of a series of filters planted at the border routers. These filters, known as transit access control lists (ACLs), are an important first line of defense against malicious activities.

The border routers of the Internet module provide the first line of defense through the deployment of inbound ACLs. These ACLs allow only permitted traffic to the DMZ server farm and for internal users to exit to the Internet. All unauthorized traffic should be dropped on the interface facing the Internet.

In general, the inbound ACLs should perform the following tasks:

- Basic filtering for private, special-use address and antispoofing measures. This task denies address space as stipulated in RFC 1918. It also prevents traffic with source addresses that belong to the special-use address space as defined in RFC 3330, *Special-Use IPv4 Addresses*. In addition, this task prevents traffic with source addresses belonging to the internal network from entering via the Internet-facing interface. You can find the antispoofing guidelines in RFC 2827, *Network Ingress Filtering: Defeating Denial of Service Attacks Which Employ IP Source Address Spoofing*.

- Explicitly permit return traffic for internal connections to the Internet. This traffic may include the following:

  — Specific Internet Control Message Protocol (ICMP) types

  — Outbound Domain Name System (DNS) query replies

  — Established TCP traffic

  — User Datagram Protocol (UDP) return traffic

  — File Transfer Protocol (FTP) data connections

- Explicitly permit external traffic destined to the DMZ or a predefined address block. These may include the following:
  - HTTP traffic
  - Virtual Private Network (VPN) traffic
  - Simple Mail Transfer Protocol (SMTP)
  - Inbound FTP data connections
  - Inbound DNS traffic
- Explicitly deny other traffic.

Example 7-1 shows a sample configuration. It is important to further develop the following to suit your network environment before implementing it.

Example 7-1 *Sample Filtering at the Internet Module*

```
Router#configure terminal
!Add anti-spoofing entries.
!Deny special-use address sources.
!Refer to RFC 3330 for additional special use addresses.
Router(config)#access-list 110 deny ip 127.0.0.0 0.255.255.255 any
Router(config)#access-list 110 deny ip 192.0.2.0 0.0.0.255 any
Router(config)#access-list 110 deny ip 224.0.0.0 31.255.255.255 any
Router(config)#access-list 110 deny ip host 255.255.255.255 any
!The deny statement below should not be configured
!on Dynamic Host Configuration Protocol (DHCP) relays.
Router(config)#access-list 110 deny ip host 0.0.0.0 any
!Filter RFC 1918 space.
Router(config)#access-list 110 deny ip 10.0.0.0 0.255.255.255 any
Router(config)#access-list 110 deny ip 172.16.0.0 0.15.255.255 any
Router(config)#access-list 110 deny ip 192.168.0.0 0.0.255.255 any
!Permit Border Gateway Protocol (BGP) to the edge router.
Router(config)#access-list 110 permit tcp host bgp_peer IP gt 1023 host edge
  router_ip eq bgp
Router(config)#access-list 110 permit tcp host bgp_peer IP eq bgp host edge
  router_ip gt 1023
!Deny your space as source (as noted in RFC 2827).
Router(config)#access-list 110 deny ip your Internet-routable subnet any
!Explicitly permit return traffic. Allow specific ICMP types.
Router(config)#access-list 110 permit icmp any any echo-reply
Router(config)#access-list 110 permit icmp any any unreachable
Router(config)#access-list 110 permit icmp any any time-exceeded
Router(config)#access-list 110 deny   icmp any any
!Outgoing DNS queries are shown below.
Router(config)#access-list 110 permit udp any eq 53  host primary DNS server IP gt
  1023
!Permit older DNS queries and replies to primary DNS server.
Router(config)#access-list 110 permit udp any eq 53  host primary DNS server IP eq 53
!Permit legitimate business traffic.
Router(config)#access-list 110 permit tcp any Internet-routable subnet established
Router(config)#access-list 110 permit udp any range 1 1023 Internet-routable subnet
  gt 1023
!Internet-sourced connections to publicly accessible servers are shown below
Router(config)#access-list 110 permit tcp any host public web server IP eq 80
```

continues

Example 7-1   *Sample Filtering at the Internet Module (Continued)*

```
Router(config)#access-list 110 permit tcp any host public web server IP eq 443
Router(config)#access-list 110 permit tcp any host public FTP server IP eq 21
!Data connections to the FTP server are allowed
!by the permit established ACE.
!Allow PASV data connections to the FTP server.
Router(config)#access-list 110 permit tcp any gt 1023 host public FTP server IP gt
  1023
Router(config)#access-list 110 permit tcp any host public SMTP server IP eq 25
!Explicitly deny all other traffic.
Router(config)#access-list 101 deny ip any any
```

Although the guidelines seem simple to follow, the difficult part in developing transit ACL is in determining what traffic or protocol is allowed and what is not allowed for your network. It is important that you find out what is applicable within your network, because not all networks are the same. Some basic protocols are common to most networks, however. For example, if you have a web server in the DMZ that provides information for external users, you need to permit TCP traffic to the DMZ via port 80. The task of developing the transit ACL is extremely important, because any mistake you make here can have drastic consequences, such as denying legitimate traffic or, in the worst case, exposing some servers or applications to hacking.

As part of the implementation of the transit ACL, here are some good points to remember:

- Never allow a direct connection to be initiated by an external host to an internal host. At no time can this rule be bent.

- In the event that you allow external hosts to initiate a connection to a host within your network, place the internal host in the DMZ.

- Be extremely careful with ICMP and UDP traffic flowing both in and out of the Internet module. Although DNS traffic, such as zone updates, may be allowed, you have to be strict with other ICMP or UDP traffic.

- Avoid an application design that makes use of tunneling or port redirection (for example, remote desktop or file system redirection).

- An antispoofing mechanism has to be applied on the Internet connection; RFC 2827 is a mandatory literature. The intent of anti-spoofing is to make sure that traffic from the Internet is not trying to spoof an internal address.

- All management traffic must be encrypted. For this, the Cisco IOS code with Secure Shell (SSH) is recommended. (SSH is a more secure alternative to Telnet.) For a device that is manageable via the web, SSL has to be implemented. For authentication and logging purposes, facilities such as Terminal Access Controller Access Control System (TACACS) have to be in place.

- NAT can be used to protect internal hosts from being directly connected via an external host.

- Traffic from the Internet should neither be sourced nor destined to a private IP address. Therefore, private IP filtering has to be in place at the border router.

- To provide remote access via the Internet, the VPN termination can be done on the firewall or parallel to the firewall, if there is a separate device. In other words, remote-access traffic needs to be scrutinized by the firewall.

- Stateful inspection has to be implemented so that packets that fail to match a proper TCP state are dropped.

- Rate limiting of traffic may be implemented based on a set threshold. Rate limiting proves useful to control traffic so as to prevent excessive bandwidth consumption.

Figure 7-8 shows the significance of the various security measures in the Internet module. Because security is a big topic by itself, you are advised to refer to documentation that offers a more in-depth discussion. A good point of reference is the Cisco SAFE Blueprint at the following URL:

http://www.cisco.com/en/US/netsol/ns340/ns394/ns171/ns128/ networking_solutions_package.html

Figure 7-8 *Various Security Measures in the Internet Module*

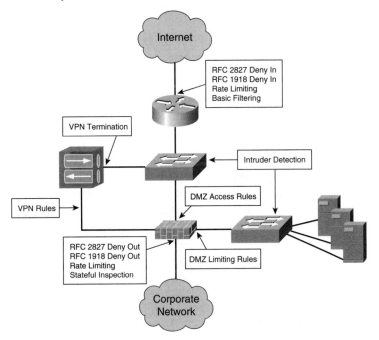

Resilient Border Gateway Protocol (BGP) Design

The BGP is an interdomain routing protocol used to exchange routing information between autonomous systems. It is the *de facto* standard for routing within the Internet.

With more and more corporate networks getting connected to the Internet, BGP is becoming an integral part of the Internet module within a corporate network's IP infrastructure. With the growing importance of ensuring continuous operation for the Internet, much research and development efforts have been spent on improving the protocol in the area of resiliency and process optimization.

Because BGP is responsible for the Internet connection for a network, its operational status is critical to the overall health of the network. One common comment about BGP as a protocol is its slowness in response to network events, and as such, its slow convergence. This is in part due to its scanner process, which is scheduled once every 60 seconds. Since its inception, BGP has not only undergone updates and expansion in features, but much work has been done on improving its response to network events and its convergence. For a good refresher on BGP, you may want to refer to *Internet Routing Architectures*, Second Edition, by Sam Halabi (Cisco Press, 2000).

The following sections illustrate some of the improvements to BGP, including soft reconfiguration, convergence optimization, next-hop address tracking, fast peering session deactivation, and IP event dampening.

BGP Soft Reconfiguration

In BGP, the exchange of routes between two autonomous systems is maintained by the eBGP peering session between the border routers. The border routers' behaviors are governed by the routing policies, which include configurations such as route map, filter list, and distribute list. Whenever there is a change in the routing policies on either side, the BGP session has to be cleared for the new policy to take effect. There are two ways to clear the BGP sessions:

- Hard reset
- Soft reset

When the BGP session is cleared with the hard reset option, the route cache of the router is flushed, causing a loss of routing information. When this happens, the router, or the network, is no longer able to forward traffic to its neighbor network. In soft reset, the routing table is not flushed and, therefore, the impact on the router is minimal. Soft reset is preferred over the hard reset because its impact on the overall network is minimal.

Soft reset can be used for both inbound and outbound updates. When it is used to generate inbound updates from a neighbor, it is called an *inbound soft reset*. There are two ways to perform an inbound soft reset:

- **Using stored routing update information** —In this method, in order not to reset the BGP session, the router needs to store all received updates from its neighbor without modifications. This requires a lot of memory resources and is an operation that is detrimental to the well-being of the router. This is also known as the soft-reconfiguration inbound feature.

- **Using dynamic soft reset**—This method is an improvement over the first, because it provides for automatic support for dynamic soft reset that does not depend on the stored routing updates. This is done through the enhancement to the BGP code within the IOS. Therefore, it requires less memory and is the preferred method. This enhancement over the first is also called the *route refresh* capability. The first method needs preconfiguration, whereas the enhanced method does not need configuration.

When the soft reset feature is used to send a new set of updates to a neighbor, it is called an *outbound soft reset*. There is only one way to perform outbound soft reset: dynamic soft reset.

With the enhanced method, no preconfiguration is required. However, you need to verify that the peer supports the route refresh capability via the **show ip bgp neighbors** command. In Figure 7-9, router R15 has an external peer, R16, that supports the soft reset capability.

Figure 7-9 *BGP Peer with Route Refresh Capability*

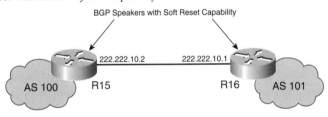

When its external peer supports this capability, the message highlighted in Example 7-2 displays on R15.

Example 7-2 *Status of BGP Peer with Route Refresh Capability*

```
R15#show ip bgp neighbors 222.222.10.1
BGP neighbor is 222.222.10.1,  remote AS 101, external link
  BGP version 4, remote router ID 222.222.10.1
  BGP state = Established, up for 00:00:24
  Last read 00:00:24, hold time is 180, keepalive interval is 60 seconds
  Neighbor capabilities:
    Route refresh: advertised and received(old & new)
    Address family BGP IPv4: advertised and received
```

With the route refresh capability, you can then issue the following command on R15 to reset the inbound routing table:

```
R15#clear ip bgp 222.222.10.1 in
```

For outbound soft reset, you can issue the following command:

```
R15#clear ip bgp 222.222.10.1 out
```

On the other hand, R14 peers with R13, which does not have the soft reset capability. The status message on R14 looks different from R15's when its peer does not support the soft reset feature, as shown in Example 7-3.

Example 7-3 *Status of BGP Peer Without Soft Reset Capability*

```
R14#show ip bgp neighbors 222.222.10.6
BGP neighbor is 222.222.10.6,  remote AS 103, external link
  BGP version 4, remote router ID 222.222.10.6
  BGP state = Established, up for 00:00:22
  Last read 00:00:22, hold time is 180, keepalive interval is 60 seconds
  Neighbor capabilities:
    Route refresh: advertised
    Address family IPv4 Unicast: advertised and received
```

In this case, the preconfiguration method (soft-reconfiguration inbound) may be considered. However, the performance impact on the router has to be examined carefully. Example 7-4 shows the preconfiguration method of inbound soft reset.

Example 7-4 *Inbound Soft Reset with Preconfiguration*

```
Router A
interface serial 1/0
ip address 222.222.10.5 255.255.255.252
router bgp 100
 neighbor 222.222.10.6 remote-as 103
 neighbor 222.222.10.6 soft-reconfiguration inbound
```

With the preconfigured inbound soft reset, the status of the peer is reflected in Example 7-5.

Example 7-5 *BGP Status with Soft Reset Preconfiguration*

```
R14#show ip bgp neighbors 5.5.5.11
BGP neighbor is 5.5.5.11,  remote AS 103, external link
  BGP version 4, remote router ID 5.5.5.11
  BGP state = Established, up for 00:00:13
  Last read 00:00:13, hold time is 180, keepalive interval is 60 seconds
  Neighbor capabilities:
    Route refresh: advertised
    Address family IPv4 Unicast: advertised and received
    IPv4 MPLS Label capability:
  Received 133 messages, 0 notifications, 0 in queue
  Sent 139 messages, 0 notifications, 0 in queue
  Default minimum time between advertisement runs is 30 seconds

 For address family: IPv4 Unicast
  BGP table version 1, neighbor version 1
  Index 3, Offset 0, Mask 0x8
  Inbound soft reconfiguration allowed
  Route refresh request: received 0, sent 0
  0 accepted prefixes consume 0 bytes
  Prefix advertised 0, suppressed 0, withdrawn 0
```

The BGP soft reconfiguration feature allows for policies to be changed without affecting the BGP session. When you maintain the BGP session, the routing of the network is kept in steady state and, thus, operation of the network is not impacted.

BGP Convergence Optimization

BGP convergence optimization refers to a series of IOS code enhancements and configuration recommendations to improve BGP's convergence performance. Basically, the IOS developers look at the various factors that are involved in the BGP operation and look for ways to improve these individual factors to contribute to the overall performance. These factors include the following:

- TCP frame optimization
- Input queues
- Maximum transmission unit (MTU) size
- Update packing
- Peer group

A BGP speaker relies on a TCP session for its interaction with its peer. Before the enhancement, the BGP process did not fully make use of the available TCP frame size for its transmission. This results in slow update propagation. Enhancement was made to the IOS code to improve on this.

From experience, a BGP speaker experiences a large number of dropped TCP acknowledgments when sending updates to multiple peers. This degrades the BGP performance and affects convergence. This is in part due to the default input queue size of the interface being swamped by the TCP acknowledgments. By changing the queue size to 4096 via the **hold-queue** command, you can greatly reduce the number of dropped TCP acknowledgments and will see a marked improvement in performance.

The default TCP maximum segment size (MSS) is 536 bytes on a router. This setting may not be efficient for today's network, especially with high-speed interfaces such as Gigabit Ethernet. The efficiency of the BGP process can be improved if the MSS is optimized with respect to the interface used. You can do this via the **ip tcp path-mtu-discovery** command.

A BGP update consists of a list of network layer reachability information (NLRI) that shares same attributes. The more NLRI sent within an update, the more efficient the BGP process will be. This is what update packing tries to achieve. The improvement to convergence varies with update packing, because this depends on the attributes and the table size.

When a BGP speaker needs to send updates to its peer, it needs to go through its table once and subject the prefixes to the outbound policies. This has to be done once on a per-peer basis. When multiple peers are involved, especially with a large prefix table, this process becomes a control-plane-intensive exercise and convergence takes a long time. The solution to this is to make use of the peer group feature. With the peer group feature, the update generation needs to be done only once and sent to a peer group leader. The update is then replicated by the leader to peer members. Update generation still requires walking through the prefix table and outbound policies, but update replication does not have to be and is more efficient. The improvement to convergence can be significant, especially with a large peer group.

You can achieve a vast improvement to the BGP convergence via the combination of the above enhancements and configuration recommendations. With a more efficient BGP process and improved convergence, the resiliency of the Internet module can be greatly improved.

BGP Next-Hop Address Tracking

The BGP next-hop address tracking feature obsoletes the BGP scanner process, and allows BGP to respond quickly to changes to the next hop so as to improve its convergence time.

As mentioned, the BGP scanner is a process that monitors the next-hop state so as to ascertain the validity of the installed routes. By default, this process does its job every 60 seconds. Therefore, any network failure that relates to the next hop will not be handled by BGP until the next scanning cycle. With the next-hop address tracking feature, any changes to the next-hop status is quickly reported to the BGP protocol. This bypasses the 60-second requirement and improves BGP's capability to respond to network events. This also removes the control-plane load introduced by the scanner process and, therefore, improves the overall performance and stability of the router.

This feature is available in Cisco IOS Releases 12.0(29)S and 12.3(14)T and later, and is enabled by default. However, you may choose to turn it off with the commands shown in Example 7-6.

Example 7-6 *Disabling BGP Next-Hop Address Tracking*

```
router#config terminal
router(config)#router bgp 100
router(config-router)#address-family ipv4 unicast
router(config-router-af)#no bgp nexthop trigger enable
```

BGP Support for Fast Peering Session Deactivation

The BGP support for the fast peering session deactivation feature is part of the overall BGP convergence improvement effort. This event-driven feature allows BGP to monitor its peering sessions with its neighbors. Upon detection of a loss of session due to whatever reason, this feature allows BGP to terminate the session immediately, bypassing the scanner cycle and the BGP hold timer, which is 3 minutes by default. This way, BGP can clean up routes in a much faster manner, and thus improve its convergence time.

This feature is available in Cisco IOS Releases 12.0(29)S and 12.3(14)T and later. Example 7-7 shows a sample configuration.

Example 7-7   *Enabling BGP Fast Peering Session Deactivation*

```
router#config terminal
router(config)#router bgp 100
router(config-router)#address-family ipv4 unicast
router(config-router-af)#neighbor 10.1.1.1 remote-as 101
router(config-router-af)#neighbor 10.1.1.1 fall-over
```

BGP Route Dampening

An observation that you can make with a router running BGP is that it goes through a series of steps to make sure all routes that it learned are in place before introducing these routes into its forwarding table, and before advertising the routes to its BGP peers. Therefore, when an external route is toggling between available and unavailable in rapid successions (better known as route flap), not only does the router need to process this change of states, but it also needs to send out the withdrawal and update messages to its peers. Route flap is bad because it causes load on the control plane of the routers running BGP, and, in the worst case, it actually has the same effect as a DoS attack on itself.

BGP route dampening is a feature that reduces the effect of route flap in the functioning of the BGP process. It introduces an exponential decay mechanism, which is configurable, so that this effect can be minimized. If the route is dampened, the BGP will not take its status into consideration until it has stopped flapping. With the route-dampening feature, the control plane of the router is protected, unnecessary network convergence can be prevented, and network stability is greatly enhanced.

Example 7-8 shows the command used to configure BGP route dampening with default values.

Example 7-8   *Configuring BGP Route Dampening*

```
R2#configure terminal
R2(config)#router bgp 100
R2(config-router)#bgp dampening
```

Example 7-9 shows the BGP dampening status of a router.

Example 7-9   *Displaying BGP Dampening Status*

```
R2#show ip bgp dampening parameters
dampening 15 750 2000 60 (DEFAULT)
  Half-life time      : 15 mins     Decay Time       : 2320 secs
  Max suppress penalty: 12000       Max suppress time: 60 mins
  Suppress penalty    :  2000       Reuse penalty    : 750
R2#
```

Nonstop Forwarding with Stateful Switchover (NSF/SSO) for BGP

The Nonstop Forwarding with Stateful Switchover (NSF/SSO) feature allows a router with dual route processors to maximize its overall availability. With NSO/SSO, when the primary route processor fails, the standby route processor can take over the operation of the router with minimal traffic disruption. As illustrated in Chapter 3, "Fundamentals of IP Resilient Networks," unlike Route Processor Redundancy Plus (RPR+), NSF/SSO allows the router to maintain the data link layer connections and continue forwarding packets during the switchover to the secondary processor. The forwarding operation continues to take place even though there is a loss in routing protocol peerings. As the router recovers, routing protocols continue to be restored dynamically in the background until everything is back to normal.

In normal BGP operation, when there is a switchover of route processors in a local router, the TCP connection between the local router and its remote peer is taken down. Therefore, the remote peer starts to clear all routes that are associated with this local router and stops forwarding traffic to it. With the NSF/SSO for BGP feature, this does not happen. It essentially allows the remote router to continue its forwarding operation to the local router when such a catastrophic event occurs. This is essentially the combination of the NSF/SSO feature and enhancements that have been made to the BGP protocol.

Suppose that you intend to turn on the NSF/SSO for BGP in your local router, which has been installed with dual route processors. For NSF/SSO for BGP to work in the local router, several conditions must be met:

- The local and remote router must agree to support the BGP graceful restart feature.
- The remote router must not prematurely declare the local router as unavailable when switchover occurs.
- The remote router must not communicate the state change (the switchover) to other peers. This is to avoid a network convergence from taking place.
- The remote router must send BGP updates to help the local router restore its BGP table.
- The remote router must have a way to tell the local router that it has finished sending the updates.
- While all this is taking place, the remote router must mark all routes associated with the local router as "stale." However, it must continue to forward traffic destined for the local router.

The NSF/SSO for BGP feature requires the participation of remote devices for it to work. However, not every device has a dual processor configuration. Therefore, new concepts have been introduced: NSF capable and NSF aware. An NSF-capable device has dual processors and is running the same feature. On the other hand, a NSF-aware device has only a single processor but is capable of participating in the protocol. Therefore, whenever a device is neither NSF capable nor NSF aware, normal BGP routing behavior takes place.

That means there will be traffic disruption when there is a processor switchover, because the TCP connections for the two peers are taken down.

Because the operation of the NSF/SSO for BGP involves maintaining states across the two route processors within the same router, it requires compatible hardware to be installed. As such, care must be taken before enabling this feature. The following are implementation guidelines:

- **Cisco 12000 series router**—Route processors must be of the same type. That is, a GRP route processor may be used only with another GRP route processor. And a PRP route processor may be used only with another PRP.

- **Cisco 10000 series router**—Route processors must be of the same type. That is, a PRE-1 route processor may be used only with another PRE-1 route processor. And PRE-2 may be used only with another PRE-2.

- **Cisco 7500 series router**—RSP-2 and RSP-4 may be used together, and RSP-8 and RSP-16 may be used together. However, these two groups of processors cannot be used together.

Figure 7-10 illustrates a sample setup for NSF/SSO for BGP between two routers, R1 and R2. R1 is configured with two route processors running in SSO mode.

Figure 7-10 *Setup for NSF/SSO for BGP*

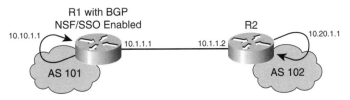

The first step in configuring NSF/SSO for BGP is to ascertain the redundancy level of the router as a whole, as shown in Example 7-10.

Example 7-10 *Determining the Redundancy Status of a Router*

```
R1#show redundancy
Redundant System Information :
------------------------------
       Available system uptime = 4 days, 4 hours, 26 minutes, 11 seconds
 Switchovers system experienced = 0
             Standby failures = 1
       Last switchover reason = none

              Hardware Mode = Duplex
   Configured Redundancy Mode = SSO
    Operating Redundancy Mode = SSO
            Maintenance Mode = Disabled
              Communications = Up
```

continues

Example 7-10 *Determining the Redundancy Status of a Router (Continued)*

```
Current Processor Information :
------------------------------
              Active Location = slot 4
        Current Software state = ACTIVE
      Uptime in current state = 4 days, 4 hours, 25 minutes, 55 seconds
                 Image Version = Cisco Internetwork Operating System Software
IOS (tm) GS Software (C12KPRP-P-M), Version 12.0(28)S1, RELEASE SOFTWARE (fc1)
Technical Support: http://www.cisco.com/techsupport
Copyright© 1986-2004 by cisco Systems, Inc.
Compiled Fri 27-Aug-04 21:13 by hqluong
                          BOOT = bootflash:c12kprp-p-mz.120-28.S1.bin,1;
                   CONFIG_FILE =
                       BOOTLDR =
        Configuration register = 0x2102

Peer Processor Information :
---------------------------
              Standby Location = slot 5
        Current Software state = STANDBY HOT
      Uptime in current state = 1 minute, 6 seconds
                 Image Version = Cisco Internetwork Operating System Software
IOS (tm) GS Software (C12KPRP-P-M), Version 12.0(28)S1, RELEASE SOFTWARE (fc1)
Technical Support: http://www.cisco.com/techsupport
Copyright© 1986-2004 by cisco Systems, Inc.
Compiled Fri 27-Aug-04 21:13 by hqluong
                          BOOT = bootflash:c12kprp-p-mz.120-28.S1.bin,1;
                   CONFIG_FILE =
                       BOOTLDR =
        Configuration register = 0x2102
R1#
```

After the redundancy of the router R1 has been confirmed, the actual configuration of the protocol can begin. Example 7-11 shows a sample configuration for NSF/SSO for BGP on router R1.

Example 7-11 *Configuring BGP with NSF/SSO on R1*

```
router bgp 101
 no synchronization
 bgp log-neighbor-changes
 bgp graceful-restart restart-time 120
 bgp graceful-restart stalepath-time 360
 bgp graceful-restart
 network 10.10.1.1 mask 255.255.255.255
 neighbor 10.1.1.2 remote-as 102
 no auto-summary
```

Example 7-12 shows a sample configuration for NSF/SSO for BGP on router R2.

Example 7-12 *Configuring BGP with NSF/SSO on R2*

```
router bgp 102
 no synchronization
 bgp log-neighbor-changes
 bgp graceful-restart restart-time 120
 bgp graceful-restart stalepath-time 360
 bgp graceful-restart
 network 10.20.1.1 mask 255.255.255.255
 neighbor 10.1.1.1 remote-as 101
 no auto-summary
```

When the eBGP peering between the two routers has been established, the BGP status of R1 is as illustrated in Example 7-13.

Example 7-13 *BGP Status of R1*

```
R1#show ip bgp neighbors 10.1.1.2
BGP neighbor is 10.1.1.2,  remote AS 102, external link
  BGP version 4, remote router ID 10.20.1.1
  BGP state = Established, up for 00:20:36
  Last read 00:00:36, hold time is 180, keepalive interval is 60 seconds
  Neighbor capabilities:
    Route refresh: advertised and received(new)
    Address family IPv4 Unicast: advertised and received
    Graceful Restart Capability: advertised and received
      Remote Restart timer is 120 seconds
      Address families preserved by peer:
        IPv4 Unicast
```

Likewise, the BGP status of R2 is as illustrated in Example 7-14.

Example 7-14 *BGP Status of R2*

```
R2#show ip bgp neighbors 10.1.1.1
BGP neighbor is 10.1.1.1,  remote AS 101, external link
  BGP version 4, remote router ID 10.10.1.1
  BGP state = Established, up for 00:21:47
  Last read 00:00:47, hold time is 180, keepalive interval is 60 seconds
  Neighbor capabilities:
    Route refresh: advertised and received(new)
    Address family IPv4 Unicast: advertised and received
    Graceful Restart Capability: advertised and received
      Remote Restart timer is 120 seconds
      Address families preserved by peer:
        IPv4 Unicast
```

Because the two routers are running with no hardware issued at the beginning, a show of BGP route status and its forwarding table in R2 is as shown in Example 7-15.

Example 7-15 *Route Status of R2*

```
R2#show ip bgp
BGP table version is 3, local router ID is 10.20.1.1
Status codes: s suppressed, d damped, h history, * valid, > best, i - internal,
              r RIB-failure, S Stale
Origin codes: i - IGP, e - EGP, ? - incomplete

   Network          Next Hop          Metric LocPrf Weight Path
*> 10.10.1.1/32     10.1.1.1               0             0 101 i
*> 10.20.1.1/32     0.0.0.0                0         32768 i

R2#show ip cef 10.10.1.1
10.10.1.1/32, version 15, epoch 0, cached adjacency 10.1.1.1
0 packets, 0 bytes
  via 10.1.1.1, 0 dependencies, recursive
    next hop 10.1.1.1, SRP0/0 via 10.1.1.1/32 (Default)
    valid cached adjacency
```

Notice that the route to the loopback interface of R1, 10.10.1.1, is reflected in BGP as a valid and best path. In addition, the forwarding table in R2 shows valid information for the route and its next-hop interface. To show the effect of turning on NSF/SSO for BGP, initiate an extended ping session from the loopback interface of R2 to the loopback interface of R1. This is to ensure that both the forwarding tables of the routers have to be utilized for this experiment. Now, suppose the primary route processor in R1 encounters a problem during the experiment and is forced to switch over to the secondary route processor. Example 7-16 shows what happens in R2.

Example 7-16 *Detecting Route Processor Switchover of Its Peer in R2*

```
R2#ping
Protocol [ip]:
Target IP address: 10.10.1.1
Repeat count [5]: 80000
Datagram size [100]:
Timeout in seconds [2]:
Extended commands [n]: y
Source address or interface: 10.20.1.1
Type of service [0]:
Set DF bit in IP header? [no]:
Validate reply data? [no]:
Data pattern [0xABCD]:
Loose, Strict, Record, Timestamp, Verbose[none]:
Sweep range of sizes [n]:
Type escape sequence to abort.
Sending 80000, 100-byte ICMP Echos to 10.10.1.1, timeout is 2 seconds:
!!!!!!!!!!!!!!!!!!!!!!!!!!!!!!!!!!!!!!!!!!!!!!!!!!!!!!!!!!!!!!!!!!!!!!!!!!!!
!!!!!!!!!!!!!!!!!!!!!!!!!!!!!!!!!!!!!!!!!!!!!!!!!!!!!!!!!!!!!!!!!!!!!!!!!!!!
!output omitted for brevity
```

Example 7-16 *Detecting Route Processor Switchover of Its Peer in R2 (Continued)*

```
4d05h: %BGP-5-ADJCHANGE: neighbor 10.1.1.1 Down NSF peer closed the
session!!!!!!!!!!!!!!!!!!!!!!!!!!!!!!!!!!!!!!!!!!!!!!!!!!!!!!!!!
!!!!!!!!!!!!!!!!!!!!!!!!!!!!!!!!!!!!!!!!!!!!!!!!!!!!!!!!!!!!!!!!!!!!!!!!
!!!!!!!!!!!!!!!!!!!!!!!!!!!!!!!!!!!!!!!!!!!!!!!!!!!!!!!!!!!!!!!!!!!!!!!!
!!!!!!!!!!!!!!!!!!!!!!!!!!!!!!!!!!!!!!!!!!!!!!!!!!!!!!!!!!!!!!!!!!!!!!!!
!!!!!!!!!!!!!!!!!!!!!!!!!!!!!!!!!!!!!!!!!!!!!!!!!!!!!!!!!!!!!!!!!!!!!!!!
!output omitted for brevity
4d05h: %BGP-5-ADJCHANGE: neighbor 10.1.1.1 Up !!!!!!!!!!!!!!!!!!!!!!
!!!!!!!!!!!!!!!!!!!!!!!!!!!!!!!!!!!!!!!!!!!!!!!!!!!!!!!!!!!!!!!!!!!!!!!!
!!!!!!!!!!!!!!!!!!!!!!!!!!!!!!!!!!!!!!!!!!!!!!!!!!!!!!!!!!!!!!!!!!!!!!!!
!!!!!!!!!!!!!!!!!!!!!!!!!!!!!!!!!!!!!!!!!!!!!!!!!!!!!!!
!!!!!!!!!!!!!!!!!!!!!!!!!!!!!!!!!!!!!!!!!!!!!!!!!!!!!!!!!!!!!!!!!!!!!!!!
!!!!!!!!!!!!!!!!!!!!!!!!!!!!!!!!!!!!!!!!!!!!!!!!!!!!!!!!!!!!!!
Success rate is 100 percent (80000/80000), round-trip min/avg/max = 1/1/4 ms
R2#
```

Notice that half way through the experiment, R2 detected that its neighbor has closed the BGP session, but it continues to forward the ping request. Likewise, R1 continues to reply to the ping request while its secondary route processor is taking over the control-plane function. Along the way, the BGP session is reestablished; the final result is seen at the bottom of the screen, which states a zero drop performance. In addition, notice that the latency is barely affected, with a range of 1 to 4 milliseconds.

As part of the NSF/SSO for BGP feature, after the BGP session is reestablished, BGP updates take place in the background so that R1 can rebuild its BGP table. This is reflected in the **debug** session of R2 shown in Example 7-17.

Example 7-17 *BGP Updates on R2*

```
Router#
4d05h: %BGP-5-ADJCHANGE: neighbor 10.1.1.1 Up
4d05h: BGP(0): Begin update run for versions 1->4 for 1 update groups
4d05h: BGPNSF(0): send End-of-RIB for IPv4 Unicast to neighbor 10.1.1.1
4d05h: BGP(0): End update run for versions 1->4 (0ms), 1/1/0 updates formatted/e
nqueued/replicated, formatting was not aborted, enqueuing was not aborted, 1 att
rs - 1 nets visited
4d05h: BGPNSF(0): rcvd End-of-RIB for IPv4 Unicast from 10.1.1.1
4d05h: BGPNSF(0): Receiving router rcvd End-of-RIB from restarting peer 10.1.1.1
4d05h: BGP(0): Reset update-group 1 versions from 4 to (cand 10.1.1.1) 4
4d05h: BGPNSF: service NSF requests for AF IPv4 Unicast
4d05h: BGPNSF: NSF processing for IPv4 Unicast paths completed
4d05h: BGPNSF: service NSF requests for AF IPv6 Unicast
4d05h: BGPNSF: NSF processing for IPv6 Unicast paths completed
4d05h: BGPNSF: service NSF requests for AF VPNv4 Unicast
4d05h: BGPNSF: NSF processing for VPNv4 Unicast paths completed
4d05h: BGPNSF: service NSF requests for AF IPv4 Multicast
4d05h: BGPNSF: NSF processing for IPv4 Multicast paths completed
4d05h: BGPNSF: service NSF requests for AF IPv6 Multicast
4d05h: BGPNSF: NSF processing for IPv6 Multicast paths completed
4d05h: BGP(0): Reset update-group 1 versions from 4 to (cand 10.1.1.1) 4
```

NSF/SSO for BGP is a big step forward in terms of improving the stability and availability of routes that rely on BGP. With this feature, traffic continues to be forwarded even though there is a switchover of the route processors because of a fault.

The various enhancements made to BGP have resulted in improved resiliency of the Internet module. With proper design and configuration of the Internet module, you can achieve highly available Internet connectivity to support the business functions.

Using Network Address Translation (NAT)

NAT, as originally defined in RFC 1631, *The IP Network Address Translator (NAT)*, was proposed to be a short-term solution to solve the Internet IP address depletion problem. The RFC is subsequently obsoleted by RFC 3022, *Traditional IP Network Address Translator (Traditional NAT)*, which introduces the term *traditional NAT* to include both the basic NAT and Network Address Port Translation (NAPT). NAPT is also commonly known as *Protocol Address Translation (PAT)*. In this section, the term NAT loosely means traditional NAT.

NAT plays an important role in the overall Internet connectivity strategy. This is especially so for small companies that have more hosts needing Internet access than the public IP addresses that have been allocated. In fact, most of the time, there is only one public address assigned by the service provider, which has to be shared. Even for large enterprises that have no issue with the availability of the public IP addresses, NAT can prove useful in other situations (for example, to prevent direct connection between a client and a server to minimize DoS attacks).

With the NAT feature playing a vital role in the Internet module, it is important that you are familiar with it and understand its implication with respect to its effect on routing and application behaviors. A good source of information is the NAT resource page from the following URL:

http://www.cisco.com/en/US/tech/tk648/tk361/tk438/tsd_technology_support_sub-protocol_home.html

Enhanced NAT Resiliency

Many enhancements have been made to the IOS NAT implementation, allowing for flexible deployment to satisfy many networking requirements. In the following sections, you learn about the enhancements that are of importance with respect to resilient IP communication:

- NAT with route map
- Static mapping with Hot Standby Routing Protocol (HSRP) support
- Stateful NAT (SNAT)
- Limiting NAT entries
- Multihoming with NAT

NAT with Route Map

Dynamic NAT can be implemented with a route map rather than an access list. With route maps, you can match traffic based on an access list, next-hop IP address, output interface, or a combination of each to determine which address pool to use.

The combination of dynamic NAT with route map enables you to implement a multihomed design. For example, you can have a design where the inside network is multihomed to different service providers. With the feature, the same inside local address can be translated to different inside global addresses, depending on which service provider the traffic is bound for.

In Figure 7-11, a router is multihomed to the Internet by connecting through interface serial 0 to Internet service provider ISP-1, which has assigned the 192.168.1.0/24 address space. It is connected through interface serial 1 to ISP-2, which has assigned the address space 172.16.1.0/24. The LAN interface of the router is connected to the corporate inside network, which belongs to the 10.0.0.0/8 network. The requirement is that the same inside host should be translated to addresses assigned by the respective ISPs when traffic is forwarded through interface serial 0 or serial 1.

Figure 7-11 *Multihomed NAT*

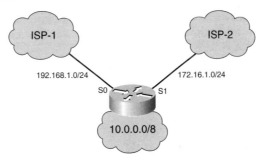

Example 7-18 shows the configuration for the border router.

Example 7-18 *Sample Configuration For Multihomed NAT*

```
interface Ethernet0
 ip address 10.1.1.1 255.0.0.0
 ip nat inside
!This connects to the corporate network, designated as the NAT inside interface.
interface Serial0
 ip address 192.168.1.1 255.255.255.252
 ip nat outside
!This connects to the Internet through ISP-1, designated as the NAT outside
 interface.

interface Serial1
 ip address 172.16.1.1 255.255.255.252
 ip nat outside
```

continues

Example 7-18 *Sample Configuration For Multihomed NAT (Continued)*

```
!This connects to the Internet through ISP-2, designated as the NAT outside
 interface.

ip nat pool ISP-1 192.168.1.3 192.168.1.254 prefix-length 24
!This creates a pool by the name ISP-1, which contains addresses assigned by ISP-1.

ip nat pool ISP-2 172.16.1.3 172.16.1.254 prefix-length 24
!This creates a pool by the name ISP-2, which contains addresses assigned by ISP-2.

ip nat inside source route-map isp-1 pool ISP-1
!The preceding line configures Dynamic NAT mapping for the inside network
10.0.0.0/8 to a global address from the pool ISP-1 to be used for traffic matched
 by the route-map isp-1.

ip nat inside source route-map isp-2 pool ISP-2
!The preceding line configures Dynamic NAT mapping for the inside network
10.0.0.0/8 to a global address from the pool ISP-2 to be used for traffic matched
 by the route-map isp-2.

access-list 1 permit 10.0.0.0 0.255.255.255
!This ACL permits traffic from all hosts in the corporate network.

route-map isp-2 permit 10
 match ip address 1
 match interface Serial1
!This route-map matches all traffic matched by ACL 1 and going out of
interface serial 1. In other words, all traffic from the corporate network to the
 Internet through ISP-2 is matched.

route-map isp-1 permit 10
 match ip address 1
 match interface Serial0
!This route-map matches all traffic matched by ACL 1 and going out of
interface serial 0. In other words, all traffic from the corporate network to the
 Internet through ISP-1 is matched.
```

Another use of dynamic NAT with a route map is in the remote-access scenario with IP Security (IPsec). For example, you may be required to use NAT and IPsec together on a router to reach the Internet and a VPN site through the same interface. In this case, this feature can be used to selectively translate packets that are bound for the Internet and not translate traffic bound for the VPN site.

Static Mapping with Hot Standby Routing Protocol (HSRP) Support

In previous examples, the NAT function has been performed by the border router, which is a single point of failure. One way to increase the availability of the border router performing NAT is to incorporate the function of HSRP.

As illustrated in Figure 7-12, when you combine the functions of HSRP and NAT, the introduction of the secondary router greatly enhances the availability of the NAT infrastructure. However, it is important to note that in this design, the two routers do not exchange states of the translations. Therefore, this design works with static mapping design only.

Figure 7-12 *NAT with HSRP Support*

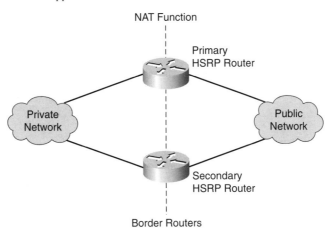

Example 7-19 illustrates the command for incorporating NAT with HSRP in the primary router.

Example 7-19 *Configuring NAT with HSRP on the Primary Router*

```
Primary_Router#configure terminal
Primary_Router(config)#interface Serial0/0
Primary_Router(config-if)#ip address 64.104.85.1 255.255.255.252
Primary_Router(config-if)#ip nat outside
Primary_Router(config-if)#interface GigabitEthernet0/1
Primary_Router(config-if)#ip address 10.1.1.253 255.255.255.0
Primary_Router(config-if)#ip nat inside
Primary_Router(config-if)#standby ip 10.1.1.254
Primary_Router(config-if)#standby priority 100
Primary_Router(config-if)#standby name Border
Primary_Router(config-if)#standby preempt
Primary_Router(config-if)#standby track Serial0/0
Primary_Router(config-if)#exit
Primary_Router(config)#ip nat inside source static 10.1.1.1 64.104.85.101
```

Example 7-20 illustrates the corresponding configuration for the secondary router.

Example 7-20 *Configuring NAT with HSRP on the Secondary Router*

```
Secondary_Router#configure terminal
Secondary_Router(config)#interface Serial0/0
Secondary_Router(config-if)#ip address 64.104.85.5 255.255.255.252
Secondary_Router(config-if)#ip nat outside
Secondary_Router(config-if)#interface GigabitEthernet0/1
Secondary_Router(config-if)#ip address 10.1.1.252 255.255.255.0
Secondary_Router(config-if)#ip nat inside
Secondary_Router(config-if)#standby ip 10.1.1.254
Secondary_Router(config-if)#standby priority 90
Secondary_Router(config-if)#standby name Border
Secondary_Router(config-if)#standby track Serial0/0
Secondary_Router(config-if)#exit
Secondary_Router(config)#ip nat inside source static 10.1.1.1 64.104.85.101
```

Stateful NAT

As you learned in the previous section, the introduction of a secondary router improves the availability of the NAT infrastructure. However, the lack of an exchange of states means only the static mapping method can be deployed. The introduction of stateful NAT solves this problem.

In stateful NAT, two or more routers function as a translation group. As in the HSRP approach, the primary router is in charge of forwarding and translating the IP addresses as required. In addition, it informs the secondary routers of the states of its translation activities. This enables the secondary routers to build the same translation tables. In the event that the primary router fails, the secondary routers take over the forwarding task with the information that is residing in the translation tables. In this case, traffic continues to flow because the same translation information is being used. The introduction of stateful NAT brings resiliency to dynamic NAT, and, of course, it continues to work for static NAT configuration.

The stateful NAT function is delivered in phases. In phase one, it supports applications that do not carry embedded IP addresses in the payload of the TCP or UDP packet. Therefore, Application Level Gateway (ALG) will not be supported in phase one. The following is a list of applications supported in phase one:

- Archie
- Finger
- HTTP
- ICMP
- Ping
- rcp, rlogin, and rsh

- TCP
- Telnet

The following applications are not supported in phase one:

- ALG
- FTP
- NetMeeting Directory
- Remote access server (RAS)
- SPA interface processor (SIP)
- Skinny
- Trivial File Transfer Protocol (TFTP)
- Asymmetrical routing

In phase two, the following application supports have been added:

- Voice over IP (VoIP)
- FTP
- DNS
- Asymmetrical routing

For a complete list of ALG support, refer to the Cisco IOS NAT Application Layer Gateway website at the following URL:

http://www.cisco.com/en/US/tech/tk648/tk361/
technologies_white_paper09186a00801af2b9.shtml

You can implement stateful NAT in two ways. One is by leveraging the HSRP method; the other is via a primary/secondary method.

Using the HSRP Method for Stateful NAT

In the HSRP method, the stateful NAT configuration is based on the usual HSRP configuration. The stateful NAT then makes use of the redundancy API built in to the Cisco IOS Software to perform its task. When this method is used, the primary and secondary NAT routers are elected according to the HSRP standby state.

Example 7-21 illustrates the configuration for the primary NAT router.

Example 7-21 *Stateful NAT Based on HSRP Configuration on the Primary Router*

```
Primary_Router#configure terminal
Primary_Router(config)#interface serial0/0
Primary_Router(config)#ip address 64.104.85.1 255.255.255.252
Primary_Router(config-if)#ip nat outside
Primary_Router(config-if)#interface GigabitEthernet0/1
```

continues

Example 7-21 *Stateful NAT Based on HSRP Configuration on the Primary Router (Continued)*

```
Primary_Router(config-if)#ip address 10.1.1.253 255.255.255.0
Primary_Router(config-if)#ip nat inside
Primary_Router(config-if)#standby ip 10.1.1.254
Primary_Router(config-if)#standby priority 100
Primary_Router(config-if)#standby name border
Primary_Router(config-if)#standby preempt
Primary_Router(config-if)#standby track Serial0/0
Primary_Router(config-if)#exit
Primary_Router(config)#ip nat pool public_pool 64.104.85.101 64.104.85.101 netmask
  255.255.255.128
Primary_Router(config)#ip nat inside source list 100 pool public_pool overload
Primary_Router(config)#access-list 100 permit ip 10.1.1.0 0.0.0.255 any
Primary_Router(config)#ip nat stateful id 1
Primary_Router(config-ipnat-snat)#redundancy border
Primary_Router(config-ipnat-snat-red)#mapping-id 10
```

Example 7-22 illustrates the corresponding configuration for the secondary router.

Example 7-22 *Stateful NAT Based on HSRP Configuration on the Secondary Router*

```
Secondary_Router#configure terminal
Secondary_Router(config)#interface serial0/0
Secondary_Router(config)#ip address 64.104.85.5 255.255.255.252
Secondary_Router(config-if)#ip nat outside
Secondary_Router(config-if)#interface GigabitEthernet0/1
Secondary_Router(config-if)#ip address 10.1.1.252 255.255.255.0
Secondary_Router(config-if)#ip nat inside
Secondary_Router(config-if)#standby ip 10.1.1.254
Secondary_Router(config-if)#standby priority 90
Secondary_Router(config-if)#standby name Border
Secondary_Router(config-if)#standby track Serial0/0
Secondary_Router(config-if)#exit
Secondary_Router(config)#ip nat pool Public_Pool 64.104.85.101 64.104.85.101
  netmask 255.255.255.128
Secondary_Router(config)#ip nat inside source list 100 pool Public_Pool overload
Secondary_Router(config)#access-list 100 permit ip 10.1.1.0 0.0.0.255 any
Secondary_Router(config)#ip nat Stateful id 2
Secondary_Router(config-ipnat-snat)#redundancy Border
Secondary_Router(config-ipnat-snat-red)#mapping-id 10
```

Using the Primary/Secondary Method for Static NAT

In the primary/secondary method, you can explicitly specify the IP address of the primary
and secondary routers (whereas in the HSRP method it was selected by the HSRP state).

Example 7-23 illustrates the configuration for the primary NAT router using the primary/
secondary method.

Example 7-23 *Stateful NAT Based on the Primary/Secondary Configuration on the Primary Router*

```
Primary_Router#configure terminal
Primary_Router(config)#interface serial0/0
Primary_Router(config-if)#ip address 64.104.85.1 255.255.255.252
Primary_Router(config-if)#ip nat outside
Primary_Router(config-if)#interface GigabitEthernet0/1
Primary_Router(config-if)#ip address 10.1.1.253 255.255.255.0
Primary_Router(config-if)#ip nat inside
Primary_Router(config-if)#standby ip 10.1.1.254
Primary_Router(config-if)#standby priority 100
Primary_Router(config-if)#standby name Border
Primary_Router(config-if)#standby preempt
Primary_Router(config-if)#standby track Serial0/0
Primary_Router(config-if)#exit
Primary_Router(config)#ip nat pool Public_Pool 64.104.85.101 64.104.85.101 netmask
  255.255.255.128
Primary_Router(config)#ip nat inside source list 100 pool Public_Pool overload
Primary_Router(config)#access-list 100 permit ip 10.1.1.0 0.0.0.255 any
Primary_Router(config)#ip nat Stateful id 1
Primary_Router(config-ipnat-snat)#primary 10.1.1.253
Primary_Router(config-ipnat-snat-pri)#peer 10.1.1.252
Primary_Router(config-ipnat-snat-pri)#mapping-id 10
```

The **primary** command is used to identify the interface that will be used by the primary NAT router to communicate with the secondary router. The **peer** command is used to identify the partner.

Example 7-24 illustrates the corresponding configuration for the secondary NAT router using the primary/secondary method.

Example 7-24 *Stateful NAT Based on a Primary/Secondary Configuration on the Secondary Router*

```
Secondary_Router#configure terminal
Secondary_Router(config)#interface serial0/0
Secondary_Router(config)#ip address 64.104.85.5 255.255.255.252
Secondary_Router(config-if)#ip nat outside
Secondary_Router(config-if)#interface GigabitEthernet0/1
Secondary_Router(config-if)#ip address 10.1.1.252 255.255.255.0
Secondary_Router(config-if)#ip nat inside
Secondary_Router(config-if)#standby ip 10.1.1.254
Secondary_Router(config-if)#standby priority 90
Secondary_Router(config-if)#standby name Border
Secondary_Router(config-if)#standby track Serial0/0
Secondary_Router(config-if)#exit
Secondary_Router(config)#ip nat pool Public_Pool 64.104.85.101 64.104.85.101
  netmask 255.255.255.128
Secondary_Router(config)#ip nat inside source list 100 pool Public_Pool overload
Secondary_Router(config)#access-list 100 permit ip 10.1.1.0 0.0.0.255 any
Secondary_Router(config)#ip nat Stateful id 2
Secondary_Router(config-ipnat-snat)primary 10.1.1.252
Secondary_Router(config-ipnat-snat-pri)#peer 10.1.1.253
Secondary_Router(config-ipnat-snat-pri)#mapping-id 10
```

Limiting NAT Entries

By now, you have realized that one of the most important resources in the translation exercise is the global address pool. When the addresses in this address pool run out, new connections to the outside network may be denied. Therefore, the global address pool becomes a prime target for the DoS attacks. In addition, because NAT is a CPU-intensive operation, the operation itself may be a target, too. Numerous viruses, worms, and DoS attacks take out NAT service. Therefore, you must introduce mechanisms to protect this important part of the network.

Rate limiting the NAT operation is one such mechanism. This feature provides you with control over how the global address pool is utilized and limits the maximum number of concurrent NAT requests on the router.

Example 7-25 illustrates the command for limiting the maximum number of NAT entries to 200 on a router.

Example 7-25 *Configuring Maximum Number of NAT Entries*

```
Router#configure terminal
Router(config)#ip nat translation max-entries 200
```

Note that in the command 200 is an arbitrary number and not a recommended configuration. You should determine the max entries based on your network requirement.

Multihoming with NAT

As described earlier in the section "ISP-Level Redundancy," acquiring multiple ISP connections is important for corporate networks that want redundant connectivity to the Internet. However, this may pose some technical challenges in terms of routing and addressing. Constructing a multihomed network is not as straightforward, because it involves some intricate addressing and routing issues. The best practices and details about the technicality of multihoming are documented in RFC 2008 and 2260.

RFC 2260 states an address allocation and routing formula for a multihomed network. Unfortunately, it suffers from drawbacks, such as requiring the corporate network to renumber its addresses when it comes time to change to another ISP. In addition, the method suggested also makes load balancing of the Internet traffic for the corporate network difficult because it lacks flexibility. However, some of these drawbacks may be overcome with the introduction of the NAT function. Multihoming with NAT is a complex operation that combines the operation of BGP with the NAT function.

Figure 7-13 illustrates the concept of *auto route injection*, which is described in RFC 2260. In Figure 7-13, the corporate network is served by two border routers, with each connecting to different ISPs. The two border routers, Border_A and Border_B, are connected to the border routers of the ISPs, ISP_A_Border and ISP_B_Border, respectively. Both Border_A and Border_B maintain an eBGP connection with their respective ISP's border router, while they maintain an iBGP connection with each other. The iBGP connection is important because it ensures that traffic is not black-holed when there is a router failure. The global address prefix allocated by ISP A is denoted by Prefix_A, and the address prefix allocated by ISP B is denoted by Prefix_B.

Figure 7-13 *Auto Route Injection Before Failure*

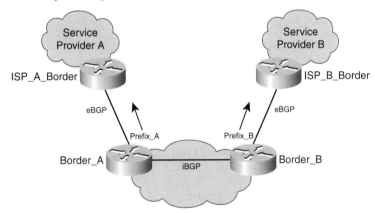

The idea behind auto route injection is such that when everything is in working order, both border routers, Border_A and Border_B, would only advertise the prefix that is allocated by the ISP to which they are connected. For example, Border_A will only advertise Prefix_A to ISP_A_Border, whereas Border_B will only advertise Prefix_B to ISP_B_Border. This is done when the set of routes Border_A receives from ISP_A_Border via the eBGP connection has a nonempty intersection with the set of routes it receives from Border_B via the iBGP connection. When the connection between Border_B and ISP_B_Border is broken, this intersection becomes empty. In this case, Border_A starts to advertise Prefix_B to ISP_A_Border. It continues to advertise Prefix_B for as long as the connection between Border_B and ISP_B_Border is broken, as illustrated in Figure 7-14.

Figure 7-14 *Auto Route Injection After Failure*

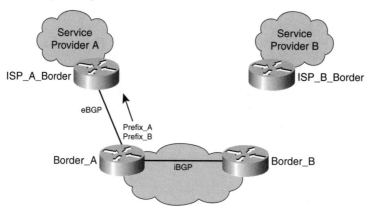

Besides running BGP to process the routes received from other peers, both the border routers, Border_A and Border_B, also run the NAT function. Running NAT in both the border routers means that the corporate network need not go through renumbering when there is a change in either of the ISPs. When there is a change in ISP, the inside address of the corporate network remains the same. The only reconfiguration that is required is the inside global address. This affects only the borders running NAT, which is a more manageable task.

When NAT is running in the border routers, they are configured with multiple pools of inside global addresses, which have been allocated by the various ISPs. An inside local address can be mapped to more than one inside global address from the multiple pools that have been created. This depends on which ISP the traffic is bound, based on the routing decision. This method of address translation is done via the route map option.

When you combine the feature of NAT and the functionality of the BGP protocol, the corporate network can increase the resiliency of its Internet connectivity.

Effects of NAT on Network and Applications

The basic concept of NAT may be just the translations of IP addresses and TCP port numbers. However, its application in the Internet module, or any other module, has a significant effect on the entire network. The following sections discuss important points that need your attention as you introduce NAT into a network.

Implications on TCP and ICMP Traffic

The function of NAPT allows for the mapping of multiple inside addresses to a single global address. This is done by including the TCP port number in the mapping decision, thus enabling a N:1 mapping. NAPT proves extremely useful for small remote office connections because service providers usually allocate only a single global address for such a network. With NAPT, all hosts within the inside network can establish connections to the outside network.

In NAPT, only TCP or UDP sessions are allowed and they must originate from the inside network. In some cases, an inbound session is required (for example, a DNS query). In this case, a statically configured well-known TCP port number may be required on the border router so that the query can be directed to a particular host within the inside network.

In addition to TCP or UDP sessions, you may have to take care of the ICMP messages. With the exception of the redirect message, the ICMP packets are translated in the same way as that of the TCP or UDP packets.

The complication with the NAPT setup is that because the global IP address and the WAN connectivity to the service provider usually share the same address, the border router has to differentiate traffic that is meant for itself from that of the inside network. The assumption here is that all inbound sessions are meant for the border router, unless the target service port has been statically mapped to a host within the inside network.

Application-Specific Gateways

The basic idea of NAT is to map the source or destination IP addresses in the IP packets so that connections can be established from the inside to the outside network. This operation is transparent to most applications except those that embed IP address information in the payload of the IP packet. One example of such an application is the FTP application. Because NAT only deals with the source or destination IP address in the IP packet, it does not take care of those embedded in the payload. Therefore, passing these applications through NAT will not work. ALGs are specially written code to handle such applications and they usually accompany the NAT feature. The FTP ALG, for one, is found in almost all NAT implementations.

The following types of ALGs are supported on the Cisco IOS Software:

- ICMP
- FTP PORT and PASV commands
- NetBIOS over TCP/IP (datagram, name, and session services)
- RealAudio
- CuSeeMe
- StreamWorks
- DNS A and PTR queries
- Netmeeting
- H.323v2-H.225/245 message types

- Session Initiation Protocol (SIP)
- Skinny Client Control Protocol (SCCP)
- Real Time Streaming Protocol (RTSP)
- VDOLive
- Vxtreme
- IP Multicast
- PPTP
- MPLS VPN (VPN routing and forwarding [VRF]-aware NAT)
- IPsec Encapsulating Security Payload (ESP) mode tunnels in PAT configuration
- SPI-matching—Multiple IPsec ESP mode tunnels

The significance of the ALG involvement in payload alteration means that the payload itself must not be encoded. Unless the ALG can decrypt the information, it will be rendered useless in this scenario and the application will break.

Effects on Voice over IP (VoIP) Traffic

Because VoIP traffic is becoming common in most networks, you must take care when the traffic is traversing through some NAT devices, especially firewalls. If you deploy a firewall with NAT features in a VoIP network, the firewall must have some additional features for the VoIP application to work. VoIP endpoints rely on signaling protocols to initiate a call. These protocols run on well-known port numbers, and, therefore, static pinholes can be created in the firewall that lies in the traffic path. However, the signaling protocols also carry information such as the IP address of the end point and the dynamic port number to be used. With the ability to inspect information deep into the signaling packet, the firewall will then open another pinhole for that dynamic port number. This new pinhole lasts as long as the duration of the conversation. For the firewall to perform this task, it needs the ALG for the signaling protocols.

After the signaling is done, the endpoints are ready to establish a connection. The voice stream is carried in RTP packets with the dynamically assigned port number. At the same time, the firewall also performs the necessary IP address translation for the RTP packets.

Obviously, if you want to deploy a VoIP application with firewall and NAT features, you must plan the design and configuration carefully. This is especially so when you have to consider the strict performance requirement of voice traffic. With the firewall and the NAT features in the path of the voice traffic, it is important that these do not affect the quality of the voice call, because implementing NAT may affect the router's processing performance.

Effects on Router Performance

When the source IP or destination IP address within the IP packet needs to be changed, the router needs to recalculate the checksum in the IP packet. For TCP and UDP payload, the checksum within the TCP and UDP headers must be updated, too. Therefore, for both basic NAT and NAPT, the router needs to make modifications to the IP packets in several parts. And this has to be done on every single packet that traverses the router. Besides making the necessary changes, the router also needs to maintain the translation table for all the sessions. Thus, the NAT feature can be quite demanding on the CPU and memory resources.

Therefore, proper sizing of the border router needs to be done prior to turning on the NAT feature. When choosing the right border router, consider the bandwidth required and the number of sessions expected. Some of the latest router products from Cisco incorporate special ASIC to offload CPU-intensive functions, including NAT. These hardware-assisted NAT features certainly help in maintaining a healthy CPU situation. Products such as the Cisco 7304 series router with NSE-100 processor support NAT through the PXF ASIC. Alternatively, you should consider the ISR range of routers that support NAT without degradation in performance when sourcing for a border router.

Effects on Network Security

NAT provides a certain degree of security for the host residing in the inside network, because its true IP address is hidden from the outside network. It is more difficult to launch a direct attack on this host, because its address cannot be directly accessed from the Internet. However, this address-masking capability means that diagnosing legitimate application problems is more difficult. You must keep track of the translations, and determine whether it was the translation itself or the payload that caused a problem. In addition, in the event that a host from the inside network is launching an attack on some host residing in the outside network, it is hard to trace the troublemaker from the outside network.

Introducing the NAT feature is not a straightforward decision. Many aspects of the network, from hardware support to application performance, will be affected and must be carefully sorted out. However, if properly worked into the network from the early design stage, NAT can be a powerful tool in contributing to the resiliency of the network.

Summary

The Internet module is responsible for connecting the entire network to the Internet. Because the Internet is used for business purposes, establishing Internet module redundancy is critical. Understanding the addressing schemes and routing policies in the Internet, and security practice, is a prerequisite to establishing a resilient design. This design is further supported by enhancements made to the BGP and NAT features within the IOS.

This chapter covers the following topics:

- Leased Line
- SONET/SDH
- Resilient Packet Ring
- Dial Backup
- Virtual Private Network

CHAPTER 8

WAN Module

WAN connectivity is a key element in the resilient IP infrastructure. Most IP networks require some form of WAN connectivity to connect two or more location together. Hence, the robustness of the WAN connectivity is important.

WAN connectivity exists in many forms, including as a simple leased circuit between two offices that are located near each other, and long-haul submarine cable systems. In this chapter, you learn about popular choices of WAN connectivity available in the industry. You also look at what the issues are, both technically and operationally, to provide a resilient IP WAN infrastructure. However, in most contexts, the choice of WAN connectivity is usually determined by availability of service and economics. In some cases, a certain WAN connectivity option that is ideal for the deployment might not be available by the local provider of such a service. In other cases, an option might not be cost-effective.

In most cases of deployment, the final choice of WAN connectivity is a good balance of cost and availability of service. In some cases, a mixture of two of more connectivity options might increase network availability and reduce the cost of operations. For instance, your WAN connectivity might be a mixture of expensive leased line and IP tunnel going through the Internet. Cost for the IP tunnel via the Internet might be significantly cheaper than the leased line. It will be cost-effective to load share the traffic across both the leased line and IP tunnel to reduce the total cost of WAN connectivity. At the same time, it reduces dependency on a single service provider and technology.

Leased Line

Leased line, or leased circuit in some cases, is the simplest form of WAN connectivity. Most service providers provide leased lined or leased circuit service to customers. Service providers provision the traffic for each of their customers in their backbone, and deliver the service to the customers with a dedicated physical circuit.

Table 8-1 summarizes the leased circuits typically available from a service provider.

Table 8-1 *Various Leased Circuits Available*

Bandwidth	Options	Interface Type
64 Kbps~512 Kbps	Sub rate T1, E1, nxDS0	X.21 serial interface V.35 serial interface
1.544 Mbps	T1	V.35 serial interface X.21 interface
2 Mbps	E1	V.35 serial interface X.21 interface
35 Mbps	E3	E3 coax BNC G.703 interface
45 Mbps	T3	T3 coax BNC

The choice of the leased circuit used depends on the network bandwidth that is required and the type of service available from the service provider.

Domestic Leased Circuit Versus International Private Leased Circuit

In general, leased circuit service can be divided into domestic leased circuit (DLC) or international private leased circuit (IPLC). *DLC* is a term used by service providers to denote a leased circuit within a country, as shown in Figure 8-1.

Figure 8-1 *Domestic Leased Circuit (DLC)*

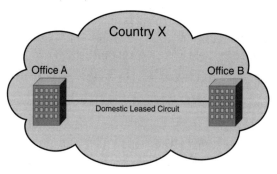

As opposed to DLC, IPLC is a leased line provided between countries. Figure 8-2 shows IPLC.

Figure 8-2 *International Private Leased Circuit (IPLC)*

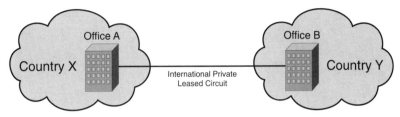

Major service providers with an international presence offer IPLC. In some cases, the user might choose to purchase a *half circuit*. The concept of half circuit is such that the user might want to purchase one end of the circuit from one service provider in one country and another end of the circuit from another service provider in another country. Figure 8-3 illustrates the concept of a half circuit.

Figure 8-3 *Half Circuit*

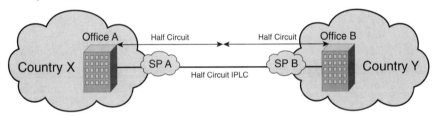

Half circuit is usually done either for cost reasons, or because the service provider within your country does not have the reach and capacity to provide the leased circuit to the target country.

Leased Circuit Encapsulation

To send the IP traffic across a leased circuit, additional lower-layer protocols are used. Both High-Level Data Link Control (HDLC) and Point-to-Point Protocol (PPP) are popular WAN encapsulation protocols. The IP packet is data carried as a payload on either an HDLC frame or a PPP packet. Figure 8-4 illustrates an HDLC frame and a PPP packet.

Figure 8-4   *Comparing HDLC and PPP*

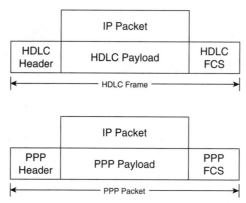

As illustrated in Figure 8-5, connecting two routers via a leased line is straightforward.

Figure 8-5   *One Leased Line Connecting Two Routers*

Example 8-1 shows the configurations required on Router A and Router B.

Example 8-1   *Two Routers Connected via a Leased Line Configuration*

```
Router A
interface serial 0
  ip address 1.1.1.1 255.255.255.0
  no shutdown

Router B
interface serial 0
  ip address 1.1.1.2 255.255.255.0
  no shutdown
```

Traditionally, the leased circuit has always been treated as the "weakest link" in network design. The assumption is that a leased circuit will never be as reliable as a LAN connection. Therefore, one solution is to provision a second leased circuit to improve the resiliency of the WAN. It is a good idea to purchase the circuits from two or more providers when possible. Doing so improves resiliency by removing the dependency on a single provider, as illustrated in Figure 8-6.

Figure 8-6   *Two Leased Lines Connecting Two Routers*

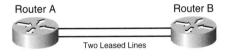

Example 8-2 shows the configuration for a dual-circuit design.

Example 8-2   *Two Routers Connected via Two Leased Circuits*

```
Router A
interface serial 0
 ip address 1.1.1.1 255.255.255.0
 no shutdown

interface serial 1
 ip address 1.1.2.1 255.255.255.0
 no shutdown

Router B
interface serial 0
  ip address 1.1.1.2 255.255.255.0
  no shutdown

interface serial 1
  ip address 1.1.2.2 255.255.255.0
  no shutdown
```

The introduction of a secondary leased circuit to increase resiliency does present some interesting questions. For example, in the case of two or more leased lines between two routers, you must distribute the traffic across those multiple leased lines. You have two possible solutions to this problem:

- Equal-cost load balancing
- Multilink Point-to-Point Protocol (MPPP)

Equal-Cost Load Balancing

Equal-cost load balancing is an algorithm dealing with multiple routes to a common destination. These routes will have the same weight such that no route is more preferred. The router treats both routes as equal cost and performs load balancing between the two routes in an alternate fashion.

In Figure 8-7, traffic between the Ethernet interfaces of Routers A and B can be load balanced via the configuration shown in Example 8-3.

Example 8-3 *Equal-Cost Load Balancing for Two Routers*

```
Router A
Interface Ethernet 0
  ip address 2.2.2.0 255.255.255.0
  no shutdown

interface serial 0
  ip address 1.1.1.1 255.255.255.0
  no shutdown

interface serial 1
  ip address 1.1.2.1 255.255.255.0
  no shutdown

ip route 0.0.0.0 0.0.0.0 serial 0
ip route 0.0.0.0 0.0.0.0 serial 1

Router B
interface ethernet 0
  ip address 2.2.3.0 255.255.255.0
  no shutdown

interface serial 0
  ip address 1.1.1.2 255.255.255.0
  no shutdown

interface serial 1
  ip address 1.1.2.2 255.255.255.0
  no shutdown

ip route 0.0.0.0 0.0.0.0 serial 0
ip route 0.0.0.0 0.0.0.0 serial 1
```

Figure 8-7 *Equal-Cost Load Balancing*

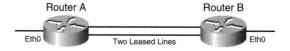

Multilink Point-to-Point Protocol (MPPP)

As opposed to the equal-cost load balancing method, MPPP is a PPP feature when two or more PPP sessions are bonded together to form a single logical connection. From the router's point of view, there is only one IP connection between the two routers. This is the main difference between the two methods.

Using Figure 8-7 as an example, the two leased circuits can be bonded via MPPP as shown in Example 8-4.

Example 8-4   *MPPP Configuration for Two Routers*

```
Router A
Interface Ethernet 0
  ip address 2.2.2.0 255.255.255.0
  no shutdown

interface multilink1
  ip address 1.1.1.1 255.255.255.0
  ppp multilink
  multilink-group 1

interface serial 0
  encapsulation ppp
  ppp multilink
  multilink-group 1

interface serial 1
  encapsulation ppp
  ppp multilink
  multilink-group 1

ip route 0.0.0.0 0.0.0.0 multilink1

Router B
interface ethernet 0
  ip address 2.2.3.0 255.255.255.0
  no shutdown

interface multilink1
  ip address 1.1.1.2 255.255.255.0
  ppp multilink
  multilink-group 1

interface serial 0
  encapsulation ppp
  ppp multilink
  multilink-group 1

interface serial 1
  encapsulation ppp
  ppp multilink
  multilink-group 1

ip route 0.0.0.0 0.0.0.0 multilink1
```

There are a few advantages of using MPPP versus equal-cost load balancing. One key advantage of MPPP is the ability to perform fragmentation of frames and interleaving of frames. Fragmentation of frames enables large packets to be fragmented into a small enough size to satisfy the delay requirement of real-time traffic, especially voice. The interleaving feature provides a special transmit queue for the smaller delay-sensitive packets, enabling them to be sent earlier than the rest of the packets. However, MPPP requires more processing power from the router's CPU, which makes it unsuitable for certain low-end routers. When using MPPP for voice, latency for both circuits has to be equal. If it is not, the packets might not arrive at the same time, which will cause the voice quality to suffer.

SONET/SDH

Synchronous Optical Network (SONET)/Synchronous Digital Hierarchy (SDH) is a common technology used by service providers to offer circuits over an optical network. The SONET specification is defined by American National Standards Institute (ANSI), under ANSI T1.105, ANSI T1.106, ANSI T1.117, and Bellcore GR-253. SDH is defined by the International Telecommunication Union Telecommunication Standardization Sector (ITU-T). In general, SONET equipment is used in North America, and SDH is generally used in the rest of the world.

Both SONET and SDH are based on a similar frame structure. SONET uses a frame structure known as Synchronous Transport Signal (STS), but SDH uses a frame structure know as Synchronous Transport Module (STM). Speed-wise, a SONET OC-3 is similar to SDH STM-1, at 155 Mbps. SONET/SDH also uses multiplexing and demultiplexing technology to transport its payload. For that, multiple STS-1 signals can be multiplexed to form a single STS-3 signal. Likewise, multiple STM-4 signals can be multiplexed into a single STM-16 signal. Table 8-2 illustrates the various SONET/SDH speeds.

Table 8-2   *SONET/SDH Speeds*

Optical Level	Electric Level	SDH	Line Rate	Payload Rate
OC-1	STS-1	--	51.84 Mbps	50.112 Mbps
OC-3	STS-3	STM-1	155.520 Mbps	150.336 Mbps
OC-12	STS-12	STM-4	622.080 Mbps	601.344 Mbps
OC-48	STS-48	STM-16	2488.320 Mbps	2405.376 Mbps
OC-192	STS-192	STM-64	9953.280 Mbps	9621.504 Mbps

Although SONET and SDH are quite similar in nature, they have differences, such as the naming conventions used in both technologies. For example, SONET uses section, line, and path, whereas SDH uses path, multiplex section, and regenerator section. A detailed explanation of those terms is beyond the scope of this book.

A typical SONET/SDH network is built using optical fiber rings, as illustrated in Figure 8-8. A single SONET/SDH ring is built with two fiber rings to improve resiliency. The network can be made up of multiple rings. A SONET/SDH ADM (add/drop multiplexer) is used to multiplex multiple rings into a single ring.

Figure 8-8   *Typical SONET/SDH Network*

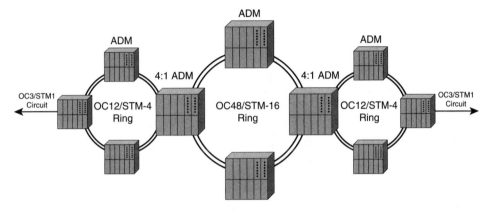

A typical service provider might build a main OC-48/STM-16 ring and extend it to multiple, smaller OC-12/STM-4 rings. Given that four OC-12/STM-4s can be multiplexed (muxed) into a single OC-48/STM-16, the service provider can build four smaller OC-12 rings. A customer circuit is provisioned on the ADM by demultiplexing on the OC-12 rings.

A OC-48/STM-16 ring can support four OC-12/STM-4 rings. One OC-12/STM-4 ring can then support four OC-3/STM-1 circuits. So, one OC-48/STM-16 ring can support 16 OC-3/STM-1 circuits. That does not sound like a large number. However, a single OC-3/STM-1 circuit can be demuxed into multiple DS-3 circuits and more T1 and E1 circuits.

In the next sections, you learn about various SONET/SDH framing and SONET/SDH multiplexing issues.

SONET/SDH Framing

A basic signal in SONET is OC-1 (Optical Channel level 1), or its electrical equivalent STS-1 (Synchronous Transport Signal level 1). The signal is organized in 9 rows and 90 columns of 8 bits (1 byte). This frame is then repeated at 8000 times in 1 second. Hence, the bandwidth will be 9 (rows) $\times$ 90 (columns) $\times$ 8000 (frame/sec) $\times$ 8 (bit) = 51.84 Mbps.

Figure 8-9 illustrates SONET framing.

Figure 8-9 *SONET Framing*

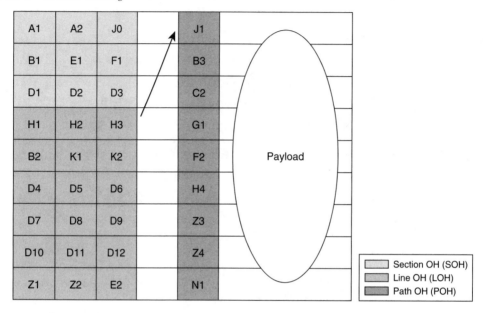

The fields in the frame are as follows:

- **A1 and A2**—Frame start
- **J0**—Section trace
- **B1**—Section error monitoring
- **E1**—Local orderwire channels
- **F1**—Reserved
- **D1 to D12**—Data communication channels
- **H1 and H2**—Synchronous payload envelope (SPE) pointers
- **H3**—Pointer action byte
- **B2**—Line error monitoring
- **K1 and K2**—Signaling for protection of multiplex section
- **Z1 and Z2**—For future use
- **E3**—Allocated for express orderwire between line entities
- **J1**—Synchronous Transport Signal (STS) path trace
- **B3**—Path error monitoring
- **C2**—Signal label

- **G1**—Path status
- **F2**—Path user channel
- **H4**—Multiframe indication
- **Z3 and Z4**—Future use
- **N1**—Tandem connection maintenance

The upper three columns contain section overhead (SOH) information. The lower six contain line overhead information. The remaining 87 columns are used for user data and carrying the SPE (synchronous payload envelope). SPE contains the path overhead (POH) and the payload. The first row of line overhead contains a pointer to the first byte of SPE.

SONET/SDH can also be multiplexed together, as illustrated in Figure 8-10.

Figure 8-10 *Multiplexing SONET*

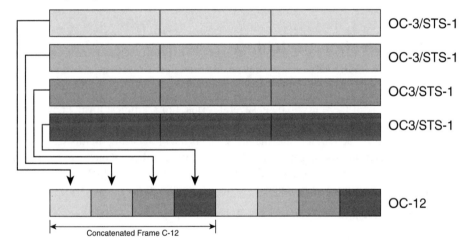

Multiple OC-3 can be multiplexed together to form an OC-12. OC-12c means concatenated payload; the virtual containers are not multiplexed.

PPP over SONET/SDH

In most cases, a SONET/SDH circuit provides a single serial bitstream. To carry IP traffic over a SONET/SDH circuit, HDLC and PPP are typically deployed.

From PPP's point of view, SONET/SDH is just a full-duplex octet bitstream. PPP packets are carried using a SONET/SDH payload in a form of SPE or an SDH virtual container (VC). Likewise, HDLC frames are carried as a SONET/SDH payload.

In Figure 8-11, the router in each site is physically connected to the ADM by the service provider. The service provider will provision the OC-3 circuits between the two sites. The router will be configured to use either PPP or HDLC framing to carry IP traffic.

Figure 8-11 *PPP over SONET/SDH Circuit for Two Sites*

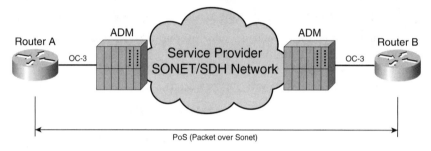

SONET/SDH Protection Switching

Most SONET/SDH networks are built using dual fiber rings in an active and protect operation. SONET/SDH offers protection switching in case of a failure in the fiber.

The topology of the ring can be in several forms. In its simplest form, known as *unidirectional self-healing ring (USHR)*, two fibers are used, as shown in Figure 8-12. The outer ring is the active ring, and the inner ring is the protect ring. In this scenario, all traffic uses the outer ring for transmission. However, during a fiber cut on the outer ring, as shown on the right of the diagram, SONET/SDH protection switching kicks in to make the inner ring the active ring. The switchover is made within 50 milliseconds (ms) of ring failure.

Figure 8-12 *SONET/SDH Network Protection*

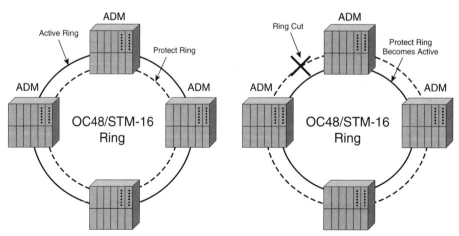

Another topology, bidirectional line switch ring (BLSR), can be built with two fibers. The difference between a USHR and BLSR is that the protection switching takes effect only on the segment when the fiber is broken. The rest of the ring segment continues to work normally.

Based on the same technology, linear automatic protection switching can be used to protect a link failure between the router and the SONET/SDH ADM.

Figure 8-13 shows a router that supports SONET/SDH Automatic Protection Switching (APS). The router is configured with an active link and a protected link to the SONET/SDH ADM. If a link failure occurs on one of the links, SONET/SDH APS kicks in and failovers the circuit to the protected link. The failover time is less than 50 ms. APS within a router does not require Layer 3 routing to reconverge. APS can also be applied across two routers when one router will be a working router and another router will be a protect router. When a switchover is required for multiple router configuration, Layer 3 routing must reconverge.

Figure 8-13 *SONET/SDH Protection Switching*

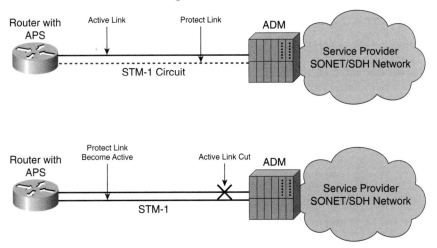

The advantage of such a configuration is that it protects against failure of the link to the SONET/SDH ADM. However, the effect of it is that the protection link will not be used unless a failover occurs. This incurs additional cost on the router port, and the general cost from the service provider to provide additional protection circuit is higher.

Figure 8-14 illustrates an example for a single router connected to a SONET ADM and running APS.

Figure 8-14 *APS for a Single Router with an ADM*

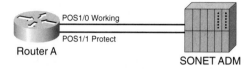

Example 8-5 shows the configuration for APS for a single router as illustrated in Figure 8-14.

Example 8-5 *Configuration of Router A*

```
Router A
interface Loopback0
ip address 10.1.1.1 255.255.255.255
!
interface POS1/0
ip address 10.1.1.2 255.255.255.0
aps group 10
aps working 1
!
interface POS1/1
ip address 10.1.1.3 255.255.255.0
aps group 10
aps revert 1
aps protect 1 10.1.1.1
```

Figure 8-15 shows APS between two routers.

Figure 8-15 *APS Between Two Routers with an ADM*

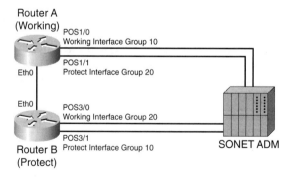

Example 8-6 shows the configuration of two routers with an ADM.

Example 8-6 *Configuration of Two Routers with an ADM*

```
Router A (Working Router)
interface Loopback0
ip address 10.1.1.1 255.255.255.255
!
```

Example 8-6 *Configuration of Two Routers with an ADM (Continued)*

```
interface POS1/0
aps group 10
aps working 1
!
interface POS1/1
aps group 20
aps protect 1 10.1.1.2

Router B (Protect Router)
interface Loopback0
ip address 10.1.1.2 255.255.255.0
!
interface POS3/0
aps group 20
aps working 1
!
interface POS3/1
aps group 10
aps protect 1 10.1.1.1
!
```

By using SONET/SDH APS, you can increase the resiliency of the links of the router.

Resilient Packet Ring

Resilient Packet Ring (RPR) technology is an emerging network architecture and technology based on-fiber ring similar to a SONET/SDH infrastructure.

RPR technology has a few key advantages:

- Offers resiliency to the existing fiber ring by having a protection switching mechanism similar to SONET/SDH.
- Supports multiple classes of service to offer traffic prioritization.
- Enables Multicast traffic to be carried efficiently without the need of packet replication.

Cisco Dynamic Packet Transport (DPT) technology is one such implementation of packet ring technology. Although RPR technology has been standardized in 2004, under the 802.17 working group, this section covers DPT rather than the 802.17 specifications.

Although DPT is a packet ring technology, Spatial Reuse Protocol is the underlying protocol that implements DPT. You will find that they might be used interchangeably.

DPT Architecture

Unlike a SONET/SDH infrastructure where there is a protection ring, which does not carry traffic unless there is a break in the working ring, DPT technology uses both fiber rings to carry traffic simultaneously. Hence, as compared with a SONET/SDH infrastructure, whereas an OC-12/STM-4 ring might just carry 622 Mbps of traffic, a corresponding DPT ring can carry 2 * 622 Mbps, or 1244 Mbps (1.2 Gbps).

DPT uses dual counter-rotating rings with multiple nodes on the ring, as shown in Figure 8-16. Data and control traffic are carried over both rings in opposite directions. Topology information is carried via control traffic such that all the nodes on the ring have a complete view of the network topology with information of the existing nodes on the ring.

Figure 8-16 *DPT with Four Routers*

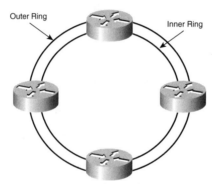

As shown in Figure 8-17, the concept of having control traffic carried in the opposite direction of data traffic is such that, in case of a fiber break along the path, control traffic can be carried effectively to tell the corresponding node to "wrap" the ring by redirecting the packets from the inner ring to the outer ring depending on the direction of the ring. The protection mechanism allows traffic to be redirected, with little or no drop in packets.

Figure 8-17 *Counter-Rotating Rings of DPT*

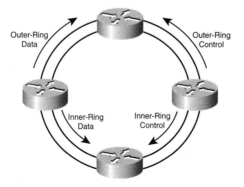

In Figure 8-18, when the outer rings break, the nodes closest to the break wrap the rings to redirect traffic and isolate the break. This protection switching is done within 50 ms, similar to SONET/SDH protection switching. When spatial reuse protocol (SRP) performs a switchover, no Layer 3 reconvergence occurs.

Figure 8-18 *Breakage in DPT Four-Node Ring*

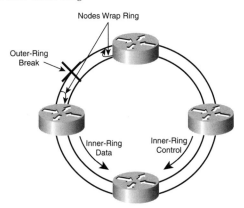

Shown in Figure 8-19, a DPT/SRP network can have multiple nodes on a single ring. Each node has two physical (PHY) interfaces and two data paths. Hence, this provides the necessary resiliency and causes the node to have two Media Access Control (MAC) addresses. When a node wants to send a packet to another node, it determines which ring has the shortest hop count to the destination based on the topology information discovered. When the packet arrives at the destination, it is removed from the ring. Therefore, bandwidth is only consumed on the span between the source node and the destination node.

Figure 8-19 *SRP MAC Architecture*

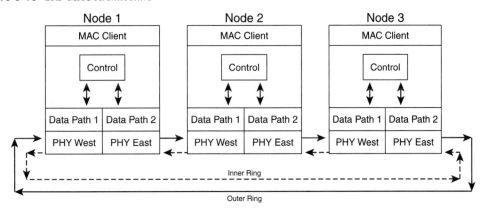

In the event of multicast traffic, the packet is inserted into the ring, and each node receives the similar packet, but the packet is not removed from the ring and instead continues to be forwarded to the next node. When the sender of the packet sees its packet arrive on itself, the packet is then stripped from the ring. The advantage of such an implementation is that each node is responsible for copying the packet to itself. No single node needs to do packet replication to other nodes on the ring. Therefore, it is scalable despite the number of nodes on the ring.

DPT/SRP Classes of Service

DPT/SRP offers two classes of service and fairness to the traffic on the ring:

- **High-priority service**—It is used to support high-priority service such as voice or video.
- **Low-priority service**—It is used for best-effort types of service.

The next sections describe SRP queuing and the fairness algorithm.

SRP Queuing

Figure 8-20 shows the general concept of how the various queues work. An RPR node typically has six different queues:

- Two queues to receive traffic for high-priority and low-priority service:
    - High-priority RX queue
    - Low-priority RX queue
- Two queues for adding traffic as either high priority or low priority:
    - High-priority TX queue
    - Low-priority TX queue
- Two transit queues:
    - High-priority transit queue
    - Low-priority transit queue

When packets must be transmitted into the ring, they are typically classified by the routers to determine the priority level and added into the respective queue to be added into the ring. When a packet arrives at the ring with a destination address of the node, it is sent to the respective receive queue to be sent to other interfaces in the router.

Transit queues are queues to hold traffic that goes through the node to another node on the ring.

Figure 8-20 *0RPR Fairness and Queuing on a Single Node*

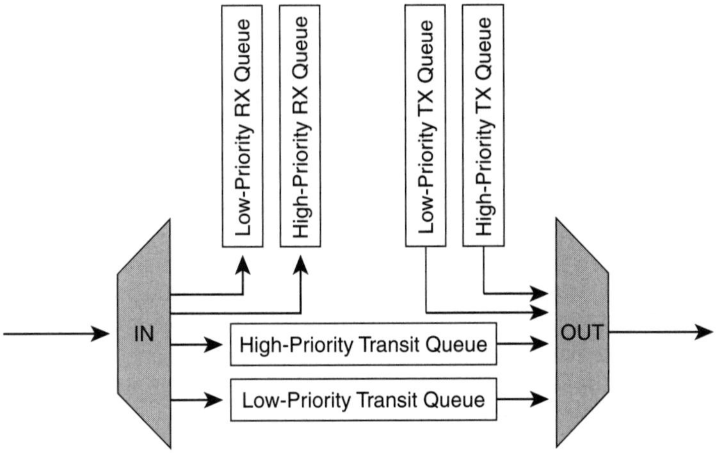

SRP Fairness Algorithm

SRP offers a fairness algorithm that ensures priority to the traffic on the ring. Transmission scheduling is done in this order, from high priority to low priority:

1 High-priority transmit (add)

2 High-priority transit

3 Low-priority transmit (add)

4 Low-priority transit

When there is congestion, feedback control messages are sent to the neighboring node to throttle down the traffic.

RPR Standards

In 2000, the IEEE 802.17 Resilient Packet Ring working group was started as a unit under the IEEE 802 LAN/MAN working group. The 802.17 working group was formed with the objective to standardize on the RPR ring type of technology.

Differences Between 802.17 and DPT/SRP

Although both the 802.17 specification and DPT/SRP are similar as packet ring technologies, the two standards do differ.

In terms of class of service, DPT/SRP defines two classes of service: high priority and low priority. 802.17 defines three class of service: Class A, B, and C. 802.17 Class A service is a high-priority service. Class B service has a lower priority than Class A service, and Class C is a best-effort service. 802.17 Class A service is similar to DPR/SRP high-priority service. However, in DPT/SRP, there is not a concept of Class B service. DPT/SRP low priority is the best fit for Class B and Class C service combined.

Although the current Cisco implementation of DPT/SRP uses an OC-12 to OC-192 physical interface, the RPR specification allows the use of SONET/SDH interfaces and Gigabit Ethernet (GE) interfaces.

Cisco DPT/SRP requires the ring speed to be similar throughout all the nodes. So, if the DPR/SRP ring is OC-12, all the interfaces between all the nodes have to be OC-12. RPR does not have that requirement. One segment of the ring can be OC-12 and another segment can be OC-48. However, mixing interface speeds on the same ring has to be handled with care.

The RPR technology may sound complex with counter-rotating rings and SONET/SDH framing. Contrary to what it seems, the configuration for RPR on the Cisco router is straightforward. Example 8-7 shows the simple configurations for a four-node DPT/SRP ring, as illustrated in Figure 8-21.

Example 8-7 *Configuration Example of Four-Router DPR/SRP Ring*

```
GSR A Configuration

GSR A:
hostname GSR-A
!
interface Loopback0
ip address 10.0.0.1 255.255.255.255
!
interface SRP1/0
ip address 10.10.10.1 255.255.255.192
!
router ospf 100
network 10.10.10.0 0.0.0.255 area 1
network 10.0.0.1 0.0.0.0 area 0
auto-cost reference-bandwidth 2488

GSR B:
hostname GSR-B
!
interface Loopback0
ip address 10.0.0.2 255.255.255.255
!
interface SRP1/0
ip address 10.10.10.2 255.255.255.192
!
router ospf 100
network 10.10.10.0 0.0.0.255 area 1
```

Example 8-7   *Configuration Example of Four-Router DPR/SRP Ring (Continued)*

```
network 10.0.0.1 255.255.255.255 area 0

GSR C:
hostname GSR-C
!
interface Loopback0
ip address 10.0.0.3 255.255.255.255

!
interface SRP1/0
ip address 10.10.10.3 255.255.255.192
!
router ospf 100
network 10.10.10.0 0.0.0.255 area 1
network 10.0.0.1 255.255.255.255 area 0

GSR D:
hostname GSR-D
!
interface Loopback0
ip address 10.0.0.4 255.255.255.255

!
interface SRP1/0
ip address 10.10.10.4 255.255.255.192
!
router ospf 100
network 10.10.10.0 0.0.0.255 area 1
network 10.0.0.1 255.255.255.255 area 0
```

Figure 8-21   *DPT/SRP Dual Ring with Four Routers*

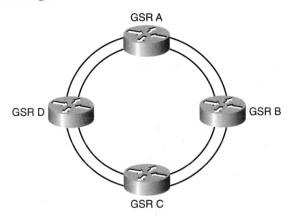

Although the DPT technology is most commonly used in a WAN deployment, it can be used in the data center, too. DPT/SRP interfaces are available in servers from vendors. This provides for both performance and resiliency, because both the interfaces are capable of transmitting traffic, as well as SDH-like protection for the IP connectivity.

Dial Backup

To achieve a resilient IP network design, you can sometimes use more than one leased circuit for redundancy. However, this solution may not make financial sense. In that case, a dial backup is one good option. Dial backup is also known as an on-demand circuit, and its concept is illustrated in Figure 8-22.

Figure 8-22 *Two Routers Using ISDN as Backup*

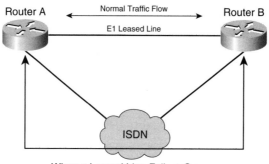

In Figure 8-22, under normal usage, traffic is carried across the E1 leased line between the two routers. Upon a failure of the leased line, the routers automatically dial up the neighboring router via an Integrated Service Digital Network (ISDN) connection. Whereas a traditional dial-up connection generally uses a copper phone line with an analog dial-up modem with up to 56 Kbps of bandwidth, an ISDN provides a digital dial-up line without the use of a modem.

Typically, there are two types of ISDN:

- ISDN Basic Rate Interface (BRI) provides 2B+1D channels; that is, two B channels of 64 kbps, and 1 D channel of 16 kbps. The B channels carry data, and the D channel is used for controling and signaling information. Because each B channel provides 64 Kbps, an ISDN BRI can carry 128 Kbps of data.

- ISDN Primary Rate Interface (PRI) depends on the physical line interface. In the United States, it is typically a T1 interface, which provides 23B+1D. However, in other parts of the world, it is usually an E1 interface, which provides 30D + a 64-Kbps D channel.

You can implement a dial backup solution in a few ways. The simplest way is to use a floating static route. A floating static route is a method of having a static route added to the neighboring router with a higher distance via the ISDN interfaces. Under a steady-state operation, the route via the serial interface is the preferred one. Upon a failure, the serial interface is marked as down, and the associated static route will not exist. Hence, the static route with the higher distance via the ISDN interface is used, as illustrated in Figure 8-23.

Figure 8-23 *Floating Static Route*

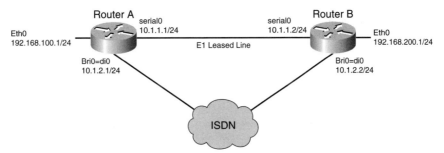

In Figure 8-23, Router A has an E1 leased line to Router B using a serial interface. In addition, Router A has an ISDN BRI to provide a backup interface. Router A has two static routes to reach the Router B Ethernet interface. The static route with a default cost routes the traffic using the serial interface, IP route 192.168.200.0/24 10.1.1.2, and the floating static route that has a higher distance of 100 will route using the ISDN BRI interface, IP route 192.168.200.0/24 10.1.2.2 100.

Example 8-8 shows the necessary configuration.

Example 8-8 *Static Route Configuration*

```
Router A
 hostname routerA
 !
 username routera password 0 <password>
 !
 isdn switch-type basic-net3
 !
 !
 interface ethernet0
 ip address 192.168.100.1 255.255.255.0
 !
 interface Serial0
 ip address 10.1.1.1 255.255.255.0
 !
 interface BRI0
 no ip address
 encapsulation ppp
 load-interval 30
 dialer pool-member 1
```

continues

Example 8-8 *Static Route Configuration (Continued)*

```
    isdn switch-type basic-net3
    ppp authentication chap
    !
    interface Dialer0
    ip address 10.1.2.1 255.255.255.0
    encapsulation ppp
    dialer pool 1
    dialer remote-name routera
    dialer string 1001
    dialer-group 1
    no cdp enable
    ppp authentication chap
    !
    ip classless
    ip route 192.168.200.0 255.255.255.0 10.1.1.2
    ip route 192.168.200.0 255.255.255.0 10.1.2.2 100
  !
    dialer-list 1 protocol ip permit
    !
    end

Router B
  hostname routerB
  !
  username routerb password 0 <password>
  !
  isdn switch-type basic-net3
  !
  !
  interface ethernet0
  ip address 192.168.200.1 255.255.255.0
  !
  interface Serial0
  ip address 10.1.1.2 255.255.255.0
  !
  interface BRI0
  no ip address
  encapsulation ppp
  load-interval 30
  dialer pool-member 1
  isdn switch-type basic-net3
  ppp authentication chap
  !
  interface Dialer0
  ip address 10.1.2.2 255.255.255.0
  encapsulation ppp
  dialer pool 1
  dialer remote-name routerb
  dialer string 1002
  dialer-group 1
  no cdp enable
  ppp authentication chap
```

Example 8-8 *Static Route Configuration (Continued)*

```
!
ip classless
ip route 192.168.100.0 255.255.255.0 10.1.1.1
ip route 192.168.100.0 255.255.255.0 10.1.2.1 100
!
dialer-list 1 protocol ip permit
!
end
```

As shown in Example 8-8, Cisco IOS uses a dialer interface to trigger the actual dial-up. The dialer interface is configured with the remote name to identity itself as the correct router. The dialer interface is configured with the dialer string that specified the number to dial.

Virtual Private Network (VPN)

Service providers in various parts of the world are pushing Virtual Private Network (VPN) services in various ways as lower-cost but effective WAN connectivity. VPN is a general concept to run a private network over a public network infrastructure. You can purchase a VPN service from your service provider, and the service provider is responsible for setting up the tunnel for you, such as Multiprotocol Label Switching (MPLS)-VPN. You can also build your own network using existing technology to do either a Layer 3 tunnel or Layer 2 tunnel.

A Layer 3 tunnel enables you to transport Layer 3 packets, such as, IP over another IP network. The carrying of an IP packet as a payload on another IP packet is essentially an IP tunnel.

A Layer 2 tunnel offers even greater flexibility by transporting Layer 2 packets over an IP network. The Layer 2 packet can be a serial HDLC frame or an Ethernet frame and can be transported over the IP network.

In this section, you learn about the following technologies:

- Layer 3 tunnel in the form of an IP tunnel
- Layer 2 tunnel using L2TPv3
- MPLS-VPN

IP Tunnel

IP tunnels transport IP packets as data payload in another IP packet. A few technologies accomplish this functionality—namely, IP in IP tunneling and Generic Routing Encapsulation (GRE). IP in IP tunneling is described in RFC 1853, and GRE is described in RFC 2784.

As shown in Figure 8-24, an IP connection can be used as a transport layer for another IP packet.

Figure 8-24 *IP Tunnel*

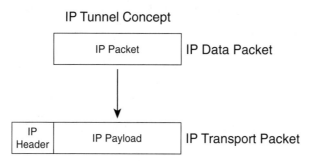

As illustrated in Figure 8-25, you might have two sites in remote locations or even located in different countries. Although IPLC will be expensive across two countries, there is an option to use an IP tunnel. Each local office can purchase an Internet transit service from the local Internet service provider (ISP). In this example, Site A is connected to its local ISP A, and Site B is connected to its local ISP B. Although the ISPs are connected via the Internet, you can set up an IP tunnel between the two sites. From a cost perspective, instead of purchasing an IPLC, the circuit can now be a virtual DLC, which is significantly cheaper.

Figure 8-25 *IP Tunnel over Internet*

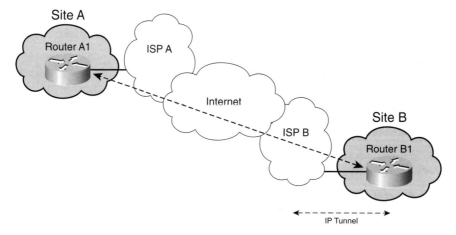

However, depending on the service level agreement given by the local ISP, the ISP might not guarantee the quality of Internet connectivity. Therefore, it is always wise to check out the quality level of the service offered by the ISP before committing to such an implementation as the primary WAN connectivity option.

As illustrated in Figure 8-26, the IP tunnel can be a very simple setup using GRE. There are two sites, Site A and Site B, connected by an IP service from a service provider. Each site's router, Router A and Router B, is connected to the service provider individually using a serial interface. A GRE tunnel is set up between the two routers, and a default route is statically defined at each end of the tunnel.

Figure 8-26 *IP Tunnel Deployment*

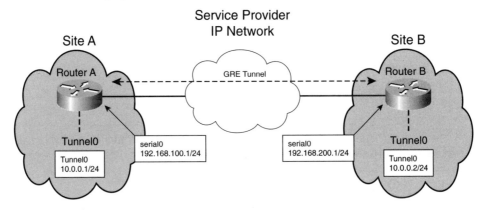

Example 8-9 shows a sample configuration for the IP tunnel.

Example 8-9 *IP Tunnel Configuration*

```
Router A
!
interface serial 0
  ip address 192.168.100.1
!
interface Tunnel0
  ip address 10.0.0.1 255.255.255.0
  tunnel source 192.168.100.1 255.255.255.0
  tunnel destination 192.168.200.1
  tunnel mode gre
!
! route tunnel destination using serial 0
!
ip route 192.168.200.0 255.255.255.0 serial 0
!
! route the rest of the traffic using tunnel interface
!
ip route 0.0.0.0 0.0.0.0 tunnel0


Router B
!
Interface serial 0
  Ip address 192.168.200.1 255.255.255.0
```

continues

Example 8-9   *IP Tunnel Configuration (Continued)*

```
!
interface Tunnel0
  ip address 10.0.0.2 255.255.255.0
  tunnel source 192.168.200.1
  tunnel destination 192.168.100.1
  tunnel mode gre
!
! route tunnel destination using serial 0
!
ip route 192.168.100.0 255.255.255.0 serial 0
!
! route the rest of the traffic using tunnel interface
!
ip route 0.0.0.0 0.0.0.0 tunnel0
```

NOTE   IP in IP tunneling is similar to a GRE tunnel. To use IP in IP tunneling, just change the command from **tunnel mode gre** to **tunnel mode ipip**.

Tunnel interfaces behave very much like an ordinary serial interface. It is also possible to run a routing protocol on it, instead of using a static route as shown. However, to prevent routing loops, it is a good idea to put an explicit static route to the tunnel destination.

When an IP packet is carried over a tunnel interface, the packet size increases with the additional overhead of the tunnel header. The increase in size might exceed the MTU (maximum transfer unit) of the given physical interface. When that happens, the router drops the packet and sends an "ICMP Destination Unreachable" message with the flag "fragmentation needed and DF set" to the sender. If Internet Control Message Protocol (ICMP) is not blocked, the ICMP message arrives at the sender and the sender must fragment the packet and resend it at a small size. However, if ICMP is blocked along the way, the Destination Unreachable message might not reach the sender, and the result is that the packet will be silently dropped.

One solution is to run an MTU path discovery on the tunnel interface with the command **tunnel path-mtu-discovery**, whereby the router will automatically reduce the MTU size of the GRE tunnel when it sees an "ICMP Destination Unreachable" message with the flag "fragmentation needed and DF set." Another solution is to manually reduce the size of the MTU on the interface itself, to force the IP packet to fragment before it reaches the tunnel interface.

L2TPv3

Layer 2 Tunnel Protocol (L2TP) is a technology to transport PPP packets over an IP network. It is defined in RFC 2661. L2TP version 3 (L2TPv3) is the standardized technology to carry any Layer 2 frame, such as a serial HDLC or Ethernet frame, over an IP network.

Figure 8-27 illustrates the concept of L2TPv3.

Figure 8-27 *L2TPv3*

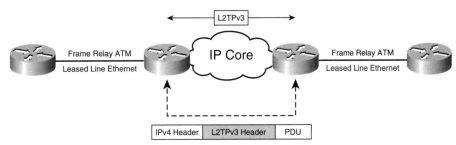

L2TPv3 Deployment

Although some service providers provide Ethernet or serial HDLC service using L2TPv3 technology, this section assumes that you will be implementing L2TPv3 yourself. Because the key advantage of L2TPv3 is the ability to transport Layer 2 frames, the deployment example in this section is based on transporting both Ethernet frames and serial HDLC frames.

The ability to transport Ethernet frames enables you to connect Ethernet switches together using a standard trunking protocol, such as Inter-Switch Link (ISL) or 802.1q. Although this simplifies the network design, take care to watch for broadcast traffic between the sites. This is especially so if the bandwidth of the IP connection between the two sites is limited.

In Figure 8-28, there are two sites in the network, Site A and Site B. Each site has a router that connects to the service provider's IP network, known as Router A2 in Site A and Router B2 in Site B. This can be a router that subscribes to an IP transit service or Internet service from the service provider.

Figure 8-28 *Deploying L2TPv3 on Two Sites*

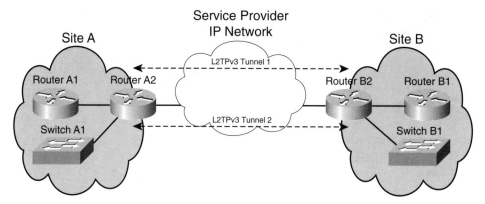

Within the network in each site, there is also one router (A1 in Site A) and one switch (A1 in Site A). These are the router and switch to which the rest of the systems connect.

Router A2 and Router B2 provide and maintain the L2TPv3 connection between the two sites. Two L2TPv3 sessions will be created: one to transport Ethernet frames and the other to transport serial HDLC frames.

Example 8-10 shows the configuration of Router A2 at Site A and the configuration of Router B2 at site B.

Example 8-10 *Configuration Example of Router A2 in Site A*

```
Router A2
!
l2tp-class l2tp-defaults
 retransmit initial retries 30
 cookie-size 8
!
! pseudowire class for ethernet
!
pseudowire-class ether-pw
 encapsulation l2tpv3
 protocol none
 ip local interface serial 0/0
!
! pseudowire class for HDLC
!
pseudowire-class hdlc-pw
 encapsulation l2tpv3
 protocol none
 ip local interface serial 0/0
!
! 2M leased line to the service provider
!
Interface serial 0/0
```

Example 8-10   *Configuration Example of Router A2 in Site A (Continued)*

```
     ip address 192.168.100.1 255.255.255.0
 !
 ! Create a L2TPv3 tunnel for the Ethernet interface
 !
 interface Ethernet 0/0
    xconnect 192.168.200.1 100 encapsulation l2tpv3 manual pw-class ether-pw
    l2tp id 200 100
    l2tp cookie local 4 54321
    l2tp cookie remote 4 12345
    l2tp hello l2tp-defaults
 !
 ! Create a L2TPv3 tunnel for the Serial interface
 !
 interface serial 1/0
    xconnect 192.168.200.1 101 encapsulation l2tpv3 manual pw-class hdlc-pw
    l2tp id 201 101
    l2tp cookie local 4 54321
    l2tp cookie remote 4 12345
    l2tp hello l2tp-defaults
 !
 ! default route to the service provider
 !
 ip route 0.0.0.0 0.0.0.0 192.168.100.2

 Router B2
 !
 l2tp-class l2tp-defaults
  retransmit initial retries 30
  cookie-size 8
 !
 ! pseudowire class for ethernet
 !
 pseudowire-class ether-pw
  encapsulation l2tpv3
  protocol none
  ip local interface serial 0/0
 !
 ! pseudowire class for HDLC
 !
 pseudowire-class hdlc-pw
  encapsulation l2tpv3
  protocol none
  ip local interface serial 0/0
 !
 ! 2M leased line to the service provider
 !
 Interface serial 0/0
    ip address 192.168.200.1 255.255.255.0
 !
 ! Create a L2TPv3 tunnel for the Ethernet interface
 !
 interface Ethernet 0/0
```

continues

Example 8-10 *Configuration Example of Router A2 in Site A (Continued)*

```
      xconnect 192.168.100.1 100 encapsulation l2tpv3 manual pw-class ether-pw
      l2tp id 100 200
      l2tp cookie local 4 12345
      l2tp cookie remote 4 54321
      l2tp hello l2tp-defaults
  !
  ! Create a L2TPv3 tunnel for the Serial interface
  !
  interface serial 1/0
      xconnect 192.168.100.1 101 encapsulation l2tpv3 manual pw-class hdlc-pw
      l2tp id 101 201
      l2tp cookie local 4 12345
      l2tp cookie remote 4 54321
      l2tp hello l2tp-defaults
  !
  ! default route to the service provider
  !
  ip route 0.0.0.0 0.0.0.0 192.168.200.2
```

Although the complication of setting up a L2TPv3 tunnel resides within Router A2 and Router B2, from Router A1's and B1's point of view, they see each other as directly connected via the serial interface. Likewise, from switch A1's and B1's point of view, they see themselves as connected via a simple Ethernet interface, as illustrated in Figure 8-29.

Figure 8-29 *View from End Nodes of L2TPv3*

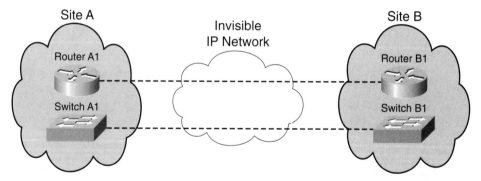

Example 8-11 shows the configurations required for Router A1 and B1. Notice that the configuration is straightforward.

Example 8-11 *End Nodes Configuration for L2TPv3*

```
Router A1
interface serial 0
   ip address 192.168.100.1 255.255.255.0

Router B1
interface serial 0
   ip address 192.168.100.2 255.255.255.0
```

Notice also that the IP addresses can be similar to that of Router A2's and Router B2's serial interfaces. The reason for this is that Router A1 and Router B1 only see each other via the tunnel. Whatever has been configured in the network in between them is invisible. Example 8-12 shows the configuration for the switches.

Example 8-12 *Switch Configuration for L2TPv3*

```
Switch A1
interface FastEthernet 0/1
  switchport trunk encapsulation dot1q
  switchport mode dynamic desirable

Switch B1
interface FastEthernet 0/1
  switchport trunk encapsulation dot1q
  switchport mode dynamic desirable
```

MPLS-VPN

Multiprotocol Label Switching (MPLS) complements IP routing technology by introducing the concept of label switching on top of the regular IP destination routing. The MPLS technology prepends labels to IP packets. A separate forwarding table is also built, and traffic forwarding relies on labels rather than on normal routing.

There are a few key features of MPLS in addition to top of IP routing technology — namely, MPLS-VPN (virtual private network), traffic engineering (TE), and quality of service (QoS). This section only focuses on MPLS-VPN.

MPLS-VPN enables the creation of a VPN on top of an existing MPLS network. Although there is recent development to create both Layer 2 and Layer 3 VPNs, this section focuses only on Layer 3 VPNs.

Although many service providers offer MPLS-VPN as an alternative WAN connectivity for an IP network, the key advantage for MPLS-VPN is the ability to create VPNs with multiple sites and with the possibility of multiple physical links.

Shown in Figure 8-30, a router sitting at the edge of an MPLS network is known as a *label edge router* (*LER*). The LER receives packets from an external normal IP router and then labels the IP packet with an MPLS label and forwards it into the MPLS network. At the heart of the MPLS network is the label switch router (LSR). When an LSR sees a labeled packet, it performs label swapping and forwards the packet to the next LSR, until it reaches the desired destination, which is another LER. The term *label switched path* (LSP) is used to describe the path taken by the packets to traverse the network using MPLS label swapping.

Figure 8-30 *MPLS Architecture*

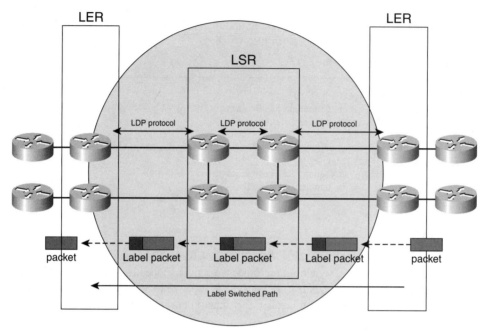

All the routers within an MPLS network run a common IGP, either OSPF or IS-IS. The router builds a routing table using this routing protocol and then uses the routing table to build a label forwarding table. A forwarding equivalence class (FEC) is used to describe a group of IP packets forwarded over the same path. The LSRs use Label Distribution Protocol (LDP) to exchange label information with each other. Hence, in a MPLS network, forwarding decisions are based on labels rather than routing information. However, routing information provided by the IGP protocol, OSPF or IS-IS, constructs the label forwarding table.

The MPLS-VPN feature enables the creation of VPNs within the MPLS network. Figure 8-31 shows a conceptual network of MPLS-VPN. Although MPLS-VPN is generally deployed by service providers, its use is not restricted to service providers only. Some large enterprises are deploying MPLS-VPN to support their business needs.

In MPLS-VPN, additional terms are introduced to describe the architecture shown in Figure 8-31:

- **Customer edge (CE) router**—The router that the customer used to connect to the service provider
- **Provider edge (PE) router**—The router with which the service provider connects to the customer router
- **Provider (P) router**—The router within the service provider MPLS network that connects to the PE routers

Figure 8-31   *MPLS-VPN Architecture*

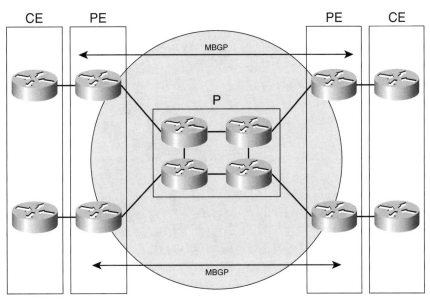

To enable MPLS-VPN, Multiprotocol BGP (MBGP) must be running between all the PE routers. MPLS-VPN uses MBGP to propagate label information on the respective VPN, as illustrated in Figure 8-32.

For a single VPN, such as the example shown in Figure 8-32, the two PE routers will have the VPN configured, and the MBGP will be used to exchange information on the VPN between the PE routers. In the example, when a packet from the CE router arrives in the PE router, the PE tags it with a VPN label. When the PE sends the packet to a P router, it tags the packet with an additional forwarding label derived from IGP. Therefore, when the packet is sent across the network, it actually contains two labels. When the packet arrives at the destination PE router, the PE router strips the labels and sends the IP packet to the target CE router. The P router does not care about the VPN label; it just forwards the packet based on the label derived from IGP.

NOTE   This section uses an example of MPLS with a single VPN. Although you can create multiple VPNs, the configuration example is restricted to only one VPN for simplicity.

In Figure 8-33, there is a single VPN known as RED VPN with two CE routers involved. The service provider's MPLS network is built up with only four routers: two P routers and two PE routers.

Figure 8-32 *Single VPN in MPLS-VPN*

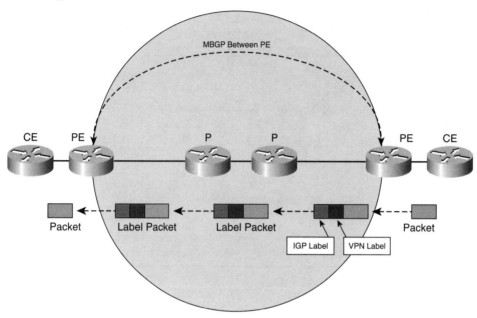

Figure 8-33 *MPLS-VPN Example*

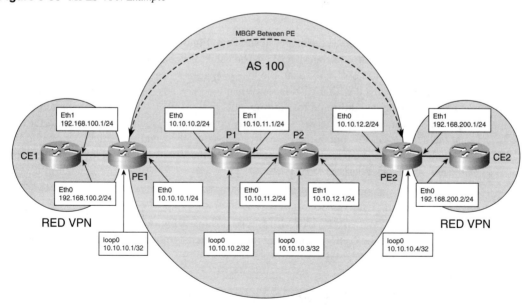

The configuration for the P routers is the simplest and is shown in Example 8-13.

Example 8-13   *Configuration for Both P Routers (P1 and P2)*

```
Router P1
!
! CEF forwarding needs to be enabled
!
ip cef
!
interface loopback0
  ip address 10.0.0.2 255.255.255.255
!
interface Ethernet 0
  ip address 10.10.10.2 255.255.255.0
  tag-switching ip
!
interface Ethernet 1
  ip address 10.10.11.1 255.255.255.0
  tag-switching ip
!
router ospf 1
  network 10.0.0.0 0.0.0.255 area 0
  network 10.10.10.0 0.0.0.255 area 0
  network 10.10.11.0 0.0.0.255 area 0

Router P2
!
! CEF forwarding needs to be enabled
!
ip cef
!
interface loopback0
  ip address 10.0.0.3 255.255.255.255
!
interface Ethernet 0
  ip address 10.10.11.2 255.255.255.0
  tag-switching ip
!
interface Ethernet 1
  ip address 10.10.12.1 255.255.255.0
  tag-switching ip
!
router ospf 1
  network 10.0.0.0 0.0.0.255 area 0
  network 10.10.11.0 0.0.0.255 area 0
  network 10.10.12.0 0.0.0.255 area 0
```

The PE router will be more complicated with MBGP running, as shown in Example 8-14.

Example 8-14 *Configuration of Both PE Routers (PE1 and PE2)*

```
Router PE1
!
! CEF forwarding needs to be enabled
!
ip cef
!
! define RED VPN
!
ip vrf RED
  rd 100:1
  route-target export 100:1000
  route-target import 100:1000
!
interface loopback0
  ip address 10.0.0.1 255.255.255.255
!
! Ethernet 0 to connect to P router
!
interface Ethernet 0
  ip address 10.10.10.1 255.255.255.0
  tag-switching ip
!
! Ethernet 1 to connect to CE router
!
interface Ethernet 1
  ip vrf forwarding RED
  ip address 192.168.100.1 255.255.255.0
!
router ospf 1
  network 10.0.0.0 0.0.0.255 area 0
  network 10.10.10.0 0.0.0.255 area 0
!
Router bgp 100
  !
  ! establish BGP session with other PE
  !
  neighbor 10.10.10.4 remote-as 100
  neighbor 10.10.10.4 update-source Loopback0
  !
  address-family vpnv4
  neighbor 10.10.10.4 activate
  neighbor 10.10.10.4 send-community both
  exit-address-family
  !
  ! command for VPN RED
  !
  address-family ipv4 vrf RED
  redistribute connected
  exit-address-family
!
```

Example 8-14   *Configuration of Both PE Routers (PE1 and PE2) (Continued)*

```
Router PE2
!
! CEF forwarding needs to be enabled
!
ip cef
!
! define RED VPN
!
ip vrf RED
  rd 100:1
  route-target export 100:1000
  route-target import 100:1000
!
interface loopback0
  ip address 10.0.0.4 255.255.255.255
!
! Ethernet 0 to connect to P router
!
interface Ethernet 0
  ip address 10.10.12.2 255.255.255.0
  tag-switching ip
!
! Ethernet 1 to connect to CE router
!
interface Ethernet 1
  ip vrf forwarding RED
  ip address 192.168.200.1 255.255.255.0
!
router ospf 1
  network 10.0.0.0 0.0.0.255 area 0
  network 10.10.12.0 0.0.0.255 area 0
!
Router bgp 100
  !
  ! establish BGP session with other PE
  !
  neighbor 10.10.10.1 remote-as 100
  neighbor 10.10.10.1 update-source Loopback0

  !
  address-family vpnv4
  neighbor 10.10.10.1 activate
  neighbor 10.10.10.1 send-community both
  exit-address-family
  !
  ! command for VPN RED
  !
  address-family ipv4 vrf RED
  redistribute connected
  exit-address-family
```

The CE router will see only the interface to the respective PE router. It does not have visibility to the MPLS network. Given that the individual CE to PE interface has its own IP subnet, the PE router routes those subnets across using MBGP. Notice that in the PE's MBGP configuration, there is a statement to **redistribute connected**. The **redistribute connected** command takes the connected routes of the CE and injects the routes into the routing table of the VPN. When the routes are available in the VPN routing table, other CEs within the VPN gain connectivity via those connected routes.

The configuration for the CE routers is simple, with a default route pointing to the respective PE routers, as shown in Example 8-15.

Example 8-15 *Configuration of the CE Routers*

```
Router CE1
!
interface Ethernet 0
  ip address 192.168.100.2 255.255.255.0
!
ip route 0.0.0.0 0.0.0.0 192.168.100.1
!

Router CE2
!
interface Ethernet 0
  ip address 192.168.200.2 255.255.255.0
!
ip route 0.0.0.0 0.0.0.0 192.168.200.1
```

One key advantage of MPLS-VPN is the ability to create a VPN of multiple sites. Figure 8-34 shows a single VPN with four sites connected to a single MPLS-VPN service provider.

Figure 8-34 *MPLS-VPN with Multiple Sites*

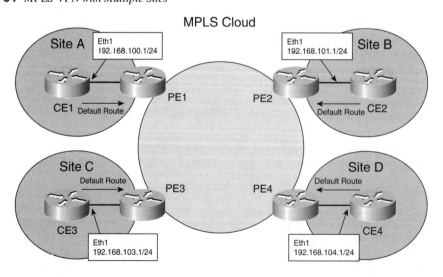

Configuration for the CE router at individual sites could be as simple as a default route to the PE routers, as shown in Example 8-16.

Example 8-16 *Configuration of the CE Router at Site A*

```
Router CE1
!
interface Ethernet 0
  ip address 192.168.100.2 255.255.255.0
!
ip route 0.0.0.0 0.0.0.0 192.168.100.1
!
```

With such configuration, the responsibility of routing multiple sites resides with the service provider network, using MBGP to route the traffic across multiple sites.

However, a single default route to the service provider does not offer the ability to have multiple paths to the other sites. You can run a routing protocol such as OSPF between the CE and PE routers to improve resiliency by allowing the CE routers to have multiple paths to each other.

Shown in Figure 8-35, a similar example to Figure 8-34, CE routers have serial leased lines to each other.

Figure 8-35 *MPLS-VPN with Multiple Sites Running OSPF with PE*

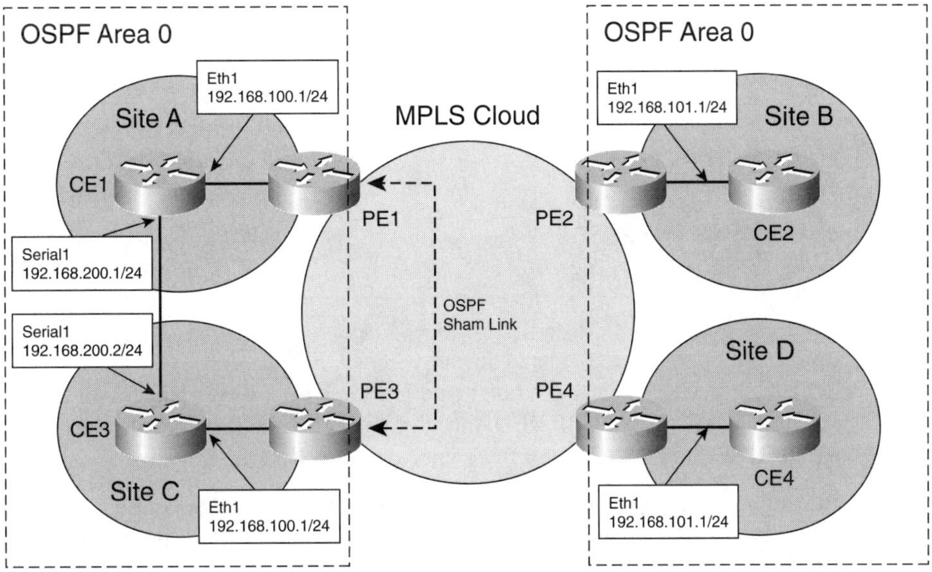

All the CE routers belong to OSPF Area 0. CE routers in Site A and Site C have a serial leased line connected to each other.

The PE routers need to have OSPF configured and running between the link and the PE and the CE, as shown in Example 8-17.

Example 8-17 *Configuration of the PE Routers Running OSPF with CE*

```
Router PE1
!
! define RED VPN
!
ip vrf RED
  rd 100:1
  route-target export 100:1000
  route-target import 100:1000
!
! Configuration for ospf for VPN RED
!
router ospf 10 vrf RED
  network 192.168.100.0 0.0.0.255 area 0
  area 0 sham-link 192.168.100.2 192.168.103.2 cost 40
  !
Router bgp 100
  !
  ! establish BGP session with other PE.
  ! One set of BGP peering command is shown for brevity
  !
  neighbor 10.10.10.4 remote-as 100
  neighbor 10.10.10.4 update-source Loopback0
!
  address-family vpnv4
  neighbor 10.10.10.4 activate
  neighbor 10.10.10.4 send-community both
  exit-address-family
  !
  ! command for VPN RED
  !
  address-family ipv4 vrf RED
  redistribute connected
  redistribute ospf 10
  exit-address-family
```

Shown in Example 8-17, a separate instance of an OSPF process has been created for VRF RED, which is the VPN ID. The command is **router ospf 10 vrf RED**. Within the configuration for MBGP for VRF RED, the additional command **redistribute ospf 10** is configured to allow OSPF routes to be injected into VRF RED.

Referring to Figure 8-34, the serial link between CE1 and CE3 becomes a backdoor link for the MPLS-VPN. OSPF treats the link through MPLS-VPN as a interarea route, and the backdoor link as a intra-area route. The intra-area route will be more preferred than the interarea route. To get around the problem, a sham link is created between the PE1 and PE3 router. A *sham link* is an intra-area link. With a sham link, the path between the MPLS-VPN will be used. As shown in Example 8-17, the sham link is configured with the command

area 0 sham-link 192.168.100.2 192.168.103.2 cost 40, where 192.168.100.2 is the address for PE1, and 192.168.203.2 is the address for PE2. A similar command has to be configured in PE2.

Example 8-18 shows the configuration for a CE router running OSPF at Site A.

Example 8-18   *Configuration of CE Router Running OSPF at Site A*

```
Router CE1
!
interface Ethernet 0
  ip address 192.168.100.2 255.255.255.0
!
Interface Serial 0
  ip address 192.168.200.1 255.255.255.0
!
router ospf 10
  network 192.168.100.0 0.0.0.255 area 0
  network 192.168.200.0 0.0.0.255 area 0
!
```

MPLS-VPN enables you to connect multiple sites together with a single VPN. At the same time, using another WAN connectivity such as leased line, you can build a resilient and cost-effective WAN network.

Summary

This chapter covered various WAN connectivity options to build a resilient IP infrastructure. The choice of WAN connectivity is determined by bandwidth requirements, but unfortunately your choices are often restricted by costs and availability. If you have multiple WAN connectivity working together, you can reduce dependency on a single element and improve resiliency of the overall IP infrastructure.

This chapter covers the following topics:

- Data Center Environmental Considerations
- Data Center Network Considerations
- Data Center Network Architecture
- Data Center Network Security
- Service Optimization
- Integrated Service Modules

CHAPTER 9

Data Center Module

Information is, perhaps, the most important asset that a company possesses. With almost all companies storing their information in digital form, data centers are becoming the most important physical asset a company has. The importance of data centers in the entire IT asset can never be underestimated. After all, the aim of the whole IT infrastructure is to transport and process information. Without information, there is not much use for the IT infrastructure. Therefore, the discussion of a resilient IP network has to include a resilient data center module.

Unlike yesteryear when data centers could just mean a room that housed some servers, the construction of a modern data center is a technical task. The power requirement, the air conditioning, and even cabling require professional and technical know-how.

As for the networking aspect, a data center module is not as straightforward as it seems. It is more than merely connecting a bunch of servers to a network. One important point to note is how the physical aspects of a data center and its network design influence each other. Each is closely related and dependent on the other. Therefore, various factors must be considered when dealing with data center resiliency. The environmental aspects of the data center include the following:

- The amount of real estate available within the data center affects rack layout.
- The amount of power and air conditioning available affects what kind of equipment that can be deployed.
- The cabling layout, if not done properly from day one, can mean a disastrous mess when expansion takes place.

Other than the environmental aspects, changes in the way people access information, and the proliferation of hacking and denial-of-service (DoS) attacks on the Internet, affect how networks are constructed within the data center. With the introduction of new Layer 2 and Layer 3 networking technology to tackle these changes, today's data center networks differ from those of the past. Technologies that address information availability and scalability have emerged in recent years. These technologies, such as content networking, have contributed to the totally new idea of making information available around the clock.

As part of the discussion on constructing the data center module, this chapter touches on some of these factors and highlights some new features that have been successfully deployed.

Data Center Environmental Considerations

This section considers how network design is influenced by environmental factors within the data center and vice versa. Not many of us have the luxury of being involved in the planning and construction of a new data center. Many of us step into an already existing data center. Therefore, you must work within the constraints of the existing data center—lack of space, a cooling problem, and so on. The following sections cover various physical aspects of data centers and discuss how they contribute to the resiliency of a data center module.

Cabling

Cabling is definitely the most "unglamorous" part when it comes to data center discussion. Often, cabling is treated as an afterthought, with jobs being done by technicians. The fact is, cabling and network design are intertwined, and it is as technical a subject as networking design can be.

A well-designed cabling plant improves operational efficiency and helps in maintaining network resiliency. It is common to walk into a data center and see cables dangling from the ceiling or snaking across the floors. These scenarios are perfect to produce a network problem. In the worst-case scenario, precious time is wasted in troubleshooting when a network manager has to sort through a cable mess to figure out which cable goes to which switch port.

This section describes important components of proper cabling:

* Tagging
* Documentation
* Discipline

Tagging

Network managers often fail to tag cables. A tagged cable on both ends helps with easy location of the connected devices. When a high-profile network breaks down, every minute counts when trying to bring the network service back up. In this type of scenario, the pressure on network managers can be great. The last thing that you want is to do cable tracing under duress. A well thought out tagging system helps to eliminate this chore and improves confidence and assurance under difficult situations. The use of different color cables and tags for different devices is an extremely helpful method. A proper cabling system from the beginning minimizes the likelihood of cable faults and aids in reducing troubleshooting time, leading to a higher availability number for the network.

Documentation

Another area that is closely related to tagging but that is mostly ignored is documentation. Besides having diagrams showing the logical network designs, it is important to have documentation of the physical connectivity, too. A detailed diagram showing which port of a router is connected to which port of a switch is extremely important, especially when it comes to remote troubleshooting of a network. Such documentation proves crucial when you are trying to ascertain the connectivity status of a particular link. It would be a disaster thinking both sides of a link are up when in actuality you are looking at the status of the wrong port. Again, this is about improving confidence and assurance during troubleshooting time.

Discipline

One word sums up the expectation when it comes to cabling: *discipline*. It is common to see a neat and tidy data center on day one, only to turn into a mess of cables within six months. This happens as new devices are added and new cables are added haphazardly, crisscrossing from rack to rack. Many network managers think tagging can wait and documentation can be followed up, but procrastination and lack of discipline are the enemies of data center operation. Therefore, strict operational procedure has to be enforced. One good policy to follow is to have regular monthly or yearly "cleanup" exercises for the data center so that a proper operating environment can be maintained.

All works that are carried out within the data center, even just the laying of a single cable, must be planned. Preparation work has to be done well before the actual work. Such preparation includes the approval, switch port assignment, proper cable run, patch panel assignment, tagging, documentation, and a scheduled time slot. All these things should be done even before the new device is brought into the data center. In reality, it is the reverse that happens. Somebody brings a new device in, powers it up, looks for a cable that is lying on the floor, runs it in the "shortest path" manner, and plugs it into a convenient switch port. For this type of operation, there is no point talking about network resiliency.

Rack Space

Many network managers may realize that a data center is about dealing with real estate. Just as real estate in a downtown area is expensive, the rack space within a data center is precious.

The importance of planning for space in the data center cannot be ignored. Proper planning for rack space means networking equipment can be located conveniently and correctly within the data center, which not only helps in operational efficiency but also ultimately contributes to network resiliency. Rack-space planning is important, especially if the data center experiences frequent change. For example, if no space allowance is provided, replacing a smaller switch with a bigger one might prove impossible, or worse, other devices might have to be remounted to make way for a new device. In such a case, moving equipment means a longer downtime.

Server Size

Server technology has undergone tremendous changes over the past few years. Two areas profoundly impact the data center network design: the physical size and performance of the server.

As shown in Figure 9-1, except for those top-end high-performance servers, most servers have experienced some downsizing in recent years. The physical dimensions of servers are getting smaller, and yet they pack the same, if not more, compute power than their predecessors. The proliferation of 1-RU servers, or rack-mount servers, has changed the look of the data center and affects how data center networks are designed.

Figure 9-1 *Changes in the Server Size*

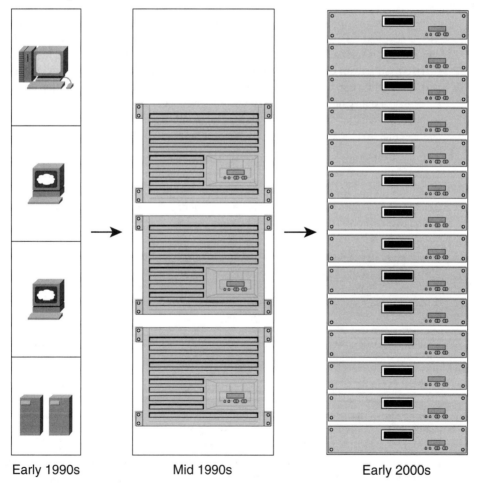

Early 1990s   Mid 1990s   Early 2000s

There are two ways to connect these 1-RU servers physically to the network. The first is to have these servers connected via unshielded twisted-pair (UTP) cables to a switch that is located in another rack, as shown in Figure 9-2. For a small number of servers, this is still manageable, especially for the rack that contains the switch. However, when many racks of servers need to be connected in this manner, cabling can become quite an issue. Imagine the load on the cable tray leading to the rack containing the switch. In addition, jamming hundreds of cables into a single rack can be a problem, to say the least.

Figure 9-2   *Running UTP Cables to an External Switch*

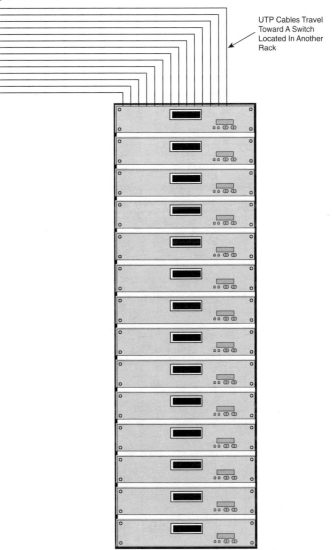

UTP Cables Travel Toward A Switch Located In Another Rack

Figure 9-3 shows another way to connect the servers to the network. In this option, all the servers are connected to a small switch within the same rack. This small form-factor switch, typically 1-RU in size, can be both Layer 2 or Layer 3, depending on the logical network design. In this case, what comes out of the server rack is just a pair of fiber that connects the small switch to its upstream connection. The upstream connections can typically be a pair of distribution switches or a pair of routers. The benefit of this option is neater cabling running within the data center. All the UTP cables, which are bulky and harder to manage, are confined within the rack. The problem with this option is the cost associated with the introduction of those 1-RU switches within the server rack. In the case of a distribution switch as upstream, it also means the introduction of the Spanning Tree Protocol (STP) between the racks. The STP introduces another factor that determines the resiliency of the server resources. From a network management perspective, this also means more devices to monitor and manage. From an inventory perspective, this might mean more parts to stock for spares, which ultimately adds to the cost. Another limitation of this design is that servers must be connected to a different switch to satisfy some requirements.

Figure 9-3 *Alternative Cabling Option*

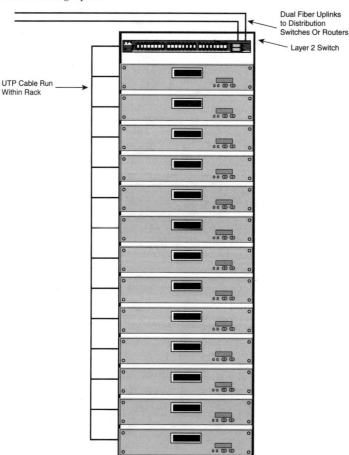

Note that physical connectivity does not affect the Layer 3 design of the data center. Therefore, it is possible to see a mix of these two options within the same data center. The point to note is that each method has its pros and cons, and it is difficult to say which is better than the other. The decision will often depend on the operational requirements, preferences, and the network manager's familiarity with a particular setup.

Power

Power is one important consideration when it comes to data center readiness. It is important to note how the new generation of networking equipment and new technologies affect the sizing of the power requirement within the data center.

Consider network speed, for example. Just a few years ago, a 100-Mbps backbone was considered high speed. Today, even a gigabit backbone pales in comparison with those that deploy a 10-Gbps network. In fact, some networks have a 40-Gbps link capacity. As network speed gets faster and faster, it is important to know that the power to drive this kind of speed is increasing, too. A power-supply module of a network device that was purchased three years ago might not be enough to drive the high-speed modules of today. Likewise, the power supply within the data center might not be adequate to drive a new network infrastructure of today.

A good example is the Cisco Catalyst 6513 switch. With a total of 13 slots, it needs a lot of power to drive those modules within the slots. The power supply for the Catalyst 6500 used to be 1000 watts (W). Today, the power-supply module of the Catalyst 6513 measures 6000 W, with an input current of 20 amps. Not many data centers can provide a 20-amp input.

Another good example is the Cisco Carrier Routing System, the CRS-1. With a power rating of 16.56 kW, it certainly needs some major power upgrading and site preparation before installation.

Another area of development that affects the power-supply requirement within a data center is IP telephony. With the introduction of IP phones, the switch not only has to provide data connectivity but also power to drive the phone. The power supply for a Catalyst switch used to be just for the modules alone. But today, more power is required to drive the IP phones attached to the switch. Imagine installing a Catalyst 6513 with the 48-port 10/100 Ethernet modules. Each of the 10/100 Ethernet ports has an IP phone attached to it. You would have to plan carefully for the power required.

Not only do you need to look into the primary power requirement, you also have to revise the standby power. For example, with a load of 6000 W power module, you must review your uninterruptible power supply (UPS). By the time a power failure occurs, it is too late to realize that you have an inadequate UPS. In addition, if you are deploying a power generator, you must make sure that you have stored enough fuel for emergency purposes. If you neglect to assess both primary and standby power needs, you compromise data center resiliency.

Next-Generation Server Architecture

In the server arena, one of the most significant developments is the introduction of the blade server products. These new products from vendors such as IBM, HP, and Dell literally change the way servers are deployed within the data center.

The blade servers are slim in size, and they slide into a common chassis, sharing power supply, fan, floppy drive, and switch ports. With their own processor, memory, and operating systems, each is an independent server. With a single chassis supporting up to 14 servers, these machines pack high-density computing power. One benefit of a blade server is that cabling becomes neater. They also come with their own mini network within their chassis. However, connecting these mini networks is something new that the network manager faces.

As shown in Figure 9-4, blade servers typically come with a dual network interface card (NIC) configuration for redundancy purposes. These NICs are connected to the backplane of the chassis, where there may be modules that aggregate these connections and provide connectivity to the outside world. These modules, sometimes called the *pass-through modules*, provide for both copper and fiber connections through special cable. Depending on the speed and distance requirements, the connections are typically 100- or 1000-Mbps Ethernet.

Figure 9-4   *Blade Server Connectivity*

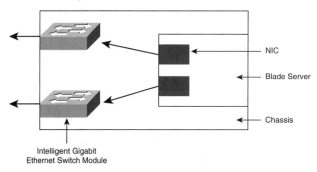

Another way to provide network connectivity to these servers is to have a mini switch, which comes in the form of a module that resides in the chassis. One example of this module is the Cisco Intelligent Gigabit Ethernet Switch Module (IGESM). It plugs into the IBM eServer Bladecenter chassis and is based on the Cisco Catalyst 2950 image. The connections out of the IGESMs are two trunk ports that connect to a pair of distribution switches. In this case, STP plays an important role in providing a loop-free Layer 2 network.

Blade servers have certainly changed the way servers are connected to the network. They introduce new challenges in areas such as power requirements, floor space loading, and cooling. In the area of network connectivity, the obvious challenge is to ensure that both Layer 2 and Layer 3 resiliency continue to work. Fortunately, products such as the IGESM ensure that feature interoperability is not an issue (because IGESM is based on the same Catalyst family of code).

So far, you have learned about only the physical aspects of data centers. Through extensive deployment experience and proper planning, the physical aspects tend to become easier to deal with than other areas, such as information security and network design. If you want to learn more about the construction of a data center, refer to *Build the Best Data Center Facility for Your Business*, by Douglas Alger (Cisco Press, 2005).

Besides the physical aspects, you must consider other factors when designing a data center network, as discussed in the following section.

Data Center Network Considerations

Designing a data center network differs from designing a normal campus-access network. It is more than just connecting a group of servers to a network. Some design considerations within a data center network are not found in other parts of a network. Besides those environmental considerations mentioned in the previous section, various important factors, such as security, server performance, fault tolerance, and multifaceted servers, need to be considered. These factors determine design philosophy and the choice of features, and ultimately influence the selection of equipment to be deployed within the data center.

Security

With important assets such as servers and databases residing within the data center, it is the center of focus for all hackers. To develop a data center network architecture that can mitigate cyber attacks, security has to be part of the network architecture from day one. It is tempting, and as a result disastrous, to treat security as an afterthought when developing a data center network. Unfortunately, many network managers ignore this advice, and they pay the hefty price of being compromised.

With the focus on securing the information infrastructure, many security features have been developed in the routing and switching products from Cisco Systems. Some of these technologies are applied solely in data center environments. These features help network managers to defend against threats and attacks. However, their use has to be factored into the architecture from day one, because ad hoc or incremental introduction might prove difficult to manage. Or worse, it might result in problems such as nonoptimized routing within the data center network. The new features are discussed in the section "Data Center Network Security."

Also, a good source of information for a security architecture is the Cisco Security Blueprint for Enterprise Networks (SAFE). It includes best practices and design recommendations for implementing security in various parts of the network. You can find more information about SAFE at the following URL:

http://www.cisco.com/go/safe

Server Performance

Server performance profoundly impacts the way data center networks are designed. In normal campus-access networks, users spend most of their time on activities such as typing and reading. During this time, the network connection is actually idling. For example, think about a 48-port access switch that connects to a group of users. Even though these users share a common 1-Gbps uplink, plenty of network bandwidth is available to serve this group of users.

Servers, however, behave differently than the end stations. Because servers are supposed to serve hundreds, if not thousands, of user connections at any given time, they are kept busy almost all the time. In addition, with the introduction of high-performance network interface cards, the new-generation servers are fully capable of generating gigabits of traffic at the line rate. If each server within a rack generates a line rate of traffic most of the time, the network architecture has to be able to address this traffic load and at the same time provide features and redundancy required to make sure information is available around the clock. Sizing of the uplink bandwidth and choice of equipment now takes on a new dimension.

The performance of these new servers affects how they should be connected to the network. For example, aggregating many high-performance servers to a single low-end access switch, typically with 1- or 2-Gb connections, may pose a serious performance issue. This issue, together with that discussed in the section "Server Size," illustrates the complexity of data center design.

Fault-Tolerant Server Features

To increase server network availability, various NIC and server vendors have developed different technologies to address this issue. The following are some of the well-known technologies:

- Cisco Fast EtherChannel (FEC)
- Cisco Gigabit EtherChannel (GEC)
- HP trunking
- HP Network Fault Tolerance (NFT)
- HP Transmit Load Balancing (TLB)
- Linux Bonding Active Backup
- Linux Bonding Round Robin
- Linux Bonding XOR
- Sun Trunking
- Microsoft Network Load Balancing (NLB)
- IBM High-Availability Cluster Multiprocessing (HACMP)

Each of these technologies works differently to achieve the same goal: to prevent a single point of failure for accessibility to the server. Although some merely provide redundancy at network connectivity level, others provide for full server redundancy. Some work at the Layer 2 level by working around the Media Access Control (MAC) address, whereas some work at the Layer 3 level on the IP address. Which of these technologies you choose to deploy will ultimately affect how the design of your logical IP network performs. Obviously, it also determines how the physical connectivity has to be carried out.

Multifaceted Server

For performance and security reasons, the data center architecture has to take on the concept of multifaceted servers. That is, servers have multiple network interfaces to serve different functions:

- A public-facing interface for serving the information to all users
- A private-facing interface for management purposes
- A backup interface for backing up vital information

The network needs to be constructed to cater to these needs. Issues that you must address include how to separate these interfaces at the Layer 3 level and how to provide physical connectivity for these interfaces. Dealing with these problems may seem straightforward when you have only a few servers; when you have hundreds or thousands of servers, however, this can be a challenging problem. In the section "Server Size," you learned about the problem of having to jam hundreds of cables into a rack. That was for one interface per server. Multiply the problem by three, and you will run into a scalability issue. Obviously, scalability is one important consideration when implementing a solution for servers because of the numbers involved.

Data Center Network Architecture

So far, you have learned about the various factors that are particular to the data center environment. By now, you should realize that designing a data center network is not as easy as it seems. To incorporate all these considerations into the architecture, you might deploy a unique design philosophy or features that are only applicable to a data center environment.

Although designing the data center module is a complex task, the basics of networking still apply. One important rule still holds true even in the data center module: modularity. Modularity helps you tackle the challenge by dividing the data center network into many subareas. This way, the complex problem can be broken down into manageable blocks that are easy to understand. Figure 9-5 shows the high-level building blocks of a data center network.

Figure 9-5 *Modular Approach to a Data Center Module*

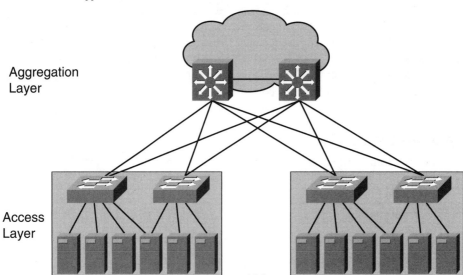

As shown in Figure 9-5, there are two portions to the data center module: the access and the aggregation layers. Both of these layers perform different functions, and they are described in the following sections.

Access Layer Design

The access layer is the point where the servers are connected to the network. Depending on the network design, the access layer may provide Layer 2 switching only or both Layer 2 and Layer 3 switching functions. In the following discussion, the phrase *server farm* may mean a single access layer block or it may mean many blocks. In general, a server farm means a group of servers under the same administrative domain. Therefore, there can be many server farms in a data center module.

From an IP network point of view, a server farm is a straightforward design. Just provide an IP subnet, assign IP addresses to the servers, and provide a default gateway function. However, the Layer 2 design may vary, depending on various factors.

For example, the number of servers may dictate how the Layer 2 should be designed. With a few servers, you can connect them to a switch and get the job done. There will be just a few cables to connect, and they will be neatly tucked within a rack. However, when you have tens or hundreds of servers to connect, real estate becomes an issue. Here, real estate points to both the number of switch ports available on a switch and the space to aggregate all the cables. The largest switch today, the Catalyst 6513, can provide 528 10/100/1000-Mbps switch ports (after reserving two slots for the supervisors). Even if you decide to connect that many servers to a single switch, dragging more than 500 UTP cables into a rack is no easy task. In addition, connecting that many servers to a single switch is unwise, because a single switch failure means a massive server outage.

When dealing with access layer design, there are two important influencing factors:

- The physical aspects of the servers, such as size and number
- The logical IP design

When trying to design the access layer, many network managers adopt one of the two design options, or some variation of both.

The first is to provide Layer 2 switching within a single rack. Such a setup is often deployed when there are many 1-RU servers within the rack. Depending on how many interfaces each server has, there can be one, two, or even three 1-RU switches within the rack to provide connectivity, as illustrated in Figure 9-6.

Figure 9-6   *Connectivity Within a Rack*

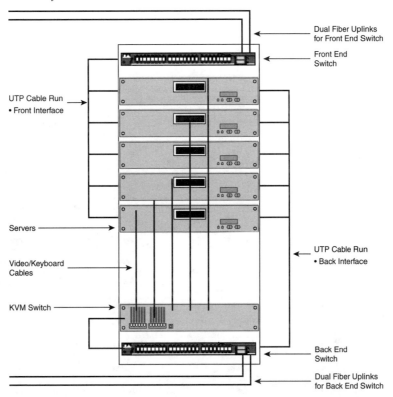

As shown in Figure 9-6, besides the servers and the switches, additional equipment may reside within the rack. A good example is a Keyboard-Video-Mouse (KVM) switch, which provides for remote control of the servers, or even an out-of-band network that provides management of the switches.

Advantages of this model include the following:

- The UTP cables are confined within the rack, which makes them easier to manage.

- There will be only a few cables leaving the rack. These are the cables that provide the uplinks from the switches within the rack to the aggregating devices, which are residing in other racks. These cables may still be UTP, or they may be fiber cables.

- The server farm scales by these self-contained racks. This type of scaling enables network managers to partition the server farm into blocks for easier management.

However, critics dislike the model for the following reasons:

- For a really large server farm, there will be too many 1-RU Layer 2 switches in the network. As in all Layer 2 networks, STP plays an important role. Having a large STP domain with too many devices may not be a good idea for a server farm. Introduction of STP also increases the complexity within the server farm.

- Extra cost is incurred in the procurement of those 1-RU switches within the rack.

The second way of connecting the server is to designate a rack to house modular switches to provide for connectivity for all servers, as illustrated in Figure 9-7.

Figure 9-7   *Connecting Servers to a Modular Access Switch*

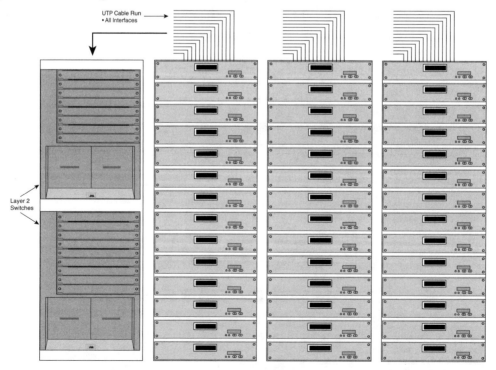

In this model, there are only servers within the rack, and perhaps the KVM switch. All the UTP cables that leave the rack are bound for the Layer 2 switches. Typically, the first rack of the row houses the switch. Therefore, all cables run toward this rack. Some network managers might prefer to place this rack in the middle of the row and thereby shorten the average length of the cable. Figure 9-8 shows these two options.

Figure 9-8   *Possible Locations of Access Switches*

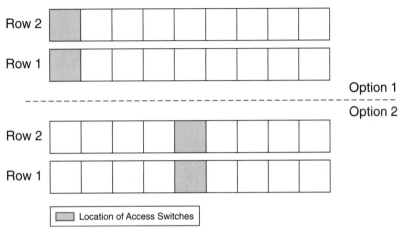

The solution proposed by the second option manages to solve some issues but introduces some cabling challenges to other network managers. This just shows that there will never be a right or wrong access layer design. Both options have their merits, and, in fact, it is very common to see data centers deploying both options. Besides the physical aspect of connectivity, the logical Layer 2 design is an important area of focus.

NIC Teaming

One of the most important influencing factors is the fault-tolerant features of the servers, as mentioned in the section "Server Performance." Although features such as the FEC and GEC provide link redundancy, their main aim is to increase overall throughput of the server. The real fault-tolerant feature, in terms of availability of information, is to have more than one network interface working together. This concept, known as NIC teaming, is shown in Figure 9-9.

Figure 9-9 *NIC Teaming*

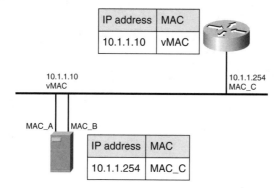

The device driver of the NICs presents a virtual MAC (vMAC) address to the Layer 2 world outside of a single virtual interface. Other devices on the same network map this vMAC address to the actual IP address of the server. This way, when the primary interface fails on the server, the secondary interface takes over. With the vMAC, the rest of the devices on the same network do not have to flush their ARP tables (which means that you can maintain continuous connections).

Figure 9-10 shows one way to achieve high availability with NIC teaming. With this design, the infrastructure is protected from a single point of failure in the area of connectivity, such as in the server NICs and switch. Note, however, the requirement for the server's VLAN to span across the switches.

Figure 9-10 *Possible Physical Connection for NIC Teaming*

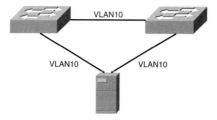

In the case of multiple-server VLANs with the same NIC teaming strategy, the STP domains can get quite complex. One good example is when the aggregation layer is introduced, as shown in Figure 9-11.

Figure 9-11 *Redundancy with NIC Teaming*

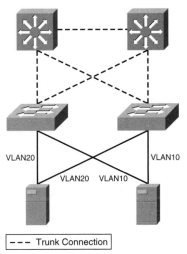

One advantage of having multiple-server VLANs is that you can limit the extent of an outage. A problem in one VLAN will not affect the rest. However, with the server VLANs spanning multiple switches, management of STP of individual VLANs becomes complicated. In this case, you might be tempted to introduce additional features such as MSTP or 802.1s. Remember, however, that introducing more features means introducing complexity (leading to troubleshooting difficulties when errors occur). Spending too much time troubleshooting a server farm VLAN issue means incurring longer downtime when problems occur.

Clustering

NIC teaming may mitigate a NIC failure scenario. However, to take the actual server failure into consideration, another technique, called *clustering*, may be introduced. Whereas NIC teaming works at the Layer 2 level, clustering works at Layer 3.

Clustering is a popular way to increase the availability of the server resource. Operating systems from Sun Microsystems, Microsoft, Novell, and Linux provide server clustering solutions. Although they work differently in detail, clustering solutions share the same concept. Figure 9-12 shows a typical clustering solution. Basically, more than one server works together, and they present to the rest of the world a single virtual server with an IP address. To keep track of each other's status, the servers are connected to each other via a private network, and deploy a *heartbeat mechanism*. The use of the heartbeat mechanism is to make sure that their partner is still functioning. The private network is a Layer 2 network.

Figure 9-12 *Server Clustering*

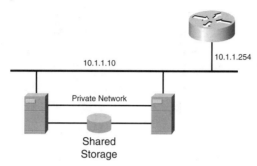

Clustering greatly improves the server farm availability by providing node-level redundancy. The significance of clustering technology is that the network design needs to step up to match the resiliency.

Aggregation Layer Design

The aggregation layer within the data center is where the server VLANs are terminated and where the Layer 3 edge begins. The function of the aggregation layer within the data center is similar to that of the distribution module discussed in the section "Distribution Layer" in Chapter 6, "Access Module."

As mentioned, the logical IP network of the server farm is straightforward. You need a pair of Layer 3 devices to provide a redundant default gateway service to a group of servers. However, you already saw in the previous sections that the physical connections can vary, even though they achieve the same logical design. The aggregation layer can provide Layer 3 services to the servers in two ways :

- Trunk ports on an aggregation switch
- Routed ports on an aggregation switch

Trunk Ports on an Aggregation Switch

Figure 9-13 shows one way to connect the server farm access layer to the aggregation layer. The links between the two layers are Layer 2 connections. The ports at both ends of the uplinks are configured as trunk ports. STP is enabled on all switches to ensure a loop-free Layer 2 topology, while the trunk ports carry all VLAN traffic.

Figure 9-13 shows the Catalyst 6500 with the Supervisor Engine 720 to be positioned at the aggregation layer. The supervisor engines in the two aggregation switches provide the Layer 3 function, and are acting as the redundant default gateways for the servers. Figure 9-14 shows the resulting Layer 3 network.

Figure 9-13 *Trunking Between the Access and Aggregation Layers*

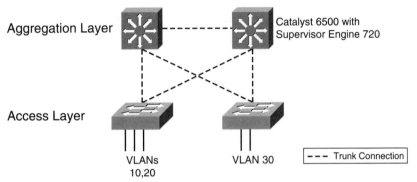

Figure 9-14 *Logical IP Network of a Server Farm*

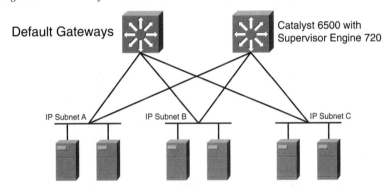

One characteristic of this design is its capability to support a VLAN that spans multiple access switches while preserving the IP logical design. However, note that spanning a VLAN across access switches is not a recommended design unless it is absolutely necessary. An example of when this can be tolerated is when a pair of fault-tolerant servers that use Layer 2 for a heartbeat needs to be on the same VLAN.

Routed Ports on an Aggregation Switch

Figure 9-15 shows another way to connect the access layer to the aggregation layer. In this design, the port on the aggregating layer facing the access layer is configured as a routing port. In other words, no STP runs between the ports at the end of the uplinks. The port at the access layer switch is configured as an access port. Even though the Layer 2 design of this option is different from that of Figure 9-13, the resulting logical IP network remains the same.

Figure 9-15   *Routed Ports Between the Access and Aggregation Layers*

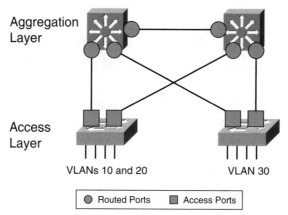

One advantage of this design is its simplicity. Because the STP is confined within the access layer, the aggregating layer runs pure routing protocols only. Even the interconnect between the two aggregating devices is a routed link. The result is a simpler configuration at the aggregating layer devices.

One drawback of this design is the restricted footprint of the VLANs. Placing a pair of fault-tolerant servers that use a Layer 2 network for a heartbeat is challenging. For example, if you want to place one of the servers in another location, the Layer 2 network has to be expanded in an awkward manner, as shown in Figure 9-16.

Figure 9-16   *Extending the Access Layer*

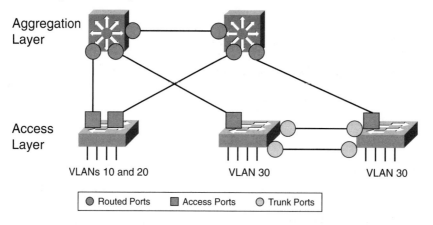

As with application layer design, both access layer design options have pros and cons. You may use a mix of both within a data center.

Architecture Scaling Consideration

Although the focus of a server farm design still revolves around switching and routing technology, many network managers mistake the design as just another typical campus design. Besides those differences discussed in the section "Data Center Network Considerations," one more factor makes designing a server farm different from a campus design: scaling.

A server farm has a unique scaling challenge simply because of bandwidth requirements. Unlike user workstations, which tend to be idle most of the time and generate bursty traffic at other times, server traffic tends to be consistently high volume. Therefore, it is easy to hit a performance issue in the server farm just because of bandwidth. Figure 9-17 shows one good example of a scaling problem.

Figure 9-17 *Scaling a High-Density Server Farm*

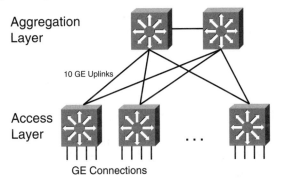

In Figure 9-17, the server farm architecture makes use of the chassis-based access layer to provide connections for the servers. Suppose that all the servers are connected at gigabit speed, and they are all capable of generating line-rate traffic. Because of the number of servers connecting to a single access switch, the network manager has decided to adopt 10 GE as the uplink standard. Now consider the number of 10 GE ports that are required on the aggregating device. You soon realize that aggregating traffic at such a speed requires a reevaluation of the hardware architecture of the aggregating devices, as well as the network design. Not many switches can support a high density of 10-GE ports. In addition, it would seem a waste of expensive resources to prevent a 10-GE uplink from forwarding traffic just because of an STP-blocked mode. Therefore, not only the hardware needs to be reevaluated to support the bandwidth required, the logical network design needs to be revisited, too. There is certainly a need to create many aggregating modules to scale the server farm.

Integrating all the aggregating modules into a common data center may mean introducing another layer. For the convenience of this discussion, this new layer is called the *core layer within the data center*. Most network managers probably have not had an opportunity to work on such a scale. Such a design is usually found in extremely huge data centers with thousands of servers. The core layer within the data center functions in the same way as an

IP core network module: it consolidates individual blocks. In this case, the individual blocks are the aggregating layers, each with hundreds of servers generating huge traffic loads, as shown in Figure 9-18.

Figure 9-18 *Core Layer Within a Data Center Module*

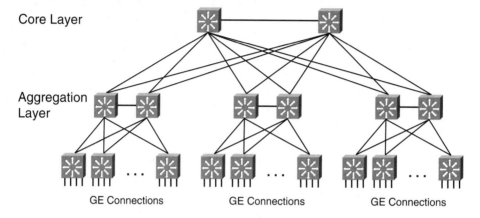

Data Center Network Security

Unlike the old days when security meant planting one or two firewalls, data center security today takes on a different dimension. With information playing a vital role in the operation of a business, the stakes are getting too high for information to be compromised. Attacks on networks are becoming more sophisticated and they are done through, but not limited to, the following techniques:

- **Packet sniffing**—An application that uses the promiscuous mode of the network adapter to capture all networks packets.

- **IP spoofing**—An attack in which a hacker assumes an IP address of others to conceal its true identity.

- **Denial-of-service (DoS) attack**—Aims to overwhelm a service so as to deny legitimate requests from being serviced. The service may be in the form of bandwidth, memory, or CPU. It is the most well-known of all Internet attacks, and efforts should be invested in understanding its mechanisms. Some of the more famous DoS attacks include the following:

  — Code Red

  — Blaster

  — Ping of Death

  — Trinity

- **Password attack**—As its name implies, this attack intends to acquire passwords to important assets so as to cause further damage. Password attacks can be achieved through other methods previously mentioned, such as IP spoofing, or they can be achieved via brute force.

- **Man-in-the-middle attack**—This type of attack happens when a hacker manages to position himself between the source and the destination of a network transaction. ARP cache poisoning is one common method.

- **Application attack**—This type of attack happens when application software holes are exploited to gain access to a computer system. The holes may be bugs or may be TCP port numbers that are exposed.

- **Port redirection attack**—This type of attack makes use of a compromised host to gain access to a network that is otherwise protected.

Understanding the mechanics of all these attacks is important, so that you know what you are up against. Such an understanding also helps you decide how the architecture should look, and what features are required in those routers and switches within the data center. In general, attacks can be launched from Layer 2 or Layer 3 perspectives, and each layer has to have some defense mechanism built in to the architecture. No longer can a network manager treat security as an afterthought. Instead, security should be an integral part of the data center architecture.

Layer 2 Security

Layer 2 security deals with protecting the network and hosts at the MAC level. Figure 9-19 shows a simple attacking mechanism that can compromise a Layer 2 network.

Figure 9-19 *Worm Attack on the Server*

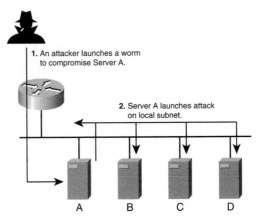

In Figure 9-19, Server A has been compromised by a worm from outside the network. When the worm strikes, it starts sending out probe packets and generating broadcast storms on the local subnet. The probe packets enable Server A to further infect other hosts, while the broadcast storm consumes all bandwidth on the subnet. This form of worm attack is the simplest to execute, but its damage can prove substantial.

One way to counter this sort of attack is to isolate the servers into different broadcast domains. With a Layer 3 partition, chances of a broadcast storm are minimized because there are fewer servers and they are protected from each other. However, this means using more subnets and, thus, wasting precious IP addresses. For example, in the most drastic implementation, you could put one server in a single IP subnet with its own default gateway. That means wasting four addresses, a /30 subnet, just to provide connectivity to a single server. In addition, a /30 subnet also means there are not enough IP addresses on the subnet to provide for a redundant gateway. When there is a shortage of public IP addresses, this might not be a good solution. Perhaps you need a solution that segregates the servers at the Layer 2 level while allowing them to share a common IP subnet. This is where the concept of private VLANs (PVLANs) comes in.

Private VLANs (PVLANs)

The PVLAN feature aims to solve the Layer 2 broadcast attack problem (and work around the IP address shortage issue).

The basic concept of a PVLAN is simple. It provides Layer 2 isolation for a group of hosts residing in the same IP subnet, as illustrated in Figure 9-20.

Figure 9-20 *Private VLAN*

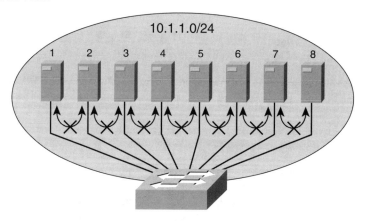

In Figure 9-20, all the servers reside within the same subnet (in this case, a /24 network). They share the same default gateway, and from a networking perspective, this is the only common entity that they can connect to. Although they reside within the same IP subnet, they have been isolated from a Layer 2 perspective. Every server behaves as if there are only two hosts on their subnet—itself and its default gateway. All communication at the Layer 2, be it broadcast or multicast, has been isolated for these servers.

With this implementation, even if one server is compromised, just as before, it will not be able to launch an attack on the rest of the servers. The probe packet will not get to the rest of the servers, and the broadcast will be contained, too. The only probable target is its default gateway. In this case, proper security measures and configuration would have been implemented on the default gateway to deal with attacks such as this.

In some cases, because of fault-tolerance requirements, certain groups of servers may need to communicate with each other via Layer 2 connectivity. In this case, PVLAN provides the concept of a community, where only servers within this community have Layer 2 communication. As a community, these servers are Layer 2 isolated from the rest of the servers within the same PVLAN. Thus, PVLAN provides protection but still allows servers to run in a fault-tolerant manner.

To support this community feature, the PVLAN feature introduces a new port role and VLAN concepts. To configure PVLAN, it is important that you understand these roles.

PVLAN Ports

There are three types of PVLAN ports:

- **Promiscuous port**—This port can communicate with all other ports within a PVLAN. This is where the default gateway for the IP subnet resides.

- **Isolated port**—This port is completely isolated from the rest of the PVLAN ports, except the promiscuous port.

- **Community ports**—These ports can communicate among themselves at Layer 2. They are separated from other community ports or isolated ports, except the promiscuous port.

Figure 9-21 shows the relationship of the three port types.

Figure 9-21 *Port Types of the Private VLAN*

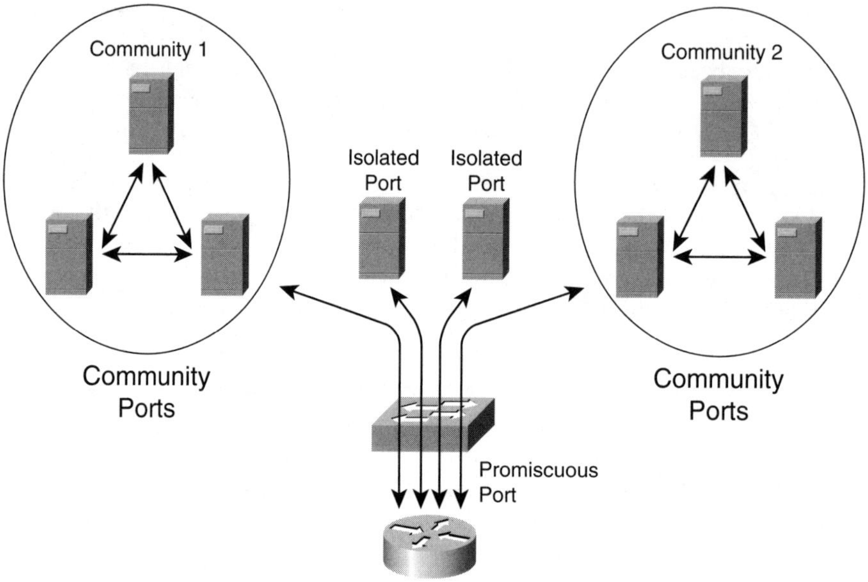

Types of VLANs

The PVLAN feature is achieved via the combination of a few special VLANs. These VLANs have to be created first before the PVLAN feature can actually work:

- **Primary VLAN**—The VLAN that carries traffic from the promiscuous port to all other ports.

- **Isolated VLAN**—The VLAN used by the isolated port to communicate with the promiscuous port. There can be multiple isolated VLANs within a PVLAN.

- **Community VLAN**—The VLAN used by the community ports to communicate among themselves and to send traffic to the promiscuous port. There can be multiple community VLANs within a PVLAN.

NOTE   Both the isolated and community VLANs are also known as *secondary VLANs*.

The construction of a PVLAN allows for these VLANs to be trunked across multiple switches as long as they support the PVLAN feature.

Configuring PVLAN

PVLAN configuration requires a few steps. Figure 9-22 shows a PVLAN configuration.

Figure 9-22 *Example of a Private VLAN*

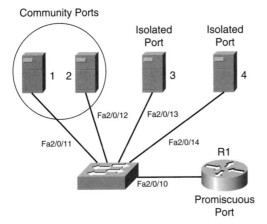

	VLAN101 Primary	VLAN102 Community	VLAN103 Private
Fa2/0/10	X	X	X
Fa2/0/11	X	X	
Fa2/0/12	X	X	
Fa2/0/13	X		X
Fa2/0/14	X		X

Suppose you are required to construct the PVLAN shown in Figure 9-22. Servers 1, 2, 3, and 4 reside within a PVLAN, where their traffic is isolated at Layer 2. Servers 1 and 2 reside within a community, because they run fault-tolerant features that require Layer 2 connectivity. All the servers share the same default gateway, which is R1.

Example 9-1 shows the steps to create the required PVLAN:

Step 1 Create a primary VLAN, VLAN101.

Step 2 Create a community VLAN, VLAN102.

Step 3 Create an isolated VLAN, VLAN103.

Step 4 Associate the secondary VLANs to the primary VLAN.

Step 5 Configure switch port Fa2/0/10 as a PVLAN promiscuous port.

Step 6 Configure switch ports Fa2/0/11 as PVLAN host ports. A host port is a switch port that participates in a PVLAN, but it is not the promiscuous port. The configuration for Fa2/0/12 to Fa2/0/14 will be the same except for their respective PVLAN assignments.

Example 9-19 *Creating a Private VLAN*

```
Step 1
Switch# configure terminal
Switch(config)# vlan 101
Switch(config-vlan)# private-vlan primary
Switch(config-vlan)# end
```

continues

Example 9-19 *Creating a Private VLAN (Continued)*

```
Switch# show vlan private-vlan
Primary Secondary Type              Interfaces
------- --------- ----------------- -----------------------------------
101               primary

Step 2
Switch# configure terminal
Switch(config)# vlan 102
Switch(config-vlan)# private-vlan community
Switch(config-vlan)# end
Switch# show vlan private-vlan


Primary Secondary Type              Interfaces
------- --------- ----------------- -----------------------------------
101               primary
        102       community

Step 3
Switch# configure terminal
Switch(config)# vlan 103
Switch(config-vlan)# private-vlan isolated
Switch(config-vlan)# end
Switch# show vlan private-vlan
Primary Secondary Type              Interfaces
------- --------- ----------------- -----------------------------------
101               primary
        102       community
        103       isolated

Step 4
Switch# configure terminal
Switch(config)# vlan 101
Switch(config-vlan)# private-vlan association 102-103
Switch(config-vlan)# end
Switch# show vlan private-vlan


Primary Secondary Type              Interfaces
------- --------- ----------------- -----------------------------------
101     102       community
101     103       isolated

Step 5
Switch# configure terminal
Switch(config)# interface fastethernet 2/0/10
Switch(config-if)# switchport mode private-vlan promiscuous
Switch(config-if)# switchport private-vlan mapping 101 add 102-103
Switch(config-if)# end

Switch#show interfaces fastethernet 2/0/10 switchport
Name: Fa2/0/10
Switchport: Enabled
Administrative Mode: private-vlan promiscuous
```

Example 9-19 *Creating a Private VLAN (Continued)*

```
Operational Mode: private-vlan promiscuous
Administrative Trunking Encapsulation: negotiate
Negotiation of Trunking: Off
Access Mode VLAN: 1 (default)
Trunking Native Mode VLAN: 1 (default)
Administrative Native VLAN tagging: enabled
Voice VLAN: none
Administrative private-vlan host-association: none
Administrative private-vlan mapping: 101 (VLAN101) 102 (VLAN102) 103 (VLAN103)
Administrative private-vlan trunk native VLAN: none
Administrative private-vlan trunk Native VLAN tagging: enabled
Administrative private-vlan trunk encapsulation: dot1q
Administrative private-vlan trunk normal VLANs: none
Administrative private-vlan trunk private VLANs: none
Operational private-vlan:
  101 (VLAN101) 102 (VLAN102) 103 (VLAN103)
Trunking VLANs Enabled: ALL
Pruning VLANs Enabled: 2-1001
Capture Mode Disabled
Capture VLANs Allowed: ALL


Step 6
Switch# configure terminal
Switch(config)# interface fastethernet 2/0/11
Switch(config-if)# switchport mode private-vlan host
Switch(config-if)# switchport private-vlan host-association 101 102
Switch(config-if)# end

Switch#show interfaces fastethernet 2/0/11 switchport
Name: Fa2/0/11
Switchport: Enabled
Administrative Mode: private-vlan promiscuous
Operational Mode: private-vlan promiscuous
Administrative Trunking Encapsulation: negotiate
Negotiation of Trunking: Off
Access Mode VLAN: 1 (default)
Trunking Native Mode VLAN: 1 (default)
Administrative Native VLAN tagging: enabled
Voice VLAN: none
Administrative private-vlan host-association: none
Administrative private-vlan mapping: 101 (VLAN101) 102 (VLAN102)
Administrative private-vlan trunk native VLAN: none
Administrative private-vlan trunk Native VLAN tagging: enabled
Administrative private-vlan trunk encapsulation: dot1q
Administrative private-vlan trunk normal VLANs: none
Administrative private-vlan trunk private VLANs: none
Operational private-vlan:
  101 (VLAN101) 102 (VLAN102)
Trunking VLANs Enabled: ALL
Pruning VLANs Enabled: 2-1001
Capture Mode Disabled
Capture VLANs Allowed: ALL
```

As you can see from Step 5's **show** command in Example 9-1, port Fa2/0/10 is associated with VLANs 101, 102, and 103, indicating that it is a promiscuous port. Step 6's **show** command shows Fa2/0/11 associated with the two VLANs, 101 and 102, indicating that it is a host port.

Catalyst Support for PVLANs

Note that not all Catalyst switches support the PVLAN feature. Those that do not support the PVLAN feature may support a subset of the PVLAN feature called the *PVLAN edge function*.

The PVLAN edge function provides port isolation on a per-switch basis. There is no protection between isolated ports on different switches. As in the isolated ports of the PVLAN feature, the PVLAN edge ports do not forward traffic to any other ports.

Table 9-1 shows the list of PVLAN features supported by the Catalyst range of products.

Table 9-1   *Range of Catalyst Switches Supporting Private VLANs*

Catalyst Platform	Isolated VLAN	Community VLAN	PVLAN Edge
6500	Yes	Yes	NA
5500	No	No	No
4500	Yes	Yes	NA
3750	Yes	Yes	Yes
3560	Yes	Yes	Yes
3550	No	No	Yes
3500XL	No	No	Yes
2970	No	No	Yes
2955	No	No	Yes
2950	No	No	Yes
2948/2980G	Yes	Yes	NA
2940	No	No	Yes
2900XL	No	No	Yes
1900	No	No	No

VLAN Access Control List (VACL)

A VLAN access control list (VACL) is another feature that assists in preventing attacks from taking place at Layer 2. This feature allows access lists to be applied at the VLAN level. This is different from the traditional access list, which is applied at the Layer 3 level.

Together with the PVLAN feature, a VACL enables network managers to exert powerful control over the security of the server farm. Figure 9-23 shows an example VACL, where Host A is not allowed to send specific traffic to Host B.

Figure 9-23   *VLAN Access Control List*

As mentioned in the section "Private VLAN," the PVLAN is made up of multiple VLANs functioning together. The traffic from the default gateway travels in one direction via the primary VLAN. Traffic from the servers travels via the secondary VLANs to the default gateway.

A VACL can be applied on the secondary VLANs only, without affecting the primary VLAN. This way, traffic from the default gateway to the servers is not affected at all, whereas traffic from the servers is subjected to further inspection. It is also possible to filter traffic on the isolated VLAN, while leaving the community VLAN untouched.

The combination of PVLAN and VACL is a powerful tool in fighting Layer 2 attacks. For example, because a server is set up to receive connection requests, it is rare for it to be initiating a high volume of requests. Under a worm attack, it is common to see servers initiating hundreds, if not thousands, of connection requests. Therefore, a VACL can be applied on the secondary VLAN so that all connections originating from the server are dropped. This way, the attack can be minimized, and the spread of the worm attack can be contained.

A VACL is implemented in hardware on the Catalyst 6500 series switches. The VACLs are configured at Layer 2 and, therefore, need only the PFC module to operate. Because the function is implemented in hardware, the performance of the switch remains the same regardless of the size of the ACL.

Port Security

Port security blocks access to a switch port based on MAC addresses. This happens when the MAC address of the station attempting to access the port differs from the list of MAC addresses that is specified for the port. The list of allowed MAC addresses can be manually keyed in or learned dynamically.

When a security violation occurs, the switch port can either be shut down permanently or only for a period of time. The port can also operate in a restrictive mode in which it drops traffic only from an offending station.

Example 9-2 shows the configuration of port security on the Catalyst 6500 switch.

Example 9-20 *Configuring Port Security*

```
Console> (enable) set port security 2/1 enable
Port 2/1 security enabled.
Console> (enable) show port 2/1
Port  Name                 Status      Vlan      Level  Duplex Speed Type
----- -------------------- ----------- --------- ------ ------ ----- ------------

 2/1                       connected   522       normal half    100 100BaseTX


Port  Security Secure-Src-Addr  Last-Src-Addr       Shutdown Trap      IfIndex
----- -------- ----------------- ------------------- -------- -------- -------

 2/1  enabled  00-90-2b-03-34-08 00-90-2b-03-34-08 No       disabled 1081


Port     Broadcast-Limit Broadcast-Drop
-------- --------------- ---------------

 2/1                   -              0


Port  Align-Err  FCS-Err    Xmit-Err   Rcv-Err    UnderSize
----- ---------- ---------- ---------- ---------- ---------

 2/1          0          0          0          0         0


Port  Single-Col Multi-Coll Late-Coll  Excess-Col Carri-Sen Runts     Giants
----- ---------- ---------- ---------- ---------- --------- --------- ---------

 2/1          0          0          0          0         0         0         0

Last-Time-Cleared
-------------------------
Fri 8 April 2005, 12:50:38
```

Port security helps mitigate attacks where a host is compromised, and the worm is generating bogus MAC addresses to flood the network.

Dynamic ARP Inspection

A man-in-the-middle attack makes use of the ARP protocol to insert itself in the middle of a conversation. *ARP cache poisoning* is a common example. To prevent such attacks from taking place, switches must ensure that only valid ARP requests and responses are forwarded. Dynamic ARP inspection works by intercepting all ARP packets and verifying that valid MAC and IP address bindings are taking place.

The dynamic ARP inspection feature determines the validity of the ARP packets by inspecting its database. This database contains information obtained from the Dynamic Host Configuration Protocol (DHCP) operation, or it may be configured manually for server connections.

When invalid ARP packets are detected in the network, the dynamic ARP inspection feature causes the switch to drop the packet. The feature also rate limits the ARP packets, such that anything above the preset threshold may be deemed a DoS attack. All ports that are connected to an end device are considered untrusted, and are therefore subject to the inspection. Ports that are connected to other switches are considered trusted and will not be inspected, because it is assumed that the traffic would have been inspected by other switches already.

Example 9-3 shows an example of configuring a dynamic ARP inspection.

Example 9-21 *Configuring a Dynamic ARP Inspection*

```
Switch# configure terminal
Enter configuration commands, one per line. End with CNTL/Z.
Switch(config)# ip arp inspection vlan 10
Switch(config)# end
Switch# show ip arp inspection vlan 10
Source Mac Validation : Disabled
Destination Mac Validation : Disabled
IP Address Validation : Disabled
Vlan Configuration Operation ACL Match Static ACL
---- ------------- --------- --------- ----------
10   Enabled     Active
Vlan ACL Logging DHCP Logging
---- ----------- -----------
10   Deny        Deny
Switch#
Switch# configure terminal
Enter configuration commands, one per line. End with CNTL/Z.
Switch(config)# interface fa6/3
Switch(config-if)# ip arp inspection trust
Switch(config-if)# end
Switch# show ip arp inspection interfaces fastEthernet 6/3
Interface       Trust State Rate (pps)
--------------- ----------- ----------
Fa6/3           Trusted     None
Switch#
```

The examples given so far demonstrate the importance of Layer 2 security within the data center network. Because it is difficult to rework the network just to implement some of these features, you must build them in to the design from day one.

Layer 3 Security

Traditionally, Layer 3 security has been a task performed by firewalls. Firewalls inspect IP packets and TCP sessions to determine whether traffic is "safe" and, therefore, should be allowed to continue its path into the network. Firewalls are essential in preventing attacks such as IP address spoofing, port scans, TCP SYNC packet flooding, and so on. It can be considered as the single point of entry to the information required and plays a vital role in maintaining the network perimeter security.

However, security is no longer just about firewalls anymore. The sophistication of attacks has evolved, and you need more than just a firewall to protect the critical resources within the server farm. No longer is the attacker just coming from outside the network; it could very well be an insider job nowadays. In addition, the trend in attacking has moved from application server to infrastructure attack. These attacks are sophisticated and require network managers to have a solid understanding of IP technology to appreciate the danger (and to know how to mitigate these threats).

Switch Forwarding Architecture

As mentioned in the section "Adopt Topology-Based Switching" in Chapter 6, switching hardware architecture can be exploited to bring down a network. This is especially so in the data center, where a high concentration of servers means there are many switches to exploit. When a server is infected by a worm, its high-performance network interface can be a deadly tool if it starts generating hundreds or thousands of flows per second. As recommended in Chapter 6, a topology-based switching architecture should be adopted for all switches in the data center.

Control Plane Policing

As mentioned in the section "Control Plane Policing" in Chapter 4, "Quality of Service," it is important to protect the control plane of the switches. This is especially important for the switches in the data center, because the consequence of a switch failure can mean taking many servers out of service. This feature is especially important for switches that serve the DMZ network, because the servers in the DMZ network are accessible from outside the network and therefore have a higher chance of being compromised.

DHCP Server Protection

A DHCP server is used widely to assign IP addresses to clients in a network in both enterprise and service provider networks. It is one of the most critical assets within an IP infrastructure. However, its importance is sometimes overlooked, because network managers pay more attention to protecting application servers.

A compromised DHCP server can mean networkwide outages, because the server can no longer assign IP addresses to the clients. Without an IP address, there will be no more network connections for new users who have just joined the network.

A DHCP server can be compromised easily. In Figure 9-24, a hacker launches an attack on the DHCP server just by generating a high number of DHCP requests. The DHCP server quickly runs out of IP addresses from its pools. Legitimate users who now try to log in to the network find that there is no connection, because no IP addresses are being assigned.

Figure 9-24 *Attacking a DHCP Server*

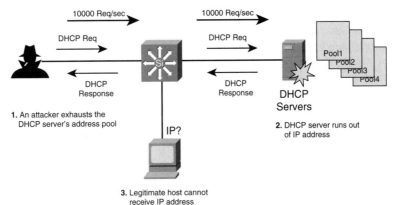

DHCP snooping is a security feature that filters untrusted DHCP messages such as those shown in Figure 9-24. Untrusted DHCP messages may originate from outside the network or from some compromised hosts within the network. The feature enforces security by building and maintaining a DHCP binding table. The table contains important information such as the MAC address, IP address, leased time, and VLAN number. With the information from the table, the feature acts like a firewall between untrusted hosts and the DHCP server.

Example 9-4 shows an example of configuring the DHCP snooping feature.

Example 9-22 *Configuring DHCP Snooping*

```
Switch(config)# ip dhcp snooping
Switch(config)# ip dhcp snooping vlan 100
Switch(config)# ip dhcp snooping information option
Switch(config)# interface fastethernet0/10
Switch(config-if)# ip dhcp snooping limit rate 50
```

In Example 9-4, the switch has the DHCP snooping function enabled on VLAN 100. It is also enforcing a rate limit of 50 packets per second on one of its ports.

Service Optimization

In the discussion of a resilient IP network, much of the focus is on the network itself, like designing the IP network for resiliency, deploying resilient hardware in a network, and enabling protocols in the network to protect from failure.

However, there is one area, called *service optimization*, that is critical to the whole resilient IP network equation, but it is not familiar territory for many network managers. Service optimization is beyond having a resilient IP network where connectivity is always available. More important, it is about highly available information, delivered in an optimized way.

Because information derives from the server farm, service optimization is about designing a server farm infrastructure such that it is fault tolerant, secured, and scalable. For example, when a company announces an online price-reduction promotion, its website can be easily overwhelmed by the sudden influx of requests, called *flash crowds*, if the server farm is not optimized for this service. So, although the IP network may still be up and running, it is not serving its purpose, because it cannot process those requests.

Special features have been developed to solve flash crowd problems, including the following:

- Server load balancing
- Global site selector
- Web caching
- Integrated service module

These features play an important part in the overall availability of information, and they are unique to the data center module.

Server Load Balancing

Server load balancing (SLB), sometimes known as *content switching*, is about server virtualization. The aim of SLB is to combine the processing power of various servers into one huge virtual server that provides information in a nonstop fashion. This is partly to mitigate the risk of losing a single server, and partly to improve the performance by having more horsepower. Another benefit of SLB is that maintenance can be performed on a single server while the rest continue to provide the information. To the clients, this virtual server behaves as if it is one huge physical server. Although many server vendors have their own high-availability architecture, they are usually proprietary in nature and costly. A network-based SLB architecture enables network managers to tackle the same problem in another way.

Figure 9-25 shows the concept of SLB. Three physical servers are connected to a router running the SLB function. These servers appear to the outside world as one virtual server with the URL http://www.acme.com and an associated virtual IP address.

Figure 9-25 *Server Load Balancing*

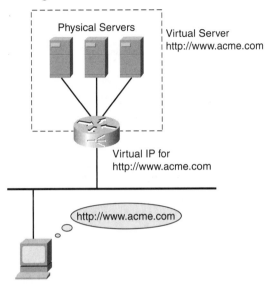

In a nutshell, SLB works by having the router or an SLB appliance intercepting all requests to a website. Based on the type of request, it then selectively assigns the physical servers located behind it to process those requests.

To understand how SLB technology works, you need to understand several critical concepts. These concepts, called *policies*, dictate how SLB will be configured and how applications will be handled:

- **Load-balancing policies**—These rules dictate how connections are distributed across the physical servers. Load-balancing policies are usually called the load-distribution algorithms, which include the following:

  - Round robin—Assigned in sequential manner, going back to the first server after the last one has been assigned.

  - Weighted round robin—Same as round robin, except weights can be assigned so that some servers can be serving more requests.

  - Least connections—The one with the least connections gets assigned.

  - Weighted least connections—Same as least connections, except weights can be assigned to influence the next in line.

  - Least loaded—Assigned based on server load.

  - Hashing—Based on information such as a source IP address or URL.

- **Persistence policies**—These rules describe requirements to ensure that requests coming to a particular physical server are maintained until web transactions, or sessions, have completed. For the SLB device to keep track of these sessions, some form of identification has to be present in the traffic stream. This information is typically found within the URL, cookie, or the SSL session ID of the request

- **Server failure policies**—These rules dictate the error-handling mechanism when a physical server fails. The server may be in the process of a web transaction. In this case, there are several ways to work around this failure:
  - Restart the transaction
  - Redirect the session to another server
  - Issue an error message from another server

- **Content-specific policies**—These rules may be implemented to direct traffic based on its content type. For example, you may want to route a request for general information to a particular server, whereas the request for an application transaction may be rerouted to another server, because application transactions require a more powerful server.

- **Device-specific policies**—These rules direct traffic based on the device types of the requestor. For example, a request from a PC browser may be directed to a particular server, whereas a request from PDA device may be directed to another server.

The physical servers reside behind the SLB device, and these are the resources that process those requests. When directing requests to these physical servers, the SLB device may modify the request packets, depending on whether the requests are forwarded to the servers through directed mode or dispatch mode.

In *directed mode*, the SLB device forwards the traffic via Network Address Translation (NAT). In this case, the destination address in the request, which is pointing to the virtual IP address residing in the SLB device, is translated to the IP address of the assigned physical server. The MAC address of the packet is also rewritten.

In *dispatch mode*, only the MAC address is rewritten; the original destination IP address is preserved. Dispatch mode proves especially useful in the scenario when the SLB device is actually load-balancing firewalls, which requires the IP address to be preserved. Depending on implementation details, other information within the packet, such as the source IP address, TCP ports, and checksums, may be modified.

Based on the SLB polices, it is possible to devise a rule for all requests that contain the following information:

Destination IP = 10.1.1.1
Protocol = TCP
Destination port = 80

Send the request to the following two servers, using a round-robin algorithm:

> 10.2.1.1, port 80
> 10.2.1.2, port 80

In this scenario, the load-balancing decision is made based on IP address, protocol, and TCP port number. Because this Layer 3 and 4 information is available, redirection can be done right from the start of the TCP connection, within the TCP SYNC packet.

It is also possible to load balance based on more complex criteria, such as the following:

> Destination IP = 10.1.1.1
> Protocol = TCP
> Destination port = 80
> URL contains ApplicationForCarLoan.html

Send the request to the following two servers, using a round-robin algorithm:

> 10.2.1.1, port 80
> 10.2.1.2, port 80

For this scenario, information provided by the TCP SYNC packet alone will not be enough for the redirection to take place. Because the content switch needs to base its decision on URL content, it must be able to read into the request first. However, the client will not send the URL request until it has terminated its TCP SYNC request. To overcome this deadlock, the SLB device needs the feature called *delayed binding*.

Figure 9-26 shows the concept of delayed binding in SLB. Unlike a direct TCP connection between a client and a server, delayed binding consists of two connections: a front end and a back end. The front-end connection consists of the client and the virtual IP address of the intended destination, which resides in the SLB device. The back-end connection is established between the SLB device and the actual server. The following steps are involved in delayed binding:

1 Client sends TCP SYNC request to the virtual IP address.
2 SLB device returns TCP SYNC/ACK to client.
3 Client sends TCP ACK to SLB device; TCP connection established.
4 Client sends HTTP Get request, which contains the URL of the web page that it is requesting. SLB device looks into the URL and decides to which server to send the request.
5 SLB sends TCP SYNC request to the assigned server.
6 Assigned server returns TCP SYNC/ACK to SLB device.
7 SLB device sends TCP ACK to assigned server, TCP connection established
8 SLB device sends the HTTP Get request to the assigned server for processing.

Figure 9-26   *TCP Delayed Binding*

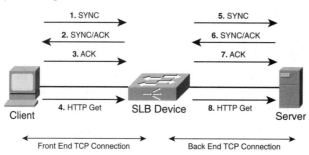

Via delayed binding, the SLB device acts as a middleman between the client and the actual server. To maintain the connectivity, the SLB device spliced both the front end and the back end together via some data structure. This way, it can keep track of which front-end connection is to be linked to which back-end connection.

SLB can be thought of as the network's way of improving information availability. It is a critical component within a resilient IP architecture, because availability of information is what counts. You might be able to build a resilient IP network, but without robust information availability, the network might not serve its purpose.

The SLB function is delivered via the Cisco CSS 11500 family of content switches. For high-performance SLB functionality, consider the Catalyst 6500 Content Switching Module (CSM).

Global Site Selector

SLB protects the network infrastructure from a physical server failure by having multiple servers working on the requests; however, it does not protect the infrastructure from a site failure. In the event that a catastrophic event happens to the entire rack containing the servers, or worse, the entire data center, users will not be able to obtain the information that they want. The global server load balancing (GSLB) technique aims to solve this problem. Whereas SLB works by load balancing traffic across servers, GSLB works by load balancing traffic across geographically dispersed data centers.

The function of GSLB is delivered via a product called the *Global Site Selector* (*GSS*). The GSS is an integral part of the DNS routing hierarchy, and works closely with the SLB devices such as the Cisco CSS 11500 family of switches or the CSM service module on the Catalyst 6500 series. The GSS improves the availability of information in the following ways:

- Monitors the health of the SLB devices, and based on a customized policies, directs user requests to an alternate SLB device.

- Detects site outages, and redirects user requests to another data center for continued processing of information.

- Sends requests to the nearest site for faster processing.

- Offloads the traditional DNS server by taking over the resolution process at a request rate of thousands per second. Because DNS resolution constitutes a major portion of delay in web traffic, an improvement in this process improves latency and cuts down response time from a user perspective.

Before you can use the GSS effectively, you must have a good understanding of the DNS resolution process.

Understanding DNS Resolution

The Domain Name System (DNS) is a distributed database of host information that maps domain names to IP addresses for the Internet. It has been used since the early 1980s, and almost all applications on the Internet today rely on DNS, including HTTP, FTP, Telnet, e-mail, and so on. With DNS, there is no need to remember the IP address of the Cisco Systems website, for example. You just need to remember www.cisco.com.

Figure 9-27 shows how www.cisco.com fits in the DNS structure. Just like a file system, the DNS structure is hierarchical and is made up of the following components:

- **DNS resolver (DNSR)**—Clients that access client name servers.

- **Client name server (CNS)**—A server running DNS software and is responsible for finding the requested website. CNS is also known as DNS proxy (D-Proxy).

- **Root name server (RNS)**—A server that resides at the top of the DNS hierarchy. These are the servers that hold the entire DNS database. There are 13 root servers in the Internet today.

- **Authoritative name server (ANS)**—A server that is run by an enterprise or a service provider. This server is the authoritative server for the domain requested. The ANS responds to the CNS with the requested IP address. It does not respond to the client directly.

- **Intermediate name server (INS)**—A server that is used for scaling the DNS infrastructure. When the RNS does not have the IP address of the ANS, it sends the requesting CNS to an INS. The INS then sends the CNS to the ANS.

Figure 9-27 *DNS Structure*

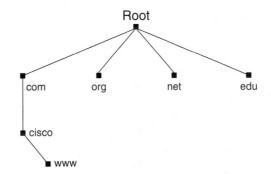

One important aspect of DNS is the process known as *delegation*. Delegation enables a network manager to locally administer the segments, or domains, yet makes it possible for the information to be made available to the entire Internet.

As illustrated in Figure 9-28, the DNS resolution process for www.cisco.com goes through the following steps:

Step 1   The client sends a request to the CNS for the IP address of www.cisco.com.

Step 2   The CNS can either reply with an IP address, if it already knows the IP address of www.cisco.com, or it will send a request to the RNS (Step 2a). There are two ways the RNS can help in the request. If it knows the ANS responsible for cisco.com, it can redirect the CNS directly to the ANS; if not, it will redirect the CNS to the INS (Step 2b). The INS will then redirect the CNS to the ANS. This process is known as an *iterated query*.

Step 3   The CNS sends a query to the ANS that is authoritative for cisco.com. This ANS is authoritative for names such as www.cisco.com and ftp.cisco.com, and so on. It sends the IP address of www.cisco.com to the CNS.

Step 4   The CNS sends the IP address of www.cisco.com to the client. The client uses the IP address to initiate a connection.

Figure 9-28 *DNS Resolution Process*

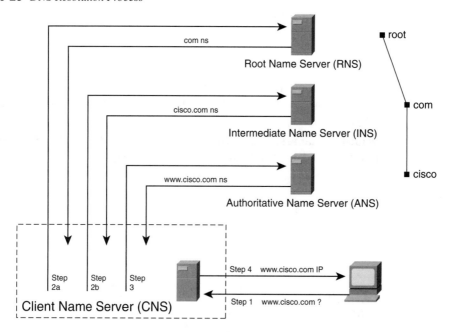

With the introduction of GSS, the DNS resolution process remains the same, except the ANS responsibility has been taken over by the GSS.

Using GSS

As the authoritative name server for a domain, GSS will return the IP address of a requested website when it receives requests from the CNS. Unlike the traditional ANS, which is usually a server, GSS formulates its reply based on certain criteria, such as the following:

- Availability of servers
- Proximity of sites
- Load of server
- Source of request
- User-specific preference

As shown in Figure 9-29, the DNS resolution process for www.cisco.com involving a GSS will be as follows:

1 The client sends a request to the CNS for the IP address of www.cisco.com.

2 The CNS is redirected to the GSS, because the GSS is the ANS for cisco.com.

3 Based on the feedback information from the SLB devices within both the data centers, GSS selects an appropriate site to serve the request (in this case, data center 2).

4 GSS returns the virtual IP address on the SLB residing in data center 2 to the CNS.

5 The CNS sends the virtual IP address to the client.

6 Client sends its request to the SLB residing in data center 2, and the SLB proceeds to handle the client request as described in the section "Server Load Balancing."

Working hand in hand, the combination of SLB and GSS improves the availability of information. The redundancy is elevated from protecting server failure to protecting data center failure.

Figure 9-29   *Global Site Selector in Action*

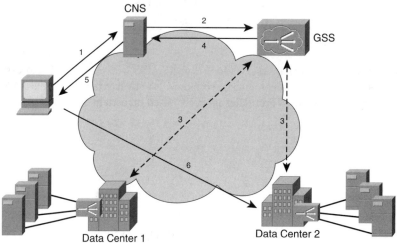

Web Cache Communication Protocol (WCCP)

Although SLB and GSS ensure the high availability of information, they may not solve some fundamental issues of Internet connectivity. With the proliferation of web traffic, the traditional 80/20 rule of traffic distribution no longer applies. In the past, it was assumed that 80 percent of traffic would stay within a network, whereas only 20 would be outbound traffic. Today, with Internet access, most of the information resides outside of the network. Therefore, network managers must solve the associated problems that arise from this phenomenon:

- **Reduce WAN congestion**—WAN connectivity gets choked with more outbound traffic. In areas such as the Asia Pacific, upgrading WAN connectivity can be costly.

- **Improve user experience**—With most traffic bound for the Internet and limited WAN connectivity, maintaining an acceptable user experience becomes an issue when congestion occurs.

Web caching is one area of server optimization where the network tries to fulfill content requests locally. In doing so, it helps to improve user experience, by accelerating the delivery of content locally, and improves WAN performance by cutting down on repeated requests. The protocol that makes web caching possible is the Web Cache Communication Protocol (WCCP).

Figure 9-30 shows the traffic flow with WCCP:

   1   Client sends HTTP request for a particular website.

2 Request is intercepted by the WCCP running in the router and is redirected to the content engine based on the protocol of the request.

3 Two options are possible, depending on whether the content is stored locally:

   a Content engine fulfils the request if it has the content stored locally.

   b For content that is not stored locally, the content engine sends the request to the actual server for the requested content.

3 Server sends content to the content engine, and the content engine stores a copy for local storage. Subsequent request will be fulfilled locally.

4 The content engine sends the content to the client.

Figure 9-30 *Web Cache Communication Protocol*

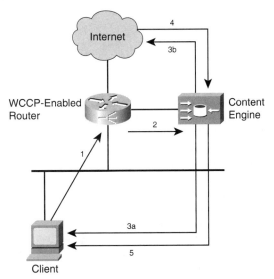

This method of caching is also known as *transparent caching* because the steps are transparent to the clients. There is no need for the client to have a special configuration in its browser or workstation. In fact, the client does not know that its request has been redirected or that the content engine exists.

Because the working of transparent caching is invisible to users, it has to take care of failure scenarios in an invisible manner, too. Potential problems that might arise include an overloading situation or failure of the cache engine.

A sudden surge in client requests might overload the cache engine; after all, the cache engine can process only a fixed number of transactions per second. In this situation, the cache engine might issue an overload bypass request, in which client requests are forwarded to the real servers. Return traffic from the servers is sent to the client directly, bypassing the cache engine in its return path.

For redundancy purposes, WCCP allows for a group of cache engines to service the redirected request. This group, called a *cache cluster*, can scale up to 32 cache engines. Cache clusters allow the caching capability to scale in a linear manner. With each cache engine supporting a certain numbers of transactions per second, adding extra cache engines increases the overall transaction's capability of the cache farm.

With WCCP version 1, only a single router services a cluster. When a cache engine is connected to the router, they communicate via UDP port number 2048. The communication between the router and the cache engine minimizes configuration and allows for new cache engines to be added to the cluster without reconfiguration. Within the cluster, the cache engine with the lowest IP address is elected the leader, and it determines how redirection should be redistributed among the caches. Only redirection of HTTP traffic (TCP port 80) is supported by WCCP version 1.

WCCP version 2 improves on the previous version by allowing a group of routers to redirect traffic to a cache cluster. This way, the caching infrastructure is greatly enhanced. WCCP version 2 introduces the concept of a service group; a subset of the cache cluster is mapped to a subset of the router with the same service. WCCP version 2 supports a variety of redirected traffic. Besides HTTP (TCP port 80), it also supports various UDP and TCP traffic, such as FTP, audio, and video applications.

Example 9-5 shows a WCCP configuration. In this example, all web traffic arriving at interface fastethernet 2/0/1 will be redirected.

Example 9-23 *Configuring a Web Cache Communication Protocol*

```
router# configure terminal
router(config)# ip wccp web-cache
router(config)# interface fastethernet 2/0/1
router(config-if)# ip wccp web-cache redirect in
Router(config-if)# exit
```

Just as a cache engine can be deployed to accelerate a client's request for content, it can be placed in front of web servers to speed up the delivery of content. This way of deploying the cache engine, called *reverse proxy caching*, is an effective way to offload traffic from the servers. Reverse proxy caching improves server capacity and website performance, thus enhancing the overall user experience. With reverse proxy caching, the most popular static web content is cached so that servers need not keep servicing the same request again and again.

The steps are involved in reverse proxy caching, as illustrated in Figure 9-31:

1 Connection from the Internet requests content from the server.

2 Router with WCCP enabled redirects the request to the content engine.

   3 Depending on whether the content is stored locally, one of the following occurs:

   a Content engine fulfills the request if it has the content stored locally.

   b For content that is not stored locally, the content engine sends the request to the actual server for the requested content.

   3 Server sends content to the content engine; content engine stores a copy for local storage. Subsequent request will be fulfilled locally.

   4 Content engine sends the content to the client.

Figure 9-31 *Reverse Proxy Caching*

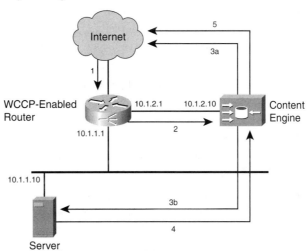

The configuration of the cache engine for the reverse proxy caching function is shown in Example 9-6.

Example 9-24 *Configuring Reverse Proxy Caching on a Cache Engine*

```
Cacheengine#config terminal
Cacheengine#(config)#wccp version 2
Cacheengine#(config)#wccp router-list 1 10.1.2.1
Cacheengine#(config)#wccp 99 reverse-proxy router-list-num 1
```

The configuration of the router for the support of reverse proxy caching is shown in Example 9-7.

Example 9-25 *Configuring Reverse Proxy Caching on a Router*

```
Router#config terminal
Router(config)#ip wccp 99
Router(config)#interface s0/0
Router(config-if)#ip wccp 99 redirect in
```

WCCP is an important component of the overall server farm architecture. When you integrate WCCP into the network, it can either optimize the WAN usage or it can improve the performance of the server farm. One point to note, however, is that WCCP is CPU intensive and, depending on the configuration, may have different impact on the performance of the router.

Integrated Service Modules

Up to this point, topics such as Layer 2 security, Layer 3 security, server load balancing, and even web caching have been discussed as individual topics. It might seem that these features are implemented via different hardware, implementations that might pose a problem within the data center. As it is, real estate in the data center is precious, and not many network managers have the luxury of working with ample rack space. This is where the concept of integrated service modules of the Cisco Catalyst 6500 and the 7600 family comes in.

The availability of the various service modules of the Catalyst 6500 family changes its role within the data center. More than just a switch with Layer 3 features, the inclusion of these service modules turned the Catalyst 6500 family into an IP service platform within the data center.

Many service modules are available on the Catalyst 6500 family, and the following are relevant to the data center environment:

- **Firewall Service Module (FWSM)**—Used to provide a high-performance firewall function at 5-Gbps throughput, 100,000 connections per second, and 1 million concurrent connections.

- **Content Switching Module (CSM)**—Used to provide load balancing of firewalls, web servers, caches, and other network devices.

- **SSL Service Module (SSM)**—Provides accelerations and increases security of web applications.

- **Anomaly Detection and Mitigation Modules**—Detects DoS attacks and blocks malicious traffic without affecting normal traffic.

- **Network Analysis Module (NAM)**—Provides visibility into the traffic flow within the data center network. The monitoring functions can help you fight DoS attacks.

The use of service modules is a relatively new concept to many network managers. Besides saving rack space and power, their benefit is in the way they work in an integrated manner, as part of the data center architecture. When used in combination, they transform the server farm into a highly scalable and secure infrastructure. However, depending on the logical IP network design, care should be taken with respect to routing and performance issues. For example, you might end up with the FWSM performing a basic routing function, when it can be done by the MSFC within the same chassis. Another example is that if you place the FWSM into a bridge mode, you might lose features such as NAT.

Because many different service modules are available within the Catalyst 6500 and Cisco 7600 families of products, you have many possibilities of deploying them. However, this also means more planning needs to be done it terms of usage. A good source of information about how to leverage the powerful combination of the service modules can be found in *Data Center Fundamentals*, by Mauricio Arregoces and Maurizio Portolani (Cisco Press, 2004).

Summary

Maintaining high availability for the data center module requires multidisciplinary knowledge such as construction, networking, server, security, and operation experience.

Constructing the data center module requires network designers and managers to have multifaceted knowledge. Professionals who are good in this area usually possess a wide array of technical expertise that spans various disciplines: construction, networking, server, storage, security, and operation experience. This chapter presented the overall challenge of building a data center module.

The data center module is closely linked to operational issues, such as fault detection and overall management of the infrastructure, which you learn about in Chapter 10, "Beyond Implementation."

This chapter covers the following topics:

- Components of Network Management
- Establishing a Baseline
- Managing Cisco IOS Deployment
- Moving Toward Proactive Management

CHAPTER 10

Beyond Implemention: Network Managment

In this final chapter, you learn about a topic of paramount importance in running a resilient IP network: network management. Unfortunately, network management is an area that is frequently neglected. Imagine flying an airplane without instrumentation. With no dials to indicate speed, altitude, and fuel level, the outcome of the flight is predictable. Likewise, it is impossible to run an IP network without a network management system.

The topic of network management, in this case, means more than just having a server running some management software with icons flashing in the background. Most network managers equate network management with polling devices via Simple Network Management Protocol (SNMP). In fact, this is just a small part of fault management, which, in turn, is a part of the network management methodology. The network management methodology is a framework encompassing various areas and requires instilling discipline and change procedures with respect to the operations of the network. This chapter covers these areas so that you will understand their purpose.

Also, as part of the effort to stay ahead of the network so that problems can be avoided, research efforts have been focusing on developing features that help in proactive management. This chapter looks into some of these features in IOS so that you understand their relevancy to your network.

Components of Network Management

The International Organization for Standardization (ISO) network management model defines five functional areas for network management:

- Fault management
- Configuration management
- Accounting management
- Performance management
- Security management

These five functional areas are commonly known as FCAPS, based on the first letter of their individual names. Each functional area focuses on different tasks that are necessary to operate and maintain the health of the network. In the building of a resilient IP network, FCAPS is as important as the actual design and construction. In fact, the budget for the FCAPS component can be as big, if not bigger, than the budget for the hardware.

Fault Management

Fault management deals with the detection, logging, notification, and correction of problems that may crop up in the network from time to time. This area is most easily understood by network managers, and so it is not surprising that it is the most widely deployed among the five functional areas.

The functioning of the fault management system relies on different components within the network to work together. A problem can be detected in several ways:

- When a device sends an SNMP trap
- When a device is polled
- When a remote monitoring (RMON) threshold is exceeded
- By a syslog message

Regardless of which way the problem is detected, a back-end management system processes these messages so that an action can be taken.

Because fault management relies on devices to send meaningful message to the management systems, it is important that the devices are configured correctly, and Management Information Base (MIB) files are compiled in the management systems. MIB files such as the RFC 1213-MIB and CISCO-PRODUCTS-MIB are the most common ones, because they are standard MIB files for Cisco routers. Some Cisco products require certain MIB files, because they deal with the basics of the device's health—for example, the CISCO-STACK-MIB for the Catalyst family of switches or the generic CISCO-ENVMON-MIB are important MIB files that provide information about the general health of the Catalyst device.

Note also that the syslog messages provide a wealth of information to minimize network downtime. Problems such as hardware failure and memory fragmentation often have indicative signs in the syslog prior to impending failure. Therefore, going through the syslog file for alarming messages should be part of the network operation.

One good strategy to minimize network downtime is to try to stay ahead of the problems that may happen in the network. Therefore, it is important to introduce proactive fault management in your network operation. This method is unlike traditional fault management where an action is taken only upon receiving notification, which is the method most network managers are familiar with. In proactive fault management, you collect statistics about the network or device health, do a trending analysis, and try to predict the behavior of the network or device. Examples of proactive fault management are collecting the CPU utilization of a router, the traffic load on a particular interface, or the memory states of the router.

Another important component of proactive fault management is the RMON specification, which allows for a device to self-monitor against a preset threshold. A good example of a tool that provides RMON capability is the Network Analysis Module (NAM) that is available in the Cisco Catalyst 6500 series. Proactive fault management requires you to obtain the latest MIB files for the devices that you are monitoring. For Cisco devices, a good source for the latest MIB files can be found at the following URL:

http://www.cisco.com/public/sw-center/netmgmt/cmtk/mibs.shtml

Proactive fault management is one of the steps required for establishing a baseline for your network. This is discussed in details in the section "Establishing a Baseline."

Configuration Management

The goal of configuration management is to keep track of both the hardware and software inventory in the network. This plays an important part in the operation of the network, especially during troubleshooting and capacity planning stages, and should be incorporated as a portion of the change control procedure. Configuration management consists mainly of three areas, as follows:

- Configuration file management
- Inventory management
- Software management

Configuration File Management

Configuration file management deals with keeping track of the actual configurations that go into each and every device in the network. Because a command that gets issued in a router can adversely affect the entire network, configuration files must be verified and certified as deployable before being implemented. Therefore, configuration file management is more than just storing up all the configuration files of devices. It is part of the elaborate engineering process whereby designs are verified, features tested, and code checked for deployment suitability. This is part of the software life cycle process, which is discussed in the section "IOS Software Life Cycle Management."

TIP   One of the most difficult tasks in configuration file management is keeping track of configuration changes. Many times, documentation falls behind actual network configuration because of time constraints or simple lack of discipline. A good tool to help in this area is Really Awesome New Cisco Config Differ (RANCID). RANCID is a free application that keeps track of router hardware and software configurations. It works by logging in to a set of routers, checking the configurations, and e-mailing any difference from the previous session to a specified e-mail address. By displaying the differences in configuration, RANCID not only helps to verify changes executed in the network, it also helps in the documentation process. You can download RANCID from the following URL:

http://www.shrubbery.net/rancid/

Inventory Management

Inventory management provides a database of all the hardware installed in the network, including chassis, modules, software, boot code, and so on. The information is important so that network managers can have an overview of all the devices deployed within the network. This information is vital for an efficient operation. For example, when a hardware vendor makes an announcement about faulty modules that need immediate replacement, you can quickly locate those modules with the inventory management information.

Another use of the information is in helping with future sparing of hardware. A good rundown of hardware inventory assists in deciding what sort of hardware (and quantity) is required for sparing.

Performing inventory management is also helpful for establishing a baseline for the network. This is discussed in the section "Establishing a Baseline."

Inventory management may seem like a tedious task, but the discovery function of most network management platforms aid in retrieving the information. By using the SNMP Get function, you can easily obtain an up-to-date copy of the information.

Software Management

Software management deals with keeping track of the software images deployed within the network. Although keeping track of versioning can be done via the inventory management function, software management goes a step further. The proper functioning of networking devices requires more than just Cisco IOS Software. Boot codes, microcodes, and Field Programmable Gate Array (FPGA) codes on the modules are necessary on certain ranges of routers and switches. Ensuring that the right versions of these codes are deployed is critical to the functioning of the entire device, and this may not be an easy task. A tool such as the CiscoWorks LAN Management Solution (LMS) comes in handy here because it eases the burden of administering the software. In addition, new versions of Cisco IOS codes come with release notes, and you need to examine them carefully. It would be disastrous just to upgrade the codes on a device without going through the release note to understand the caveats and new feature support. Therefore, software management encompasses a strict process of downloading the correct code, backing up current running code, making sure that the hardware configuration matches the software code, and then finally loading for production use. For this, it is absolutely critical that network managers understand the software life cycle management aspects of Cisco IOS software. You will learn more about this in the section "Managing Cisco IOS Deployment."

Accounting Management

Accounting management provides deep insight into the network usage patterns of users or application systems. Usually, the need for accounting management arises because of the requirement for chargeback or interdepartmental billing. Depending on how the funding for the network comes about, some users may be charged based on how much network resources they consume. This concept shares the same characteristic as that of a phone bill, on which individual calls can be listed and the total charge tabulated based on usage.

The accounting management function is achieved when individual network connections are recorded and stored for later tabulation. The Cisco NetFlow technology provides this capability via the NetFlow agents and collector. The NetFlow features can be turned on in the router or switches, so that individual network connections can be recorded and sent in bulk to the NetFlow collector. As opposed to equipment that does localized traffic sniffing, NetFlow provides a holistic view of the traffic flow, because it can provide more detailed information. The NetFlow collector is usually software running in an external server that provides number-crunching capability on the data collected. An example of a NetFlow collector is the cflowd program.

Another method of providing an accounting function is via the Cisco IOS command **ip accounting.** This command is issued at the interface level and provides statistics on the traffic that is transited through a router. Information such as the number of packets and byte counts is available. However, note that enabling this feature may potentially cause performance degradation, so care must be taken when enabling this command.

The function of accounting management has expanded to help fight distributed denial-of-service (DDoS) attacks. Because account management enables you to get detailed information down to the per-traffic flow level, you can use this function as a building block for many anti-DDoS techniques, such as Unicast Reverse Path Forwarding (uRPF) and identifying and classifying threats. Anti-DDoS products include the Cisco Traffic Anomaly Detector service module on the Catalyst 6500 series switches.

Performance Management

The goal of performance management is to ensure that adequate networking resources are available to support user needs. Performance management measures the various components of the network, including throughput, response times, and interface utilization. This functional area ensures that the user experience is maintained.

Implementing performance management occurs in three main steps:

- Know what information of interest to gather.
- Establish a baseline for the network in a normal operation environment, and understand when peak period occurs in the network.
- Determine a threshold to help decide what course of action to take when the threshold is exceeded.

One of the driving forces behind the need for performance management is the service level agreement (SLA) between the network operation and its end users. An SLA is basically a contract between the network operator and its end users specifying the expected performance and services delivered by the network. It is usually based on a preset group of metrics that is attainable and measurable. The metrics may include information such as round-trip response time between two endpoints, one-way transmission time, and jitter and latency characteristics. These metrics usually derive from application requirements. For example, a Voice over IP (VoIP) application may require a one-way delay of 150 milliseconds (ms) with less than 1 percent packet loss. In this case, these requirements translate to the metrics within the SLA.

To honor the SLA, network managers must rely on statistics collected from the network. Besides the standard interface utilization and CPU load, other information, such as the input queue drops, output queue drops, and ignored packets, can prove to be extremely useful. Up to this point, the statistics are collected from a single device. However, more data is required if information such as user or application profiling is required. This is when technologies such as remote monitoring (RMON) can prove to be extremely helpful.

The RMON technology works in a distributed fashion whereby agents, either embedded within the device to be monitored or via an external probe, are deployed within the network. These agents send vital information about the traffic flowing within the network to a central network management station. The RMON technology was first specified in RFC 1513, *Token Ring Extensions to the Remote Network Monitoring MIB*, and has since been updated. In RFC 2021, *Remote Network Monitoring Management Information Base Version 2 Using SMIv2*, the RMON specification has moved beyond the usual Media Access Control (MAC) layer to the application layer, where applications such as web, Network File System (NFS), and e-mail can be monitored.

With the introduction of applications such as VoIP that demand stringent performance characteristics from the network, monitoring the performance on a device-by-device basis or even RMON may not be adequate anymore. More sophisticated features that take measurements from a holistic point of view are required. Features such as the IP SLA have been introduced in Cisco IOS to cater to this new requirement. IP SLA is discussed later in this chapter.

Security Management

Security management is a very broad topic, and it often means different things to different people. This book confines security management to mean controlling access to network resources. The control is essential so that only authorized personnel can perform certain tasks and not cause service disruption to the operation of the network.

There are various ways to control access to the network resources. The following are some examples:

- Access control lists (ACLs)
- User IDs and passwords
- Terminal Access Controller Access Control System (TACACS)

ACLs

An ACL is a simple method whereby network devices only accept connections such as Telnet from a certain predetermined IP addresses. These IP addresses may belong to the workstations within the network operating center or network management stations.

User IDs and Passwords

User IDs and passwords represent another way to implement security. With the concept of an ID level, different job roles may be assigned to different ID levels. For example, a person with an operator status may only issue monitoring and **show** commands, whereas another person with an administrator job role may override existing configurations. More important, as opposed to common IDs and passwords, different IDs (based on user roles) provide accountability, and this is important during troubleshooting time.

TACACS

TACACS, defined in RFC 1492, *An Access Control Protocol, Sometimes Called TACACS*, is a security protocol that runs between network devices and a TACACS server. It is used to authenticate users seeking access to network devices based on a database. As opposed to a RADIUS server, TACACS supports more functionalities, such as the authorization of commands, and maintains a log of commands issued. Variations of TACACS include the TACACS+, the authentication, authorization, and accounting (AAA) architecture that separates authentication, authorization, and accounting functions. In the realm of security management, these three functions are important concepts that need to be understood.

Within the AAA architecture, authentication is the process of identifying a user via an ID and a password. Based on a successful authentication process, the user is then allowed to access the network.

Authorization is closely related to authentication. It limits access control to network resources based on user credentials. For example, a Cisco router provides 16 levels of authorization, with 0 being the lowest and 15 the highest. Typically, the more authorization privileges a user has, the stronger the authentication should be.

Accounting is the process that collects information such as user session start and stop times and a list of executed commands. This vital information is required for troubleshooting break-ins, or for tracing back events when you are trying to troubleshoot a network problem.

Establishing a Baseline

Establishing a baseline for the network is the beginning of many of the functional areas in network management. This is like going on an expedition. To decide on a direction to take to reach a certain destination, you have to locate where you are on the map first. Just like an expedition, running a network successfully requires you to know how the network is currently performing. This is the purpose of establishing a baseline.

Complacency is always an enemy in IP network management. Often, network managers claim that there are no problems in the network, without realizing that there is a problem brewing somewhere waiting to explode. Just because a certain feature runs successfully now does not mean that a problem will not occur in the future. Because traffic load is dynamic, the network is an evolving environment, where the burden imposed on the devices, or load, changes from day to day. One of the key success factors in running a high-availability network is to know when the load on the devices becomes too much to bear. This ability to predict the future behavior of the network is what makes a high-availability network different from the rest. The prerequisite in having this ability is establishing a baseline.

A simple rule to remember when establishing a baseline is that all resources are limited within the network. Examples of resources include the CPU of a switch, bandwidth of a particular interface, forwarding rate of a router, and so on. A baseline process helps in identifying the status of these resources and planning for action in the event that these resources run out. From a high-level perspective, you need to watch two types of resources:

- The control-plane resources
- The data-plane resources

Control-plane resources refer to entities such as CPU utilization, memory consumption, and buffer utilization. As mentioned in Chapter 3, "Fundamentals of IP Resilient Networks," the control-plane function takes care of the well-being of the entire router or switch. When a router or switch runs out of CPU resources, it cannot process protocol keepalives or do proper housekeeping. This is when it begins to drop packets and, in a worst-case scenario, completely malfunctions.

Data-plane resources are simpler to understand, because they are related to link utilizations. A good example is a WAN link connecting a remote branch to the head office. With more applications being introduced and traffic load increasing, there will come a time when the WAN link simply cannot cope with the load anymore. In this case, the only way to avoid congestion is to upgrade the WAN link.

Baselining is a process to establish the current state of a network. By having an insight into how the network is performing, you can gain valuable information. The process includes the following:

- Collecting hardware and software inventory
- Determining the current utilization of both control and data planes
- Identifying current resource deficits
- Predicting future resource deficits

Figure 10-1 illustrates the concept of establishing a baseline for the network. As the network load increases over time, there will come a point when the network can no longer service requests. Therefore, another way to look at establishing a baseline is to determine where the current network is located on the curve line and how much longer before the network encounters problem. This effectively tells you how much time you have before a problem blows up.

Figure 10-1 *Establishing a Network Baseline*

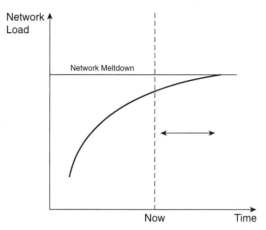

It is important that you are familiar with SNMP because establishing a baseline means collecting statistics. Other than to perform specific commands on the command prompts, the most effective way to collect statistics is via SNMP. This is especially so when you are dealing with a large network with many devices. Therefore, familiarity with management system software, such as the HP Overview or MIB Walking shareware, is useful.

To establish a baseline, follow these five steps:

Step 1 Take a snapshot of inventory.

Step 2 Collect relevant data.

Step 3 Analyze data.

Step 4 Prioritize problem areas.

Step 5 Determine a course of action.

The next sections describe each step in detail.

Step 1: Take a Snapshot of Inventory

The first step in establishing a baseline is to have an inventory of the hardware and software within the network. There are several reasons why inventory is required:

- Certain MIBs are supported only in some versions of IOS. As IOS codes are updated over time, new MIBs may have been added or deleted. Therefore, it is important to know which versions of IOS are running on the network.

- Different hardware has different performance characteristics. A 60 percent CPU load on a high-end router may mean something different than a 60 percent CPU load on a low-end router. Knowing what hardware is running on the network enables you to tailor different threshold analysis to each individual platform.

- Keep an inventory of the configuration files of the network, because as a change in configuration takes place, it is important to have a versioning control. This enables rollback to be performed and provides more information during troubleshooting.

- Know what features are enabled and track the resources they consume. The release notes that accompany the feature contain caveats that have to be considered.

Step 2: Collect Relevant Data

To do a good analysis, you must first decide what to poll. As mentioned in the beginning of the section "Establishing a Baseline," two areas are of interest: the control plane and the data plane. The control plane affects the general health of a device, and, therefore, you are interested in the status of entities such as CPU, memory, and buffers. The data plane deals with bandwidth, so you are interested in information such as link utilization.

After knowing what information to collect, you must decide how often to collect the information and for how long. For example, a five-minute interval poll of CPU utilization over a period of one month will give a good indication of the utilization pattern of the CPU resources of a device. After collecting the information, you can then analyze it.

You need two important tools for data collection: the MIB entries in the devices, which contain the information you need; and a tool such as the Multi-Router Traffic Grapher (MRTG) for collecting the information.

MIB Entries and Object Identifiers

Before you can actually collect information, you must ensure that the specific MIB information is supported by the device. In addition, collecting of information requires you to know the object identifier (OID) of the MIB object. Table 10-1 shows an example of the

OIDs of the MIB file CISCO-PROCESS-MIB. This MIB provides information to the runtime status of the CPU of a router.

Table 10-1   *IDs Within the CISCO-PROCESS-MIB*

Object Name	OID
org	1.3
dod	1.3.6
internet	1.3.6.1
directory	1.3.6.1.1
mgmt	1.3.6.1.2
experimental	1.3.6.1.3
private	1.3.6.1.4
enterprises	1.3.6.1.4.1
cisco	1.3.6.1.4.1.9
ciscoMgmt	1.3.6.1.4.1.9.9
ciscoProcessMIB	1.3.6.1.4.1.9.9.109
ciscoProcessMIBObjects	1.3.6.1.4.1.9.9.109.1
ciscoProcessMIBNotifPrefix	1.3.6.1.4.1.9.9.109.2
ciscoProcessMIBConformance	1.3.6.1.4.1.9.9.109.3
cpmCPU	1.3.6.1.4.1.9.9.109.1.1
cpmProcess	1.3.6.1.4.1.9.9.109.1.2
cpmCPUTotalTable	1.3.6.1.4.1.9.9.109.1.1.1
cpmCPUTotalEntry	1.3.6.1.4.1.9.9.109.1.1.1.1
cpmCPUTotalIndex	1.3.6.1.4.1.9.9.109.1.1.1.1.1
cpmCPUTotalPhysicalIndex	1.3.6.1.4.1.9.9.109.1.1.1.1.2
cpmCPUTotal5sec	1.3.6.1.4.1.9.9.109.1.1.1.1.3
cpmCPUTotal1min	1.3.6.1.4.1.9.9.109.1.1.1.1.4
cpmCPUTotal5min	1.3.6.1.4.1.9.9.109.1.1.1.1.5"
cpmCPUTotal5secRev	1.3.6.1.4.1.9.9.109.1.1.1.1.6"
cpmCPUTotal1minRev	1.3.6.1.4.1.9.9.109.1.1.1.1.7"
cpmCPUTotal5minRev	1.3.6.1.4.1.9.9.109.1.1.1.1.8"
cpmCPUMonInterval	1.3.6.1.4.1.9.9.109.1.1.1.1.9"

Table 10-2 shows some useful MIB entries related to the control plane and their corresponding OID.

Table 10-2 *Important Control-Plane MIBs and Their Corresponding OIDs*

MIB Entry	Description	OID
cpmCPUTotal5min	Overall CPU busy percentage in the last five-minute period	1.3.6.1.4.1.9.9.109.1.1.1.5
ciscoMemoryPoolFree	The number of bytes from the memory pool that are currently unused	1.3.6.1.4.1.9.9.48.1.1.1.6
ciscoMemoryPoolLargestFree	The largest number of contiguous bytes from the memory pool that are currently unused	1.3.6.1.4.1.9.9.48.1.1.1.7
bufferElMiss	The number of buffer element misses	1.3.6.1.4.1.9.2.1.12
bufferFail	The number of buffer allocation failures	1.3.6.1.4.1.9.2.1.46
bufferNoMem	The number of buffers create failures due to lack of memory	1.3.6.1.4.1.9.2.1.47

For the data plane, you may be interested in information pertaining to link utilization. Table 10-3 shows an example of information that is worth collecting for a serial link.

Table 10-3 *Important Data-Plane MIBs and Their Corresponding OIDs*

MIB Entry	Description	OID
ifInOctets	The total number of octets received on the interface, including framing characters	1.3.6.1.2.1.2.2.1.10
ifOutOctets	The total number of octets transmitted out of the interface, including framing characters	1.3.6.1.2.1.2.2.1.16
locIfInPktsSec	Five-minute exponentially decayed moving average of input packets per second	1.3.6.1.4.1.9.2.2.1.1.7
locIfOutPktsSec	Five-minute exponentially decayed moving average of output packets per second	1.3.6.1.4.1.9.2.2.1.1.9
locIfInputQueueDrops	The number of packets dropped because the input queue was full	1.3.6.1.4.1.9.2.2.1.1.26
locIfOutputQueueDrops	The number of packets dropped because the input queue was full	1.3.6.1.4.1.9.2.2.1.1.27
locIfInCRC	The number of input packets that had cyclic redundancy checksum errors	1.3.6.1.4.1.9.2.2.1.1.12

Multi-Router Traffic Grapher

At this point, it is important to point out an important tool that all network managers need as part of their toolkit: the Multi-Router Traffic Grapher (MRTG). MRTG is a tool that collects any SNMP data and generates HTML information pages, as well as graphs to give a visual representation of the data collected. By keeping a log of what has been collected, MRTG can generate visual graphs over a period of time. This is extremely useful in trying to understand usage trends of important resources. Figure 10-2 shows a snapshot of MRTG providing information on the utilization of an interface.

Figure 10-2 *MRTG Graph*

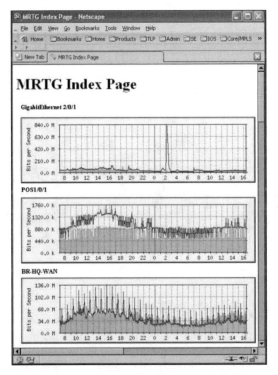

| **TIP** | If you are unfamiliar with the MRTG tool, get one today and experiment with it. You can find more information about MRTG at the following URL:

http://people.ee.ethz.ch/~oetiker/webtools/mrtg |

Step 3: Analyze Data

After the relevant information has been collected, the next step is to analyze the data. Use the data that has been collected to plot a graph. A graphical representation of information gives a good visual indication of the trend of usage. From the graph, you can easily find out how often usage has exceeded a preset threshold. For example, if you set the upper bound of the CPU threshold of a particular router to be 70 percent, drawing a line across the 70 percent mark gives you an indication of how often the router crosses the upper-bound threshold. Crossing an upper-bound threshold constantly may indicate severe control-plane overloading and should be looked into immediately. Figure 10-3 shows an example of upper-bound trending for a router.

Figure 10-3   *Analyzing Threshold*

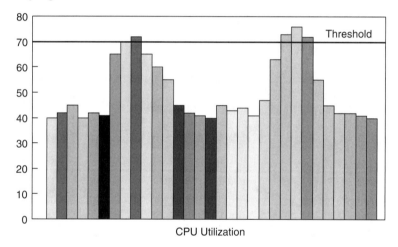

The most difficult part about this step is doing the "what-if" analysis. For example, how do you decide whether a 70 percent CPU utilization is considered trivial, high, or alarming? The answer to this question depends on several other factors—such as whether the high utilization is to be expected because of configuration and feature deployment, or whether the high utilization follows a trend: daily, weekly, or monthly basis. A good bet is to check with the hardware vendor to determine the acceptable upper-bound value. Remember, even different products from the same vendor will have different recommended values.

After a recommended upper-bound threshold has been decided for a particular hardware platform, the next thing to do is to set a lower-bound threshold. A lower-bound threshold is a value lower than the upper bound. A lower-bound threshold can be set so that if the utilization exceeds this threshold, some actions can be started within a given period of time, before it crosses the upper-bound threshold. Some of these actions may be exploring alternative configuration of the hardware or, in the worst-case scenario, an upgrade. By keeping track of the lower-bound threshold, you will always be ahead of the impending utilization problem of a hardware device. Thus, you can avoid overloading and prevent an eventual network meltdown.

Step 4: Prioritize Problem Areas

After you have completed the data analysis, you will have a good idea which part of the network has hit a lower-bound threshold, or worse, which one needs immediate attention. At this point, a baseline has been established. By focusing on those that need immediate attention, you avoid potential catastrophic network problems.

As for those that have crossed the lower-bound threshold, analysis must be carried out to predict the continued usage trend and determine a timeline for the upper bound to be breached. This way, you can buy more time to work on a potential problem. In addition, this information gives a good indication of what new hardware platforms are required in the next budgeting cycle.

Step 5: Determine a Course of Action

After a baseline has been established, you might have a list of actions that need to be taken. Often, these involve redesign or configuration changes. You might even have to perform a Cisco IOS Software upgrade for some of the devices. This might be because of new feature requirements or just based on a recommendation from Cisco Technical Assistance Center (TAC) to deal with fixes. At this point, it is always good to have discussions with hardware vendors to determine all your options.

Upgrading Cisco IOS Software may seem trivial, but it involves more than just downloading the latest software. It requires you to have a thorough understanding of the Cisco IOS Software, even down to its naming convention. In fact, you need to have a deployment strategy, as you learn in the following sections.

By prioritizing problem areas in your network, you can stay ahead of the potential issues that affect the availability of the network. When the steps are completed, the whole cycle repeats over again. Therefore, establishing a baseline is an ongoing process.

Managing Cisco IOS Deployment

Throughout this book, you have learned about the technology and features that make an IP network resilient. However, the resiliency of the network also depends on the successful deployment of the Cisco IOS Software. Often, network managers introduce a new device into the network without realizing the implication of running a particular version of IOS in that box.

Proper control processes should be in place with the deployment of IOS in the network. If you look at the entire IP infrastructure as a whole, the Cisco IOS Software allows the network to be part of the application and service-delivery mechanism. Through network design and activations of features, Cisco IOS Software allows the network to deliver the connectivity and be an application enabler. Therefore, it is an integral part of the entire IP infrastructure and should be handled the same way as you would handle the applications.

In other words, there should be some software life cycle control with regard to its deployment, just as you would with database software. Before you apply the software life cycle control to Cisco IOS Software, you have to have a thorough understanding of the IOS release and its naming convention.

Overview of IOS Releases

Understanding the Cisco IOS release process helps you make informed decisions about its deployment in your network. Different IOS releases serve different network environments, so it is important that you be familiar with them. These releases can be grouped into the following categories:

- Early Deployment (ED) release
- Major release
- Limited Deployment (LD) release
- General Deployment (GD) release

Each of these releases is used differently by the IOS development team to support its customers. For example, the ED release is used to introduce new features rapidly to serve customers who rely on features to operate in a competitive market. On the other hand, the GD release is used to serve customers who look for software with extensive field exposure and proven quality.

In addition to understanding the different IOS releases, it is important to understand the different milestones that each release goes through:

1 **End of Sales (EOS)**—Indicates last day of purchase

2 **End of Engineering (EOE)**—Indicates the date for last maintenance release

3 **End of Life (EOL)**—Indicates the date when no support will be made available

Understanding the different milestones will help you to determine the status of the IOS codes that are running within your network with respect to their individual software life cycle. For example, if you are using a release with an EOE announcement, you have to start to study its impact and start investigating newer IOS releases for your network. You have to ensure that the network is not running a code that is fast approaching its EOL date. A good source of information on the IOS releases and milestones can be found at the following URL :

http://www.cisco.com/en/US/products/sw/iosswrel/ps1828/
products_white_paper09186a008018305e.shtml

Understanding IOS Naming Convention

By now you realize the importance of identifying which Cisco IOS version is currently running in your network. First, however, you need to understand the naming convention.

The naming convention used by the IOS images provides a complete description of the release history. You can derive which train it belongs to and which business unit within Cisco is responsible for its development and the maintenance release version. The format of the naming convention is as follows:

$$[x.y(z[p])][A][o[u\{v[p]\}]]$$

Table 10-4 explains the information provided by each of the naming convention sections.

Table 10-4   *IOS Naming Convention*

Naming Convention Section	Description
x.y	A combination of two digits separated by a period (.) that identifies the major release. Example: 12.1
z	One to three digits that identify the maintenance release of x.y. This occurs every eight weeks. The values are 0 at beta, 1 at FCS, and 2 for the first maintenance release. Example: 12.1(2)
p	One alphabetic character that identifies a rebuild of x.y(z). The character starts with a lowercase *a* for the first rebuild, then *b*, and so on. Example: 12.1(2a)
A	One to three alphabetic characters that are the designators of the release train and are mandatory for CTED, STED, and X releases. It also identifies a family of products or platforms. Technology ED releases use two letters. The first letter represents the technology, and the second letter is used for differentiation. For example: • Cisco IOS Software Release 12.2B—A stands for access server/dial technology • Cisco IOS Software Release 12.2B—B stands for broadband • Cisco IOS Software Release 12.2DA—D stands for xDSL technology • Cisco IOS Software Release 12.1E—E stands for enterprise feature set • Cisco IOS Software Release 11.3HA—H stands for SDH/SONET technology • Cisco IOS Software Release 11.3NA—N stands for voice, multimedia conference • Cisco IOS Software Release 12.2MB—M stands for mobile • Cisco IOS Software Release 12.0S—S stands for service provider • Cisco IOS Software Release 12.2T—T stands for consolidated technology • Cisco IOS Software Release 12.0W—W stands for ATM/LAN switching/ Layer 3. An *X* in the first position of the release name identifies a one-time release based on the CTED T train (for example, XA, XB, XC, and so on). An *X* or *Y* in the second position of the release name identifies a short-lived ED release based on, or affiliated with, an STED release (for example, 11.3NX [based on 11.3NA], 11.3WX [based on 11.3WA], and so on).

continues

Table 10-4 *IOS Naming Convention (Continued)*

Naming Convention Section	Description
o	Optional 1- or 2-digit designator that identifies a rebuild of a particular release value. It is blank if it is not a rebuild. Example: 11.1(2)T1
u	1- or 2-digit designator that identifies the functionality of the BU-specific release. This value is determined by the BU. Example: 11.3(6)WA4
v	1- or 2-digit designator that identifies the maintenance release of the BU-specific code. The values are 0 at beta, 1 at FCS, and 2 as the first maintenance release. Example : 12.0(1)W5(6)
p	One alphabetic character designator that identifies a rebuild of a specific technology release. The value starts with a lowercase *a* for the first rebuild, then *b*, and so on. Example : 11.3(6)WA4(9a) would be a rebuild of 11.3(6)WA4(9)

Based on the naming convention, you can decipher the IOS versions that are running within your network. Figure 10-4 shows the significance of each of the naming convention sections.

Figure 10-4 *Deciphering the IOS Naming Convention*

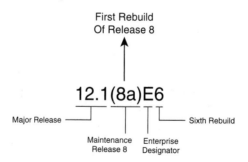

IOS Software Life Cycle Management

The IOS software life cycle management refers to the way to manage the deployment of the Cisco IOS Software. This section is based on a Cisco white paper titled "Cisco IOS Management for High-Availability Networking: Best Practices White Paper." You can find the white paper at http://www.cisco.com/en/US/tech/tk869/tk769/technologies_white_paper09186a00800a998b.shtml.

By following a structured series of steps, the Cisco IOS Software life cycle management helps you achieve successful deployment avoid known bugs, and contributes to high network availability. There are five stages in the life cycle management:

- Planning
- Design
- Testing
- Implementation
- Operation

Planning

The first stage in the Cisco IOS Software life cycle management is planning. This stage begins by examining current deployment procedures and documenting current deployment problems that are plaguing the network. The next step is to have a clear goal of what this exercise is trying to achieve. Goals may include decreasing unsuccessful deployment, consolidating the number of IOS versions running in the network, or increasing network availability through the certification process, and so on.

In the planning stage, you also need to develop a software upgrade process. Criteria and procedures have to be established on when a software upgrade is necessary and how to go about achieving that. In addition, some endorsement has to be in place so that a certain version of IOS is the *de facto* version within the network. Having a *de facto* version helps in keeping deployment consistent and simple, and helps you maintain the quality of the code running in the network. The planning step lays the framework for the entire life cycle management and is an important step in determining what has to follow.

Design

The second stage in the Cisco IOS Software life cycle management is design. The goal is to select the right IOS version for deployment and test it to ensure its suitability. For this, a thorough understanding of the various releases of IOS, and its naming conventions, is critical.

Having a process to note the feature and performance requirements is the first step in the design stage. Based on the information, a selection process will then determine the right release and version of IOS to be considered. At this step, it is always a good idea to get a Cisco Systems engineering representative involved so that selection can be confirmed via tools such as the Feature Navigator in Cisco.com, and a proper bug scrub can be performed.

Another activity that is compulsory in this step is to read up on the release notes of the candidate IOS code to understand the caveats and possible workarounds.

Testing

The third stage is to subject the candidate IOS code to a series of tests. A test network is required to perform this task, and it can never be stressed enough that you need a proper test lab. Often, network managers perform feature or new IOS testing on a live network. This is totally unacceptable. Although cost tends to be a major concern, the test network should be constructed in a manner that represents the actual network. At the very least, the equipment used in the test lab should have the same configuration as that of the production network, although not in the same quantity.

In the testing stage, the hardware, software, configurations, and applications are put together to go through a series of test criteria. These tests enable you to verify the network design, understand the impact of feature deployment, and understand the behavior of the network under extreme conditions. Remember, the more problems you discover during the testing stage, the fewer headaches you will have during live deployment.

At the completion of this stage, you will have selected and validated the right release and version of Cisco IOS Software to deploy in your network.

Implementation

The fourth stage in the Cisco IOS Software life cycle management is implementation. This stage usually begins with a pilot deployment of new IOS code in a selected portion of the network. This way, the effect and quality of the new code can be ascertained before a full-scale deployment. Some of the activities that need to be completed in this stage include developing rollback procedures in the event that unforeseen problems occur, arranging for out-of-band access or on-site personnel standby, and establishing acceptance criteria for full-scale deployment. It is also important to choose an appropriate timing for the implementation. *Never* introduce this stage when it is the seasonal peak period for the network.

Operation

The final stage in the Cisco IOS Software life cycle management is operation. A successful implementation of IOS deployment is just one step in achieving network high availability. As mentioned at the beginning of this chapter, this is the stage where the instrumentation panel has to be monitored constantly. Proactive management is necessary in this stage. Syslog monitoring, SNMP traps management, and problem management have to be in place so that the network can be monitored for any faults. It is also important to establish processes to help keep the IOS versions in check, and to help keep the configuration files consistent across devices that run the same functions. In addition, you must establish a process whereby emergency upgrades can be performed, such as when there is a Product Security Incident Response Team (PSIRT) alert from Cisco that highlights a new vulnerability in protocols. When a PSIRT is issued, the accompanying information includes hardware and software versions affected by the vulnerability. This is when a proper inventory of the network is critical. You should not be wasting time trying to find out what is deployed.

Finally, network statistic collection has to be performed so that data is made available for analysis. This will help further increase the availability of the network by identifying potential problems.

Moving Toward Proactive Management

Until recently, resiliency in IP networks focused on service restoration; meaning, as long as an alternative path existed, it was good enough. Nobody was paying much attention to the time it takes to restore the service. The Internet is one good example. The traditional applications such as e-mail, FTP, and web run on TCP, which provides for recovery capability to a certain extent. However, with the introduction of applications such as VoIP and video broadcasting, network managers are finding it harder to manage the IP network. Network faults and downtimes are easily noticed by end users nowadays because of these new applications. Challenges such as jitter and latency, which were not an issue in the past, suddenly become a problem. No longer is a connected link good enough, because it may not be sufficient to an application that requires stringent performance parameters. Network managers are beginning to realize that even the traditional network management strategy and tools need to be reexamined.

Over the years, the IOS code has been enhanced to tackle this ever-changing network environment. New features have been introduced to tackle the various challenges that have risen because of the introduction of new applications. Each of these new features solves a different component within the network, but collectively, they support the entire back-end operation to contribute to the overall network resiliency. In fact, the demand for new network features is so different nowadays that a new software infrastructure needs to be introduced.

New features have been introduced in IOS to support proactive management. The aim is to enable you to gather information on how well the network is supporting the new-generation applications, as well as outage measurement that will aid in determining network availability. These features include the following:

- IP Service Level Agreement (IP SLA)
- Component Outage Online (COOL) measurement
- Embedded Event Manager (EEM)

IP Service Level Agreement

As mentioned in the section "Accounting Management," the introduction of new applications such as VoIP requires more sophisticated measurement capability from the network. Rather than trying to stitch together performance data from various individual devices, a holistic approach needs to be taken. Remember, it is the user experience that counts. Therefore, it is important to be able to gather information that represents the user experience. This cannot be achieved by just relying on individual device providing localized performance statistics.

IP SLA, previously known as Service Assurance Agent (SAA), aims to achieve that "user experience" measurement. It is used to send measurement data within the IP network to find out the performance characteristics of the network. By simulating data and IP services, it collects information such as the following:

- Response time
- Latency
- Jitter
- Packet loss
- Packet sequencing
- Voice quality scoring
- Server response time
- Application response time
- Website response time

The construction of the simulated traffic is flexible enough so that you can specify network and application layer information, including the following:

- Source and destination IP address
- TCP port numbers
- UDP port numbers
- Type of service (ToS) byte
- Virtual route forwarding (VRF) instance
- URL

The information collected is stored by the device being monitored and can be later retrieved via the command line or the CISCO-RTTMON-MIB. IP SLA works closely with the SNMP process running within the device so that whenever an IP SLA threshold has been breached, SNMP notifications can be sent to a network management system.

The concept of IP SLA is illustrated in Figure 10-5. IP SLA relies on the interaction of four key components to work:

- IP SLA source
- IP SLA responder
- IP device
- Network management system

Figure 10-5 *IP Service Level Agreement*

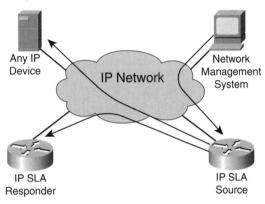

IP SLA relies on a device running the IP SLA source function to send out probes to its target to determine the network conditions, such as reachability and performance characteristics. The target in this case can be a device running the IP SLA responder function or just a normal IP device. The information collected by the IP SLA source is then collected by the network management system for data analysis.

Through the interactions of these four components, three types of IP SLA operations are performed:

- ICMP based
- Responder based
- Nonresponder based

The next sections describe each type of operation and examples of each.

ICMP-Based IP SLA Operation

The ICMP-based operation is the most basic of all and can be used for any IP devices. The IP SLA source sends ICMP packets to the destination and waits for a reply. By using the time stamp within the messages, the IP SLA source is able to calculate the response time. This operation, called the *ICMP echo*, is the same as issuing the extended **ping** command

and measures only the response time between a source and a destination. Other ICMP operations such as ICMP path echo, which uses the Traceroute utility, can be used to map out the whole traffic path.

Responder-Based IP SLA Operation

In the responder-based scenario, the IP SLA responder feature is enabled in the destination device to provide for more detailed information. This option provides for unidirectional operation and gives more accurate information in certain operations. For example, it can consider processing delay at the destination to better reflect the actual transmission delay of the network. The use of the responder is mandatory for measurement of UDP jitter, but it is optional for the other operations such as UDP echo and TCP connect operations.

Nonresponder-Based IP SLA Operation

The nonresponder-based operation is used for measuring specific applications, such as HTTP, FTP, and DHCP, as long as the destination device supports it. Whereas the ICMP-based operation focuses more on network performance, the nonresponder-based operation focuses on the application layer performance. Because the IP SLA source can craft the source packet, flexibility is built in with respect to what to measure. For example, the IP SLA source can be used to monitor the availability of a website by checking on the connection status of the URL.

Examples of IP SLA Operations

Table 10-5 shows the various IP SLA operations that can be performed.

Table 10-5   *IP SLA Operations*

IP SLA Operation	Measures	Application
UDP Jitter	Round-trip delay, one-way delay, one-way jitter, one-way packet loss, and connectivity testing for UDP traffic	Voice and network performance
ICMP Path Jitter	Hop-by-hop jitter, packet loss, and delay in an IP network	General IP performance
UDP Jitter for VoIP	Round-trip delay, one-way delay, one-way jitter, and one-way packet loss for VoIP traffic; Codec simulations for G.711u-law, G.711 a-law, and G.729A; MOS and ICPIF voice-scoring capability	VoIP network
UDP Echo	Round-trip delay of UDP traffic	Server and application connectivity testing
ICMP Echo	Round-trip delay	Basic connectivity

Table 10-5   *IP SLA Operations (Continued)*

IP SLA Operation	Measures	Application
ICMP Path Echo	Round-trip delay and hop-by-hop round-trip delay	Basic connectivity and identify bottleneck
TCP Connect	Time taken to terminate TCP connection	Server performance
HTTP	Round-trip time to retrieve a web page	Web server availability and performance
FTP	Round-trip time to transfer a file	FTP server availability and performance
DHCP	Round-trip time to receive an IP address from the DHCP server	DHCP server availability and performance
DNS	DNS lookup time	DNS server availability and performance

The main advantage of IP SLA is that it is widely available in Cisco devices, because it is embedded in the IOS code. IP SLA can be deployed in the network without the need for external probes.

Component Outage Online (COOL) Measurement

In Chapter 2, "Establishing a High-Availability Network," you learned the important concepts of mean time between failure (MTBF) and mean time to repair (MTTR). Traditionally, network managers have relied on equipment manufacturers to provide component and system reliability figures. These figures are obtained via statistics obtained within a controlled environment and may not truly reflect system behavior in a customer's environment.

The Cisco Component Outage Online (COOL) measurement is a feature that enables a network device to perform outage monitoring, event notification, and storing of outage data. The information is stored in the CISCO-OUTAGE-MONITOR MIB and is later retrieved by an external network management system for further analysis.

The CISCO-OUTAGE-MONITOR MIB contains information relating to outages of hardware, software, both physical and logical interfaces, and directly connected next-hop interfaces. By leveraging the information, you can determine the actual MTBF and MTTR values of the system. With these values, you can then decide whether the logical network design needs revisiting to boost network availability.

The target of COOL measurement is an object, which can be a physical or logical component. The types of objects COOL measures, as illustrated in Figure 10-6, are as follows:

- **Physical entity objects**—The entire network device, including the field replaceable units (FRUs). FRU includes line cards, processors, switch fabrics, power supplies, and the chassis. These objects are defined in the ENTITY-MIB.

- **Interface objects**—Physical, logical interfaces as well as channelized interfaces of the network device. These objects are defined in the IF-MIB.

- **Remote objects**—The Layer 3 interface of a directly connected remote device.

- **Software objects**—Cisco IOS processes that are running the router processor. The MIN-IOS-SW and MAX-IOS-SW are the default software objects used to measure the lower and upper bound of software-caused outages.

Figure 10-6   *Component Outage Online Measurement*

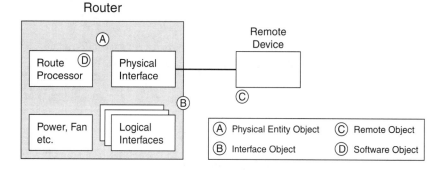

The concept of COOL measurement relies on two metrics:

- Accumulated outage time (AOT) since measurement started. This is the time for a given measurement interval.

- Number of accumulated failures (NAF) since measurement started. This is the frequency of failure for a given measurement interval.

By collecting and storing these two metrics, the MTTR and MTBF value of a system can be determined. In Figure 10-7, the total AOT for a particular object is 8 minutes (5 + 3 minutes), and the NAF is two, because there were two failures. The total measurement interval is 525,600 minutes, which is one year.

Figure 10-7   *Calculating the MTBF Figure Using COOL*

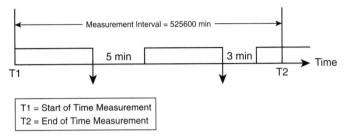

You can derive the MTBF of the object as follows:

$$\begin{aligned} \text{MTBF} &= (\text{T2} - \text{T1})/\text{NAF} \\ &= 525,600/2 \\ &= 262,800 \text{ minutes} \\ &= 4380 \text{ hours} \end{aligned}$$

Obviously, with an MTBF of 4380 hours, the figure pales in comparison to the typical MTBF figures quoted in the hardware brochure. However, bear in mind that the information is collected via a live deployment. As the device continues to function, the MTBF figure should improve over time. If the MTBF figure continues to be low, however, it might indicate an issue about product quality, an environmental issue, or even a network design problem. This figure should provide a good basis for a discussion with the hardware vendor to determine the root cause of the problem.

Example 10-1 shows an example of enabling COOL measurement on a Cisco 12406 GSR. Notice that when COOL is enabled, object tables are created to store the information being measured.

Example 10-1 *Enabling COOL on the GSR*

```
12406#show cool object-table
 cool has not been enabled
 Please, first do 1) clear cool persist-files
    before do 2) config ---> cool run
12406#
12406#clear cool persist-files
12406#config terminal
12406(config)#cool run
12406(config)#exit
12406#show cool object-table
**** COOL Object Table ****
 type index status last-change AOT    NAF  object-name
 2  1   1    1112884533  0     0    Router-Device
 2  2   1    1112884534  0     0    MIN-IOS-SW5
 2  3   1    1112884535  0     0    MAX-IOS-SW5
12406#
```

Because COOL has been enabled on the router, the system also creates a persistent file on the Flash card, as shown in Example 10-2.

Example 10-2 *Displaying a COOL Persistent File*

```
12406#dir
Directory of disk0:/
  1 -rw-  18964648 Oct 26 2004 17:57:06 +00:00 c12kprp-p-mz.120-26.S4.bin

  2 -rw-        73 Apr 7 2005 14:37:34 +00:00 outage_data_persist_file
63845376 bytes total (44834816 bytes free)
12406#
```

Example 10-3 shows how to add a physical interface to the COOL measurement.

Example 10-3 *Adding Physical Interface to a COOL Measurement*

```
12406#config terminal
12406(config)#cool interface gig 2/0
12406(config)#exit
12406#show cool object-table
 **** COOL Object Table ****
 type index status last-change AOT    NAF  object-name
 1   36  2    1112884860  6      1     GigabitEthernet2/0
 2   1   1    1112884533  0      0     Router-Device
 2   2   1    1112884534  0      0     MIN-IOS-SW5
 2   3   1    1112884535  0      0     MAX-IOS-SW5
12406#
```

Embedded Event Manager (EEM)

So far, the concept of network management has been that of a centralized and hierarchical model running on SNMP. In this model, the assumption is that all managed devices are passive. They will only report events, via traps, to a central network management system located somewhere within the network. In turn, the network management system consolidates all these traps. Depending on the severity of the traps, the network management system may or may not send instructions back to the managed devices for remedy actions. This centralized model has been around for a long time and has been working well. However, some characteristics are worth noting, and perhaps some solutions required.

First, the centralized model depends on the network management system receiving the traps before any action can be taken. In fact, the traps will be received only if the network is running. Before a trap is received, a predetermined action has to be defined. This requires network managers to predict what sort of errors may occur and for each error, what specific action needs to be taken. The problem is, sometimes the network management system is flooded with traps, and deciphering these messages becomes a problem. For example, a device might keep sending traps to the network management system because of a flapping link. It is not uncommon to see problems such as this when the event console is flooded with both Link-Down and Link-Up traps. Events such as this usually render the corrective action useless, because correlation is required and it can be quite complex for certain events.

Second, the centralized model assumes that all end devices are passive, or dumb. This might be true for older equipment with limited CPU resource and intelligence. However, with improvement in CPU and memory technology, most modern devices have enough horse-power to rival the high-end equipment of yesteryear. For that matter, you might be able to expect these devices to perform some sort of self-diagnostic, or even self-recovery. After all, these devices already have an extensive self-diagnostic capability during boot time. In addition, during runtime, valuable operation data and transient information may be harnessed.

The Embedded Event Manager (EEM) within the IOS code is designed based on the new intelligence of the end devices. By leveraging end devices with sufficient intelligence to manage themselves, EEM distributes the managements responsibility throughout the network, thereby increasing the network's capability to work around problems.

As part of the Cisco IOS Software infrastructure renewal exercise, EEM will be included in various IOS trains in phases. EEM version 1.0 is available from releases 12.0(26)S and 12.3.(4)T. In this version, EEM provides a device running IOS with the capability to invoke a customized action in reaction to syslog and SNMP events.

The architecture of EEM version 1.0 is illustrated in Figure 10-8. Two event detectors, the syslog and SNMP, are deployed to capture specific events happening within the network from the device's perspective. The syslog event detector enables action to be triggered based on the matching of regular expressions of IOS syslog messages. On the other hand, the SNMP event detector enables action to be triggered based on MIB variable changes. The EEM acts as a central depository for all events and provides a mechanism to trigger certain action through an IOS command-line interface (CLI) applet for each event received. The CLI applets are EEM policies that have been programmed via prior network knowledge.

Figure 10-8   *Embedded Event Manager*

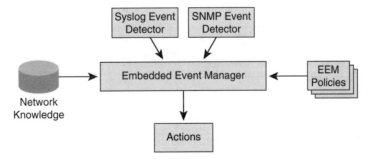

For EEM version 1.0, the following actions can be triggered:

- Generate prioritized syslog messages
- Generate a Cisco Networking Services (CNS) event to be processed by a CNS device
- Reload the device
- Switch to a secondary processor, if there is one available

Figure 10-9 illustrates the architecture of EEM version 2.0. Besides adding more event detectors, EEM version 2.0 provides more flexibility in deployment, as well as programmable action through the Tool Command Language (TCL). TCL provides a powerful environment in which environmental variables can be referenced to determine the specific status of the device.

Figure 10-9   *Embedded Event Manager Version 2.0*

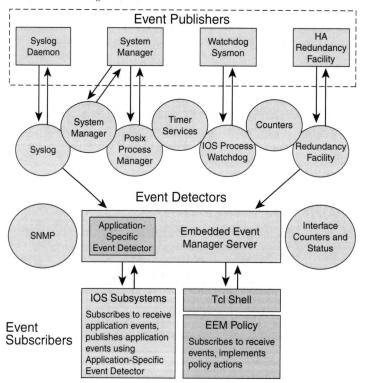

Besides having more event detectors and the TCL scripting subsystem, EEM version 2.0 also added two new components:

- Event Publisher
- Event Subscriber

These new components enable EEM detectors to interact with each other and perform subsequent actions. When a specific event is detected, besides triggering the original intended action, this detection can be published by the Event Publisher. Other event detectors, EEM policies, or even IOS processes may retrieve the published events to trigger further actions. These routines are categorized as Event Subscribers. Table 10-6 shows the list of event detectors made available in version 2.0.

Table 10-6   *Event Detectors in EEM Version 2.0*

Event Detector	Description
IOS CLI Event Detector	Triggers policies based on commands entered via the CLI. It uses a regular expression for matching.
IOS Counter Event Detector	Triggers policies based on a change of the designated counter. Used to manipulate counters internal to EEM.
IOS Redundancy Facility (RF) Event Detector	Triggers policies based on the RF state change. The RF is used to provide for the detection of hardware and software failure related to Stateful Switchover (SSO). Also used to initiate a switchover as a result of a policy action.
IOS Resource Threshold Event Detector	Triggers policies based on global platform values and thresholds. Includes resources such as CPU, memory, and buffers capacities.
IOS Timer Services Event Detector	Policies can be scheduled to occur at the designated time or interval. Provides time-based triggers, just like the UNIX CRON facility.
IOS Watchdog/System Monitor Event Detector	Triggers policies based on certain conditions relative to a certain IOS process or subsystem's activity.
EEM Application-Specific Event Detector	Application-specific events can be detected or set by an IOS subsystem or a policy. This provides the ability for one policy to trigger another policy.
Interface Counter Event Detector	Triggers policies based on the specific interface counter, including thresholding.
Online Insertion and Removal (OIR) Event Detector	Triggers policies based on hardware installation and removal activities.
Routing Event Detector	Triggers policies based on routing protocol events.
SNMP Event Detector	Triggers policies based on SNMP MIB variables and threshold.
Syslog Event Detector	Triggers policies based on regular expression matching of the syslog messages.
System Manager Event Detector	Triggers policies based on certain conditions relative to a certain IOS process or subsystem's activity. This is only available to the microkernel-based OS in 12.2(18)S and later.

Example 10-4 shows a configuration of EEM version 1.0 on a Cisco 12400 GSR. In this example, an applet called Mem_Check ensures that in the event that the memory pool falls below 512 KB, a warning message is sent to a syslog server. In addition, a forced switchover of the router processor is performed.

NOTE   Note that the second action step is for illustration purposes only in this example. From an operational perspective, you would want to investigate further before performing such a drastic action.

Example 10-4 *Configuring EEM on Cisco 12400 GSR*

```
GSR-TOP#configure terminal
Enter configuration commands, one per line. End with CNTL/Z.
GSR-TOP(config)#event manager applet Mem_Check
GSR-TOP(config-applet)#event snmp oid 1.3.6.1.4.1.9.9.48.1.1.1.6.1 get-
  type exact entry-op lt entry-val 5120000 poll-interval 10
GSR-TOP(config-applet)#action 1.0 syslog priority critical msg "Low Memory Warning
  - $_snmp_oid_val bytes available "
GSR-TOP(config-applet)#action 2.0 force-switchover
GSR-TOP(config-applet)#exit
GSR-TOP#show event manager policy registered
No. Type  Event Type     Time Registered       Name
1  applet snmp        Thu May 5 17:10:08 2005 Mem_Check
 oid {1.3.6.1.4.1.9.9.48.1.1.1.6.1} get-type exact entry-op lt entry-val {5120000}
 poll-interval 10.000
 action 1.0 syslog priority critical msg Low Memory Warning - $_snmp_oid_val bytes
 available
 action 2.0 force-switchover
GSR-TOP#
```

As mentioned earlier in this section, the customized action can be programmed through the TCL scripting language. TCL allows the devices to self-manage even if the network management system is down. Therefore, in a way, the device achieves independence through its self-management capability.

Next-Generation IOS Architecture

With the advent of a new converged infrastructure taking shape in various major networks around the world, the operating system of the router is also undergoing its own evolution. Figure 10-10 shows a fundamental change in the router's operating system architecture.

Figure 10-10   *Router OS Evolution*

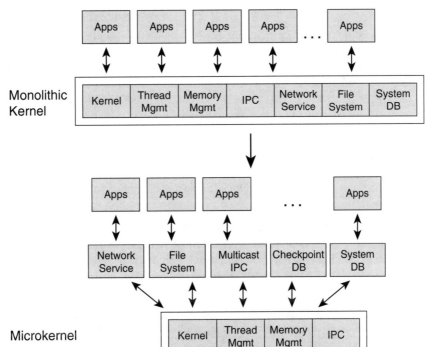

Until recently, the router's operating system was based on a monolithic kernel, with a centralized comprising system, forwarding, and network stack functions. What this means is that the various processes running within the router affect each other's operations. When a process malfunctions or fails, there is a high chance of it corrupting the health of other processes. Although enhancements to protocols through the concept of Nonstop Forwarding help to minimize downtime, the overall architecture of the router still lacks the fundamental concept of a high-availability system. Next-generation router design has expanded the concept of a highly available router from just providing redundant hardware, such as the route processors, line cards, and power supplies, to its very heart: the operating system architecture.

The new generation of router operating systems, such as Cisco IOS-XR, runs on a microkernel. The microkernel-based operating system changes the way the router hardware behaves and provides the following functions that were not possible before:

- Preemptive scheduling, with support for process priority
- Protected memory architecture for both system and application processes
- Fault containment for both system and application processes

- Fault protection for the file system, host stack, and device driver
- In-service software upgrade (ISSU) for the system and applications

The preceding functions provide the hardware with new building block capabilities to implement features that would have been almost impossible to implement in the old model. For example, the new system architecture allows the control, data, and management planes to operate independently. By having this capability, the router continues to forward traffic even if there is a temporary setback to the control-plane function. When the control plane recovers, the routing and forwarding tables are updated with fresh updates while traffic continues to pass through the router.

Another important feature is the ability to restart processes independently. This feature is key to the router being able to recover from faults without reloading the entire system. Fault containment is also the building block for the router's ability to perform in-service software upgrades.

With ISSU, the maintenance window and service impact are minimized, which enables you to maintain the overall availability of the router. Check-pointing is also a key feature that helps maintain high availability. With check-pointing, the system is able to maintain configuration and runtime system states, so that a backup resource can take over operation in the event that the primary resource fails.

With the concept of hardware component redundancy and the new-generation router operating system architecture, the router is beginning to rival the reliability reputation of the traditional voice switches. Moving forward, you should examine these new features and the new router operating system architecture to see how they can fit into your network.

Summary

Building a network from scratch now seems easy as compared to operating it to achieve high availability. The ISO management model gives you an indication of just how much has to be done in the back end. Network management is an integral part of the network operation, and instilling discipline and processes, such as establishing a baseline for the network and practicing software life cycle management, is key to success.

By being proactive, you can avoid many network problems and positively affect the overall availability of the network. You might wonder how some major service providers can maintain an almost perfect track record in their operations. Besides having more resources and technical ability, one thing for sure is that they treat network management as the most critical component of their operations.

End Notes

The section "IOS Software Life Cycle Management" was based on a Cisco white paper titled "Cisco IOS Management for High-Availability Networking: Best Practices White Paper." It is available at the following URL:

http://www.cisco.com/en/US/tech/tk869/tk769/
technologies_white_paper09186a00800a998b.shtml

APPENDIX **A**

Calculating Network Availability

This appendix discusses mathematical calculations to calculate network availability. The percentage method specifies the expected amount of system downtime. The defects-per-million method specifies the actual system performance. The availability method enables you to calculate theoretical availability based on manufacture information. This appendix also includes an availability-calculation example for a simple network topology.

The Percentage M ethod

The percentage method describes availability based on a percentage of the total number of minutes in one year (525,960 minutes, a figure that takes leap years into account). Table A-1 shows the availability percentages.

Table A-1 *Fives-Nines Availability*

Number of Nines	Availability %	Minutes of Downtime	Annual Downtime
1	90.000	52,596	36 days, 12 hours, 36 minutes
2	99.000	5259.6	3 days, 15 hours, 40 minutes
3	99.900	525.96	8 hours, 46 minutes
4	99.990	52.596	52 minutes, 36 seconds
5	99.999	5.2596	5 minutes, 15 seconds
6	99.9999	0.52596	32 seconds

The Defects-per-Million Method

The defects-per-million (DPM) method is another way to measure availability. It measures the number of failures that occurred within a million hours of operational time. For example, the following determines availability given two failures in one month:

    Hours per year   = 8766
    Number of devices   = 1000
    Accumulated hours per year = 8766 * 1000
                              = 8,766,000

Accumulated hours per month = 8,766,000/12
= 730,500 hours
Converting to defects per million = (2/730,500)*1,000,000
= 2.7378 DPM

Theoretical Availability of a Device

Based on the mean time between failure (MTBF) figure given by the manufacturer and the mean time to repair (MTTR), you can derive the availability of a device via the following equation:

Availability = MTBF / (MTBF + MTTR)

where:

- MTBF is the average time taken for a component to transit from an operation state to a failure state.

- MTTR is the average time taken to reinstate a failed component to a functioning state.

Because MTTR depends on a vendor service contract, it is a variable number. The service contract guarantees diagnostics and parts replacement, if necessary.

For example, consider a device with an MTBF of 200,000 hours and an MTTR value of 6 hours, based on the availability equation:

Availability = 200,000 / 200,006 = 0.99997

Use the following to derive downtime from availability:

1 year   = 525,960 minutes
Downtime = (1 – Availability) * 525,960
= 0.00003 * 525,960
= 15.7788

Therefore, a device with an availability of 0.99997 will suffer from 15.7788 minutes of downtime.

Although determining the availability of a single device is straightforward, determining the availability of groups of devices might not be so straightforward.

Availability of a Group of Serial Devices

You can calculate the availability of a group of components arranged in a serial fashion by using the following equation:

$$SerialAvailability = \prod_{i=1}^{n} ComponentAvailability(i)$$

where:

- i = component
- n = total number of components

For example, if you have two individual components each with an availability of 0.99999 and 0.99994 and you build a system with these two components by lining them up in a serial fashion. The availability of the system is as follows:

$$\begin{aligned} System\ availability &= 0.99 * 0.999 \\ &= 0.98901 \end{aligned}$$

For a system made up of components arranged in a serial fashion, the resultant system availability is less than any of the individual components.

Availability of a Group of Parallel Devices

You can calculate the availability of a group of components by using the following equation:

$$ParallelAvailability = 1 - \left(\prod_{i=1}^{n} (1 - ComponentAvailability_{(2)}) \right)$$

For example, if you arrange the previous two components in a parallel fashion, the resultant system has an availability as follows:

$$\begin{aligned} System\ availability &= 1 - ((1 - 0.99) * (1 - 0.999)) \\ &= 1 - (0.01 * 0.001) \\ &= 1 - 0.00001 \\ &= 0.99999 \end{aligned}$$

For a system made up of components arranged in a parallel fashion, the resultant system availability is more than any of the individual components. It is also interesting to note that a "five-nines" system can be constructed out of less reliable components.

Calculating a Simple System Availability

Figure A-1 shows simple network connectivity from Network A to Network B via a single system with two power supplies, a motherboard, and two interface cards.

Figure A-1 *Calculating Availability for a Simple System*

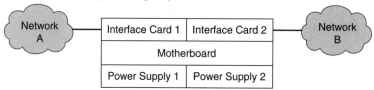

Assume that the availability of the individual components is as follows:

- Each power supply = 0.999
- Motherboard = 0.99994
- Each interface card = 0.9995

The availability from Network A to Network B is calculated by deriving the parallel availability of the power supplies and the serial availability of the resultant power supplies, motherboard, and interface cards' availability:

$$\text{Availability for power supplies} = 1 - (\,(1-0.999) * (1-0.999)\,)$$
$$= 1 - 0.000001$$
$$= 0.999999$$

Availability from Network A to Network B = $0.999999 * 0.99994 * 0.9995 * 0.9995$
$= 0.998939$

$$\text{Downtime} = (1 - \text{Availability}) * 525{,}960$$
$$= 0.001061 * 525{,}960$$
$$= 558 \text{ minutes}$$

Calculating Availability for a Simple Network Topology

Figure A-2 shows a simple network topology.

Figure A-2 *Calculating Availability for a Simple Network Topology*

The availability calculation for this simple network topology is the same as that of the previous example.

Assume that the availability of Router A and of Router B is 0.9995, and that of the individual switch is 0.9999. For simplicity, also assume that all links never fail. Then the availability of the network from segment A to the server is as follows:

0.9999 * 0.9995 * 0.9995 * 0.9999
= 0.9988

Downtime = (1 − Availability) * 525,960
= 0.0012 * 525,960
= 631 minutes

As you can see, the resultant availability might not be as impressive as you want.

To improve on the availability of the network, you could introduce a parallel path, as shown in Figure A-3

Figure A-3   *Improving Availability for a Simple Network*

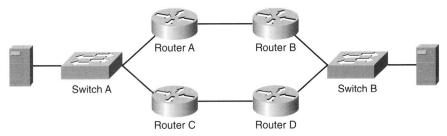

Assume the availability of the individual components are the same. Derive the new availability by first calculating the serial availability of the router pairs:

Serial availability = 0.9995 * 0.9995
= 0.999

The availability of the parallel path is calculated as follows:

Parallel availability = 1 − ((1 − 0.999) * (1 − 0.999))
= 1 − 0.000001
= 0.999999

The overall availability of the network is, therefore, as follows:

0.9999 * 0.999999 * 0.9999
= 0.999799

Downtime = (1 − Availability) * 525,960
= 0.000201 * 525,960
= 105 minutes

As compared to the single-path solution, the introduction of the secondary path has greatly improved the total availability of the whole network. Of course, the additional equipment creates an investment expense.

Summary

The calculations shown in this appendix are the basic building blocks to determine the availability of a complex network. For more detailed discussions about availability-calculation methodology, refer to *High Availability Network Fundamentals* by Chris Oggerino (Cisco Press, 2001).

RFCs Relevant to Building a Resilient IP Network

This appendix lists Requests For Comments (RFCs) that are relevant to building resilient IP networks. You can find a complete list of RFCs on the Internet Engineering Task Force (IETF) website at http://www.ietf.org.

Each RFC falls into one of the following categories, as indicated in the table:

- S   Standard
- I   Informational
- BCP   Best Current Practices
- PS   Proposed Standard
- DS   Draft Standard

RFC	Title	Status
IP		
791	*Internet Protocol*	S
894	*Standard for the Transmission of IP Datagrams over Ethernet Networks*	S
919	*Broadcasting Internet Datagrams*	S
922	*Broadcasting Internet Datagrams in the Presence of Subnets*	S
950	*Internet Standard Subnetting Procedure*	S
1042	*Standard for the Transmission of IP Datagrams over IEEE 802 Networks*	S
1055	*Nonstandard for Transmission of IP Datagrams over Serial Lines: SLIP*	S
1088	*Standard for the Transmission of IP Datagrams over NetBIOS Networks*	S
1201	*Transmitting IP Traffic over ARCNET Networks*	S
1209	*Transmission of IP Datagrams over the SMDS Service*	S
1390	*Transmission of IP and ARP over FDDI Networks*	S
3717	*IP over Optical Networks: A Framework*	I
3819	*Advice for Internet Subnetwork Designers*	BCP

RFC	Title	Status
TCP		
793	*Transmission Control Protocol*	S
2018	*TCP Selective Acknowledgment Options*	PS
2398	*Some Testing Tools for TCP Implementors*	I
2415	*Simulation Studies of Increased Initial TCP Window Size*	I
2488	*Enhancing TCP over Satellite Channels Using Standard Mechanisms*	PS
2525	*Known TCP Implementation Problems*	BCP
2581	*TCP Congestion Control*	PS
2883	*An Extension to the Selective Acknowledgment (SACK) Option for TCP*	PS
2923	*TCP Problems with Path MTU Discovery*	I
2988	*Computing TCP's Retransmission Timer*	PS
3042	*Enhancing TCP's Loss Recovery Using Limited Transmit*	PS
3155	*End-to-End Performance Implications of Links with Errors*	BCP
3360	*Inappropriate TCP Resets Considered Harmful*	BCP
3390	*Increasing TCP's Initial Window*	PS
ICMP		
792	*Internet Control Message Protocol*	S
1256	*ICMP Router Discovery Messages*	PS
Differentiated Services		
2474	*Definition of the Differentiated Services Field (DS Field) in the IPv4 and IPv6 Headers*	PS
2475	*An Architecture for Differentiated Service*	PS
2597	*Assured Forwarding PHB Group*	PS
2697	*A Single-Rate, Three-Color Marker*	I
2698	*A Two-Rate, Three-Color Marker*	I
2963	*A Rate Adaptive Shaper for Differentiated Services*	I
2983	*Differentiated Services and Tunnels*	I
3086	*Definition of Differentiated Services Per Domain Behaviors and Rules for Their Specification*	I
3140	*Per Hop Behavior Identification Codes*	PS
3246	*An Expedited Forwarding PHB*	PS

RFC	Title	Status
Differentiated Services		
3247	*Supplemental Information for the New Definition of the EF PHB (Expedited Forwarding Per-Hop Behavior)*	I
3270	*MPLS Support of Differentiated Services*	PS
3287	*Remote Monitoring MIB Extensions for Differentiated Services*	PS
3289	*Management Information Base for the Differentiated Services Architecture*	PS
3290	*An Informal Management Model for Diffserv Routers*	I
3308	*Layer 2 Tunneling Protocol (L2TP) Differentiated Services Extension*	PS
3317	*Differentiated Services Quality of Service Policy Information Base*	I
3644	*Policy Quality of Service (QoS) Information Model*	PS
3662	*A Lower Effort Per-Domain Behavior (PDB) for Differentiated Services*	I
3747	*The Differentiated Services Configuration MIB*	PS
Integrated Services		
1633	*Integrated Services in the Internet Architecture: An Overview*	I
1727	*A Vision of an Integrated Internet Information Service*	I
2210	*The Use of RSVP with IETF Integrated Services*	PS
2211	*Specification of the Controlled-Load Network Element Service*	PS
2212	*Specification of Guaranteed Quality of Service*	PS
2213	*Integrated Services Management Information Base Using SMIv2*	PS
2214	*Integrated Services Management Information Base Guaranteed Service Extensions Using SMIv2*	PS
2215	*General Characterization Parameters for Integrated Service Network Elements*	PS
2382	*A Framework for Integrated Services and RSVP over ATM*	I
2688	*Integrated Services Mappings for Low-Speed Networks*	PS
2689	*Providing Integrated Services over Low-Bitrate Links*	I
2815	*Integrated Service Mappings on IEEE 802 Networks*	PS
2998	*A Framework for Integrated Services Operation over Diffserv Networks*	I
3006	*Integrated Services in the Presence of Compressible Flows*	PS

RFC	Title	Status
OSPF		
1586	*Guidelines for Running OSPF over Frame Relay Networks*	I
1793	*Extending OSPF to Support Demand Circuits*	PS
1850	*OSPF Version 2 Management Information Base*	DS
2328	*OSPF Version 2*	S
29	*OSPF Standardization Report*	I
2370	*The OSPF Opaque LSA Option*	PS
3101	*The OSPF Not-So-Stubby Area (NSSA) Option*	PS
3137	*OSPF Stub Router Advertisement*	I
3509	*Alternative Implementations of OSPF Area Border Routers*	I
3623	*Graceful OSPF Restart*	PS
3630	*Traffic Engineering (TE) Extensions to OSPF Version 2*	PS
3883	*Detecting Inactive Neighbors over OSPF Demand Circuits*	PS
IS-IS		
1142	*OSI IS-IS Intradomain Routing Protocol*	I
1195	*Use of OSI IS-IS for Routing in TCP/IP and Dual Environments*	PS
2966	*Domain-Wide Prefix Distribution with Two-Level IS-IS*	I
2973	*IS-IS Mesh Groups*	I
3277	*Intermediate System to Intermediate System (IS-IS) Transient Blackhole Avoidance*	I
3359	*Reserved Type, Length and Value (TLV) Codepoints in Intermediate System to Intermediate System*	I
3373	*Three-Way Handshake for Intermediate System to Intermediate System (IS-IS) Point-to-Point Adjacencies*	I
3567	*Intermediate System to Intermediate System (IS-IS) Cryptography Authentication*	I
3719	*Recommendations for Interoperable Networks Using Intermediate System to Intermediate System (IS-IS)*	I
3784	*Intermediate System to Intermediate System (IS-IS) Extensions For Traffic Engineering (TE)*	I
3786	*Extending The Number of Intermediate System to Intermediate System (IS-IS) Link-State PDU Fragments Beyond the 256 Limit*	I

RFC	Title	Status
IS-IS		
3787	*Recommendations for Interoperable IP Networks Using Intermediate System to Intermediate System (IS-IS)*	I
3847	*Restart Signaling for Intermediate System to Intermediate System (IS-IS)*	I
BGP		
1657	*Definitions of Managed Objects for the Fourth Version of the Border Gateway Protocol Using SMIv2*	DS
1771	*A Border Gateway Protocol 4 (BGP-4)*	DS
1772	*Application of the Border Gateway Protocol in the Internet*	DS
1773	*Experience with the BGP-4 Protocol*	I
1774	*BGP-4 Protocol Analysis*	I
1930	*Guidelines for Creation, Selection, and Registration of an Autonomous System (AS)*	BCP
1997	*BGP Communities Attribute*	PS
1998	*An Application of the BGP Community Attribute in Multihome Routing*	I
2042	*Registering New BGP Attribute Types*	I
2270	*Using a Dedicated AS for Sites Homed to a Single Provider*	I
2385	*Protection of BGP Sessions Via the TCP MD5 Signature Option*	PS
2439	*BGP Route Flap Damping*	PS
2519	*A Framework for Interdomain Route Aggregation*	I
2547	*BGP/MPLS VPNs*	I
2796	*BGP Route Reflection - An Alternative to Full-Mesh IBGP*	PS
2858	*Multiprotocol Extensions for BGP-4*	PS
2918	*Route Refresh Capability for BGP-4*	PS
3065	*Autonomous System Confederation for BGP*	PS
3107	*Carrying Label Information in BGP-4*	PS
3345	*Border Gateway Protocol (BGP) Persistent Route Oscillation Condition*	I
3392	*Capabilities Advertisement with BGP-4*	DS
3562	*Key Management Considerations for the TCP MD5 Signature Option*	I
3765	*NOPEER Community for BGP Route Scope Control*	I
3882	*Configuring BGP to Block Denial-of-Service Attacks*	I

RFC	Title	Status
First-Hop Redundancy		
3768	*Virtual Router Redundancy Protocol (VRRP)*	DS
MPLS		
2430	*A Provider Architecture for Differentiated Services and Traffic Engineering (PASTE)*	I
2547	*BGP/MPLS VPNs*	I
2702	*Requirement for Traffic Engineering over MPLSs*	I
3031	*Multiprotocol Label Switching Architecture*	PS
3032	*MPLS Label Stacking Encoding*	PS
3034	*Use of Label Switching on Frame Relay Networks Specification*	PS
3035	*MPLS Using LDP and ATM VC Switching*	PS
3270	*Multiprotocol Label Switching (MPLS) Support of Differentiated Services*	PS
3346	*Applicability Statement for Traffic Engineering With MPLS*	I
3429	*Assignment of the "OAM Alert Label" for MPLS OAM Functions*	I
3443	*Time To Live (TTL) Processing in MPLS Networks*	PS
3468	*The Multiprotocol Label Switching (MPLS) Working Group Decision on MPLS Signaling Protocols*	I
3469	*Framework for MPLS-Based Recovery*	I
3477	*Signalling Unnumbered Links in Resource Reservation Protocol-Traffic Engineering (RSVP-TE)*	PS
3478	*Graceful Restart Mechanism for Label Distribution Protocol*	PS
3479	*Fault Tolerance for the Label Distribution Protocol (LDP)*	PS
3496	*Protocol Extension for Support of Asynchronous Transfer Mode (ATM) Service Class-aware MPLS Traffic Engineering*	I
3564	*Requirement for Support of Differentiated Services-Aware MPLS Traffic Engineering*	I
3612	*Applicability Statement for Restart Mechanisms for the Label Distribution Protocol (LDP)*	I
3785	*Use of Interior Gateway Protocol (IGP) Metric as a Second MPLS TE Metric*	BCP
3812	*MPLS Traffic Engineering (TE) Management Information Base (MIB)*	PS

RFC	Title	Status
MPLS		
3813	*MPLS Label Switching Router (LSR) Management Information Base (MIB)*	PS
3814	*MPLS Forwarding Equivalent Class to Next-Hop Label Forwarding Entry (FEC-To-NHLFE) Management Information Base (MIB)*	PS
3815	*Definitions of Managed Objects for the MPLS Label Distribution Protocol (LDP)*	PS

The Cisco Powered Network Checklist

Cisco Systems awards a Cisco Powered Network certification to service providers that demonstrate the ability to maintain high standards of network availability for their services. A Cisco Powered Network certification not only guarantees certain network performance criteria, it also recognizes excellence in network security and operations.

In the course of working with the major service providers around the world, the Cisco Powered Network program has developed checklists to guide its members toward best practices in design and construction of networks and data centers.

The following is an extract of the Cisco Powered Network data center best practices checklist. You can find the checklist at Cisco.com (http://www.cisco.com/en/US/netsol/ ns206/networking_solutions_white_paper0900aecd80122977.shtml). You should include this checklist in the evaluation criteria when constructing a resilient IP network.

Facility and Physical Requirements

- ☐ Multiple, physically separate connections to public power grid substations.
- ☐ Continuous power supply with backup uninterruptible power supply (UPS) systems:
    - ☐ Adequate UPS capacity including air conditioning and lights.
    - ☐ UPS systems tested at full load on monthly schedule.
    - ☐ Fuel for UPS generators (48 hours worth) kept on premise and monitored for local environmental compliance.
- ☐ Conform to or exceed applicable local structure building codes utilizing standards such as bulletproof glass, fire doors, and reinforced walls and complying with disaster-proof design:
    - ☐ Comply with all local zoning ordinances.
    - ☐ Certify not located in a 100-year flood plain.
    - ☐ Earthquake and hurricane bracing on all racks and cable trays, where appropriate.

- [ ] Adequate multizone air conditioning, including a backup system for the multizone air conditioning:
  - [ ] Climate control including humidity sensors and control.
- [ ] Heat and smoke detectors that meet or exceed all local fire code regulations:
  - [ ] Very Early Smoke Detection Alarm (VESDA).
  - [ ] FM200 [ETG5] fire suppression system in data center and NOC.
  - [ ] Separate dectection/FM200 zone under raised floors.
- [ ] Preaction dry pipe system zoned to release water only where needed.
- [ ] Easily removable access panels in raised flooring.
- [ ] Flood sensors and monitoring under raised floors and in other critical areas.
- [ ] Separate grounding systems to prevent grounding loops; true ground versus green wire ground.
- [ ] Sealed cable vault entrances to facility, remotely monitored.
- [ ] Formalized physical facility preventive maintenance program:
  - [ ] Sub-breakers per relay rack or lineup.
  - [ ] 48 VDC power converters, 220 VAC, 20A, 30A, 40A.
  - [ ] Power filtering in UPS system.

Physical Security

- [ ] Written security policies readily accessible:
  - [ ] Badge sharing and piggyback entry rules.
  - [ ] All visitors must be admitted through receptions.
  - [ ] Written statement of work upon sign-in.
- [ ] Building access procedures:
  - [ ] Limited number of building entrances in compliance with local fire ordinance.
  - [ ] Provide access to limited and managed security policies for all facility entrances.
  - [ ] 24×7 on-site security guards.
  - [ ] Visitor-logging procedure.
  - [ ] Card-key, biometric, or similar entry locks.
  - [ ] ID-badge system for all employees and visitors.
  - [ ] Staff and visitors must wear badges at all times on premises.

☐ Equipment locations:

  ☐ Video surveillance and motion sensors for entrances, interior doors, equipment cages, and critical equipment locations within the building.

  ☐ Locked cages with ceilings, locking cabinets with climate control for those wanting more privacy.

  ☐ Secure rooms available.

  ☐ Managed firewall services with 24×7 monitoring available.

  ☐ Backup lighting systems for entryways and cable vaults.

  ☐ Individual cabinet locks, master key in network operation center, key list from customer.

Network Security

☐ Written network access security policies readily accessible:

  ☐ Password policies (such as not sharing, lengths, forced renewal, and aging).

  ☐ Acceptable use. (ISP not allowed to run programs that are illicit or illegal; use of sniffers or cracking/hacking programs not permitted.)

  ☐ Documented user responsibilities on security in-company policies and reinforced by education.

  ☐ Asset protection.

☐ Network security infrastructure in place:

  ☐ Perimeter protection (firewalls, filtering router).

  ☐ Intrusion detection.

  ☐ Authentication and authorization (passwords, RADIUS/TACACS, secure IDs).

  ☐ Backup and recovery systems to restore after a problem, such as load balancing, failover protection.

  ☐ Regular assessment of network infrastructure.

  ☐ Assessment of network expansions or additions.

  ☐ Tape or media storage off-site backup.

  ☐ Regulars scheduled security audits.

  ☐ Server antivirus software protection.

Operations

☐ Database of all installed equipment and configurations.

☐ Toll-free telephone support.

☐ Supported monitoring:

  ☐ 24×7 monitoring of dedicated servers and network equipment. (Note both frequency and method, such as ping, SNMP poll.)

  ☐ 24×7 monitoring of the health of the equipment with alarms and pager alerts for network failure and failovers.

  ☐ 24×7 monitoring firewall services available.

  ☐ Alternate NOC available.

  ☐ Second-tier support personnel located nearby.

☐ Trouble ticket processes:

  ☐ Created and logged for all unusual or unexpected events.

☐ Automated case escalation procedures in place including escalation time frames.

☐ Reporting that provides trending statistics on trouble tickets and minutes to facilitate quality and customer reports.

☐ Performance reporting and end-user impact monitoring.

☐ Periodic and exception reports provided to customers (including usage and problem reports).

☐ Spare equipment for key networking equipment available in case of hardware failure.

☐ Business continuity plan:

  ☐ Daily site backups.

  ☐ Tape vaults or other secure storage facilities in case of natural disaster.

  ☐ On-site and off-site storage available.

☐ Customer callout and escalation database.

☐ Intercom system.

☐ Written procedures on alarm handling for each customer.

Cabling

☐ All cable runs located under raised flooring and appropriately marked.

☐ All cable runs to be physically protected via tie down.

☐ All cabling designed to Category 6 specifications.

☐ Communications cabling raceways separate from electrical, no intersections.

☐ Shielded cabling for T1/T3s. DSX panels for XCONN, demarcation, and test points.

☐ All cabling on raceways, tied down.

You can find more information about the Cisco Powered Network program at the following website:

http://www.cisco.com/en/US/netsol/ns206/networking_solutions_program_category_home.html

INDEX

Numerics

M

T

Safari®
BOOKS ONLINE
ENABLED

THIS BOOK IS SAFARI ENABLED

INCLUDES FREE 45-DAY ACCESS TO THE ONLINE EDITION

The Safari® Enabled icon on the cover of your favorite technology book means the book is available through Safari Bookshelf. When you buy this book, you get free access to the online edition for 45 days.

Safari Bookshelf is an electronic reference library that lets you easily search thousands of technical books, find code samples, download chapters, and access technical information whenever and wherever you need it.

TO GAIN 45-DAY SAFARI ENABLED ACCESS TO THIS BOOK:

- Go to **http://www.ciscopress.com/safarienabled**

- Enter the ISBN of this book (shown on the back cover, above the bar code)

- Log in or Sign up (site membership is required to register your book)

- Enter the coupon code found in the front of this book before the "Contents at a Glance" page

If you have difficulty registering on Safari Bookshelf or accessing the online edition, please e-mail customer-service@safaribooksonline.com.

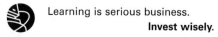

CISCO SYSTEMS

Cisco Press

NETWORK BUSINESS SERIES

JUSTIFY YOUR NETWORK INVESTMENT

Understand the business case for technologies with Network Business books from Cisco Press. Designed to support anyone **searching for optimal network systems,** Network Business titles help you justify your network investments.

1-58720-121-6

Look for Network Business titles at your favorite bookseller

The Business Case for E-Learning
Kelly / Nanjiani • ISBN: 1-58720-086-4

The Business Case for Network Security
Paquet / Saxe • ISBN: 1-58720-121-6

The Business Case for Storage Networks
Williams • ISBN: 1-58720-118-6

The Case for Virtual Business Processes
Young / Jude • ISBN: 1-58720-087-2

IP Telephony Unveiled
Brown • ISBN: 1-58720-075-9

Power Up Your Small-Medium Business
Aber • ISBN: 1-58705-135-4

The Road to IP Telephony
Carhee • ISBN: 1-58720-088-0

Taking Charge of Your VoIP Project
Walker / Hicks • ISBN: 1-58720-092-9

Coming in Fall 2005

The Business Case for Enterprise-Class Wireless LANs
Castaneda / Alasdair / Vinckier • ISBN: 1-58720-125-9

MPLS for Decision Makers
Sayeed / Morrow • ISBN: 1-58720-120-8

Network Business Series.   **Justify Your Network Investment.**

Visit **www.ciscopress.com/netbus** for details about the Network Business series and a complete list of titles.

Cisco Press

3 STEPS TO LEARNING

STEP 1

First-Step

STEP 2

Fundamentals

STEP 3

**Networking
Technology Guides**

STEP 1 **First-Step**—Benefit from easy-to-grasp explanations.
No experience required!

STEP 2 **Fundamentals**—Understand the purpose, application,
and management of technology.

STEP 3 **Networking Technology Guides**—Gain the knowledge
to master the challenge of the network.

NETWORK BUSINESS SERIES

The Network Business series helps professionals tackle the
business issues surrounding the network. Whether you are a
seasoned IT professional or a business manager with minimal
technical expertise, this series will help you understand the
business case for technologies.

Justify Your Network Investment.

Look for Cisco Press titles at your favorite bookseller today.

Visit **www.ciscopress.com/series** for details on each of these book series.